The Data Warehouse Toolkit
Second Edition

The Data Warehouse Toolkit

Second Edition

The Complete Guide to Dimensional Modeling

Ralph Kimball
Margy Ross

Wiley Computer Publishing

John Wiley & Sons, Inc.

NEW YORK • CHICHESTER • WEINHEIM • BRISBANE • SINGAPORE • TORONTO

Publisher: Robert Ipsen
Editor: Robert Elliott
Assistant Editor: Emilie Herman
Managing Editor: John Atkins
Associate New Media Editor: Brian Snapp
Text Composition: John Wiley Composition Services

This publication is designed to provide accurate and authoritative information in regard to the subject matter covered. It is sold with the understanding that the publisher is not engaged in professional services. If professional advice or other expert assistance is required, the services of a competent professional person should be sought.

Library of Congress Cataloging-in-Publication Data:

Kimball, Ralph.
   The data warehouse toolkit : the complete guide to dimensional modeling /
Ralph Kimball, Margy Ross. — 2nd ed.
     p. cm.
"Wiley Computer Publishing."
Includes index.
ISBN 0-471-20024-7
  1. Database design. 2. Data warehousing. I. Ross, Margy, 1959– II. Title.

QA76.9.D26 K575 2002
658.4'038'0285574—dc21   2002002284

Printed in the United States of America.

10 9 8

CONTENTS

ACKNOWLEDGMENTS

First of all, we want to thank the thousands of you who have read our *Toolkit* books, attended our courses, and engaged us in consulting projects. We have learned as much from you as we have taught. As a group, you have had a profoundly positive impact on the data warehousing industry. Congratulations!

This book would not have been written without the assistance of our business partners. We want to thank Julie Kimball of Ralph Kimball Associates for her vision and determination in getting the project launched. While Julie was the catalyst who got the ball rolling, Bob Becker of DecisionWorks Consulting helped keep it in motion as he drafted, reviewed, and served as a general sounding board. We are grateful to them both because they helped an enormous amount.

We wrote this book with a little help from our friends, who provided input or feedback on specific chapters. We want to thank Bill Schmarzo of Decision-Works, Charles Hagensen of Attachmate Corporation, and Warren Thornthwaite of InfoDynamics for their counsel on Chapters 6, 7, and 16, respectively.

Bob Elliott, our editor at John Wiley & Sons, and the entire Wiley team have supported this project with skill, encouragement, and enthusiasm. It has been a pleasure to work with them. We also want to thank Justin Kestelyn, editor-in-chief at *Intelligent Enterprise* for allowing us to adapt materials from several of Ralph's articles for inclusion in this book.

To our families, thanks for being there for us when we needed you and for giving us the time it took. Spouses Julie Kimball and Scott Ross and children Sara Hayden Smith, Brian Kimball, and Katie Ross all contributed a lot to this book, often without realizing it. Thanks for your unconditional support.

The data warehousing industry certainly has matured since Ralph Kimball published the first edition of *The Data Warehouse Toolkit* (Wiley) in 1996. Although large corporate early adopters paved the way, since then, data warehousing has been embraced by organizations of all sizes. The industry has constructed thousands of data warehouses. The volume of data continues to grow as we populate our warehouses with increasingly atomic data and update them with greater frequency. Vendors continue to blanket the market with an ever-expanding set of tools to help us with data warehouse design, development, and usage. Most important, armed with access to our data warehouses, business professionals are making better decisions and generating payback on their data warehouse investments.

Since the first edition of *The Data Warehouse Toolkit* was published, dimensional modeling has been broadly accepted as the dominant technique for data warehouse presentation. Data warehouse practitioners and pundits alike have recognized that the data warehouse presentation must be grounded in simplicity if it stands any chance of success. Simplicity is the fundamental key that allows users to understand databases easily and software to navigate databases efficiently. In many ways, dimensional modeling amounts to holding the fort against assaults on simplicity. By consistently returning to a business-driven perspective and by refusing to compromise on the goals of user understandability and query performance, we establish a coherent design that serves the organization's analytic needs. Based on our experience and the overwhelming feedback from numerous practitioners from companies like your own, we believe that dimensional modeling is absolutely critical to a successful data warehousing initiative.

Dimensional modeling also has emerged as the only coherent architecture for building distributed data warehouse systems. When we use the conformed dimensions and conformed facts of a set of dimensional models, we have a practical and predictable framework for incrementally building complex data warehouse systems that have no center.

For all that has changed in our industry, the core dimensional modeling techniques that Ralph Kimball published six years ago have withstood the test of time. Concepts such as slowly changing dimensions, heterogeneous products, factless fact tables, and architected data marts continue to be discussed in data warehouse design workshops around the globe. The original concepts have been embellished and enhanced by new and complementary techniques. We decided to publish a second edition of Kimball's seminal work because we felt that it would be useful to pull together our collective thoughts on dimensional modeling under a single cover. We have each focused exclusively on decision support and data warehousing for over two decades. We hope to share the dimensional modeling patterns that have emerged repeatedly during the course of our data warehousing careers. This book is loaded with specific, practical design recommendations based on real-world scenarios.

The goal of this book is to provide a one-stop shop for dimensional modeling techniques. True to its title, it is a toolkit of dimensional design principles and techniques. We will address the needs of those just getting started in dimensional data warehousing, and we will describe advanced concepts for those of you who have been at this a while. We believe that this book stands alone in its depth of coverage on the topic of dimensional modeling.

Intended Audience

This book is intended for data warehouse designers, implementers, and managers. In addition, business analysts who are active participants in a warehouse initiative will find the content useful.

Even if you're not directly responsible for the dimensional model, we believe that it is important for all members of a warehouse project team to be comfortable with dimensional modeling concepts. The dimensional model has an impact on most aspects of a warehouse implementation, beginning with the translation of business requirements, through data staging, and finally, to the unveiling of a data warehouse through analytic applications. Due to the broad implications, you need to be conversant in dimensional modeling regardless whether you are responsible primarily for project management, business analysis, data architecture, database design, data staging, analytic applications, or education and support. We've written this book so that it is accessible to a broad audience.

For those of you who have read the first edition of this book, some of the familiar case studies will reappear in this edition; however, they have been updated significantly and fleshed out with richer content. We have developed vignettes for new industries, including health care, telecommunications, and electronic commerce. In addition, we have introduced more horizontal, cross-industry case studies for business functions such as human resources, accounting, procurement, and customer relationship management.

The content in this book is mildly technical. We discuss dimensional modeling in the context of a relational database primarily. We presume that readers have basic knowledge of relational database concepts such as tables, rows, keys, and joins. Given that we will be discussing dimensional models in a non-denominational manner, we won't dive into specific physical design and tuning guidance for any given database management systems.

Chapter Preview

The book is organized around a series of business vignettes or case studies. We believe that developing the design techniques by example is an extremely effective approach because it allows us to share very tangible guidance. While not intended to be full-scale application or industry solutions, these examples serve as a framework to discuss the patterns that emerge in dimensional modeling. In our experience, it is often easier to grasp the main elements of a design technique by stepping away from the all-too-familiar complexities of one's own applications in order to think about another business. Readers of the first edition have responded very favorably to this approach.

The chapters of this book build on one another. We will start with basic concepts and introduce more advanced content as the book unfolds. The chapters are to be read in order by every reader. For example, Chapter 15 on insurance will be difficult to comprehend unless you have read the preceding chapters on retailing, procurement, order management, and customer relationship management.

Those of you who have read the first edition may be tempted to skip the first few chapters. While some of the early grounding regarding facts and dimensions may be familiar turf, we don't want you to sprint too far ahead. For example, the first case study focuses on the retailing industry, just as it did in the first edition. However, in this edition we advocate a new approach, making a strong case for tackling the atomic, bedrock data of your organization. You'll miss out on this rationalization and other updates to fundamental concepts if you skip ahead too quickly.

Navigation Aids

We have laced the book with tips, key concepts, and chapter pointers to make it more usable and easily referenced in the future. In addition, we have provided an extensive glossary of terms.

You can find the tips sprinkled throughout this book by flipping through the chapters and looking for the lightbulb icon.

We begin each chapter with a sidebar of key concepts, denoted by the key icon.

Purpose of Each Chapter

Before we get started, we want to give you a chapter-by-chapter preview of the concepts covered as the book unfolds.

Chapter 1: Dimensional Modeling Primer

The book begins with a primer on dimensional modeling. We explore the components of the overall data warehouse architecture and establish core vocabulary that will be used during the remainder of the book. We dispel some of the myths and misconceptions about dimensional modeling, and we discuss the role of normalized models.

Chapter 2: Retail Sales

Retailing is the classic example used to illustrate dimensional modeling. We start with the classic because it is one that we all understand. Hopefully, you won't need to think very hard about the industry because we want you to focus on core dimensional modeling concepts instead. We begin by discussing the four-step process for designing dimensional models. We explore dimension tables in depth, including the date dimension that will be reused repeatedly throughout the book. We also discuss degenerate dimensions, snowflaking, and surrogate keys. Even if you're not a retailer, this chapter is required reading because it is chock full of fundamentals.

Chapter 3: Inventory

We remain within the retail industry for our second case study but turn our attention to another business process. This case study will provide a very vivid example of the data warehouse bus architecture and the use of conformed dimensions and facts. These concepts are critical to anyone looking to construct a data warehouse architecture that is integrated and extensible.

Chapter 4: Procurement

This chapter reinforces the importance of looking at your organization's value chain as you plot your data warehouse. We also explore a series of basic and advanced techniques for handling slowly changing dimension attributes.

Chapter 5: Order Management

In this case study we take a look at the business processes that are often the first to be implemented in data warehouses as they supply core business performance metrics—what are we selling to which customers at what price? We discuss the situation in which a dimension plays multiple roles within a schema. We also explore some of the common challenges modelers face when dealing with order management information, such as header/line item considerations, multiple currencies or units of measure, and junk dimensions with miscellaneous transaction indicators. We compare the three fundamental types of fact tables: transaction, periodic snapshot, and accumulating snapshot. Finally, we provide recommendations for handling more real-time warehousing requirements.

Chapter 6: Customer Relationship Management

Numerous data warehouses have been built on the premise that we need to better understand and service our customers. This chapter covers key considerations surrounding the customer dimension, including address standardization, managing large volume dimensions, and modeling unpredictable customer hierarchies. It also discusses the consolidation of customer data from multiple sources.

Chapter 7: Accounting

In this totally new chapter we discuss the modeling of general ledger information for the data warehouse. We describe the appropriate handling of year-to-date facts and multiple fiscal calendars, as well as the notion of consolidated dimensional models that combine data from multiple business processes.

Chapter 8: Human Resources Management

This new chapter explores several unique aspects of human resources dimensional models, including the situation in which a dimension table begins to behave like a fact table. We also introduce audit and keyword dimensions, as well as the handling of survey questionnaire data.

Chapter 9: Financial Services

The banking case study explores the concept of heterogeneous products in which each line of business has unique descriptive attributes and performance metrics. Obviously, the need to handle heterogeneous products is not unique to financial services. We also discuss the complicated relationships among accounts, customers, and households.

Chapter 10: Telecommunications and Utilities

This new chapter is structured somewhat differently to highlight considerations when performing a data model design review. In addition, we explore the idiosyncrasies of geographic location dimensions, as well as opportunities for leveraging geographic information systems.

Chapter 11: Transportation

In this case study we take a look at related fact tables at different levels of granularity. We discuss another approach for handling small dimensions, and we take a closer look at date and time dimensions, covering such concepts as country-specific calendars and synchronization across multiple time zones.

Chapter 12: Education

We look at several factless fact tables in this chapter and discuss their importance in analyzing what didn't happen. In addition, we explore the student application pipeline, which is a prime example of an accumulating snapshot fact table.

Chapter 13: Health Care

Some of the most complex models that we have ever worked with are from the health care industry. This new chapter illustrates the handling of such complexities, including the use of a bridge table to model multiple diagnoses and providers associated with a patient treatment.

Chapter 14: Electronic Commerce

This chapter provides an introduction to modeling clickstream data. The concepts are derived from *The Data Webhouse Toolkit* (Wiley 2000), which Ralph Kimball coauthored with Richard Merz.

Chapter 15: Insurance

The final case study serves to illustrate many of the techniques we discussed earlier in the book in a single set of interrelated schemas. It can be viewed as a pulling-it-all-together chapter because the modeling techniques will be layered on top of one another, similar to overlaying overhead projector transparencies.

Chapter 16: Building the Data Warehouse

Now that you are comfortable designing dimensional models, we provide a high-level overview of the activities that are encountered during the lifecycle of a typical data warehouse project iteration. This chapter could be considered a lightning tour of *The Data Warehouse Lifecycle Toolkit* (Wiley 1998) that we coauthored with Laura Reeves and Warren Thornthwaite.

Chapter 17: Present Imperatives and Future Outlook

In this final chapter we peer into our crystal ball to provide a preview of what we anticipate data warehousing will look like in the future.

Glossary

We've supplied a detailed glossary to serve as a reference resource. It will help bridge the gap between your general business understanding and the case studies derived from businesses other than your own.

Companion Web Site

You can access the book's companion Web site at www.kimballuniversity.com. The Web site offers the following resources:

- Register for *Design Tips* to receive ongoing, practical guidance about dimensional modeling and data warehouse design via electronic mail on a periodic basis.
- Link to all Ralph Kimball's articles from *Intelligent Enterprise* and its predecessor, *DBMS Magazine*.
- Learn about Kimball University classes for quality, vendor-independent education consistent with the authors' experiences and writings.

Summary

The goal of this book is to communicate a set of standard techniques for dimensional data warehouse design. Crudely speaking, if you as the reader get nothing else from this book other than the conviction that your data warehouse must be driven from the needs of business users and therefore built and presented from a simple dimensional perspective, then this book will have served its purpose. We are confident that you will be one giant step closer to data warehousing success if you buy into these premises.

Now that you know where we are headed, it is time to dive into the details. We'll begin with a primer on dimensional modeling in Chapter 1 to ensure that everyone is on the same page regarding key terminology and architectural concepts. From there we will begin our discussion of the fundamental techniques of dimensional modeling, starting with the tried-and-true retail industry.

Dimensional Modeling Primer

I n this first chapter we lay the groundwork for the case studies that follow. We'll begin by stepping back to consider data warehousing from a macro perspective. Some readers may be disappointed to learn that it is not all about tools and techniques—first and foremost, the data warehouse must consider the needs of the business. We'll drive stakes in the ground regarding the goals of the data warehouse while observing the uncanny similarities between the responsibilities of a data warehouse manager and those of a publisher. With this big-picture perspective, we'll explore the major components of the warehouse environment, including the role of normalized models. Finally, we'll close by establishing fundamental vocabulary for dimensional modeling. By the end of this chapter we hope that you'll have an appreciation for the need to be half DBA (database administrator) and half MBA (business analyst) as you tackle your data warehouse.

Chapter 1 discusses the following concepts:

- **Business-driven goals of a data warehouse**
- **Data warehouse publishing**
- **Major components of the overall data warehouse**
- **Importance of dimensional modeling for the data warehouse presentation area**
- **Fact and dimension table terminology**
- **Myths surrounding dimensional modeling**
- **Common data warehousing pitfalls to avoid**

Different Information Worlds

One of the most important assets of any organization is its information. This asset is almost always kept by an organization in two forms: the operational systems of record and the data warehouse. Crudely speaking, the operational systems are where the data is put in, and the data warehouse is where we get the data out.

The users of an operational system *turn* the wheels of the organization. They take orders, sign up new customers, and log complaints. Users of an operational system almost always deal with one record at a time. They repeatedly perform the same operational tasks over and over.

The users of a data warehouse, on the other hand, *watch* the wheels of the organization turn. They count the new orders and compare them with last week's orders and ask why the new customers signed up and what the customers complained about. Users of a data warehouse almost never deal with one row at a time. Rather, their questions often require that hundreds or thousands of rows be searched and compressed into an answer set. To further complicate matters, users of a data warehouse continuously change the kinds of questions they ask.

In the first edition of *The Data Warehouse Toolkit* (Wiley 1996), Ralph Kimball devoted an entire chapter to describe the dichotomy between the worlds of operational processing and data warehousing. At this time, it is widely recognized that the data warehouse has profoundly different needs, clients, structures, and rhythms than the operational systems of record. Unfortunately, we continue to encounter supposed data warehouses that are mere copies of the operational system of record stored on a separate hardware platform. While this may address the need to isolate the operational and warehouse environments for performance reasons, it does nothing to address the other inherent differences between these two types of systems. Business users are underwhelmed by the usability and performance provided by these pseudo data warehouses. These imposters do a disservice to data warehousing because they don't acknowledge that warehouse users have drastically different needs than operational system users.

Goals of a Data Warehouse

Before we delve into the details of modeling and implementation, it is helpful to focus on the fundamental goals of the data warehouse. The goals can be developed by walking through the halls of any organization and listening to business management. Inevitably, these recurring themes emerge:

- "We have mountains of data in this company, but we can't access it."
- "We need to slice and dice the data every which way."
- "You've got to make it easy for business people to get at the data directly."
- "Just show me what is important."
- "It drives me crazy to have two people present the same business metrics at a meeting, but with different numbers."
- "We want people to use information to support more fact-based decision making."

Based on our experience, these concerns are so universal that they drive the bedrock requirements for the data warehouse. Let's turn these business management quotations into data warehouse requirements.

The data warehouse must make an organization's information easily accessible. The contents of the data warehouse must be understandable. The data must be intuitive and obvious to the business user, not merely the developer. Understandability implies legibility; the contents of the data warehouse need to be labeled meaningfully. Business users want to separate and combine the data in the warehouse in endless combinations, a process commonly referred to as *slicing and dicing.* The tools that access the data warehouse must be simple and easy to use. They also must return query results to the user with minimal wait times.

The data warehouse must present the organization's information consistently. The data in the warehouse must be credible. Data must be carefully assembled from a variety of sources around the organization, cleansed, quality assured, and released only when it is fit for user consumption. Information from one business process should match with information from another. If two performance measures have the same name, then they must mean the same thing. Conversely, if two measures don't mean the same thing, then they should be labeled differently. Consistent information means high-quality information. It means that all the data is accounted for and complete. Consistency also implies that common definitions for the contents of the data warehouse are available for users.

The data warehouse must be adaptive and resilient to change. We simply can't avoid change. User needs, business conditions, data, and technology are all subject to the shifting sands of time. The data warehouse must be designed to handle this inevitable change. Changes to the data warehouse should be graceful, meaning that they don't invalidate existing data or applications. The existing data and applications should not be changed or disrupted when the business community asks new questions or new data is added to the warehouse. If descriptive data in the warehouse is modified, we must account for the changes appropriately.

The data warehouse must be a secure bastion that protects our information assets. An organization's informational crown jewels are stored in the data warehouse. At a minimum, the warehouse likely contains information about what we're selling to whom at what price—potentially harmful details in the hands of the wrong people. The data warehouse must effectively control access to the organization's confidential information.

The data warehouse must serve as the foundation for improved decision making. The data warehouse must have the right data in it to support decision making. There is only one true output from a data warehouse: the decisions that are made after the data warehouse has presented its evidence. These decisions deliver the business impact and value attributable to the warehouse. The original label that predates the data warehouse is still the best description of what we are designing: a decision support system.

The business community must accept the data warehouse if it is to be deemed successful. It doesn't matter that we've built an elegant solution using best-of-breed products and platforms. If the business community has not embraced the data warehouse and continued to use it actively six months after training, then we have failed the acceptance test. Unlike an operational system rewrite, where business users have no choice but to use the new system, data warehouse usage is sometimes optional. Business user acceptance has more to do with simplicity than anything else.

As this list illustrates, successful data warehousing demands much more than being a stellar DBA or technician. With a data warehousing initiative, we have one foot in our information technology (IT) comfort zone, while our other foot is on the unfamiliar turf of business users. We must straddle the two, modifying some of our tried-and-true skills to adapt to the unique demands of data warehousing. Clearly, we need to bring a bevy of skills to the party to behave like we're a hybrid DBA/MBA.

The Publishing Metaphor

With the goals of the data warehouse as a backdrop, let's compare our responsibilities as data warehouse managers with those of a publishing editor-in-chief. As the editor of a high-quality magazine, you would be given broad latitude to manage the magazine's content, style, and delivery. Anyone with this job title likely would tackle the following activities:

- Identify your readers demographically.
- Find out what the readers want in this kind of magazine.
- Identify the "best" readers who will renew their subscriptions and buy products from the magazine's advertisers.

- Find potential new readers and make them aware of the magazine.
- Choose the magazine content most appealing to the target readers.
- Make layout and rendering decisions that maximize the readers' pleasure.
- Uphold high quality writing and editing standards, while adopting a consistent presentation style.
- Continuously monitor the accuracy of the articles and advertiser's claims.
- Develop a good network of writers and contributors as you gather new input to the magazine's content from a variety of sources.
- Attract advertising and run the magazine profitably.
- Publish the magazine on a regular basis.
- Maintain the readers' trust.
- Keep the business owners happy.

We also can identify items that should be nongoals for the magazine editor-in-chief. These would include such things as building the magazine around the technology of a particular printing press, putting management's energy into operational efficiencies exclusively, imposing a technical writing style that readers don't easily understand, or creating an intricate and crowded layout that is difficult to peruse and read.

By building the publishing business on a foundation of serving the readers effectively, your magazine is likely to be successful. Conversely, go through the list and imagine what happens if you omit any single item; ultimately, your magazine would have serious problems.

The point of this metaphor, of course, is to draw the parallel between being a conventional publisher and being a data warehouse manager. We are convinced that the correct job description for a data warehouse manager is *publisher of the right data*. Driven by the needs of the business, data warehouse managers are responsible for publishing data that has been collected from a variety of sources and edited for quality and consistency. Your main responsibility as a data warehouse manager is to serve your readers, otherwise known as business users. The publishing metaphor underscores the need to focus outward to your customers rather than merely focusing inward on products and processes. While you will use technology to deliver your data warehouse, the technology is at best a means to an end. As such, the technology and techniques you use to build your data warehouses should not appear directly in your top job responsibilities.

Let's recast the magazine publisher's responsibilities as data warehouse manager responsibilities:

- Understand your users by business area, job responsibilities, and computer tolerance.

- Determine the decisions the business users want to make with the help of the data warehouse.

- Identify the "best" users who make effective, high-impact decisions using the data warehouse.

- Find potential new users and make them aware of the data warehouse.

- Choose the most effective, actionable subset of the data to present in the data warehouse, drawn from the vast universe of possible data in your organization.

- Make the user interfaces and applications simple and template-driven, explicitly matching to the users' cognitive processing profiles.

- Make sure the data is accurate and can be trusted, labeling it consistently across the enterprise.

- Continuously monitor the accuracy of the data and the content of the delivered reports.

- Search for new data sources, and continuously adapt the data warehouse to changing data profiles, reporting requirements, and business priorities.

- Take a portion of the credit for the business decisions made using the data warehouse, and use these successes to justify your staffing, software, and hardware expenditures.

- Publish the data on a regular basis.

- Maintain the trust of business users.

- Keep your business users, executive sponsors, and boss happy.

If you do a good job with all these responsibilities, you will be a great data warehouse manager! Conversely, go down through the list and imagine what happens if you omit any single item. Ultimately, your data warehouse would have serious problems. We urge you to contrast this view of a data warehouse manager's job with your own job description. Chances are the preceding list is much more oriented toward user and business issues and may not even sound like a job in IT. In our opinion, this is what makes data warehousing interesting.

Components of a Data Warehouse

Now that we understand the goals of a data warehouse, let's investigate the components that make up a complete warehousing environment. It is helpful to understand the pieces carefully before we begin combining them to create a data warehouse. Each warehouse component serves a specific function. We need to learn the strategic significance of each component and how to wield it effectively to win the data warehousing game. One of the biggest threats to data warehousing success is confusing the components' roles and functions.

As illustrated in Figure 1.1, there are four separate and distinct components to be considered as we explore the data warehouse environment—operational source systems, data staging area, data presentation area, and data access tools.

Operational Source Systems

These are the operational systems of record that capture the transactions of the business. The source systems should be thought of as outside the data warehouse because presumably we have little to no control over the content and format of the data in these operational legacy systems. The main priorities of the source systems are processing performance and availability. Queries against source systems are narrow, one-record-at-a-time queries that are part of the normal transaction flow and severely restricted in their demands on the operational system. We make the strong assumption that source systems are not queried in the broad and unexpected ways that data warehouses typically are queried. The source systems maintain little historical data, and if you have a good data warehouse, the source systems can be relieved of much of the responsibility for representing the past. Each source system is often a natural stovepipe application, where little investment has been made to sharing common data such as product, customer, geography, or calendar with other operational systems in the organization. It would be great if your source systems were being reengineered with a consistent view. Such an enterprise application integration (EAI) effort will make the data warehouse design task far easier.

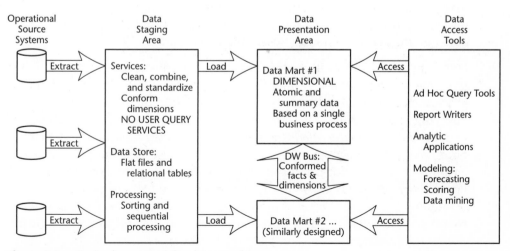

Figure 1.1 Basic elements of the data warehouse.

Data Staging Area

The data staging area of the data warehouse is both a storage area and a set of processes commonly referred to as *extract-transformation-load* (ETL). The data staging area is everything between the operational source systems and the data presentation area. It is somewhat analogous to the kitchen of a restaurant, where raw food products are transformed into a fine meal. In the data warehouse, raw operational data is transformed into a warehouse deliverable fit for user query and consumption. Similar to the restaurant's kitchen, the backroom data staging area is accessible only to skilled professionals. The data warehouse kitchen staff is busy preparing meals and simultaneously cannot be responding to customer inquiries. Customers aren't invited to eat in the kitchen. It certainly isn't safe for customers to wander into the kitchen. We wouldn't want our data warehouse customers to be injured by the dangerous equipment, hot surfaces, and sharp knifes they may encounter in the kitchen, so we prohibit them from accessing the staging area. Besides, things happen in the kitchen that customers just shouldn't be privy to.

The key architectural requirement for the data staging area is that it is off-limits to business users and does *not* provide query and presentation services.

Extraction is the first step in the process of getting data into the data warehouse environment. Extracting means reading and understanding the source data and copying the data needed for the data warehouse into the staging area for further manipulation.

Once the data is extracted to the staging area, there are numerous potential transformations, such as cleansing the data (correcting misspellings, resolving domain conflicts, dealing with missing elements, or parsing into standard formats), combining data from multiple sources, deduplicating data, and assigning warehouse keys. These transformations are all precursors to loading the data into the data warehouse presentation area.

Unfortunately, there is still considerable industry consternation about whether the data that supports or results from this process should be instantiated in physical normalized structures prior to loading into the presentation area for querying and reporting. These normalized structures sometimes are referred to in the industry as the *enterprise data warehouse*; however, we believe that this terminology is a misnomer because the warehouse is actually much more encompassing than this set of normalized tables. The enterprise's data warehouse more accurately refers to the conglomeration of an organization's data warehouse staging and presentation areas. Thus, throughout this book, when we refer to the enterprise data warehouse, we mean the union of all the diverse data warehouse components, not just the backroom staging area.

The data staging area is dominated by the simple activities of sorting and sequential processing. In many cases, the data staging area is not based on relational technology but instead may consist of a system of flat files. After you validate your data for conformance with the defined one-to-one and many-to-one business rules, it may be pointless to take the final step of building a full-blown third-normal-form physical database.

However, there are cases where the data arrives at the doorstep of the data staging area in a third-normal-form relational format. In these situations, the managers of the data staging area simply may be more comfortable performing the cleansing and transformation tasks using a set of normalized structures. A normalized database for data staging storage is acceptable. However, we continue to have some reservations about this approach. The creation of both normalized structures for staging and dimensional structures for presentation means that the data is extracted, transformed, and loaded twice—once into the normalized database and then again when we load the dimensional model. Obviously, this two-step process requires more time and resources for the development effort, more time for the periodic loading or updating of data, and more capacity to store the multiple copies of the data. At the bottom line, this typically translates into the need for larger development, ongoing support, and hardware platform budgets. Unfortunately, some data warehouse project teams have failed miserably because they focused all their energy and resources on constructing the normalized structures rather than allocating time to development of a presentation area that supports improved business decision making. While we believe that enterprise-wide data consistency is a fundamental goal of the data warehouse environment, there are equally effective and less costly approaches than physically creating a normalized set of tables in your staging area, if these structures don't already exist.

It is acceptable to create a normalized database to support the staging processes; however, this is not the end goal. The normalized structures must be off-limits to user queries because they defeat understandability and performance. As soon as a database supports query and presentation services, it must be considered part of the data warehouse presentation area. By default, normalized databases are excluded from the presentation area, which should be strictly dimensionally structured.

Regardless of whether we're working with a series of flat files or a normalized data structure in the staging area, the final step of the ETL process is the loading of data. Loading in the data warehouse environment usually takes the form of presenting the quality-assured dimensional tables to the bulk loading facilities of each data mart. The target data mart must then index the newly arrived data for query performance. When each data mart has been freshly loaded, indexed, supplied with appropriate aggregates, and further quality assured, the user community is notified that the new data has been published. Publishing includes communicating the nature of any changes that have occurred in the underlying dimensions and new assumptions that have been introduced into the measured or calculated facts.

Data Presentation

The data presentation area is where data is organized, stored, and made available for direct querying by users, report writers, and other analytical applications. Since the backroom staging area is off-limits, the presentation area *is* the data warehouse as far as the business community is concerned. It is all the business community sees and touches via data access tools. The prerelease working title for the first edition of *The Data Warehouse Toolkit* originally was *Getting the Data Out*. This is what the presentation area with its dimensional models is all about.

We typically refer to the presentation area as a series of integrated data marts. A data mart is a wedge of the overall presentation area pie. In its most simplistic form, a data mart presents the data from a single business process. These business processes cross the boundaries of organizational functions.

We have several strong opinions about the presentation area. First of all, we insist that the data be presented, stored, and accessed in dimensional schemas. Fortunately, the industry has matured to the point where we're no longer debating this mandate. The industry has concluded that dimensional modeling is the most viable technique for delivering data to data warehouse users.

Dimensional modeling is a new name for an old technique for making databases simple and understandable. In case after case, beginning in the 1970s, IT organizations, consultants, end users, and vendors have gravitated to a simple dimensional structure to match the fundamental human need for simplicity. Imagine a chief executive officer (CEO) who describes his or her business as, "We sell products in various markets and measure our performance over time." As dimensional designers, we listen carefully to the CEO's emphasis on product, market, and time. Most people find it intuitive to think of this business as a cube of data, with the edges labeled product, market, and time. We can imagine slicing and dicing along each of these dimensions. Points inside the cube are where the measurements for that combination of product, market, and time are stored. The ability to visualize something as abstract as a set of data in a concrete and tangible way is the secret of understandability. If this perspective seems too simple, then good! A data model that starts by being simple has a chance of remaining simple at the end of the design. A model that starts by being complicated surely will be overly complicated at the end. Overly complicated models will run slowly and be rejected by business users.

Dimensional modeling is quite different from third-normal-form (3NF) modeling. 3NF modeling is a design technique that seeks to remove data redundancies. Data is divided into many discrete entities, each of which becomes a table in the relational database. A database of sales orders might start off with a record for each order line but turns into an amazingly complex spiderweb diagram as a 3NF model, perhaps consisting of hundreds or even thousands of normalized tables.

The industry sometimes refers to 3NF models as *ER models*. ER is an acronym for *entity relationship*. Entity-relationship diagrams (ER diagrams or ERDs) are drawings of boxes and lines to communicate the relationships between tables. Both 3NF and dimensional models can be represented in ERDs because both consist of joined relational tables; the key difference between 3NF and dimensional models is the degree of normalization. Since both model types can be presented as ERDs, we'll refrain from referring to 3NF models as ER models; instead, we'll call them *normalized models* to minimize confusion.

Normalized modeling is immensely helpful to operational processing performance because an update or insert transaction only needs to touch the database in one place. Normalized models, however, are too complicated for data warehouse queries. Users can't understand, navigate, or remember normalized models that resemble the Los Angeles freeway system. Likewise, relational database management systems (RDBMSs) can't query a normalized model efficiently; the complexity overwhelms the database optimizers, resulting in disastrous performance. The use of normalized modeling in the data warehouse presentation area defeats the whole purpose of data warehousing, namely, intuitive and high-performance retrieval of data.

There is a common syndrome in many large IT shops. It is a kind of sickness that comes from overly complex data warehousing schemas. The symptoms might include:

- A $10 million hardware and software investment that is performing only a handful of queries per day

- An IT department that is forced into a kind of priesthood, writing all the data warehouse queries

- Seemingly simple queries that require several pages of single-spaced Structured Query Language (SQL) code

- A marketing department that is unhappy because it can't access the system directly (and still doesn't know whether the company is profitable in Schenectady)

- A restless chief information officer (CIO) who is determined to make some changes if things don't improve dramatically

Fortunately, dimensional modeling addresses the problem of overly complex schemas in the presentation area. A dimensional model contains the same information as a normalized model but packages the data in a format whose design goals are user understandability, query performance, and resilience to change.

Our second stake in the ground about presentation area data marts is that they must contain detailed, atomic data. Atomic data is required to withstand assaults from unpredictable ad hoc user queries. While the data marts also may contain performance-enhancing summary data, or aggregates, it is not sufficient to deliver these summaries without the underlying granular data in a dimensional form. In other words, it is completely unacceptable to store only summary data in dimensional models while the atomic data is locked up in normalized models. It is impractical to expect a user to drill down through dimensional data almost to the most granular level and then lose the benefits of a dimensional presentation at the final step. In Chapter 16 we will see that any user application can descend effortlessly to the bedrock granular data by using aggregate navigation, but only if all the data is available in the same, consistent dimensional form. While users of the data warehouse may look infrequently at a single line item on an order, they may be very interested in last week's orders for products of a given size (or flavor, package type, or manufacturer) for customers who first purchased within the last six months (or reside in a given state or have certain credit terms). We need the most finely grained data in our presentation area so that users can ask the most precise questions possible. Because users' requirements are unpredictable and constantly changing, we must provide access to the exquisite details so that they can be rolled up to address the questions of the moment.

All the data marts must be built using common dimensions and facts, which we refer to as *conformed*. This is the basis of the data warehouse bus architecture, which we'll elaborate on in Chapter 3. Adherence to the bus architecture is our third stake in the ground regarding the presentation area. Without shared, conformed dimensions and facts, a data mart is a standalone stovepipe application. Isolated stovepipe data marts that cannot be tied together are the bane of the data warehouse movement. They merely perpetuate incompatible views of the enterprise. If you have any hope of building a data warehouse that is robust and integrated, you must make a commitment to the bus architecture. In this book we will illustrate that when data marts have been designed with conformed dimensions and facts, they can be combined and used together. The data warehouse presentation area in a large enterprise data warehouse ultimately will consist of 20 or more very similar-looking data marts. The dimensional models in these data marts also will look quite similar. Each data mart may contain several fact tables, each with 5 to 15 dimension tables. If the design has been done correctly, many of these dimension tables will be shared from fact table to fact table.

Using the bus architecture is the secret to building distributed data warehouse systems. Let's be real—most of us don't have the budget, time, or political power to build a fully centralized data warehouse. When the bus architecture is used as a framework, we can allow the enterprise data warehouse to develop in a decentralized (and far more realistic) way.

💡 **Data in the queryable presentation area of the data warehouse must be dimensional, must be atomic, and must adhere to the data warehouse bus architecture.**

If the presentation area is based on a relational database, then these dimensionally modeled tables are referred to as *star schemas.* If the presentation area is based on multidimensional database or online analytic processing (OLAP) technology, then the data is stored in *cubes.* While the technology originally wasn't referred to as OLAP, many of the early decision support system vendors built their systems around the cube concept, so today's OLAP vendors naturally are aligned with the dimensional approach to data warehousing. Dimensional modeling is applicable to both relational and multidimensional databases. Both have a common logical design with recognizable dimensions; however, the physical implementation differs. Fortunately, most of the recommendations in this book pertain, regardless of the database platform. While the capabilities of OLAP technology are improving continuously, at the time of this writing, most large data marts are still implemented on relational databases. In addition, most OLAP cubes are sourced from or drill into relational dimensional star schemas using a variation of aggregate navigation. For these reasons, most of the specific discussions surrounding the presentation area are couched in terms of a relational platform.

Contrary to the original religion of the data warehouse, modern data marts may well be updated, sometimes frequently. Incorrect data obviously should be corrected. Changes in labels, hierarchies, status, and corporate ownership often trigger necessary changes in the original data stored in the data marts that comprise the data warehouse, but in general, these are managed-load updates, not transactional updates.

Data Access Tools

The final major component of the data warehouse environment is the *data access tool(s).* We use the term tool loosely to refer to the variety of capabilities that can be provided to business users to leverage the presentation area for analytic decision making. By definition, all data access tools query the data in the data warehouse's presentation area. Querying, obviously, is the whole point of using the data warehouse.

A data access tool can be as simple as an ad hoc query tool or as complex as a sophisticated data mining or modeling application. Ad hoc query tools, as powerful as they are, can be understood and used effectively only by a small percentage of the potential data warehouse business user population. The majority of the business user base likely will access the data via prebuilt parameter-driven analytic applications. Approximately 80 to 90 percent of the potential users will be served by these canned applications that are essentially finished templates that do not require users to construct relational queries directly. Some of the more sophisticated data access tools, like modeling or forecasting tools, actually may upload their results back into operational source systems or the staging/presentation areas of the data warehouse.

Additional Considerations

Before we leave the discussion of data warehouse components, there are several other concepts that warrant discussion.

Metadata

Metadata is all the information in the data warehouse environment that is not the actual data itself. Metadata is akin to an encyclopedia for the data warehouse. Data warehouse teams often spend an enormous amount of time talking about, worrying about, and feeling guilty about metadata. Since most developers have a natural aversion to the development and orderly filing of documentation, metadata often gets cut from the project plan despite everyone's acknowledgment that it is important.

Metadata comes in a variety of shapes and forms to support the disparate needs of the data warehouse's technical, administrative, and business user groups. We have operational source system metadata including source schemas and copybooks that facilitate the extraction process. Once data is in the staging area, we encounter staging metadata to guide the transformation and loading processes, including staging file and target table layouts, transformation and cleansing rules, conformed dimension and fact definitions, aggregation definitions, and ETL transmission schedules and run-log results. Even the custom programming code we write in the data staging area is metadata.

Metadata surrounding the warehouse DBMS accounts for such items as the system tables, partition settings, indexes, view definitions, and DBMS-level security privileges and grants. Finally, the data access tool metadata identifies business names and definitions for the presentation area's tables and columns as well as constraint filters, application template specifications, access and usage statistics, and other user documentation. And of course, if we haven't included it already, don't forget all the security settings, beginning with source transactional data and extending all the way to the user's desktop.

The ultimate goal is to corral, catalog, integrate, and then leverage these disparate varieties of metadata, much like the resources of a library. Suddenly, the effort to build dimensional models appears to pale in comparison. However, just because the task looms large, we can't simply ignore the development of a metadata framework for the data warehouse. We need to develop an overall metadata plan while prioritizing short-term deliverables, including the purchase or construction of a repository for keeping track of all the metadata.

Operational Data Store

Some of you probably are wondering where the operational data store (ODS) fits in our warehouse components diagram. Since there's no single universal definition for the ODS, if and where it belongs depend on your situation. ODSs are frequently updated, somewhat integrated copies of operational data. The frequency of update and degree of integration of an ODS vary based on the specific requirements. In any case, the O is the operative letter in the ODS acronym.

Most commonly, an ODS is implemented to deliver operational reporting, especially when neither the legacy nor more modern on-line transaction processing (OLTP) systems provide adequate operational reports. These reports are characterized by a limited set of fixed queries that can be hard-wired in a reporting application. The reports address the organization's more tactical decision-making requirements. Performance-enhancing aggregations, significant historical time series, and extensive descriptive attribution are specifically excluded from the ODS. The ODS as a reporting instance may be a stepping-stone to feed operational data into the warehouse.

In other cases, ODSs are built to support real-time interactions, especially in customer relationship management (CRM) applications such as accessing your travel itinerary on a Web site or your service history when you call into customer support. The traditional data warehouse typically is not in a position to support the demand for near-real-time data or immediate response times. Similar to the operational reporting scenario, data inquiries to support these real-time interactions have a fixed structure. Interestingly, this type of ODS sometimes leverages information from the data warehouse, such as a customer service call center application that uses customer behavioral information from the data warehouse to precalculate propensity scores and store them in the ODS.

In either scenario, the ODS can be either a third physical system sitting between the operational systems and the data warehouse or a specially administered hot partition of the data warehouse itself. Every organization obviously needs operational systems. Likewise, every organization would benefit from a data warehouse. The same cannot be said about a physically distinct ODS unless the other two systems cannot answer your immediate operational questions. Clearly, you shouldn't allocate resources to construct a third physical system unless your business needs cannot be supported by either the operational data-collection system or the data warehouse. For these reasons, we believe that the trend in data warehouse design is to deliver the ODS as a specially administered portion of the conventional data warehouse. We will further discuss hot-partition-style ODSs in Chapter 5.

Finally, before we leave this topic, some have defined the ODS to mean the place in the data warehouse where we store granular atomic data. We believe that this detailed data should be considered a natural part of the data warehouse's presentation area and not a separate entity. Beginning in Chapter 2, we will show how the lowest-level transactions in a business are the foundation for the presentation area of the data warehouse.

Dimensional Modeling Vocabulary

Throughout this book we will refer repeatedly to fact and dimension tables. Contrary to popular folklore, Ralph Kimball didn't invent this terminology. As best as we can determine, the terms *dimensions* and *facts* originated from a joint research project conducted by General Mills and Dartmouth University in the 1960s. In the 1970s, both AC Nielsen and IRI used these terms consistently to describe their syndicated data offerings, which could be described accurately today as dimensional data marts for retail sales data. Long before simplicity was a lifestyle trend, the early database syndicators gravitated to these concepts for simplifying the presentation of analytic information. They understood that a database wouldn't be used unless it was packaged simply.

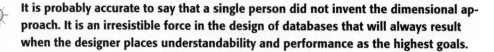 It is probably accurate to say that a single person did not invent the dimensional approach. It is an irresistible force in the design of databases that will always result when the designer places understandability and performance as the highest goals.

Fact Table

A fact table is the primary table in a dimensional model where the numerical performance measurements of the business are stored, as illustrated in Figure 1.2. We strive to store the measurement data resulting from a business process in a single data mart. Since measurement data is overwhelmingly the largest part of any data mart, we avoid duplicating it in multiple places around the enterprise.

Daily Sales Fact Table
Date Key (FK)
Product Key (FK)
Store Key (FK)
Quantity Sold
Dollar Sales Amount

Figure 1.2 Sample fact table.

We use the term *fact* to represent a business measure. We can imagine standing in the marketplace watching products being sold and writing down the quantity sold and dollar sales amount each day for each product in each store. A measurement is taken at the intersection of all the dimensions (day, product, and store). This list of dimensions defines the *grain* of the fact table and tells us what the scope of the measurement is.

> **A row in a fact table corresponds to a measurement. A measurement is a row in a fact table. All the measurements in a fact table must be at the same grain.**

The most useful facts are numeric and additive, such as dollar sales amount. Throughout this book we will use dollars as the standard currency to make the case study examples more tangible—please bear with the authors and substitute your own local currency if it doesn't happen to be dollars.

Additivity is crucial because data warehouse applications almost never retrieve a single fact table row. Rather, they bring back hundreds, thousands, or even millions of fact rows at a time, and the most useful thing to do with so many rows is to add them up. In Figure 1.2, no matter what slice of the database the user chooses, we can add up the quantities and dollars to a valid total. We will see later in this book that there are facts that are semiadditive and still others that are nonadditive. Semiadditive facts can be added only along some of the dimensions, and nonadditive facts simply can't be added at all. With nonadditive facts we are forced to use counts or averages if we wish to summarize the rows or are reduced to printing out the fact rows one at a time. This would be a dull exercise in a fact table with a billion rows.

> **The most useful facts in a fact table are numeric and additive.**

We often describe facts as continuously valued mainly as a guide for the designer to help sort out what is a fact versus a dimension attribute. The dollar sales amount fact is continuously valued in this example because it can take on virtually any value within a broad range. As observers, we have to stand out in the marketplace and wait for the measurement before we have any idea what the value will be.

It is theoretically possible for a measured fact to be textual; however, the condition arises rarely. In most cases, a textual measurement is a description of something and is drawn from a discrete list of values. The designer should make every effort to put textual measures into dimensions because they can be correlated more effectively with the other textual dimension attributes and will consume much less space. We do not store redundant textual information in fact tables. Unless the text is unique for every row in the fact table, it belongs in the dimension table. A true text fact is rare in a data warehouse because the unpredictable content of a text fact, like a free text comment, makes it nearly impossible to analyze.

In our sample fact table (see Figure 1.2), if there is no sales activity on a given day in a given store for a given product, we leave the row out of the table. It is very important that we do not try to fill the fact table with zeros representing nothing happening because these zeros would overwhelm most of our fact tables. By only including true activity, fact tables tend to be quite sparse. Despite their sparsity, fact tables usually make up 90 percent or more of the total space consumed by a dimensional database. Fact tables tend to be deep in terms of the number of rows but narrow in terms of the number of columns. Given their size, we are judicious about fact table space utilization.

As we develop the examples in this book, we will see that all fact table grains fall into one of three categories: transaction, periodic snapshot, and accumulating snapshot. Transaction grain fact tables are among the most common. We will introduce transaction fact tables in Chapter 2, periodic snapshots in Chapter 3, and accumulating snapshots in Chapter 5.

All fact tables have two or more foreign keys, as designated by the FK notation in Figure 1.2, that connect to the dimension tables' primary keys. For example, the product key in the fact table always will match a specific product key in the product dimension table. When all the keys in the fact table match their respective primary keys correctly in the corresponding dimension tables, we say that the tables satisfy *referential integrity*. We access the fact table via the dimension tables joined to it.

The fact table itself generally has its own primary key made up of a subset of the foreign keys. This key is often called a *composite* or *concatenated key*. Every fact table in a dimensional model has a composite key, and conversely, every table that has a composite key is a fact table. Another way to say this is that in a dimensional model, every table that expresses a many-to-many relationship must be a fact table. All other tables are dimension tables.

Fact tables express the many-to-many relationships between dimensions in dimensional models.

Only a subset of the components in the fact table composite key typically is needed to guarantee row uniqueness. There are usually about a half dozen dimensions that have robust many-to-many relationships with each other and uniquely identify each row. Sometimes there are as few as two dimensions, such as the invoice number and the product key. Once this subset has been identified, the rest of the dimensions take on a single value in the context of the fact table row's primary key. In other words, they go along for the ride. In most cases, there is no advantage to introducing a unique ROWID key to serve as the primary key in the fact table. Doing so makes your fact table larger, while any index on this artificial ROWID primary key would be worthless. However, such a key may be required to placate the database management system, especially if you can legitimately, from a business perspective, load multiple identical rows into the fact table.

Dimension Tables

Dimension tables are integral companions to a fact table. The dimension tables contain the textual descriptors of the business, as illustrated in Figure 1.3. In a well-designed dimensional model, dimension tables have many columns or attributes. These attributes describe the rows in the dimension table. We strive to include as many meaningful textlike descriptions as possible. It is not uncommon for a dimension table to have 50 to 100 attributes. Dimension tables tend to be relatively shallow in terms of the number of rows (often far fewer than 1 million rows) but are wide with many large columns. Each dimension is defined by its single primary key, designated by the PK notation in Figure 1.3, which serves as the basis for referential integrity with any given fact table to which it is joined.

Dimension attributes serve as the primary source of query constraints, groupings, and report labels. In a query or report request, attributes are identified as the *by* words. For example, when a user states that he or she wants to see dollar sales by week by brand, week and brand must be available as dimension attributes.

Dimension table attributes play a vital role in the data warehouse. Since they are the source of virtually all interesting constraints and report labels, they are key to making the data warehouse usable and understandable. In many ways, the data warehouse is only as good as the dimension attributes. The power of the data warehouse is directly proportional to the quality and depth of the dimension attributes. The more time spent providing attributes with verbose business terminology, the better the data warehouse is. The more time spent populating the values in an attribute column, the better the data warehouse is. The more time spent ensuring the quality of the values in an attribute column, the better the data warehouse is.

Dimension tables are the entry points into the fact table. Robust dimension attributes deliver robust analytic slicing and dicing capabilities. The dimensions implement the user interface to the data warehouse.

The best attributes are textual and discrete. Attributes should consist of real words rather than cryptic abbreviations. Typical attributes for a product dimension would include a short description (10 to 15 characters), a long description (30 to 50 characters), a brand name, a category name, packaging type, size, and numerous other product characteristics. Although the size is probably numeric, it is still a dimension attribute because it behaves more like a textual description than like a numeric measurement. Size is a discrete and constant descriptor of a specific product.

Sometimes when we are designing a database it is unclear whether a numeric data field extracted from a production data source is a fact or dimension attribute. We often can make the decision by asking whether the field is a measurement that takes on lots of values and participates in calculations (making it a fact) or is a discretely valued description that is more or less constant and participates in constraints (making it a dimensional attribute). For example, the standard cost for a product seems like a constant attribute of the product but may be changed so often that eventually we decide that it is more like a measured fact. Occasionally, we can't be certain of the classification. In such cases, it may be possible to model the data field either way, as a matter of designer's prerogative.

Product Dimension Table
Product Key (PK)
Product Description
SKU Number (Natural Key)
Brand Description
Category Description
Department Description
Package Type Description
Package Size
Fat Content Description
Diet Type Description
Weight
Weight Units of Measure
Storage Type
Shelf Life Type
Shelf Width
Shelf Height
Shelf Depth
... and many more

Figure 1.3   Sample dimension table.

We strive to minimize the use of codes in our dimension tables by replacing them with more verbose textual attributes. We understand that you may have already trained the users to make sense of operational codes, but going forward, we'd like to minimize their reliance on miniature notes attached to their computer monitor for code translations. We want to have standard decodes for the operational codes available as dimension attributes so that the labeling on data warehouse queries and reports is consistent. We don't want to encourage decodes buried in our reporting applications, where inconsistency is inevitable. Sometimes operational codes or identifiers have legitimate business significance to users or are required to communicate back to the operational world. In these cases, the codes should appear as explicit dimension attributes, in addition to the corresponding user-friendly textual descriptors. We have identified operational, natural keys in the dimension figures, as appropriate, throughout this book.

Operational codes often have intelligence embedded in them. For example, the first two digits may identify the line of business, whereas the next two digits may identify the global region. Rather than forcing users to interrogate or filter on the operational code, we pull out the embedded meanings and present them to users as separate dimension attributes that can be filtered, grouped, or reported on easily.

Dimension tables often represent hierarchical relationships in the business. In our sample product dimension table, products roll up into brands and then into categories. For each row in the product dimension, we store the brand and category description associated with each product. We realize that the hierarchical descriptive information is stored redundantly, but we do so in the spirit of ease of use and query performance. We resist our natural urge to store only the brand code in the product dimension and create a separate brand lookup table. This would be called a *snowflake*. Dimension tables typically are highly denormalized. They are usually quite small (less than 10 percent of the total data storage requirements). Since dimension tables typically are geometrically smaller than fact tables, improving storage efficiency by normalizing or snowflaking has virtually no impact on the overall database size. We almost always trade off dimension table space for simplicity and accessibility.

Bringing Together Facts and Dimensions

Now that we understand fact and dimension tables, let's bring the two building blocks together in a dimensional model. As illustrated in Figure 1.4, the fact table consisting of numeric measurements is joined to a set of dimension tables filled with descriptive attributes. This characteristic starlike structure is often called a *star join schema*. This term dates back to the earliest days of relational databases.

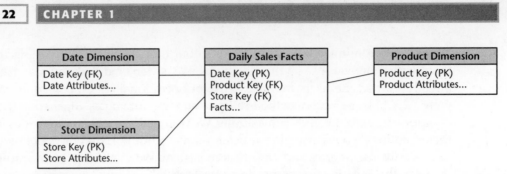

Figure 1.4 Fact and dimension tables in a dimensional model.

The first thing we notice about the resulting dimensional schema is its simplicity and symmetry. Obviously, business users benefit from the simplicity because the data is easier to understand and navigate. The charm of the design in Figure 1.4 is that it is highly recognizable to business users. We have observed literally hundreds of instances where users agree immediately that the dimensional model *is* their business. Furthermore, the reduced number of tables and use of meaningful business descriptors make it less likely that mistakes will occur.

The simplicity of a dimensional model also has performance benefits. Database optimizers will process these simple schemas more efficiently with fewer joins. A database engine can make very strong assumptions about first constraining the heavily indexed dimension tables, and then attacking the fact table all at once with the Cartesian product of the dimension table keys satisfying the user's constraints. Amazingly, using this approach it is possible to evaluate arbitrary *n*-way joins to a fact table in a single pass through the fact table's index.

Finally, dimensional models are gracefully extensible to accommodate change. The predictable framework of a dimensional model withstands unexpected changes in user behavior. Every dimension is equivalent; all dimensions are symmetrically equal entry points into the fact table. The logical model has no built-in bias regarding expected query patterns. There are no preferences for the business questions we'll ask this month versus the questions we'll ask next month. We certainly don't want to adjust our schemas if business users come up with new ways to analyze the business.

We will see repeatedly in this book that the most granular or atomic data has the most dimensionality. Atomic data that has not been aggregated is the most expressive data; this atomic data should be the foundation for every fact table design in order to withstand business users' ad hoc attacks where they pose unexpected queries. With dimensional models, we can add completely new dimensions to the schema as long as a single value of that dimension is defined for each existing fact row. Likewise, we can add new, unanticipated facts to the fact table, assuming that the level of detail is consistent with the existing fact table. We can supplement preexisting dimension tables with new, unanticipated attributes. We also can break existing dimension rows down to a lower level of granularity from a certain point in time forward. In each case, existing tables can be changed in place either simply by adding new data rows in the table or by executing an SQL ALTER TABLE command. Data would not have to be reloaded. All existing data access applications continue to run without yielding different results. We'll examine this graceful extensibility of our dimensional models more fully in Chapter 2.

Another way to think about the complementary nature of fact and dimension tables is to see them translated into a report. As illustrated in Figure 1.5, dimension attributes supply the report labeling, whereas the fact tables supply the report's numeric values.

Finally, as we've already stressed, we insist that the data in the presentation area be dimensionally structured. However, there is a natural relationship between dimensional and normalized models. The key to understanding the relationship is that a single normalized ER diagram often breaks down into multiple dimensional schemas. A large normalized model for an organization may have sales calls, orders, shipment invoices, customer payments, and product returns all on the same diagram. In a way, the normalized ER diagram does itself a disservice by representing, on a single drawing, multiple business processes that never coexist in a single data set at a single point in time. No wonder the normalized model seems complex.

If you already have an existing normalized ER diagram, the first step in converting it into a set of dimensional models is to separate the ER diagram into its discrete business processes and then model each one separately. The second step is to select those many-to-many relationships in the ER diagrams that contain numeric and additive nonkey facts and designate them as fact tables. The final step is to denormalize all the remaining tables into flat tables with single-part keys that join directly to the fact tables. These tables become the dimension tables.

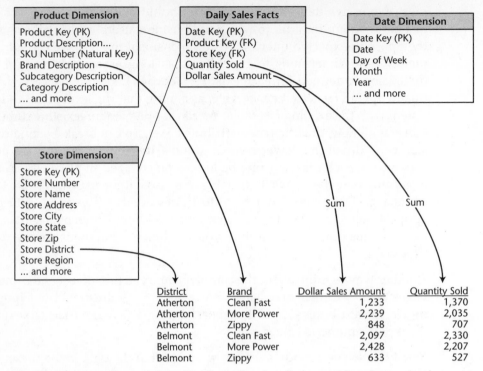

Figure 1.5 Dragging and dropping dimensional attributes and facts into a simple report.

Dimensional Modeling Myths

Despite the general acceptance of dimensional modeling, some misperceptions continue to be disseminated in the industry. We refer to these misconceptions as *dimensional modeling myths*.

Myth 1. *Dimensional models and data marts are for summary data only*. This first myth is the root cause of many ill-designed dimensional models. Because we can't possibly predict all the questions asked by business users, we need to provide them with queryable access to the most detailed data so that they can roll it up based on the business question at hand. Data at the lowest level of detail is practically impervious to surprises or changes. Our data marts also will include commonly requested summarized data in dimensional schemas. This summary data should complement the granular detail solely to provide improved performance for common queries, but not attempt to serve as a replacement for the details.

A related corollary to this first myth is that only a limited amount of historical data should be stored in dimensional structures. There is nothing about a dimensional model that prohibits the storage of substantial history. The amount of history available in data marts must be driven by the business's requirements.

Myth 2. *Dimensional models and data marts are departmental, not enterprise, solutions.* Rather than drawing boundaries based on organizational departments, we maintain that data marts should be organized around business processes, such as orders, invoices, and service calls. Multiple business functions often want to analyze the same metrics resulting from a single business process. We strive to avoid duplicating the core measurements in multiple databases around the organization.

Supporters of the normalized data warehouse approach sometimes draw spiderweb diagrams with multiple extracts from the same source feeding into multiple data marts. The illustration supposedly depicts the perils of proceeding without a normalized data warehouse to feed the data marts. These supporters caution about increased costs and potential inconsistencies as changes in the source system of record would need to be rippled to each mart's ETL process.

This argument falls apart because no one advocates multiple extracts from the same source. The spiderweb diagrams fail to appreciate that the data marts are process-centric, not department-centric, and that the data is extracted once from the operational source and presented in a single place. Clearly, the operational system support folks would frown on the multiple-extract approach. So do we.

Myth 3. *Dimensional models and data marts are not scalable.* Modern fact tables have many billions of rows in them. The dimensional models within our data marts are extremely scalable. Relational DBMS vendors have embraced data warehousing and incorporated numerous capabilities into their products to optimize the scalability and performance of dimensional models.

A corollary to myth 3 is that dimensional models are only appropriate for retail or sales data. This notion is rooted in the historical origins of dimensional modeling but not in its current-day reality. Dimensional modeling has been applied to virtually every industry, including banking, insurance, brokerage, telephone, newspaper, oil and gas, government, manufacturing, travel, gaming, health care, education, and many more. In this book we use the retail industry to illustrate several early concepts mainly because it is an industry to which we have all been exposed; however, these concepts are extremely transferable to other businesses.

Myth 4. *Dimensional models and data marts are only appropriate when there is a predictable usage pattern.* A related corollary is that dimensional models aren't responsive to changing business needs. On the contrary, because of their symmetry, the dimensional structures in our data marts are extremely flexible and adaptive to change. The secret to query flexibility is building the fact tables at the most granular level. In our opinion, the source of myth 4 is the designer struggling with fact tables that have been prematurely aggregated based on the designer's unfortunate belief in myth 1 regarding summary data. Dimensional models that only deliver summary data are bound to be problematic. Users run into analytic brick walls when they try to drill down into details not available in the summary tables. Developers also run into brick walls because they can't easily accommodate new dimensions, attributes, or facts with these prematurely summarized tables. The correct starting point for your dimensional models is to express data at the lowest detail possible for maximum flexibility and extensibility.

Myth 5. *Dimensional models and data marts can't be integrated and therefore lead to stovepipe solutions*. Dimensional models and data marts most certainly can be integrated if they conform to the data warehouse bus architecture. Presentation area databases that don't adhere to the data warehouse bus architecture will lead to standalone solutions. You can't hold dimensional modeling responsible for the failure of some organizations to embrace one of its fundamental tenets.

Common Pitfalls to Avoid

While we can provide positive recommendations about dimensional data warehousing, some readers better relate to a listing of common pitfalls or traps into which others have already stepped. Borrowing from a popular late-night television show, here is our favorite top 10 list of common errors to avoid while building your data warehouse. These are all quite lethal errors—one alone may be sufficient to bring down your data warehouse initiative. We'll further elaborate on these in Chapter 16; however, we wanted to plant the seeds early on while we have your complete attention.

Pitfall 10. Become overly enamored with technology and data rather than focusing on the business's requirements and goals.

Pitfall 9. Fail to embrace or recruit an influential, accessible, and reasonable management visionary as the business sponsor of the data warehouse.

Pitfall 8. Tackle a galactic multiyear project rather than pursuing more manageable, while still compelling, iterative development efforts.

Pitfall 7. Allocate energy to construct a normalized data structure, yet run out of budget before building a viable presentation area based on dimensional models.

Pitfall 6. Pay more attention to backroom operational performance and ease of development than to front-room query performance and ease of use.

Pitfall 5. Make the supposedly queryable data in the presentation area overly complex. Database designers who prefer a more complex presentation should spend a year supporting business users; they'd develop a much better appreciation for the need to seek simpler solutions.

Pitfall 4. Populate dimensional models on a standalone basis without regard to a data architecture that ties them together using shared, conformed dimensions.

Pitfall 3. Load only summarized data into the presentation area's dimensional structures.

Pitfall 2. Presume that the business, its requirements and analytics, and the underlying data and the supporting technology are static.

Pitfall 1. Neglect to acknowledge that data warehouse success is tied directly to user acceptance. If the users haven't accepted the data warehouse as a foundation for improved decision making, then your efforts have been exercises in futility.

Summary

In this chapter we discussed the overriding goals for the data warehouse and the differences between data warehouses and operational source systems. We explored the major components of the data warehouse and discussed the permissible role of normalized ER models in the staging area, but not as the end goal. We then focused our attention on dimensional modeling for the presentation area and established preliminary vocabulary regarding facts and dimensions. Stay tuned as we put these concepts into action in our first case study in the next chapter.

Retail Sales

The best way to understand the principles of dimensional modeling is to work through a series of tangible examples. By visualizing real cases, we can hold the particular design challenges and solutions in our minds much more effectively than if they are presented abstractly. In this book we will develop examples from a range of businesses to help move past one's own detail and come up with the right design.

To learn dimensional modeling, please *read all the chapters* in this book, even if you don't manage a retail business or work for a telecommunications firm. The chapters are *not* intended to be full-scale solution handbooks for a given industry or business function. Each chapter is a metaphor for a characteristic set of dimensional modeling problems that comes up in nearly every kind of business. Universities, insurance companies, banks, and airlines alike surely will need the techniques developed in this retail chapter. Besides, thinking about someone else's business is refreshing at times. It is too easy to let historical complexities derail us when we are dealing with data from our own companies. By stepping outside our own organizations and then returning with a well-understood design principle (or two), it is easier to remember the spirit of the design principles as we descend into the intricate details of our businesses.

Chapter 2 discusses the following concepts:

- Four-step process for designing dimensional models
- Transaction-level fact tables
- Additive and non-additive facts
- Sample dimension table attributes
- Causal dimensions, such as promotion
- Degenerate dimensions, such as the transaction ticket number
- Extending an existing dimension model
- Snowflaking dimension attributes
- Avoiding the "too many dimensions" trap
- Surrogate keys
- Market basket analysis

Four-Step Dimensional Design Process

Throughout this book we will approach the design of a dimensional database by consistently considering four steps in a particular order. The meaning of these four steps will become more obvious as we proceed with the various designs, but we'll provide initial definitions at this time.

1. Select the business process to model. A process is a natural business activity performed in your organization that typically is supported by a source data-collection system. Listening to your users is the most efficient means for selecting the business process. The performance measurements that they clamor to analyze in the data warehouse result from business measurement processes. Example business processes include raw materials purchasing, orders, shipments, invoicing, inventory, and general ledger.

   It is important to remember that we're not referring to an organizational business department or function when we talk about business processes. For example, we'd build a single dimensional model to handle orders data rather than building separate models for the sales and marketing departments, which both want to access orders data. By focusing on business processes, rather than on business departments, we can deliver consistent information more economically throughout the organization. If we establish departmentally bound dimensional models, we'll inevitably duplicate data with different labels and terminology. Multiple data flows into separate dimensional models will make us vulnerable to data inconsistencies. The best way to ensure consistency is to publish the data once. A single publishing run also reduces the extract-transformation-load (ETL) development effort, as well as the ongoing data management and disk storage burden.

2. Declare the grain of the business process. Declaring the grain means specifying *exactly* what an individual fact table row represents. The grain conveys the level of detail associated with the fact table measurements. It provides the answer to the question, "How do you describe a single row in the fact table?"

Example grain declarations include:

- An individual line item on a customer's retail sales ticket as measured by a scanner device

- A line item on a bill received from a doctor

- An individual boarding pass to get on a flight

- A daily snapshot of the inventory levels for each product in a warehouse

- A monthly snapshot for each bank account

Data warehouse teams often try to bypass this seemingly unnecessary step of the process. Please don't! It is extremely important that everyone on the design team is in agreement regarding the fact table granularity. It is virtually impossible to reach closure in step 3 without declaring the grain. We also should warn you that an inappropriate grain declaration will haunt a data warehouse implementation. Declaring the grain is a critical step that can't be taken lightly. Having said this, you may discover in steps 3 or 4 that the grain statement is wrong. This is okay, but then you must return to step 2, redeclare the grain correctly, and revisit steps 3 and 4 again.

3. Choose the dimensions that apply to each fact table row. Dimensions fall out of the question, "How do businesspeople describe the data that results from the business process?" We want to decorate our fact tables with a robust set of dimensions representing all possible descriptions that take on single values in the context of each measurement. If we are clear about the grain, then the dimensions typically can be identified quite easily. With the choice of each dimension, we will list all the discrete, textlike attributes that will flesh out each dimension table. Examples of common dimensions include date, product, customer, transaction type, and status.

4. Identify the numeric facts that will populate each fact table row. Facts are determined by answering the question, "What are we measuring?" Business users are keenly interested in analyzing these business process performance measures. All candidate facts in a design must be true to the grain defined in step 2. Facts that clearly belong to a different grain must be in a separate fact table. Typical facts are numeric additive figures such as quantity ordered or dollar cost amount.

Throughout this book we will keep these four steps in mind as we develop each of the case studies. We'll apply a user's understanding of the business to decide what dimensions and facts are needed in the dimensional model. Clearly, we need to consider both our business users' requirements and the realities of our source data in tandem to make decisions regarding the four steps, as illustrated in Figure 2.1. We strongly encourage you to resist the temptation to model the data by looking at source data files alone. We realize that it may be much less intimidating to dive into the file layouts and copybooks rather than interview a businessperson; however, they are no substitute for user input. Unfortunately, many organizations have attempted this path-of-least-resistance data-driven approach, but without much success.

Retail Case Study

Let's start with a brief description of the retail business that we'll use in this case study to make dimension and fact tables more understandable. We begin with this industry because it is one to which we can all relate. Imagine that we work in the headquarters of a large grocery chain. Our business has 100 grocery stores spread over a five-state area. Each of the stores has a full complement of departments, including grocery, frozen foods, dairy, meat, produce, bakery, floral, and health/beauty aids. Each store has roughly 60,000 individual products on its shelves. The individual products are called *stock keeping units* (SKUs). About 55,000 of the SKUs come from outside manufacturers and have bar codes imprinted on the product package. These bar codes are called *universal product codes* (UPCs). UPCs are at the same grain as individual SKUs. Each different package variation of a product has a separate UPC and hence is a separate SKU.

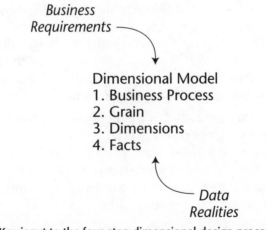

Figure 2.1   Key input to the four-step dimensional design process.

The remaining 5,000 SKUs come from departments such as meat, produce, bakery, or floral. While these products don't have nationally recognized UPCs, the grocery chain assigns SKU numbers to them. Since our grocery chain is highly automated, we stick scanner labels on many of the items in these other departments. Although the bar codes are not UPCs, they are certainly SKU numbers.

Data is collected at several interesting places in a grocery store. Some of the most useful data is collected at the cash registers as customers purchase products. Our modern grocery store scans the bar codes directly into the point-of-sale (POS) system. The POS system is at the front door of the grocery store where consumer takeaway is measured. The back door, where vendors make deliveries, is another interesting data-collection point.

At the grocery store, management is concerned with the logistics of ordering, stocking, and selling products while maximizing profit. The profit ultimately comes from charging as much as possible for each product, lowering costs for product acquisition and overhead, and at the same time attracting as many customers as possible in a highly competitive pricing environment. Some of the most significant management decisions have to do with pricing and promotions. Both store management and headquarters marketing spend a great deal of time tinkering with pricing and promotions. Promotions in a grocery store include temporary price reductions, ads in newspapers and newspaper inserts, displays in the grocery store (including end-aisle displays), and coupons. The most direct and effective way to create a surge in the volume of product sold is to lower the price dramatically. A 50-cent reduction in the price of paper towels, especially when coupled with an ad and display, can cause the sale of the paper towels to jump by a factor of 10. Unfortunately, such a big price reduction usually is not sustainable because the towels probably are being sold at a loss. As a result of these issues, the visibility of all forms of promotion is an important part of analyzing the operations of a grocery store.

Now that we have described our business case study, we'll begin to design the dimensional model.

Step 1. Select the Business Process

The first step in the design is to decide what business process(es) to model by combining an understanding of the business requirements with an understanding of the available data.

 The first dimensional model built should be the one with the most impact—it should answer the most pressing business questions and be readily accessible for data extraction.

In our retail case study, management wants to better understand customer purchases as captured by the POS system. Thus the business process we're going to model is POS retail sales. This data will allow us to analyze what products are selling in which stores on what days under what promotional conditions.

Step 2. Declare the Grain

Once the business process has been identified, the data warehouse team faces a serious decision about the granularity. What level of data detail should be made available in the dimensional model? This brings us to an important design tip.

 Preferably you should develop dimensional models for the most atomic information captured by a business process. Atomic data is the most detailed information collected; such data cannot be subdivided further.

Tackling data at its lowest, most atomic grain makes sense on multiple fronts. Atomic data is highly dimensional. The more detailed and atomic the fact measurement, the more things we know for sure. All those things we know for sure translate into dimensions. In this regard, atomic data is a perfect match for the dimensional approach.

Atomic data provides maximum analytic flexibility because it can be constrained and rolled up in every way possible. Detailed data in a dimensional model is poised and ready for the ad hoc attack by business users.

Of course, you can always declare higher-level grains for a business process that represent an aggregation of the most atomic data. However, as soon as we select a higher-level grain, we're limiting ourselves to fewer and/or potentially less detailed dimensions. The less granular model is immediately vulnerable to unexpected user requests to drill down into the details. Users inevitably run into an analytic wall when not given access to the atomic data. As we'll see in Chapter 16, aggregated summary data plays an important role as a performance-tuning tool, but it is not a substitute for giving users access to the lowest-level details. Unfortunately, some industry pundits have been confused on this point. They claim that dimensional models are only appropriate for summarized data and then criticize the dimensional modeling approach for its supposed need to anticipate the business question. This misunderstanding goes away when detailed, atomic data is made available in a dimensional model.

In our case study, the most granular data is an individual line item on a POS transaction. To ensure maximum dimensionality and flexibility, we will proceed with this grain. It is worth noting that this granularity declaration represents a change from the first edition of this text. Previously, we focused on POS data, but rather than representing transaction line item detail in the dimensional model, we elected to provide sales data rolled up by product and promotion in a store on a day. At the time, these daily product totals represented the state of the art for syndicated retail sales databases. It was unreasonable to expect then-current hardware and software to deal effectively with the volumes of data associated with individual POS transaction line items.

Providing access to the POS transaction information gives us with a very detailed look at store sales. While users probably are not interested in analyzing single items associated with a specific POS transaction, we can't predict all the ways that they'll want to cull through that data. For example, they may want to understand the difference in sales on Monday versus Sunday. Or they may want to assess whether it's worthwhile to stock so many individual sizes of certain brands, such as cereal. Or they may want to understand how many shoppers took advantage of the 50-cents-off promotion on shampoo. Or they may want to determine the impact in terms of decreased sales when a competitive diet soda product was promoted heavily. While none of these queries calls for data from one specific transaction, they are broad questions that require detailed data sliced in very precise ways. None of them could have been answered if we elected only to provide access to summarized data.

A data warehouse almost always demands data expressed at the lowest possible grain of each dimension not because queries want to see individual low-level rows, but because queries need to cut through the details in very precise ways.

Step 3. Choose the Dimensions

Once the grain of the fact table has been chosen, the date, product, and store dimensions fall out immediately. We assume that the calendar date is the date value delivered to us by the POS system. Later, we will see what to do if we also get a time of day along with the date. Within the framework of the primary dimensions, we can ask whether other dimensions can be attributed to the data, such as the promotion under which the product is sold. We express this as another design principle:

A careful grain statement determines the primary dimensionality of the fact table. It is then often possible to add more dimensions to the basic grain of the fact table, where these additional dimensions naturally take on only one value under each combination of the primary dimensions. If the additional dimension violates the grain by causing additional fact rows to be generated, then the grain statement must be revised to accommodate this dimension.

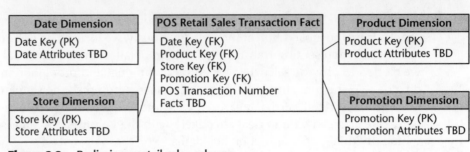

Figure 2.2 Preliminary retail sales schema.

"TBD" means "to be determined."

In our case study we've decided on the following descriptive dimensions: date, product, store, and promotion. In addition, we'll include the POS transaction ticket number as a special dimension. More will be said on this later in the chapter.

We begin to envision the preliminary schema as illustrated in Figure 2.2. Before we delve into populating the dimension tables with descriptive attributes, let's complete the final step of the process. We want to ensure that you're comfortable with the complete four-step process—we don't want you to lose sight of the forest for the trees at this stage of the game.

Step 4. Identify the Facts

The fourth and final step in the design is to make a careful determination of which facts will appear in the fact table. Again, the grain declaration helps anchor our thinking. Simply put, the facts must be true to the grain: the individual line item on the POS transaction in this case. When considering potential facts, you again may discover that adjustments need to be made to either our earlier grain assumptions or our choice of dimensions.

The facts collected by the POS system include the sales quantity (e.g., the number of cans of chicken noodle soup), per unit sales price, and the sales dollar amount. The sales dollar amount equals the sales quantity multiplied by the unit price. More sophisticated POS systems also provide a standard dollar cost for the product as delivered to the store by the vendor. Presuming that this cost fact is readily available and doesn't require a heroic activity-based costing initiative, we'll include it in the fact table. Our fact table begins to take shape in Figure 2.3.

Three of the facts, sales quantity, sales dollar amount, and cost dollar amount, are beautifully additive across all the dimensions. We can slice and dice the fact table with impunity, and every sum of these three facts is valid and correct.

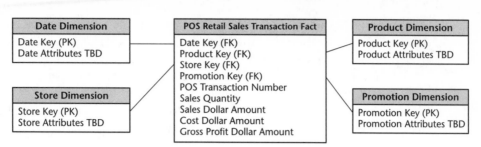

Figure 2.3 Measured facts in the retail sales schema.

We can compute the gross profit by subtracting the cost dollar amount from the sales dollar amount, or revenue. Although computed, this gross profit is also perfectly additive across all the dimensions—we can calculate the gross profit of any combination of products sold in any set of stores on any set of days. Dimensional modelers sometimes question whether a calculated fact should be stored physically in the database. We generally recommend that it be stored physically. In our case study, the gross profit calculation is straight-forward, but storing it eliminates the possibility of user error. The cost of a user incorrectly representing gross profit overwhelms the minor incremental storage cost. Storing it also ensures that all users and their reporting applications refer to gross profit consistently. Since gross profit can be calculated from adjacent data within a fact table row, some would argue that we should perform the calculation in a view that is indistinguishable from the table. This is a reasonable approach if *all* users access the data via this view and *no* users with ad hoc query tools can sneak around the view to get at the physical table. Views are a reasonable way to minimize user error while saving on storage, but the DBA must allow no exceptions to data access through the view. Likewise, some organizations want to perform the calculation in the query tool. Again, this works if *all* users access the data using a common tool (which is seldom the case in our experience).

The gross margin can be calculated by dividing the gross profit by the dollar revenue. Gross margin is a nonadditive fact because it can't be summarized along any dimension. We can calculate the gross margin of any set of products, stores, or days by remembering to add the revenues and costs before dividing. This can be stated as a design principle:

Percentages and ratios, such as gross margin, are nonadditive. The numerator and denominator should be stored in the fact table. The ratio can be calculated in a data access tool for any slice of the fact table by remembering to calculate the *ratio of the sums*, not the sum of the ratios.

Unit price is also a nonadditive fact. Attempting to sum up unit price across any of the dimensions results in a meaningless, nonsensical number. In order to analyze the average selling price for a product in a series of stores or across a period of time, we must add up the sales dollars and sales quantities before dividing the total dollars by the total quantity sold. Every report writer or query tool in the data warehouse marketplace should automatically perform this function correctly, but unfortunately, some still don't handle it very gracefully.

At this early stage of the design, it is often helpful to estimate the number of rows in our largest table, the fact table. In our case study, it simply may be a matter of talking with a source system guru to understand how many POS transaction line items are generated on a periodic basis. Retail traffic fluctuates significantly from day to day, so we'll want to understand the transaction activity over a reasonable period of time. Alternatively, we could estimate the number of rows added to the fact table annually by dividing the chain's annual gross revenue by the average item selling price. Assuming that gross revenues are $4 billion per year and that the average price of an item on a customer ticket is $2.00, we calculate that there are approximately 2 billion transaction line items per year. This is a typical engineer's estimate that gets us surprisingly close to sizing a design directly from our armchairs. As designers, we always should be triangulating to determine whether our calculations are reasonable.

Dimension Table Attributes

Now that we've walked through the four-step process, let's return to the dimension tables and focus on filling them with robust attributes.

Date Dimension

We will start with the date dimension. The date dimension is the one dimension nearly guaranteed to be in every data mart because virtually every data mart is a time series. In fact, date is usually the first dimension in the underlying sort order of the database so that the successive loading of time intervals of data is placed into virgin territory on the disk.

For readers of the first edition of *The Data Warehouse Toolkit* (Wiley 1996), this dimension was referred to as the *time dimension* in that text. Rather than sticking with that more ambiguous nomenclature, we use the *date dimension* in this book to refer to daily-grained dimension tables. This helps distinguish the date and time-of-day dimensions, which we'll discuss later in this chapter.

Unlike most of our other dimensions, we can build the date dimension table in advance. We may put 5 or 10 years of rows representing days in the table so that we can cover the history we have stored, as well as several years in the future. Even 10 years' worth of days is only about 3,650 rows, which is a relatively small dimension table. For a daily date dimension table in a retail environment, we recommend the partial list of columns shown in Figure 2.4.

Each column in the date dimension table is defined by the particular day that the row represents. The day-of-week column contains the name of the day, such as Monday. This column would be used to create reports comparing the business on Mondays with Sunday business. The day number in calendar month column starts with 1 at the beginning of each month and runs to 28, 29, 30, or 31, depending on the month. This column is useful for comparing the same day each month. Similarly, we could have a month number in year (1, ... , 12). The day number in epoch is effectively a Julian day number (that is, a consecutive day number starting at the beginning of some epoch). We also could include

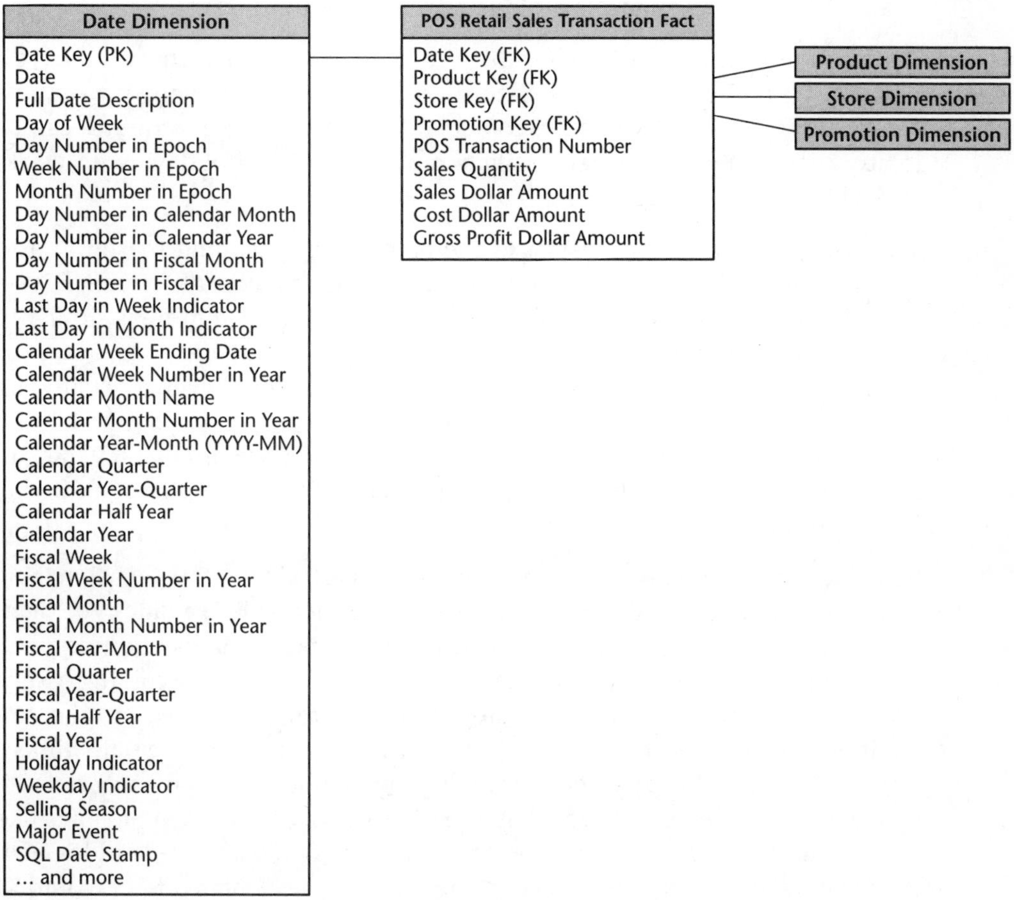

Date Dimension	**POS Retail Sales Transaction Fact**
Date Key (PK)	Date Key (FK)
Date	Product Key (FK)
Full Date Description	Store Key (FK)
Day of Week	Promotion Key (FK)
Day Number in Epoch	POS Transaction Number
Week Number in Epoch	Sales Quantity
Month Number in Epoch	Sales Dollar Amount
Day Number in Calendar Month	Cost Dollar Amount
Day Number in Calendar Year	Gross Profit Dollar Amount
Day Number in Fiscal Month	
Day Number in Fiscal Year	**Product Dimension**
Last Day in Week Indicator	**Store Dimension**
Last Day in Month Indicator	**Promotion Dimension**
Calendar Week Ending Date	
Calendar Week Number in Year	
Calendar Month Name	
Calendar Month Number in Year	
Calendar Year-Month (YYYY-MM)	
Calendar Quarter	
Calendar Year-Quarter	
Calendar Half Year	
Calendar Year	
Fiscal Week	
Fiscal Week Number in Year	
Fiscal Month	
Fiscal Month Number in Year	
Fiscal Year-Month	
Fiscal Quarter	
Fiscal Year-Quarter	
Fiscal Half Year	
Fiscal Year	
Holiday Indicator	
Weekday Indicator	
Selling Season	
Major Event	
SQL Date Stamp	
… and more	

Figure 2.4   Date dimension in the retail sales schema.

absolute week and month number columns. All these integers support simple date arithmetic between days across year and month boundaries. For reporting, we would want a month name with values such as January. In addition, a year-month (YYYY-MM) column is useful as a report column header. We likely also will want a quarter number (Q1, ... , Q4), as well as a year quarter, such as 2001-Q4. We would have similar columns for the fiscal periods if they differ from calendar periods.

The holiday indicator takes on the values of Holiday or Nonholiday. Remember that the dimension table attributes serve as report labels. Simply populating the holiday indicator with a Y or an N would be far less useful. Imagine a report where we're comparing holiday sales for a given product versus non-holiday sales. Obviously, it would be helpful if the columns had meaningful values such as Holiday/Nonholiday versus a cryptic Y/N. Rather than decoding cryptic flags into understandable labels in a reporting application, we prefer that the decode be stored in the database so that a consistent value is available to all users regardless of their reporting environment.

A similar argument holds true for the weekday indicator, which would have a value of Weekday or Weekend. Saturdays and Sundays obviously would be assigned the Weekend value. Of course, multiple date table attributes can be jointly constrained, so we can easily compare weekday holidays with weekend holidays, for example.

The selling season column is set to the name of the retailing season, if any. Examples in the United States could include Christmas, Thanksgiving, Easter, Valentine's Day, Fourth of July, or None. The major event column is similar to the season column and can be used to mark special outside events such as Super Bowl Sunday or Labor Strike. Regular promotional events usually are not handled in the date table but rather are described more completely by means of the promotion dimension, especially since promotional events are not defined solely by date but usually are defined by a combination of date, product, and store.

Some designers pause at this point to ask why an explicit date dimension table is needed. They reason that if the date key in the fact table is a date-type field, then any SQL query can directly constrain on the fact table date key and use natural SQL date semantics to filter on month or year while avoiding a supposedly expensive join. This reasoning falls apart for several reasons. First of all, if our relational database can't handle an efficient join to the date dimension table, we're already in deep trouble. Most database optimizers are quite efficient at resolving dimensional queries; it is not necessary to avoid joins like the plague. Also, on the performance front, most databases don't index SQL date calculations, so queries constraining on an SQL-calculated field wouldn't take advantage of an index.

In terms of usability, the typical business user is not versed in SQL date semantics, so he or she would be unable to directly leverage inherent capabilities associated with a date data type. SQL date functions do not support filtering by attributes such as weekdays versus weekends, holidays, fiscal periods, seasons, or major events. Presuming that the business needs to slice data by these nonstandard date attributes, then an explicit date dimension table is essential. At the bottom line, calendar logic belongs in a dimension table, not in the application code. Finally, we're going to suggest that the date key is an integer rather than a date data type anyway. An SQL-based date key typically is 8 bytes, so you're wasting 4 bytes in the fact table for every date key in every row. More will be said on this later in this chapter.

Figure 2.5 illustrates several rows from a partial date dimension table.

Data warehouses always need an explicit date dimension table. There are many date attributes not supported by the SQL date function, including fiscal periods, seasons, holidays, and weekends. Rather than attempting to determine these nonstandard calendar calculations in a query, we should look them up in a date dimension table.

If we wanted to access the time of the transaction for day-part analysis (for example, activity during the evening after-work rush or third shift), we'd handle it through a separate time-of-day dimension joined to the fact table. Date and time are almost completely independent. If we combined the two dimensions, the date dimension would grow significantly; our neat date dimension with 3,650 rows to handle 10 years of data would expand to 5,256,000 rows if we tried to handle time by minute in the same table (or via an outrigger). Obviously, it is preferable to create a 3,650-row date dimension table and a separate 1,440-row time-of-day by minute dimension.

In Chapter 5 we'll discuss the handling of multiple dates in a single schema. We'll explore international date and time considerations in Chapters 11 and 14.

Date Key	Date	Full Date Description	Day of Week	Calendar Month	Calendar Year	Fiscal Year-Month	Holiday Indicator	Weekday Indicator
1	01/01/2002	January 1, 2002	Tuesday	January	2002	F2002-01	Holiday	Weekday
2	01/02/2002	January 2, 2002	Wednesday	January	2002	F2002-01	Non-Holiday	Weekday
3	01/03/2002	January 3, 2002	Thursday	January	2002	F2002-01	Non-Holiday	Weekday
4	01/04/2002	January 4, 2002	Friday	January	2002	F2002-01	Non-Holiday	Weekday
5	01/05/2002	January 5, 2002	Saturday	January	2002	F2002-01	Non-Holiday	Weekend
6	01/06/2002	January 6, 2002	Sunday	January	2002	F2002-01	Non-Holiday	Weekend
7	01/07/2002	January 7, 2002	Monday	January	2002	F2002-01	Non-Holiday	Weekday
8	01/08/2002	January 8, 2002	Tuesday	January	2002	F2002-01	Non-Holiday	Weekday

Figure 2.5   Date dimension table detail.

Product Dimension

The product dimension describes every SKU in the grocery store. While a typical store in our chain may stock 60,000 SKUs, when we account for different merchandising schemes across the chain and historical products that are no longer available, our product dimension would have at least 150,000 rows and perhaps as many as a million rows. The product dimension is almost always sourced from the operational product master file. Most retailers administer their product master files at headquarters and download a subset of the file to each store's POS system at frequent intervals. It is headquarters' responsibility to define the appropriate product master record (and unique SKU number) for each new UPC created by packaged goods manufacturers. Headquarters also defines the rules by which SKUs are assigned to such items as bakery goods, meat, and produce. We extract the product master file into our product dimension table each time the product master changes.

An important function of the product master is to hold the many descriptive attributes of each SKU. The merchandise hierarchy is an important group of attributes. Typically, individual SKUs roll up to brands. Brands roll up to categories, and categories roll up to departments. Each of these is a many-to-one relationship. This merchandise hierarchy and additional attributes are detailed for a subset of products in Figure 2.6.

For each SKU, all levels of the merchandise hierarchy are well defined. Some attributes, such as the SKU description, are unique. In this case, there are at least 150,000 different values in the SKU description column. At the other extreme, there are only perhaps 50 distinct values of the department attribute. Thus, on average, there are 3,000 repetitions of each unique value in the department attribute. This is all right! We do not need to separate these repeated values into a second normalized table to save space. Remember that dimension table space requirements pale in comparison with fact table space considerations.

Product Key	Product Description	Brand Description	Category Description	Department Description	Fat Content
1	Baked Well Light Sourdough Fresh Bread	Baked Well	Bread	Bakery	Reduced Fat
2	Fluffy Sliced Whole Wheat	Fluffy	Bread	Bakery	Regular Fat
3	Fluffy Light Sliced Whole Wheat	Fluffy	Bread	Bakery	Reduced Fat
4	Fat Free Mini Cinnamon Rolls	Light	Sweeten Bread	Bakery	Non-Fat
5	Diet Lovers Vanilla 2 Gallon	Coldpack	Frozen Desserts	Frozen Foods	Non-Fat
6	Light and Creamy Butter Pecan 1 Pint	Freshlike	Frozen Desserts	Frozen Foods	Reduced Fat
7	Chocolate Lovers 1/2 Gallon	Frigid	Frozen Desserts	Frozen Foods	Regular Fat
8	Strawberry Ice Creamy 1 Pint	Icy	Frozen Desserts	Frozen Foods	Regular Fat
9	Icy Ice Cream Sandwiches	Icy	Frozen Desserts	Frozen Foods	Regular Fat

Figure 2.6 Product dimension table detail.

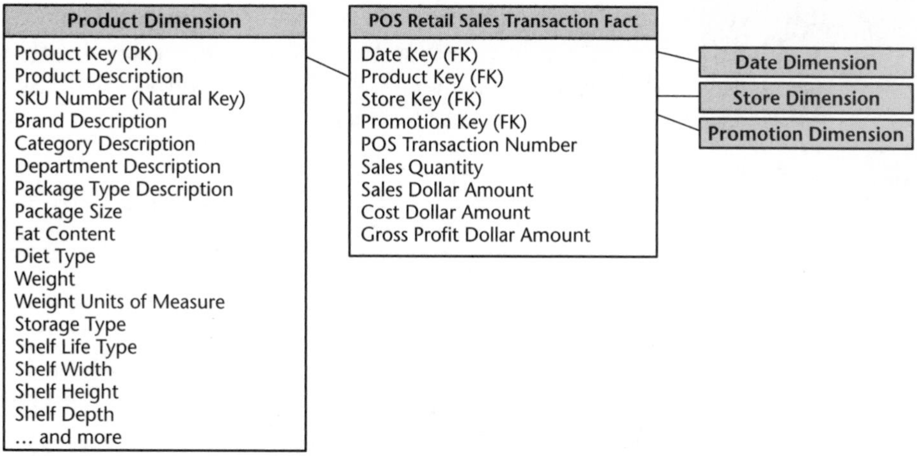

Product Dimension	POS Retail Sales Transaction Fact	
Product Key (PK)	Date Key (FK)	**Date Dimension**
Product Description	Product Key (FK)	**Store Dimension**
SKU Number (Natural Key)	Store Key (FK)	**Promotion Dimension**
Brand Description	Promotion Key (FK)	
Category Description	POS Transaction Number	
Department Description	Sales Quantity	
Package Type Description	Sales Dollar Amount	
Package Size	Cost Dollar Amount	
Fat Content	Gross Profit Dollar Amount	
Diet Type		
Weight		
Weight Units of Measure		
Storage Type		
Shelf Life Type		
Shelf Width		
Shelf Height		
Shelf Depth		
… and more		

Figure 2.7   Product dimension in the retail sales schema.

Many of the attributes in the product dimension table are not part of the merchandise hierarchy. The package-type attribute, for example, might have values such as Bottle, Bag, Box, or Other. Any SKU in any department could have one of these values. It makes perfect sense to combine a constraint on this attribute with a constraint on a merchandise hierarchy attribute. For example, we could look at all the SKUs in the Cereal category packaged in Bags. To put this another way, we can browse among dimension attributes whether or not they belong to the merchandise hierarchy, and we can drill up and drill down using attributes whether or not they belong to the merchandise hierarchy. We can even have more than one explicit hierarchy in our product dimension table.

A recommended partial product dimension for a retail grocery data mart would look similar to Figure 2.7.

A reasonable product dimension table would have 50 or more descriptive attributes. Each attribute is a rich source for constraining and constructing row headers. Viewed in this manner, we see that drilling down is nothing more than asking for a row header that provides more information. Let's say we have a simple report where we've summarized the sales dollar amount and quantity by department.

Department Description	Sales Dollar Amount	Sales Quantity
Bakery	$12,331	5,088
Frozen Foods	$31,776	15,565

If we want to drill down, we can drag virtually any other attribute, such as brand, from the product dimension into the report next to department, and we automatically drill down to this next level of detail. A typical drill down within the merchandise hierarchy would look like this:

Department Description	Brand Description	Sales Dollar Amount	Sales Quantity
Bakery	Baked Well	$3,009	1,138
Bakery	Fluffy	$3,024	1,476
Bakery	Light	$6,298	2,474
Frozen Foods	Coldpack	$5,321	2,640
Frozen Foods	Freshlike	$10,476	5,234
Frozen Foods	Frigid	$7,328	3,092
Frozen Foods	Icy	$2,184	1,437
Frozen Foods	QuickFreeze	$6,467	3,162

Or we could drill down by the fat-content attribute, even though it isn't in the merchandise hierarchy roll-up.

Department Description	Fat Content	Sales Dollar Amount	Sales Quantity
Bakery	Non-Fat	$6,298	2,474
Bakery	Reduced Fat	$5,027	2,086
Bakery	Regular Fat	$1,006	528
Frozen Foods	Non-Fat	$5,321	2,640
Frozen Foods	Reduced Fat	$10,476	5,234
Frozen Foods	Regular Fat	$15,979	7,691

We have belabored the examples of drilling down in order to make a point, which we will express as a design principle.

 Drilling down in a data mart is nothing more than adding row headers from the dimension tables. Drilling up is removing row headers. We can drill down or up on attributes from more than one explicit hierarchy and with attributes that are part of no hierarchy.

The product dimension is one of the two or three primary dimensions in nearly every data mart. Great care should be taken to fill this dimension with as many descriptive attributes as possible. A robust and complete set of dimension attributes translates into user capabilities for robust and complete analysis. We'll further explore the product dimension in Chapter 4, where we'll also discuss the handling of product attribute changes.

Store Dimension

The store dimension describes every store in our grocery chain. Unlike the product master file that is almost guaranteed to be available in every large grocery business, there may not be a comprehensive store master file. The product master needs to be downloaded to each store every time there's a new or changed product. However, the individual POS systems do not require a store master. Information technology (IT) staffs frequently must assemble the necessary components of the store dimension from multiple operational sources at headquarters.

The store dimension is the primary geographic dimension in our case study. Each store can be thought of as a location. Because of this, we can roll stores up to any geographic attribute, such as ZIP code, county, and state in the United States. Stores usually also roll up to store districts and regions. These two different hierarchies are both easily represented in the store dimension because both the geographic and store regional hierarchies are well defined for a single store row.

It is not uncommon to represent multiple hierarchies in a dimension table. Ideally, the attribute names and values should be unique across the multiple hierarchies.

A recommended store dimension table for the grocery business is shown in Figure 2.8.

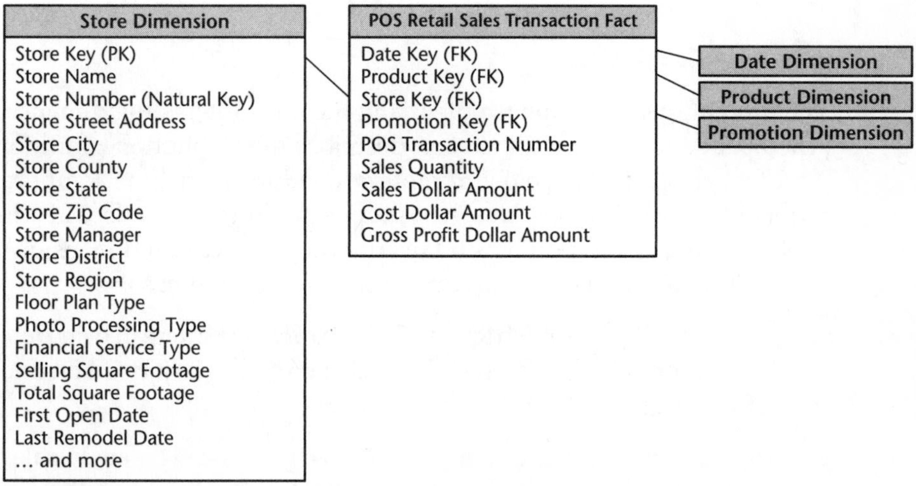

Store Dimension
Store Key (PK)
Store Name
Store Number (Natural Key)
Store Street Address
Store City
Store County
Store State
Store Zip Code
Store Manager
Store District
Store Region
Floor Plan Type
Photo Processing Type
Financial Service Type
Selling Square Footage
Total Square Footage
First Open Date
Last Remodel Date
… and more

POS Retail Sales Transaction Fact
Date Key (FK)
Product Key (FK)
Store Key (FK)
Promotion Key (FK)
POS Transaction Number
Sales Quantity
Sales Dollar Amount
Cost Dollar Amount
Gross Profit Dollar Amount

Date Dimension
Product Dimension
Promotion Dimension

Figure 2.8   Store dimension in the retail sales schema.

The floor plan type, photo processing type, and finance services type are all short text descriptors that describe the particular store. These should not be one-character codes but rather should be 10- to 20-character standardized descriptors that make sense when viewed in a pull-down list or used as a report row header.

The column describing selling square footage is numeric and theoretically additive across stores. One might be tempted to place it in the fact table. However, it is clearly a constant attribute of a store and is used as a report constraint or row header more often than it is used as an additive element in a summation. For these reasons, we are confident that selling square footage belongs in the store dimension table.

The first open date and last remodel date typically are join keys to copies of the date dimension table. These date dimension copies are declared in SQL by the VIEW construct and are semantically distinct from the primary date dimension. The VIEW declaration would look like

```
CREATE VIEW FIRST_OPEN_DATE (FIRST_OPEN_DAY_NUMBER, FIRST_OPEN_MONTH ...)
    AS SELECT DAY_NUMBER, MONTH, ...
    FROM DATE
```

Now the system acts as if there is another physical copy of the date dimension table called FIRST_OPEN_DATE. Constraints on this new date table have nothing to do with constraints on the primary date dimension table. The first open date view is a permissible outrigger to the store dimension. Notice that we have carefully relabeled all the columns in the view so that they cannot be confused with columns from the primary date dimension. We will further discuss outriggers in Chapter 6.

Promotion Dimension

The promotion dimension is potentially the most interesting dimension in our schema. The promotion dimension describes the promotion conditions under which a product was sold. Promotion conditions include temporary price reductions, end-aisle displays, newspaper ads, and coupons. This dimension is often called a *causal* dimension (as opposed to a casual dimension) because it describes factors thought to cause a change in product sales.

Managers at both headquarters and the stores are interested in determining whether a promotion is effective or not. Promotions are judged on one or more of the following factors:

- Whether the products under promotion experienced a gain in sales during the promotional period. This is called the *lift*. The lift can only be measured if the store can agree on what the baseline sales of the promoted products would have been without the promotion. Baseline values can be estimated from prior sales history and, in some cases, with the help of sophisticated mathematical models.

■ Whether the products under promotion showed a drop in sales just prior to or after the promotion, canceling the gain in sales during the promotion (time shifting). In other words, did we transfer sales from regularly priced products to temporarily reduced-priced products?

■ Whether the products under promotion showed a gain in sales but other products nearby on the shelf showed a corresponding sales decrease (cannibalization).

■ Whether all the products in the promoted category of products experienced a net overall gain in sales taking into account the time periods before, during, and after the promotion (market growth).

■ Whether the promotion was profitable. Usually the profit of a promotion is taken to be the incremental gain in profit of the promoted category over the baseline sales taking into account time shifting and cannibalization, as well as the costs of the promotion, including temporary price reductions, ads, displays, and coupons.

The causal conditions potentially affecting a sale are not necessarily tracked directly by the POS system. The transaction system keeps track of price reductions and markdowns. The presence of coupons also typically is captured with the transaction because the customer either presents coupons at the time of sale or does not. Ads and in-store display conditions may need to be linked from other sources.

The various possible causal conditions are highly correlated. A temporary price reduction usually is associated with an ad and perhaps an end-aisle display. Coupons often are associated with ads. For this reason, it makes sense to create one row in the promotion dimension for each combination of promotion conditions that occurs. Over the course of a year, there may be 1,000 ads, 5,000 temporary price reductions, and 1,000 end-aisle displays, but there may only be 10,000 combinations of these three conditions affecting any particular product. For example, in a given promotion, most of the stores would run all three promotion mechanisms simultaneously, but a few of the stores would not be able to deploy the end-aisle displays. In this case, two separate promotion condition rows would be needed, one for the normal price reduction plus ad plus display and one for the price reduction plus ad only. A recommended promotion dimension table is shown in Figure 2.9.

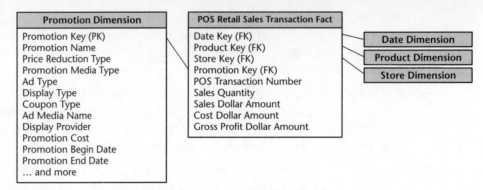

Figure 2.9 Promotion dimension in the retail sales schema.

From a purely logical point of view, we could record very similar information about the promotions by separating the four major causal mechanisms (price reductions, ads, displays, and coupons) into four separate dimensions rather than combining them into one dimension. Ultimately, this choice is the designer's prerogative. The tradeoffs in favor of keeping the four dimensions together include the following:

■ Since the four causal mechanisms are highly correlated, the combined single dimension is not much larger than any one of the separated dimensions would be.

■ The combined single dimension can be browsed efficiently to see how the various price reductions, ads, displays, and coupons are used together. However, this browsing only shows the possible combinations. Browsing in the dimension table does not reveal which stores or products were affected by the promotion. This information is found in the fact table.

The tradeoffs in favor of separating the four causal mechanisms into distinct dimension tables include the following:

■ The separated dimensions may be more understandable to the business community if users think of these mechanisms separately. This would be revealed during the business requirement interviews.

■ Administration of the separate dimensions may be more straightforward than administering a combined dimension.

Keep in mind that there is no difference in the information content in the data warehouse between these two choices.

Typically, many sales transaction line items involve products that are not being promoted. We will need to include a row in the promotion dimension, with its own unique key, to identify "No Promotion in Effect" and avoid a null promotion key in the fact table. Referential integrity is violated if we put a null in a fact table column declared as a foreign key to a dimension table. In addition to the referential integrity alarms, null keys are the source of great confusion to our users because they can't join on null keys.

You must avoid null keys in the fact table. A proper design includes a row in the corresponding dimension table to identify that the dimension is not applicable to the measurement.

Promotion Coverage Factless Fact Table

Regardless of the handling of the promotion dimension, there is one important question that cannot be answered by our retail sales schema: What products were on promotion but did not sell? The sales fact table only records the SKUs actually sold. There are no fact table rows with zero facts for SKUs that didn't sell because doing so would enlarge the fact table enormously. In the relational world, a second promotion coverage or event fact table is needed to help answer the question concerning what didn't happen. The promotion coverage fact table keys would be date, product, store, and promotion in our case study. This obviously looks similar to the sales fact table we just designed; however, the grain would be significantly different. In the case of the promotion coverage fact table, we'd load one row in the fact table for each product on promotion in a store each day (or week, since many retail promotions are a week in duration) regardless of whether the product sold or not. The coverage fact table allows us to see the relationship between the keys as defined by a promotion, independent of other events, such as actual product sales. We refer to it as a *factless fact table* because it has no measurement metrics; it merely captures the relationship between the involved keys. To determine what products where on promotion but didn't sell requires a two-step process. First, we'd query the promotion coverage table to determine the universe of products that were on promotion on a given day. We'd then determine what products sold from the POS sales fact table. The answer to our original question is the set difference between these two lists of products. Stay tuned to Chapter 12 for more complete coverage of factless fact tables; we'll illustrate the promotion coverage table and provide the set difference SQL. If you're working with data in a multidimensional online analytical processing (OLAP) cube environment, it is often easier to answer the question regarding what didn't sell because the cube typically contains explicit cells for nonbehavior.

Degenerate Transaction Number Dimension

The retail sales fact table contains the POS transaction number on every line item row. In a traditional parent-child database, the POS transaction number would be the key to the transaction header record, containing all the information valid for the transaction as a whole, such as the transaction date and store identifier. However, in our dimensional model, we have already extracted this interesting header information into other dimensions. The POS transaction number is still useful because it serves as the grouping key for pulling together all the products purchased in a single transaction.

Although the POS transaction number looks like a dimension key in the fact table, we have stripped off all the descriptive items that might otherwise fall in a POS transaction dimension. Since the resulting dimension is empty, we refer to the POS transaction number as a *degenerate dimension* (identified by the DD notation in Figure 2.10). The natural operational ticket number, such as the POS transaction number, sits by itself in the fact table without joining to a dimension table. Degenerate dimensions are very common when the grain of a fact table represents a single transaction or transaction line item because the degenerate dimension represents the unique identifier of the parent. Order numbers, invoice numbers, and bill-of-lading numbers almost always appear as degenerate dimensions in a dimensional model.

Degenerate dimensions often play an integral role in the fact table's primary key. In our case study, the primary key of the retail sales fact table consists of the degenerate POS transaction number and product key (assuming that the POS system rolls up all sales for a given product within a POS shopping cart into a single line item). Often, the primary key of a fact table is a subset of the table's foreign keys. We typically do not need every foreign key in the fact table to guarantee the uniqueness of a fact table row.

Operational control numbers such as order numbers, invoice numbers, and bill-of-lading numbers usually give rise to empty dimensions and are represented as degenerate dimensions (that is, dimension keys without corresponding dimension tables) in fact tables where the grain of the table is the document itself or a line item in the document.

If, for some reason, one or more attributes are legitimately left over after all the other dimensions have been created and seem to belong to this header entity, we would simply create a normal dimension record with a normal join. However, we would no longer have a degenerate dimension.

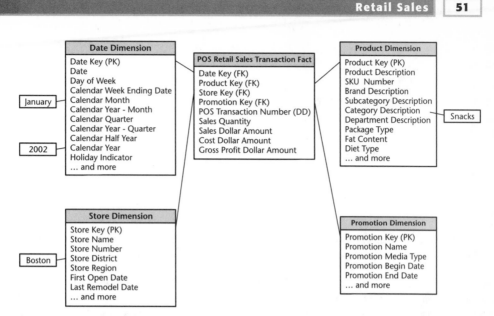

Figure 2.10 Querying the retail sales schema.

Retail Schema in Action

With our retail POS schema designed, let's illustrate how it would be put to use in a query environment. A business user might be interested in better understanding weekly sales dollar volume by promotion for the snacks category during January 2002 for stores in the Boston district. As illustrated in Figure 2.10, we would place query constraints on month and year in the date dimension, district in the store dimension, and category in the product dimension.

If the query tool summed the sales dollar amount grouped by week-ending date and promotion, the query results would look similar to those below. You can plainly see the relationship between the dimensional model and the associated query. High-quality dimension attributes are crucial because they are the source of query constraints and result set labels.

Calendar Week Ending Date	Promotion Name	Sales Dollar Amount
January 6, 2002	No Promotion	22,647
January 13, 2002	No Promotion	4,851
January 20, 2002	Super Bowl Promotion	7,248
January 27, 2002	Super Bowl Promotion	13,798

If you are using a data access tool with more functionality, the results may appear as a cross-tabular report. Such reports are more appealing to business users than the columnar data resulting from an SQL statement.

Calendar Week Ending Date	Super Bowl Promotion Sales Dollar Amount	No Promotion Sales Dollar Amount
January 6, 2002	0	22,647
January 13, 2002	0	4,851
January 20, 2002	7,248	0
January 27, 2002	13,793	0

Retail Schema Extensibility

Now that we've completed our first dimensional model, let's turn our attention to extending the design. Assume that our retailer decides to implement a frequent shopper program. Now, rather than knowing that an unidentified shopper had 26 items in his or her shopping cart, we're able to see exactly what a specific shopper, say, Julie Kimball, purchases on a weekly basis. Just imagine the interest of business users in analyzing shopping patterns by a multitude of geographic, demographic, behavioral, and other differentiating shopper characteristics.

The handling of this new frequent shopper information is relatively straightforward. We'd create a frequent shopper dimension table and add another foreign key in the fact table. Since we can't ask shoppers to bring in all their old cash register receipts to tag our historical sales transactions with their new frequent shopper number, we'd substitute a shopper key corresponding to a "Prior to Frequent Shopper Program" description on our historical fact table rows. Likewise, not everyone who shops at the grocery store will have a frequent shopper card, so we'd also want to include a "Frequent Shopper Not Identified" row in our shopper dimension. As we discussed earlier with the promotion dimension, we must avoid null keys in the fact table.

As we embellished our original design with a frequent shopper dimension, we also could add dimensions for the time of day and clerk associated with the transaction, as illustrated in Figure 2.11. Any descriptive attribute that has a single value in the presence of the fact table measurements is a good candidate to be added to an existing dimension or be its own dimension. The decision regarding whether a dimension can be attached to a fact table should be a binary yes/no based on the declared grain. If you are in doubt, it's time to revisit step 2 of the design process.

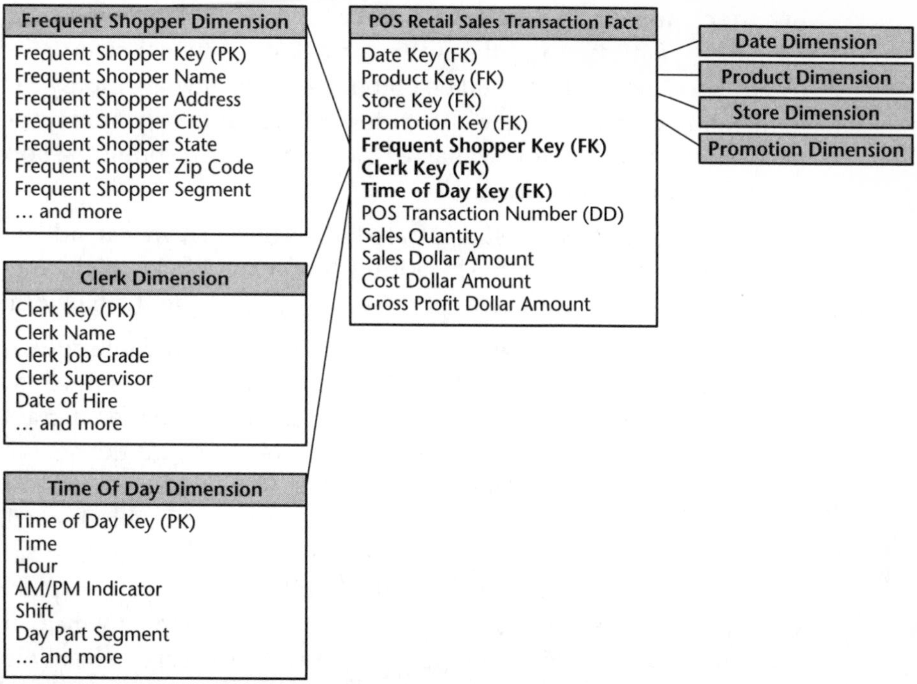

Frequent Shopper Dimension

Frequent Shopper Key (PK)
Frequent Shopper Name
Frequent Shopper Address
Frequent Shopper City
Frequent Shopper State
Frequent Shopper Zip Code
Frequent Shopper Segment
... and more

Clerk Dimension

Clerk Key (PK)
Clerk Name
Clerk Job Grade
Clerk Supervisor
Date of Hire
... and more

Time Of Day Dimension

Time of Day Key (PK)
Time
Hour
AM/PM Indicator
Shift
Day Part Segment
... and more

POS Retail Sales Transaction Fact

Date Key (FK)
Product Key (FK)
Store Key (FK)
Promotion Key (FK)
Frequent Shopper Key (FK)
Clerk Key (FK)
Time of Day Key (FK)
POS Transaction Number (DD)
Sales Quantity
Sales Dollar Amount
Cost Dollar Amount
Gross Profit Dollar Amount

Date Dimension

Product Dimension

Store Dimension

Promotion Dimension

Figure 2.11 Embellished retail sales schema.

Our original schema gracefully extends to accommodate these new dimensions largely because we chose to model the POS transaction data at its most granular level. The addition of dimensions that apply at that granularity did not alter the existing dimension keys or facts; all preexisting applications continue to run without unraveling or changing. If we had declared originally that the grain would be daily retail sales (transactions summarized by day, store, product, and promotion) rather than at transaction line detail, we would not have been able to easily incorporate the frequent-shopper, time-of-day, or clerk dimensions. Premature summarization or aggregation inherently limits our ability to add supplemental dimensions because the additional dimensions often don't apply at the higher grain.

Obviously, there are some changes that can never be handled gracefully. If a data source ceases to be available and there is no compatible substitute, then the data warehouse applications depending on this source will stop working. However, the predictable symmetry of dimensional models allow them to absorb some rather significant changes in source data and/or modeling assumptions without invalidating existing applications. We'll describe several of these unexpected modification categories, starting with the simplest:

New dimension attributes. If we discover new textual descriptors of a product, for example, we add these attributes to the dimension as new columns. All existing applications will be oblivious to the new attributes and continue to function. If the new attributes are available only after a specific point in time, then "Not Available" or its equivalent should be populated in the old dimension records.

New dimensions. As we just illustrated in Figure 2.11, we can add a dimension to an existing fact table by adding a new foreign key field and populating it correctly with values of the primary key from the new dimension.

New measured facts. If new measured facts become available, we can add them gracefully to the fact table. The simplest case is when the new facts are available in the same measurement event and at the same grain as the existing facts. In this case, the fact table is altered to add the new columns, and the values are populated into the table. If the ALTER TABLE statement is not viable, then a second fact table must be defined with the additional columns and the rows copied from the first. If the new facts are only available from a point in time forward, then null values need to be placed in the older fact rows. A more complex situation arises when new measured facts occur naturally at a different grain. If the new facts cannot be allocated or assigned to the original grain of the fact table, it is very likely that the new facts belong in their own fact table. It is almost always a mistake to mix grains in the same fact table.

Dimension becoming more granular. Sometimes it is desirable to increase the granularity of a dimension. In most cases, the original dimension attributes can be included in the new, more granular dimension because they roll up perfectly in a many-to-one relationship. The more granular dimension often implies a more granular fact table. There may be no alternative but to drop the fact table and rebuild it. However, all the existing applications would be unaffected.

Addition of a completely new data source involving existing dimensions as well as unexpected new dimensions. Almost always, a new source of data has its own granularity and dimensionality, so we create a new fact table. We should avoid force-fitting new measurements into an existing fact table of consistent measurements. The existing applications will still work because the existing fact and dimension tables are untouched.

Resisting Comfort Zone Urges

With our first dimensional design behind us, let's directly confront several of the natural urges that tempt modelers coming from a more normalized background. We're consciously breaking some traditional modeling rules because we're focused on delivering business value through ease of use and performance, not on transaction processing efficiencies.

Dimension Normalization (Snowflaking)

The flattened, denormalized dimension tables with repeating textual values may make a normalization modeler uncomfortable. Let's revisit our case study product dimension table. The 150,000 products roll up into 50 distinct departments. Rather than redundantly storing the 20-byte department description in the product dimension table, modelers with a normalized upbringing want to store a 2-byte department code and then create a new department dimension for the department decodes. In fact, they would feel more comfortable if all the descriptors in our original design were normalized into separate dimension tables. They argue that this design saves space because we're only storing cryptic codes in our 150,000-row dimension table, not lengthy descriptors.

In addition, some modelers contend that the normalized design for the dimension tables is easier to maintain. If a department description changes, they'd only need to update the one occurrence rather than the 3,000 repetitions in our original product dimension. Maintenance often is addressed by normalization disciplines, but remember that all this happens back in the staging area, long before the data is loaded into a presentation area's dimensional schema.

Dimension table normalization typically is referred to as *snowflaking*. Redundant attributes are removed from the flat, denormalized dimension table and placed in normalized secondary dimension tables. Figure 2.12 illustrates the partial snowflaking of our original schema. If the schema were fully snowflaked, it would appear as a full third-normal-form entity-relationship diagram. The contrast between Figure 2.12 and the earlier design in Figure 2.10 is startling. While the fact tables in both figures are identical, the plethora of dimension tables (even in our simplistic representation) is overwhelming.

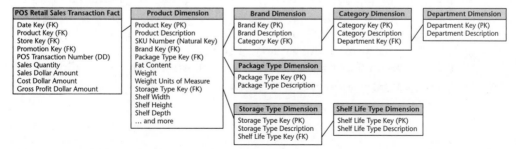

Figure 2.12   Partially snowflaked product dimension.

While snowflaking is a legal extension of the dimensional model, in general, we encourage you to resist the urge to snowflake given our two primary design drivers, ease of use and performance.

- The multitude of snowflaked tables makes for a much more complex presentation. Users inevitably will struggle with the complexity. Remember that simplicity is one of the primary objectives of a denormalized dimensional model.

- Likewise, database optimizers will struggle with the complexity of the snowflaked schema. Numerous tables and joins usually translate into slower query performance. The complexities of the resulting join specifications increase the chances that the optimizer will get sidetracked and choose a poor strategy.

- The minor disk space savings associated with snowflaked dimension tables are insignificant. If we replaced the 20-byte department description in our 150,000-row product dimension table with a 2-byte code, we'd save a whopping 2.7 MB (150,000 x 18 bytes), but we may have a 10-GB fact table! Dimension tables are almost always geometrically smaller than fact table. Efforts to normalize most dimension tables in order to save disk space are a waste of time.

- Snowflaking slows down the users' ability to browse within a dimension. Browsing often involves constraining one or more dimension attributes and looking at the distinct values of another attribute in the presence of these constraints. Browsing allows users to understand the relationship between dimension attribute values.

  Obviously, a snowflaked product dimension table would respond well if we just wanted a list of the category descriptions. However, if we wanted to see all the brands within a category, we'd need to traverse the brand and category dimensions. If we then wanted to also list the package types for each brand in a category, we'd be traversing even more tables. The SQL needed to perform these seemingly simple queries is quite complex, and we haven't even touched the other dimensions or fact table.

- Finally, snowflaking defeats the use of bitmap indexes. Bitmap indexes are very useful when indexing low-cardinality fields, such as the category and department columns in our product dimension tables. They greatly speed the performance of a query or constraint on the single column in question. Snowflaking inevitably would interfere with your ability to leverage this performance-tuning technique.

The dimension tables should remain as flat tables physically. Normalized, snowflaked dimension tables penalize cross-attribute browsing and prohibit the use of bit-mapped indexes. Disk space savings gained by normalizing the dimension tables typically are less than 1 percent of the total disk space needed for the overall schema. We knowingly sacrifice this dimension table space in the spirit of performance and ease-of-use advantages.

There are times when snowflaking is permissible, such as our earlier example with the date outrigger on the store dimension, where a clump of correlated attributes is used repeatedly in various independent roles. We just urge you to be conservative with snowflaked designs and use them only when they are obviously called for.

Too Many Dimensions

The fact table in a dimensional schema is naturally highly normalized and compact. There is no way to further normalize the extremely complex many-to-many relationships among the keys in the fact table because the dimensions are not correlated with each other. Every store is open every day. Sooner or later, almost every product is sold on promotion in most or all of our stores.

Interestingly, while uncomfortable with denormalized dimension tables, some modelers are tempted to denormalize the fact table. Rather than having a single product foreign key on the fact table, they include foreign keys for the frequently analyzed elements on the product hierarchy, such as brand, subcategory, category, and department. Likewise, the date key suddenly turns into a series of keys joining to separate week, month, quarter, and year dimension tables. Before you know it, our compact fact table has turned into an unruly monster that joins to literally dozens of dimension tables. We affectionately refer to these designs as *centipedes* because the fact tables appear to have nearly 100 legs, as shown in Figure 2.13. Clearly, the centipede design has stepped into the too-many-dimensions trap.

Remember, even with its tight format, the fact table is the behemoth in a dimensional design. Designing a fact table with too many dimensions leads to significantly increased fact table disk space requirements. While we're willing to use extra space for dimension tables, fact table space consumption concerns us because it is our largest table by orders of magnitude. There is no way to index the enormous multipart key effectively in our centipede example. The numerous joins are an issue for both usability and query performance.

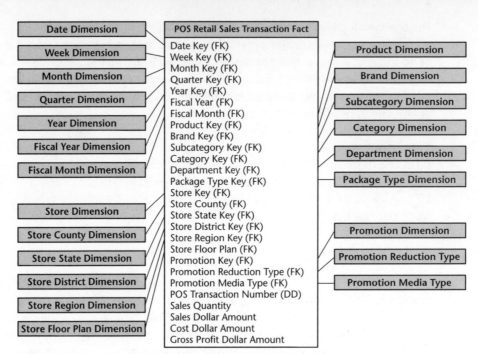

Figure 2.13 Centipede fact table with too many dimensions.

Most business processes can be represented with less than 15 dimensions in the fact table. If our design has 25 or more dimensions, we should look for ways to combine correlated dimensions into a single dimension. Perfectly correlated attributes, such as the levels of a hierarchy, as well as attributes with a reasonable statistical correlation, should be part of the same dimension. You have made a good decision to combine dimensions when the resulting new single dimension is noticeably smaller than the Cartesian product of the separate dimensions.

> A very large number of dimensions typically is a sign that several dimensions are not completely independent and should be combined into a single dimension. It is a dimensional modeling mistake to represent elements of a hierarchy as separate dimensions in the fact table.

Surrogate Keys

We strongly encourage the use of surrogate keys in dimensional models rather than relying on operational production codes. Surrogate keys go by many other aliases: *meaningless keys, integer keys, nonnatural keys, artificial keys, synthetic keys*, and so on. Simply put, surrogate keys are integers that are assigned sequentially as needed to populate a dimension. For example, the first product record is assigned a product surrogate key with the value of 1, the next product record is assigned product key 2, and so forth. The surrogate keys merely serve to join the dimension tables to the fact table.

Modelers sometimes are reluctant to give up their natural keys because they want to navigate the fact table based on the operational code while avoiding a join to the dimension table. Remember, however, that dimension tables are our entry points to the facts. If the fifth through ninth characters in the operational code identify the manufacturer, then the manufacturer's name should be included as a dimension table attribute. In general, we want to avoid embedding intelligence in the data warehouse keys because any assumptions that we make eventually may be invalidated. Likewise, queries and data access applications should not have any built-in dependency on the keys because the logic also would be vulnerable to invalidation.

Every join between dimension and fact tables in the data warehouse should be based on meaningless integer surrogate keys. You should avoid using the natural operational production codes. None of the data warehouse keys should be smart, where you can tell something about the row just by looking at the key.

Initially, it may be faster to implement a dimensional model using operational codes, but surrogate keys definitely will pay off in the long run. We sometimes think of them as being similar to a flu shot for the data warehouse—like an immunization, there's a small amount of pain to initiate and administer surrogate keys, but the long-run benefits are substantial.

One of the primary benefits of surrogate keys is that they buffer the data warehouse environment from operational changes. Surrogate keys allow the warehouse team to maintain control of the environment rather than being whipsawed by operational rules for generating, updating, deleting, recycling, and reusing production codes. In many organizations, historical operational codes (for example, inactive account numbers or obsolete product codes) get reassigned after a period of dormancy. If account numbers get recycled following 12 months of inactivity, the operational systems don't miss a beat because their business rules prohibit data from hanging around for that long. The data warehouse, on the other hand, will retain data for years. Surrogate keys provide the warehouse with a mechanism to differentiate these two separate instances of the same operational account number. If we rely solely on operational codes, we also are vulnerable to key overlap problems in the case of an acquisition or consolidation of data. Surrogate keys allow the data warehouse team to integrate data from multiple operational source systems, even if they lack consistent source keys.

There are also performance advantages associated with the use of surrogate keys. The surrogate key is as small an integer as possible while ensuring that it will accommodate the future cardinality or maximum number of rows in the dimension comfortably. Often the operational code is a bulky alphanumeric character string. The smaller surrogate key translates into smaller fact tables, smaller fact table indices, and more fact table rows per block input-output operation. Typically, a 4-byte integer is sufficient to handle most dimension situations. A 4-byte integer is a single integer, not four decimal digits. It has 32 bits and therefore can handle approximately 2 billion positive values (2^{32-1}) or 4 billion total positive and negative values (-2^{32-1} to $+2^{32-1}$). As we said, this is more than enough for just about any dimension. Remember, if you have a large fact table with 1 billion rows of data, every byte in each fact table row translates into another gigabyte of storage.

As we mentioned earlier, surrogate keys are used to record dimension conditions that may not have an operational code, such as the "No Promotion in Effect" condition. By taking control of the warehouse's keys, we can assign a surrogate key to identify this condition despite the lack of operational coding.

Similarly, you may find that your dimensional models have dates that are yet to be determined. There is no SQL date value for "Date to be Determined" or "Date Not Applicable." This is another reason we advocate using surrogate keys for your date keys rather than SQL date data types (as if our prior rationale wasn't convincing enough).

The date dimension is the one dimension where surrogate keys should be assigned in a meaningful, sequential order. In other words, January 1 of the first year would be assigned surrogate key value 1, January 2 would be assigned surrogate key 2, February 1 would be assigned surrogate key 32, and so on. We don't want to embed extensive calendar intelligence in these keys (for example, YYYY-MM-DD) because doing so may encourage people to bypass the date lookup dimension table. And, of course, in using this smart format, we would again have no way to represent "Hasn't happened yet" and other common date situations. We just want our fact table rows to be in sequential order. Treating the surrogate date key as a date sequence number will allow the fact table to be physically partitioned on the basis of the date key. Partitioning a large fact table on the basis of date is highly effective because it allows old data to be removed gracefully and new data to be loaded and indexed without disturbing the rest of the fact table.

Finally, surrogate keys are needed to support one of the primary techniques for handling changes to dimension table attributes. This is actually one of the most important reasons to use surrogate keys. We'll devote a whole section in Chapter 4 to using surrogate keys for slowly changing dimensions.

Of course, some effort is required to assign and administer surrogate keys, but it's not nearly as intimidating as many people imagine. We'll need to establish and maintain a cross-reference table in the staging area that will be used to substitute the appropriate surrogate key on each fact and dimension table row. In Chapter 16 we lay out a flow diagram for administering and processing surrogate keys in our dimensional schemas.

Before we leave the topic of keys, we want to discourage the use of concatenated or compound keys for dimension tables. We can't create a truly surrogate key simply by gluing together several natural keys or by combining the natural key with a time stamp. Also, we want to avoid multiple parallel joins between the dimension and fact tables, sometimes referred to as *double-barreled joins*, because they have an adverse impact on performance.

While we don't typically assign surrogate keys to degenerate dimensions, you should evaluate each situation to determine if one is required. A surrogate key is necessary if the transaction control numbers are not unique across locations or get reused. For example, our retailer's POS system may not assign unique transaction numbers across stores. The system may wrap back to zero and reuse previous control numbers once its maximum has been reached. Also, your transaction control number may be a bulky 24-byte alphanumeric column. In such cases, it would be advantageous to use a surrogate key. Technically, control number dimensions modeled in this way are no longer degenerate.

For the moment, let's assume that the first version of the retail sales schema represents both the logical and physical design of our database. In other words, the relational database contains only five actual tables: retail sales fact table and date, product, store, and promotion dimension tables. Each of the dimension tables has a primary key, and the fact table has a composite key made up of these four foreign keys, in addition to the degenerate transaction number. Perhaps the most striking aspect of the design at this point is the simplicity of the fact table. If the four foreign keys are tightly administered consecutive integers, we could reserve as little as 14 bytes for all four keys (4 bytes each for date, product, and promotion and 2 bytes for store). The transaction number might require an additional 8 bytes. If the four facts in the fact table were each 4-byte integers, we would need to reserve only another 16 bytes. This would make our fact table row only 38 bytes wide. Even if we had a billion rows, the fact table would occupy only about 38 GB of primary data space. Such a streamlined fact table row is a very typical result in a dimensional design.

Our embellished retail sales schema, illustrated in Figure 2.11, has three additional dimensions. If we allocate 4 bytes each for shopper and clerk and 2 bytes for the time of day (to the nearest minute), then our fact table width grows to only 48 bytes. Our billion-row fact table occupies just 48 GB.

Market Basket Analysis

The retail sales schema tells us in exquisite detail what was purchased at each store and under what conditions. However, the schema doesn't allow us to very easily analyze which products were sold in the same market basket together. This notion of analyzing the combination of products that sell together is known by data miners as *affinity grouping* but more popularly is called *market basket analysis*. Market basket analysis gives the retailer insights about how to merchandise various combinations of items. If frozen pasta dinners sell well with cola products, then these two products perhaps should be located near each other or marketed with complementary pricing. The concept of market basket analysis can be extended easily to other situations. In the manufacturing environment, it is useful to see what products are ordered together because we may want to offer product bundles with package pricing.

The retail sales fact table cannot be used easily to perform market basket analyses because SQL was never designed to constrain and group across line item fact rows. Data mining tools and some OLAP products can assist with market basket analysis, but in the absence of these tools, we'll describe a more direct approach below. Be forewarned that this is a rather advanced technique; if you are not doing market basket analysis today, simply skim this section to get a general sense of the techniques involved.

In Figure 2.14 we illustrate a market basket fact table that was derived from retail sales transactions. The market basket fact table is a periodic snapshot representing the pairs of products purchased together during a specified time period. The facts include the total number of baskets (customer tickets) that included products A and B, the total number of product A dollars and units in this subset of purchases, and the total number of product B dollars and units purchased. The basket count is a semiadditive fact. For example, if a customer ticket contains line items for pasta, soft drinks, and peanut butter in the market basket fact table, this single order is counted once on the pasta-soft drinks fact row, once on the row for the pasta-peanut butter combination, and so on. Obviously, care must be taken to avoid summarizing purchase counts for more than one product.

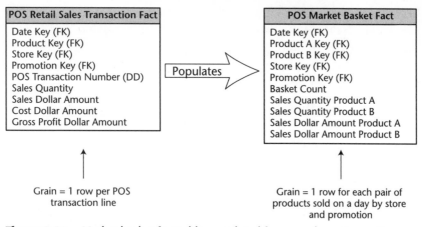

Figure 2.14 Market basket fact table populated from purchase transactions.

You will notice that there are two generalized product keys (product keys A and B) in the market basket fact table. Here we have built a single product dimension table that contains entries at multiple levels of the hierarchy, such as individual products, brands, and categories. This specialized variant of our normal product dimension table contains a small number of rather generic attributes. The surrogate keys for the various levels of the product hierarchy have been assigned so that they don't overlap.

Conceptually, the idea of recording market basket correlations is simple, but the sheer number of product combinations makes the analysis challenging. If we have N products in our product portfolio and we attempt to build a table with every possible pair of product keys encountered in product orders, we will approach N^2 product combinations [actually $N \times (N - 1)$ for the mathematicians among you]. In other words, if we have 10,000 products in our portfolio, there would be nearly 100,000,000 pairwise combinations. The number of possible combinations quickly approaches absurdity when we're dealing with a large number of products. If a retail store sells 100,000 SKUs, there are 10 billion possible SKU combinations.

The key to realistic market basket analysis is to remember that the primary goal is to understand the *meaningful* combinations of products sold together. Thinking about our market basket fact table, we would first be interested in rows with high basket counts. Since these product combinations are observed frequently, they warrant further investigation. Second, we would look for situations where the dollars or units for products A and B were in reasonable balance. If the dollars or units are far out of balance, all we've done is find high-selling products coupled with insignificant secondary products, which wouldn't be very helpful in making major merchandising or promotion decisions.

In order to avoid the combinatorial explosion of product pairs in the market basket fact table, we rely on a progressive pruning algorithm. We begin at the top of the product hierarchy, which we'll assume is category. We first enumerate all the category-to-category market basket combinations. If there are 25 categories, this first step generates 625 market basket rows. We then prune this list for further analysis by selecting only the rows that have a reasonably high order count and where the dollars and units for products A and B (which are categories at this point) are reasonably balanced. Experimentation will tell you what the basket count threshold and balance range should be.

We then push down to the next level of detail, which we'll assume is brand. Starting with the pruned set of combinations from the last step, we drill down on product A by enumerating all combinations of brand (product A) by category (product B). Similarly, we drill down one level of the hierarchy for product B by looking at all combinations of brand (product A) by brand (product B). Again, we prune the lists to those with the highest basket count frequencies and dollar or unit balance and then drill down to the next level in the hierarchy.

As we descend the hierarchy, we produce rows with smaller and smaller basket counts. Eventually, we find no basket counts greater than the reasonable threshold for relevance. It is permissible to stop at any time once we've satisfied the analyst's curiosity. One of the advantages of this top-down approach is that the rows found at each point are those with the highest relevance and impact. Progressively pruning the list provides more focus to already relevant results. One can imagine automating this process, searching the product hierarchy downward, ignoring the low basket counts, and always striving for balanced dollars and units with the high basket counts. The process could halt when the number of product pairs reached some desired threshold or when the total activity expressed in basket count, dollars, or units reached some lower limit.

A variation on this approach could start with a specific category, brand, or even a product. Again, the idea would be to combine this specific product first with all the categories and then to work down the hierarchy. Another twist would be to look at the mix of products purchased by a given customer during a given time period, regardless of whether they were in the same basket. In any case, much of the hard work associated with market basket analysis has been off-loaded to the staging area's ETL processes in order to simplify the ultimate query and presentation aspects of the analysis.

Summary

In this chapter we got our first exposure to designing a dimensional model. Regardless of industry, we strongly encourage the four-step process for tackling dimensional model designs. Remember that it is especially important that we clearly state the grain associated with our dimensional schema. Loading the fact table with atomic data provides the greatest flexibility because we can summarize that data "every which way." As soon as the fact table is restricted to more aggregated information, we'll run into walls when the summarization assumptions prove to be invalid. Also remember that it is vitally important to populate our dimension tables with verbose, robust descriptive attributes.

In the next chapter we'll remain within the retail industry to discuss techniques for tackling a second business process within the organization, ensuring that we're leveraging our earlier efforts while avoiding stovepipes.

Inventory

I n Chapter 2 we developed a dimensional model for the sales transactions in a large grocery chain. We remain within the same industry in this chapter but move up the value chain to tackle the inventory process. The designs developed in this chapter apply to a broad set of inventory pipelines both inside and outside the retail industry.

Even more important, this chapter provides a thorough discussion of the data warehouse bus architecture. The bus architecture is essential to creating an integrated data warehouse from a distributed set of related business processes. It provides a framework for planning the overall warehouse, even though we will build it incrementally. Finally, we will underscore the importance of using common, conformed dimensions and facts across the warehouse's dimensional models.

Chapter 3 discusses the following concepts:

- **Value chain implications**
- **Inventory periodic snapshot model, as well as transaction and accumulating snapshot models**
- **Semi-additive facts**
- **Enhanced inventory facts**
- **Data warehouse bus architecture and matrix**
- **Conformed dimensions and facts**

Introduction to the Value Chain

Most organizations have an underlying value chain consisting of their key business processes. The value chain identifies the natural, logical flow of an organization's primary activities. For example, in the case of a retailer, the company may issue a purchase order to a product manufacturer. The products are delivered to the retailer's warehouse, where they are held in inventory. A delivery is then made to an individual store, where again the products sit in inventory until a consumer makes a purchase. We have illustrated this subset of a retailer's value chain in Figure 3.1. Obviously, products sourced from a manufacturer that delivers directly to the retail store would bypass the warehousing steps of the value chain.

Operational source systems typically produce transactions or snapshots at each step of the value chain, generating interesting performance metrics along the way. The primary objective of most analytic decision support systems is to monitor the performance results of key processes. Since each business process produces unique metrics at unique time intervals with unique granularity and dimensionality, each process typically spawns one or more fact tables. To this end, the value chain provides high-level insight into the overall enterprise data warehouse. We'll devote more time to this topic later in this chapter.

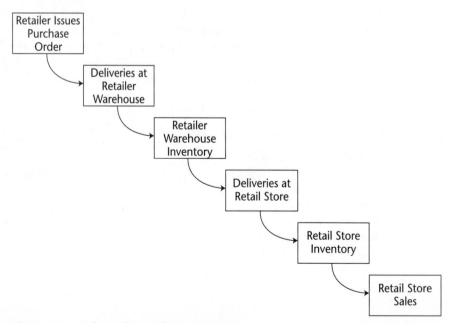

Figure 3.1 Subset of a retailer's value chain.

Inventory Models

In the meantime, we'll delve into several complementary inventory models. The first is the inventory periodic snapshot. Every day (or at some other regular time interval), we measure the inventory levels of each product and place them as separate rows in a fact table. These periodic snapshot rows appear over time as a series of data layers in the dimensional model, much like geologic layers represent the accumulation of sediment over long periods of time. We'll explore this common inventory model in some detail. We'll also discuss briefly a second inventory model where we record every transaction that has an impact on inventory levels as products move through the warehouse. Finally, in the third model, we'll touch on the inventory accumulating snapshot, where we build one fact table row for each product delivery and update the row until the product leaves the warehouse. Each of the three inventory models tells a different story. In some inventory applications, two or even all three models may be appropriate simultaneously.

Inventory Periodic Snapshot

Let's return to our retail case study. Optimized inventory levels in the stores can have a major impact on chain profitability. Making sure the right product is in the right store at the right time minimizes out-of-stocks (where the product isn't available on the shelf to be sold) and reduces overall inventory carrying costs. The retailer needs the ability to analyze daily quantity-on-hand inventory levels by product and store.

It is time to put the four-step process for designing dimensional models to work again. The business process we're interested in analyzing is the retail store inventory. In terms of granularity, we want to see daily inventory by product at each individual store, which we assume is the atomic level of detail provided by the operational inventory system. The dimensions immediately fall out of this grain declaration: date, product, and store. We are unable to envision additional descriptive dimensions at this granularity. Inventory typically is not associated with a retail promotion dimension. Although a store promotion may be going on while the products are sitting in inventory, the promotion usually is not associated with the product until it is actually sold. After the promotion has ended, the products still may be sitting in inventory. Typically, promotion dimensions are associated with product movement, such as when the product is ordered, received, or sold.

The simplest view of inventory involves only a single fact: quantity on hand. This leads to an exceptionally clean dimensional design, as shown in Figure 3.2.

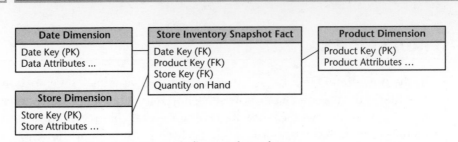

Figure 3.2   Store inventory periodic snapshot schema.

The date dimension table in this case study is identical to the table developed in the earlier case for retail store sales. The product and store dimensions also may be identical. Alternatively, we may want to further decorate these dimension tables with additional attributes that would be useful for inventory analysis. For example, the product dimension could be enhanced to include columns such as the minimum reorder quantity, assuming that they are constant and discrete descriptors of each product stock keeping unit (SKU). Likewise, in the store dimension, in addition to the selling square-footage attribute we discussed in Chapter 2, we also might include attributes to identify the frozen and refrigerated storage square footages. We'll talk more about the implications of adding these dimension attributes later in this chapter.

If we are analyzing inventory levels at the retailer's warehouse rather than at the store location, the schema would look quite similar to Figure 3.2. Obviously, the store dimension would be replaced with a warehouse dimension. When monitoring inventory levels at the warehouse, normally we do not retain the store dimension as a fourth dimension unless the warehouse inventory has been allocated to a specific store.

Even a schema as simple as this one can be very useful. Numerous insights can be derived if inventory levels are measured frequently for many products in many storage locations. If we're analyzing the in-store inventory levels of a mass merchandiser, this database could be used to balance store inventories each night after the stores close.

This periodic snapshot fact table faces a serious challenge that Chapter 2's sales transaction fact table did not. The sales fact table was reasonably sparse because only about 10 percent of the products in each of our hypothetical stores actually sold each day. If a product didn't sell in a store on a given day, then there was no row in the fact table for that combination of keys. Inventory, on the other hand, generates dense snapshot tables. Since the retailer strives to avoid out-of-stock situations where the product is not available for sale, there is a row in the fact table for virtually every product in every store every day.

We may well include the zero measurements as explicit records. For our grocery retailer with 60,000 products stocked in 100 stores, we would insert approximately 6 million rows (60,000 products x 100 stores) with each fact table load. With a row width of just 14 bytes, the fact table would grow by 84 MB each time we append more fact table rows. A year's worth of daily snapshots would consume over 30 GB. The denseness of inventory snapshots sometimes mandates some compromises.

Perhaps the most obvious compromise is to reduce the snapshot frequencies over time. It may be acceptable to keep the last 60 days of inventory at the daily level and then revert to less granular weekly snapshots for historical data. In this way, instead of retaining 1,095 snapshots during a 3-year period, the number could be reduced to 208 total snapshots (60 daily + 148 weekly snapshots in two separate fact tables given their unique periodicity). We have reduced the total data size by more than a factor of 5.

Semiadditive Facts

We stressed the importance of fact additivity in Chapter 2. When we modeled the flow of product past a point at the checkout cash register, only the products that actually sold were measured. Once a product was sold, it couldn't be counted again in a subsequent sale. This made most of the measures in the retail sales schema perfectly additive across all dimensions.

In the inventory snapshot schema, the quantity on hand can be summarized across products or stores and result in a valid total. Inventory levels, however, are not additive across dates because they represent snapshots of a level or balance at one point in time. It is not possible to tell whether yesterday's inventory is the same or different from today's inventory solely by looking at inventory levels. Because inventory levels (and all forms of financial account balances) are additive across some dimensions but not all, we refer to them as *semiadditive facts*.

The semiadditive nature of inventory balance facts is even more understandable if we think about our checking account balances. On Monday, let's presume that you have $50 in your account. On Tuesday, the balance remains unchanged. On Wednesday, you deposit another $50 into your account so that the balance is now $100. The account has no further activity through the end of the week. On Friday, you can't merely add up the daily balances during the week and declare that your balance is $400 (based on $50 + 50 + 100 + 100 + 100). The most useful way to combine account balances and inventory levels across dates is to average them (resulting in an $80 average balance in the checking example). We are all familiar with our bank referring to the average daily balance on our monthly account summary.

All measures that record a static level (inventory levels, financial account balances, and measures of intensity such as room temperatures) are inherently nonadditive across the date dimension and possibly other dimensions. In these cases, the measure may be aggregated usefully across time, for example, by averaging over the number of time periods.

The last few words in this design principle contain a trap. Unfortunately, you cannot use the SQL AVG function to calculate the average over time. The SQL AVG function averages over all the rows received by the query, not just the number of dates. For example, if a query requested the average inventory for a cluster of three products in four stores across seven dates (that is, what is the average daily inventory of a brand in a geographic region during a given week), the SQL AVG function would divide the summed inventory value by 84 (3 products x 4 stores x 7 dates). Obviously, the correct answer is to divide the summed inventory value by 7, which is the number of daily time periods. Because SQL has no standard functionality such as an AVG_DATE_SUM operator that would compute the average over just the date dimension, inventory calculations are burdened with additional complexity. A proper inventory application must isolate the date constraint and retrieve its cardinality alone (in this case, the 7 days comprising the requested week). Then the application must divide the final summed inventory value by the date constraint cardinality. This can be done with an embedded SQL call within the overall SQL statement or by querying the date dimension separately and then storing the resulting value in an application that is passed to the overall SQL statement.

Enhanced Inventory Facts

The simplistic view of inventory we developed in our periodic snapshot fact table allows us to see a time series of inventory levels. For most inventory analysis, quantity on hand isn't enough. Quantity on hand needs to be used in conjunction with additional facts to measure the velocity of inventory movement and develop other interesting metrics such as the number of turns, number of days' supply, and gross margin return on inventory (GMROI, pronounced "jem-roy").

If we added quantity sold (or equivalently, quantity depleted or shipped if we're dealing with a warehouse location) to each inventory fact row, we could calculate the number of turns and days' supply. For daily inventory snapshots, the number of turns measured each day is calculated as the quantity sold divided by the quantity on hand. For an extended time span, such as a year, the number of turns is the total quantity sold divided by the daily average quantity on hand. The number of days' supply is a similar calculation. Over a time span, the number of days' supply is the final quantity on hand divided by the average quantity sold.

In addition to the quantity sold, we probably also can supply the extended value of the inventory at cost, as well as the value at the latest selling price. The difference between these two values is the gross profit, of course. The gross margin is equal to the gross profit divided by the value at the latest selling price.

Finally, we can multiply the number of turns by the gross margin to get the GMROI, as expressed in the following formula:

$$\text{GMROI} = \frac{\text{total quantity sold x (value at latest selling price} - \text{value at cost)}}{\text{daily average quantity on hand x value at the latest selling price}}$$

Although this formula looks complicated, the idea behind GMROI is simple. By multiplying the gross margin by the number of turns, we create a measure of the effectiveness of our inventory investment. A high GMROI means that we are moving the product through the store quickly (lots of turns) and are making good money on the sale of the product (high gross margin). A low GMROI means that we are moving the product slowly (low turns) and aren't making very much money on it (low gross margin). The GMROI is a standard metric used by inventory analysts to judge a company's quality of investment in its inventory.

If we want to be more ambitious than our initial design in Figure 3.2, then we should include the quantity sold, value at cost, and value at the latest selling price columns in our snapshot fact table, as illustrated in Figure 3.3. Of course, if some of these metrics exist at different granularity in separate fact tables, a requesting application would need to retrieve all the components of the GMROI computation at the same level.

Notice that quantity on hand is semiadditive but that the other measures in our advanced periodic snapshot are all fully additive across all three dimensions. The quantity sold amount is summarized to the particular grain of the fact table, which is daily in this case. The value columns are extended, additive amounts. We do not store GMROI in the fact table because it is not additive. We can calculate GMROI from the constituent columns across any number of fact rows by adding the columns up before performing the calculation, but we are dead in the water if we try to store GMROI explicitly because we can't usefully combine GMROIs across multiple rows.

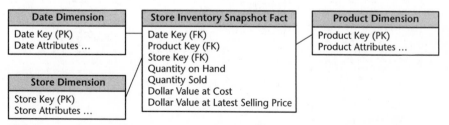

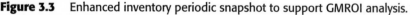

Figure 3.3   Enhanced inventory periodic snapshot to support GMROI analysis.

The periodic snapshot is the most common inventory schema. We'll touch briefly on two alternative perspectives to complement the inventory snapshot just designed. For a change of pace, rather than describing these models in the context of the retail in-store inventory, we'll move up the value chain to discuss the inventory located in our warehouses.

Inventory Transactions

A second way to model an inventory business process is to record every transaction that affects inventory. Inventory transactions at the warehouse might include the following:

- Receive product
- Place product into inspection hold
- Release product from inspection hold
- Return product to vendor due to inspection failure
- Place product in bin
- Authorize product for sale
- Pick product from bin
- Package product for shipment
- Ship product to customer
- Receive product from customer
- Return product to inventory from customer return
- Remove product from inventory

Each inventory transaction identifies the date, product, warehouse, vendor, transaction type, and in most cases, a single amount representing the inventory quantity impact caused by the transaction. Assuming that the granularity of our fact table is one row per inventory transaction, the resulting schema is illustrated in Figure 3.4.

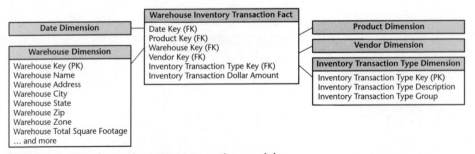

Figure 3.4 Warehouse inventory transaction model.

Even though the transaction-level fact table is again very simple, it contains the most detailed information available about inventory because it mirrors fine-scale inventory manipulations. The transaction-level fact table is useful for measuring the frequency and timing of specific transaction types. For instance, only a transaction-grained inventory fact table can answer the following questions:

- How many times have we placed a product into an inventory bin on the same day we picked the product from the same bin at a different time?

- How many separate shipments did we receive from a given vendor, and when did we get them?

- On which products have we had more than one round of inspection failures that caused return of the product to the vendor?

Even so, it is impractical to use this table as the sole basis for analyzing inventory performance. Although it is theoretically possible to reconstruct the exact inventory position at any moment in time by rolling all possible transactions forward from a known inventory position, it is too cumbersome and impractical for broad data warehouse questions that span dates or products.

> **Remember that there's more to life than transactions alone. Some form of snapshot table to give a more cumulative view of a process often accompanies a transaction fact table.**

Inventory Accumulating Snapshot

The final inventory model that we'll explore briefly is the accumulating snapshot. In this model we place one row in the fact table for a shipment of a particular product to the warehouse. In a single fact table row we track the disposition of the product shipment until it has left the warehouse. The accumulating snapshot model is only possible if we can reliably distinguish products delivered in one shipment from those delivered at a later time. This approach is also appropriate if we are tracking disposition at very detailed levels, such as by product serial number or lot number.

Let's assume that the inventory goes through a series of well-defined events or milestones as it moves through the warehouse, such as receiving, inspection, bin placement, authorization to sell, picking, boxing, and shipping. The philosophy behind the accumulating snapshot fact table is to provide an updated status of the product shipment as it moves through these milestones. Each fact table row will be updated until the product leaves the warehouse. As illustrated in Figure 3.5, the inventory accumulating snapshot fact table with its multitude of dates and facts looks quite different from the transaction or periodic snapshot schemas.

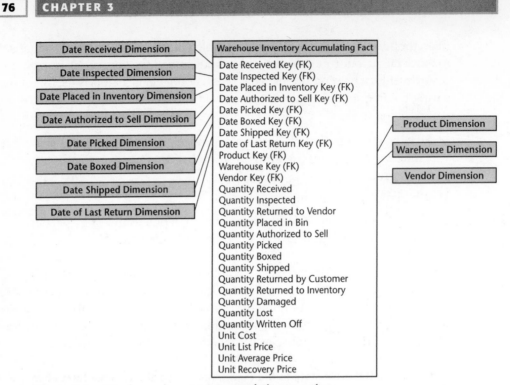

Figure 3.5 Warehouse inventory accumulating snapshot.

Accumulating snapshots are the third major type of fact table. They are interesting both because of the multiple date-valued foreign keys at the beginning of the key list and also because we revisit and modify the same fact table records over and over. Since the accumulating snapshot rarely is used in long-running, continuously replenished inventory processes, rather than focusing on accumulating snapshots at this time, we'll provide more detailed coverage in Chapter 5. The alert reader will notice the four non-additive metrics at the end of the fact table. Again, stay tuned for Chapter 5.

Value Chain Integration

Now that we've completed the design of three inventory model variations, let's revisit our earlier discussion about the retailer's value chain. Both the business and IT organizations typically are very interested in value chain integration. Low-level business analysts may not feel much urgency, but those in the higher ranks of management are very aware of the need to look across the business to better evaluate performance. Numerous data warehouse projects have focused recently on management's need to better understand customer relationships from an end-to-end perspective. Obviously, this requires the ability to look consistently at customer information across processes, such as quotes, orders, invoicing, payments, and customer service. Even if your management's vision is not so lofty, business users certainly are tired of getting reports that don't match from different systems or teams.

IT managers know all too well that integration is needed to deliver on the promises of data warehousing. Many consider it their fiduciary responsibility to manage the organization's information assets. They know that they're not fulfilling their responsibilities if they allow standalone, nonintegrated databases to proliferate. In addition to better addressing the business's needs, the IT organization also benefits from integration because it allows the organization to better leverage scarce resources and gain efficiencies through the use of reusable components.

Fortunately, the folks who typically are most interested in integration also have the necessary organizational influence and economic willpower to make it happen. If they don't place a high value on integration, then you're facing a much more serious organizational challenge. It shouldn't be the sole responsibility of the data warehouse manager to garner organizational consensus for an integrated warehouse architecture across the value chain. The political support of senior management is very important. It takes the data warehouse manager off the hook and places the burden of the decision-making process on senior management's shoulders, where it belongs.

In Chapters 1 and 2 we modeled data from several processes of the value chain. While separate fact tables in separate data marts represent the data from each process, the models share several common business dimensions, namely, date, product, and store. We've logically represented this dimension sharing in Figure 3.6. Using shared, common dimensions is absolutely critical to designing data marts that can be integrated. They allow us to combine performance measurements from different processes in a single report. We use multipass SQL to query each data mart separately, and then we outer join the query results based on a common dimension attribute. This linkage, often referred to as *drill across,* is straightforward if the dimension table attributes are identical.

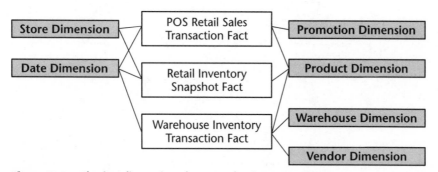

Figure 3.6 Sharing dimensions between business processes.

Data Warehouse Bus Architecture

Obviously, building the enterprise's data warehouse in one step is too daunting, yet building it as isolated pieces defeats the overriding goal of consistency. For long-term data warehouse success, we need to use an architected, incremental approach to build the enterprise's warehouse. The approach we advocate is the data warehouse bus architecture.

The word *bus* is an old term from the electrical power industry that is now used commonly in the computer industry. A bus is a common structure to which everything connects and from which everything derives power. The bus in your computer is a standard interface specification that allows you to plug in a disk drive, CD-ROM, or any number of other specialized cards or devices. Because of the computer's bus standard, these peripheral devices work together and usefully coexist, even though they were manufactured at different times by different vendors.

💡 **By defining a standard bus interface for the data warehouse environment, separate data marts can be implemented by different groups at different times. The separate data marts can be plugged together and usefully coexist if they adhere to the standard.**

If we think back to the value chain diagram in Figure 3.1, we can envision many business processes plugging into the data warehouse bus, as illustrated in Figure 3.7. Ultimately, all the processes of an organization's value chain will create a family of dimensional models that share a comprehensive set of common, conformed dimensions. We'll talk more about conformed dimensions later in this chapter, but for now, assume that the term means *similar*.

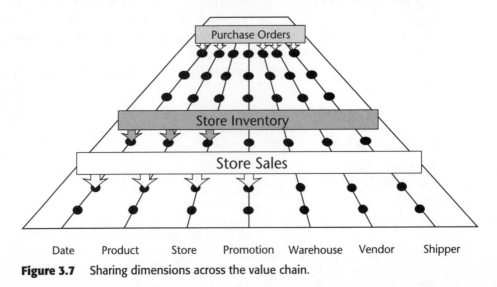

Figure 3.7 Sharing dimensions across the value chain.

The data warehouse bus architecture provides a rational approach to decomposing the enterprise data warehouse planning task. During the limited-duration architecture phase, the team designs a master suite of standardized dimensions and facts that have uniform interpretation across the enterprise. This establishes the data architecture framework. We then tackle the implementation of separate data marts in which each iteration closely adheres to the architecture. As the separate data marts come on line, they fit together like the pieces of a puzzle. At some point, enough data marts exist to make good on the promise of an integrated enterprise data warehouse.

The bus architecture allows data warehouse managers to get the best of both worlds. They have an architectural framework that guides the overall design, but the problem has been divided into bite-sized data mart chunks that can be implemented in realistic time frames. Separate data mart development teams follow the architecture guidelines while working fairly independently and asynchronously.

The bus architecture is independent of technology and the database platform. All flavors of relational and online analytical processing (OLAP)-based data marts can be full participants in the data warehouse bus if they are designed around conformed dimensions and facts. Data warehouses will inevitably consist of numerous separate machines with different operating systems and database management systems (DBMSs). If designed coherently, they will share a uniform architecture of conformed dimensions and facts that will allow them to be fused into an integrated whole.

Data Warehouse Bus Matrix

The tool we use to create, document, and communicate the bus architecture is the data warehouse bus matrix, which we've illustrated in Figure 3.8.

COMMON DIMENSIONS

BUSINESS PROCESSES	Date	Product	Store	Promotion	Warehouse	Vendor	Contract	Shipper
Retail Sales	X	X	X	X				
Retail Inventory	X	X	X					
Retail Deliveries	X	X	X					
Warehouse Inventory	X	X			X	X		
Warehouse Deliveries	X	X			X	X		
Purchase Orders	X	X			X	X	X	X

Figure 3.8 Sample data warehouse bus matrix.

Working in a tabular fashion, we lay out the business processes of the organization as matrix rows. It is important to remember that we are identifying the business processes closely identified with sources of data, not the organization's business departments. The matrix rows translate into data marts based on the organization's primary activities. We begin by listing the data marts that are derived from a single primary source system, commonly known as *first-level data marts*. These data marts are recognizable complements to their operational source.

💡 **The rows of the bus matrix correspond to data marts. You should create separate matrix rows if the sources are different, the processes are different, or if the matrix row represents more than what can reasonably be tackled in a single implementation iteration.**

Once it is time to begin a data mart development project, we recommend starting the actual implementation with first-level data marts because they minimize the risk of signing up for an implementation that is too ambitious. Most of the overall risk of failure comes from biting off too much of the extract-transformation-load (ETL) data staging design and development effort. In many cases, first-level data marts provide users with enough interesting data to keep them happy and quiet while the data mart teams keep working on more difficult issues.

Once we've fully enumerated the list of first-level data marts, then we can identify more complex multisource marts as a second step. We refer to these data marts as *consolidated data marts* because they typically cross business processes. While consolidated data marts are immensely beneficial to the organization, they are more difficult to implement because the ETL effort grows alarmingly with each additional major source that's integrated into a single dimensional model. It is prudent to focus on the first-level data marts as dimensional building blocks before tackling the task of consolidating. In some cases the consolidated data mart is actually more than a simple union of data sets from the first-level data marts.

Profitability is a classic example of a consolidated data mart where separate revenue and cost factors are combined from different process marts to provide a complete view of profitability. While a highly granular profitability mart is exciting because it provides visibility into product and customer profit performance, it is definitely not the first mart you should attempt to implement. You could easily drown while attempting to stage all the components of revenue and cost. If you are absolutely forced to focus on profitability as your first mart, then you should begin by allocating costs on a rule-of-thumb basis rather than doing the complete job of sourcing all the underlying cost detail. Even so, attempting to get organization consensus on allocation rules may be a project showstopper given the sensitive (and perhaps wallet-impacting) nature of the allocations. One of the project prerequisites, outside the scope of the warehouse project team's responsibilities, should be business agreement on the allocation rules. It is safe to say that it is best to avoid dealing with the complexities of profitability until you have some data warehousing successes under your belt.

The columns of the matrix represent the common dimensions used across the enterprise. It is often helpful to create a comprehensive list of dimensions before filling in the matrix. When you start with a large list of potential dimensions, it becomes a useful creative exercise to determine whether a given dimension possibly could be associated with a data mart.

The shaded cells indicate that the dimension column is related to the business process row. The resulting matrix will be surprisingly dense. Looking across the rows is revealing because you can see the dimensionality of each data mart at a glance. However, the real power of the matrix comes from looking at the columns as they depict the interaction between the data marts and common dimensions.

The matrix is a very powerful device for both planning and communication. Although it is relatively straightforward to lay out the rows and columns, in the process, we're defining the overall data architecture for the warehouse. We can see immediately which dimensions warrant special attention given their participation in multiple data marts. The matrix helps prioritize which dimensions should be tackled first for conformity given their prominent roles.

The matrix allows us to communicate effectively within and across data mart teams, as well as upward and outward throughout the organization. The matrix is a succinct deliverable that visually conveys the entire plan at once. It is a tribute to its simplicity that the matrix can be used effectively to directly communicate with senior IT and business management.

Creating the data warehouse bus matrix is one of the most important up-front deliverables of a data warehouse implementation. It is a hybrid resource that is part technical design tool, part project management tool, and part communication tool.

It goes without saying that it is unacceptable to build separate data marts that ignore a framework to tie the data together. Isolated, independent data marts are worse than simply a lost opportunity for analysis. They deliver access to irreconcilable views of the organization and further enshrine the reports that cannot be compared with one another. Independent data marts become legacy implementations in their own right; by their very existence, they block the development of a coherent warehouse environment.

So what happens if you're not starting with a blank data warehousing slate? Perhaps several data marts have been constructed already without regard to an architecture of conformed dimensions. Can you rescue your stovepipes and convert them to the bus architecture? To answer this question, you should start first with an honest appraisal of your existing nonintegrated data marts. This typically entails a series of face-to-face meetings with the separate teams (including the clandestine teams within business organizations) to determine the gap between the current environment and the organization's architected goal. Once the gap is understood, you need to develop an incremental plan to convert the data marts to the enterprise architecture. The plan needs to be sold internally. Senior IT and business management must understand the current state of data chaos, the risks of doing nothing, and the benefits of moving forward according to your game plan. Management also needs to appreciate that the conversion will require a commitment of support, resources, and funding.

If an existing data mart is based on a sound dimensional design, perhaps you can simply map an existing dimension to a standardized version. The original dimension table would be rebuilt using a cross-reference map. Likewise, the fact table also would need to be reprocessed to replace the original dimension keys with the conformed dimension keys. Of course, if the original and conformed dimension tables contain different attributes, rework of the preexisting queries is inevitable. More typically, existing data marts are riddled with dimensional modeling errors beyond just the lack of adherence to standardized dimensions. In some cases, the stovepipe data mart already has outlived its useful life. Isolated data marts often are built for a specific functional area. When others try to leverage the environment, they typically discover that the data mart was implemented at an inappropriate level of granularity and is missing key dimensionality. The effort required to retrofit these data marts into the warehouse architecture may exceed the effort to start over from scratch. As difficult as it is to admit, stovepipe data marts often have to be shut down and rebuilt in the proper bus architecture framework.

Conformed Dimensions

Now that you understand the importance of the bus architecture, let's further explore the standardized conformed dimensions that serve as the cornerstone of the warehouse bus. Conformed dimensions are either identical or strict mathematical subsets of the most granular, detailed dimension. Conformed dimensions have consistent dimension keys, consistent attribute column names, consistent attribute definitions, and consistent attribute values (which translates into consistent report labels and groupings). Dimension tables are not conformed if the attributes are labeled differently or contain different values. If a customer or product dimension is deployed in a nonconformed manner, then either the separate data marts cannot be used together or, worse, attempts to use them together will produce invalid results.

Conformed dimensions come in several different flavors. At the most basic level, conformed dimensions mean the exact same thing with every possible fact table to which they are joined. The date dimension table connected to the sales facts is identical to the date dimension table connected to the inventory facts. In fact, the conformed dimension may be the same physical table within the database. However, given the typical complexity of our warehouse's technical environment with multiple database platforms, it is more likely that the dimensions are duplicated synchronously in each data mart. In either case, the date dimensions in both data marts will have the same number of rows, same key values, same attribute labels, same attribute definitions, and same attribute values. There is consistent data content, data interpretation, and user presentation.

Most conformed dimensions are defined naturally at the most granular level possible. The grain of the customer dimension naturally will be the individual customer. The grain of the product dimension will be the lowest level at which products are tracked in the source systems. The grain of the date dimension will be the individual day.

Sometimes dimensions are needed at a rolled-up level of granularity. Perhaps the roll-up dimension is required because the fact table represents aggregated facts that are associated with aggregated dimensions. This would be the case if we had a weekly inventory snapshot in addition to our daily snapshot. In other situations, the facts simply may be generated by another business process at a higher level of granularity. One business process, such as sales, captures data at the atomic product level, whereas forecasting generates data at the brand level. You couldn't share a single product dimension table across the two business process schemas because the granularity is different. The product and brand dimensions still would conform if the brand table were a strict subset of the atomic product table. Attributes that are common to both the detailed and rolled-up dimension tables, such as the brand and category descriptions, should be labeled, defined, and valued identically in both tables, as illustrated in Figure 3.9.

Roll-up dimensions conform to the base-level atomic dimension if they are a strict subset of that atomic dimension.

We may encounter other legitimate conformed dimension subsets with dimension tables at the same level of granularity. For example, in the inventory snapshot schema we added supplemental attributes to the product and store dimensions that may not be useful to the sales transaction schema. The product dimension tables used in these two data marts still conform if the keys and

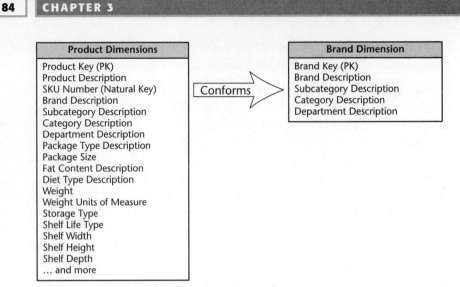

Figure 3.9 Conforming roll-up dimension subsets.

common columns are identical. Of course, given that the supplemental attributes were limited to the inventory data mart, we would be unable to look across processes using these add-on attributes.

Another case of conformed dimension subsetting occurs when two dimensions are at the same level of detail but one represents only a subset of rows. For example, we may have a corporate product dimension that contains data for our full portfolio of products across multiple disparate lines of business, as illustrated in Figure 3.10. Analysts in the separate businesses may want to view only their subset of the corporate dimension, restricted to the product rows for their business. By using a subset of rows, they aren't encumbered with the entire product set for the organization. Of course, the fact table joined to this subsetted dimension must be limited to the same subset of products. If a user attempts to use a subset dimension while accessing a fact table consisting of the complete product set, he or she may encounter unexpected query results. Technically, referential integrity would be violated. We need to be cognizant of the potential opportunity for user confusion or error with dimension row subsetting. We will further elaborate on dimension subsets when we discuss heterogeneous products in Chapter 9.

The conformed date dimension in our daily sales and monthly forecasting scenario is a unique example of both row and column dimension subsetting. Obviously, we can't simply use the same date dimension table because of the difference in roll-up granularity. However, the month dimension may consist of strictly the month-end daily date table rows with the exclusion of all columns that don't apply at the monthly granularity. Excluded columns would include daily date columns such as the date description, day number in epoch, weekday/weekend indicator, week-ending date, holiday indicator, day number within year, and others. You might consider including a month-end indicator on the daily date dimension to facilitate creation of this monthly table.

Conformed dimensions will be replicated either logically or physically throughout the enterprise; however, they should be built once in the staging area. The responsibility for each conformed dimension is vested in a group we call the *dimension authority*. The dimension authority has responsibility for defining, maintaining, and publishing a particular dimension or its subsets to all the data mart clients who need it. They take responsibility for staging the gold-standard dimension data. Ultimately, this may involve sourcing from multiple operational systems to publish a complete, high-quality dimension table.

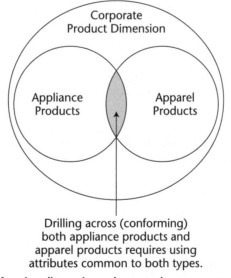

Drilling across (conforming)
both appliance products and
apparel products requires using
attributes common to both types.

Figure 3.10 Conforming dimension subsets at the same granularity.

The major responsibility of the centralized dimension authority is to establish, maintain, and publish the conformed dimensions to all the client data marts.

Once a set of master conformed dimensions has been defined for the enterprise, it is extremely important that the data mart teams actually use these dimensions. The commitment to use conformed dimensions is more than a technical decision; it is a business policy decision that is key to making the enterprise data warehouse function. Agreement on conformed dimensions faces far more political challenges than technical hurdles. Given the political issues surrounding them, conformed dimensions must be supported from the outset by the highest levels of the organization. Business executives must stress the importance to their teams, even if the conformed dimension causes some compromises. The CIO also should appreciate the importance of conformed dimensions and mandate that each data mart team takes the pledge to always use them.

Obviously, conformed dimensions require implementation coordination. Modifications to existing attributes or the addition of new attributes must be reviewed with all the data mart teams employing the conformed dimension. You will also need to determine your conformed dimension release strategy. Changes to identical dimensions should be replicated synchronously to all associated data marts. This push approach to dimension publishing maintains the requisite consistency across the organization.

Now that we've preached about the importance of conformed dimensions, we'll discuss the situation where it may not be realistic or necessary to establish conformed dimensions for the organization. If you are a conglomerate with subsidiaries that span widely varied industries, there may be little point in trying to integrate. If you don't want to cross-sell the same customers from one line of business to another, sell products that span lines of business, or assign products from multiple lines of business to a single salesperson, then it may not make sense to attempt a comprehensive data warehouse architecture. There likely isn't much perceived business value to conform your dimensions. The willingness to seek a common definition for product or customer is a major litmus test for an organization theoretically intent on building an enterprise data warehouse. If the organization is unwilling to agree on common definitions across all data marts, the organization shouldn't attempt to build a data warehouse that spans these marts. You would be better off building separate, self-contained data warehouses for each subsidiary.

In our experience, while many organizations find it currently mission impossible to combine data across their disparate lines of business, some degree of integration is typically an ultimate goal. Rather than throwing your hands in the air and declaring that it can't possibly be done, we suggest starting down the path toward conformity. Perhaps there are a handful of attributes that can be conformed across disparate lines of business. Even if it is merely a product description, category, and line of business attribute that is common to all businesses, this least-common-denominator approach is still a step in the right direction. You don't have to get all your businesses to agree on everything related to a dimension before proceeding.

Conformed Facts

Thus far we have talked about the central task of setting up conformed dimensions to tie our data marts together. This is 90 percent of the up-front data architecture effort. The remaining effort goes into establishing conformed fact definitions.

Revenue, profit, standard prices, standard costs, measures of quality, measures of customer satisfaction, and other key performance indicators (KPIs) are facts that must be conformed. In general, fact table data is not duplicated explicitly in multiple data marts. However, if facts do live in more than one location, such as in first-level and consolidated marts, the underlying definitions and equations for these facts must be the same if they are to be called the same thing. If they are labeled identically, then they need to be defined in the same dimensional context and with the same units of measure from data mart to data mart.

> We must be disciplined in our data naming practices. If it is impossible to conform a fact exactly, then you should give different names to the different interpretations. This makes it less likely that incompatible facts will be used in a calculation.

Sometimes a fact has a natural unit of measure in one fact table and another natural unit of measure in another fact table. For example, the flow of product down the retail value chain may best be measured in shipping cases at the warehouse but in scanned units at the store. Even if all the dimensional considerations have been taken into account correctly, it would be difficult to use these two incompatible units of measure in one drill-across report. The usual solution to this kind of problem is to refer the user to a conversion factor buried in the product dimension table and hope that the user can find the conversion factor and use it correctly. This is unacceptable in terms of both overhead and vulnerability to error. The correct solution is to carry the fact in both units of measure so that a report can easily glide down the value chain, picking off comparable facts. We'll talk more about multiple units of measure in Chapter 5.

Summary

Inventory is an important process to measure and monitor in many industries. In this chapter we developed dimensional models for the three complementary views of inventory. Either the periodic or accumulating snapshot model will serve as a good stand-alone depiction of inventory. The periodic snapshot would be chosen for long-running, continuously replenished inventory scenarios. The accumulating snapshot would be used for one-time, finite inventory situations with a definite beginning and end. More in-depth inventory applications will want to augment one or both of these models with the transaction model.

We introduced key concepts surrounding the data warehouse bus architecture and matrix. Each business process of the value chain, supported by a primary source system, translates into a data mart, as well as a row in the bus matrix. The data marts share a surprising number of standardized, conformed dimensions. Developing and adhering to the bus architecture is an absolute must if you intend to build a data warehouse composed of an integrated set of data marts.

Procurement

We'll explore the procurement process in this chapter. This topic has obvious cross-industry appeal because it is applicable to anyone who acquires products or services for either use or resale. In addition to developing several purchasing models in this chapter, we will provide in-depth coverage of the techniques for handling changes to our dimension table attributes. While the descriptive attributes in dimension tables are relatively static, they are subject to change over time. Product lines are restructured, causing product hierarchies to change. Customers move, causing their geographic information to change. Sales reps are realigned, causing territory assignments to change. We'll discuss several approaches to dealing with these inevitable changes in our dimension tables.

Chapter 4 discusses the following concepts:

- **Value chain reinforcement**
- **Blended versus separate transaction schemas**
- **Slowly changing dimension techniques, both basic and advanced**

Procurement Case Study

Thus far we have studied downstream retail sales and inventory processes in the value chain. We understand the importance of mapping out the data warehouse bus architecture where conformed dimensions are used across process-centric fact tables. In this chapter we'll extend these concepts as we work our way further up the value chain to the procurement process.

For many companies, procurement is a critical business activity. Effective procurement of products at the right price for resale is obviously important to retailers such as our grocery chain. Procurement also has strong bottom-line implications for any large organization that buys products as raw materials for manufacturing. Significant cost-savings opportunities are associated with reducing the number of suppliers and negotiating agreements with preferred suppliers.

Demand planning drives efficient materials management. Once demand is forecasted, procurement's goal is to source the appropriate materials/products in the most economical manner. Procurement involves a wide range of activities from negotiating contracts to issuing purchase requisitions and purchase orders (POs) to tracking receipts and authorizing payments. The following list gives you a better sense of a procurement organization's common analytic requirements:

- Which materials or products are purchased most frequently? How many vendors supply these products? At what prices? In what units of measure (such as bulk or drum)?

- Looking at demand across the enterprise (rather than at a single physical location), are there opportunities to negotiate favorable pricing by consolidating suppliers, single sourcing, or making guaranteed buys?

- Are our employees purchasing from the preferred vendors or skirting the negotiated vendor agreements (maverick spending)?

- Are we receiving the negotiated pricing from our vendors (vendor contract purchase price variance)?

- How are our vendors performing? What is the vendor's fill rate? On-time delivery performance? Late deliveries outstanding? Percent of orders backordered? Rejection rate based on receipt inspection?

Procurement Transactions

As we begin working through the four-step design process, we first decide that procurement is the business process to be modeled. We study the process in detail and observe a flurry of procurement transactions, such as purchase requisitions, purchase orders, shipping notifications, receipts, and payments. Similar to the approach we took in Chapter 3 with the inventory transactions, we first elect to build a fact table with the grain of one row per procurement transaction. We identify transaction date, product, vendor, contract terms, and procurement transaction type as our key dimensions. Procured units and transaction amount are the facts. The resulting design looks similar to Figure 4.1.

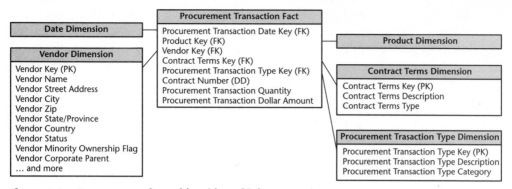

Figure 4.1 Procurement fact table with multiple transaction types.

If we are still working for the same grocery retailer, then the transaction date and product dimensions are the same conformed dimensions we developed originally in Chapter 2. If we're working with manufacturing procurement, the raw materials products likely are located in a separate raw materials dimension table rather than included in the product dimension for salable products. The vendor, contract terms, and procurement transaction type dimensions are new to this schema. The vendor dimension contains one row for each vendor, along with interesting descriptive attributes to support a variety of vendor analyses. The contract terms dimension contains one row for each generalized set of terms negotiated with a vendor, similar to the promotion dimension in Chapter 2. The procurement transaction type dimension allows us to group or filter on transaction types, such as purchase orders. The contract number is a degenerate dimension. It would be used to determine the volume of business conducted under each negotiated contract.

Multiple- versus Single-Transaction Fact Tables

As we review the initial procurement schema design with business users, we are made aware of several new details. First of all, we learn that the business users describe the various procurement transactions differently. To the business, purchase orders, shipping notices, warehouse receipts, and vendor payments are all viewed as separate and unique processes.

It turns out that several of the procurement transactions actually come from different source systems. There is no single procurement system to source all the procurement transactions. Instead, there is a purchasing system that provides purchase requisitions and purchase orders, a warehousing system that provides shipping notices and warehouse receipts, and an accounts payable system that deals with vendor payments.

We further discover that several of our transaction types have different dimensionality. For example, discounts taken are applicable to vendor payments but not to the other transaction types. Similarly, the name of the warehouse clerk who received the goods at the warehouse applies to receipts but doesn't make sense elsewhere.

We also learn about a variety of interesting control numbers, such as purchase order and payment check numbers, that are created at various steps in the procurement process. These control numbers are perfect candidates for degenerate dimensions. For certain transaction types, more than one control number may apply.

While we sort through these new details, we are faced with a design decision. Should we build a blended transaction fact table with a transaction type dimension to view all our procurement transactions together, or do we build separate fact tables for each transaction type? This is a common design quandary that surfaces in many transactional situations, not just procurement.

As dimensional modelers, we need to make design decisions based on a thorough understanding of the business requirements weighed against the trade-offs of the available options. In this case, there is no simple formula to make the definite determination of whether to use a single or multiple fact tables. A single fact table may be the most appropriate solution in some situations, whereas multiple fact tables are most appropriate in others. When faced with this design decision, we look to the following considerations to help us sort things out:

- First, what are the users' analytic requirements? As designers, our goal is to reduce complexity in order to present the data in the most effective form for the business users. How will the business users most commonly analyze this data? Do the required analyses often require multiple transaction types together, leading us to consider a single blended fact table? Or do they more frequently look solely at a single transaction type in an analysis, causing us to favor separate fact tables for each type of transaction?

- Are there really multiple unique business processes? In our procurement example, it seems that buying products (purchase orders) is distinctly different from receiving products (receipts). The existence of separate control numbers for each step in the process is a clue that we are dealing with separate processes. Given this situation, we would lean toward separate fact tables. In Chapter 3's inventory example, all the varied inventory transactions clearly related to a single inventory process, resulting in a single fact table design.

- Are multiple source systems involved? In our example, we're dealing with three separate source systems: purchasing, warehousing, and accounts payable. Again, this would suggest separate fact tables. The data staging activities required to source the single-transaction fact table from three separate source systems is likely daunting.

- What is the dimensionality of the facts? In our procurement example we discovered several dimensions that applied to some transaction types but not to others. This would again lead us to separate fact tables.

In our hypothetical case study we decide to implement multiple transaction fact tables as illustrated in Figure 4.2. We have separate fact tables for purchase requisitions, purchase orders, shipping notices, warehouse receipts, and vendor payments. We arrived at this decision because the users view these activities as separate and distinct business processes, the data comes from different source systems, and there is unique dimensionality for the various transaction types. Multiple fact tables allow us to provide richer, more descriptive dimensions and attributes. As we progress from purchase requisitions all the way to vendor payments, we inherit date dimensions and degenerate dimensions from the previous steps. The single fact table approach would have required generalization of the labeling for some dimensions. For example, purchase order date and receipt date likely would have been generalized to transaction date. Likewise, purchasing agent and receiving clerk would become employee. In another organization with different business requirements, source systems, and data dimensionality, the single blended fact table may be more appropriate.

We understand that multiple fact tables may require more time to manage and administer because there are more tables to load, index, and aggregate. Some would argue that this approach increases the complexity of the data staging processes. In fact, it may simplify the staging activities. Since the operational data exist in separate source systems, we would need multiple staging processes in either fact table scenario. Loading the data into separate fact tables likely will be less complex than attempting to integrate data from the multiple sources into a single fact table.

Complementary Procurement Snapshot

Separate from the decision regarding procurement transaction fact tables, we may find that we also need to develop some sort of snapshot fact table to fully address the needs of the business. As we suggested in Chapter 3, an accumulating snapshot that crosses processes would be extremely useful if the business is interested in monitoring product movement as it proceeds through the procurement pipeline (including the duration or lag at each stage). We'll spend more time on this topic in Chapter 5.

Date Dimension

Vendor Dimension

Employee Dimension

Purchase Requisition Fact
Requisition Date Key (FK)
Requested Date Key (FK)
Product Key (FK)
Vendor Key (FK)
Contract Terms Key (FK)
Requested By Key (FK)
Contract Number (DD)
Purchase Requisition Number (DD)
Purchase Requisition Quantity
Purchase Requisition Dollar Amount

Product Dimension

Contract Terms Dimension

Received Condition Dimension

Discount Taken Dimension

Purchase Order Fact
Requisition Date Key (FK)
Requested Date Key (FK)
Purchase Order Date Key (FK)
Product Key (FK)
Vendor Key (FK)
Contract Terms Key (FK)
Requested By Key (FK)
Purchase Agent Key (FK)
Contract Number (DD)
Purchase Requisition Number (DD)
Purchase Order Number (DD)
Purchase Order Quantity
Purchase Order Dollar Amount

Shipping Notices Fact
Shipping Notification Date Key (FK)
Ship Date Key (FK)
Requested Date Key (FK)
Product Key (FK)
Vendor Key (FK)
Contract Terms Key (FK)
Requested By Key (FK)
Purchase Agent Key (FK)
Contract Number (DD)
Purchase Requisition Number (DD)
Purchase Order Number (DD)
Shipping Notification Number (DD)
Shipped Quantity

Warehouse Receipts Fact
Warehouse Receipt Date Key (FK)
Ship Date Key (FK)
Requested Date Key (FK)
Product Key (FK)
Vendor Key (FK)
Received Condition Key (FK)
Warehouse Clerk (FK)
Purchase Requisition Number (DD)
Purchase Order Number (DD)
Shipping Notification Number (DD)
Received Quantity

Vendor Payment Fact
Payment Date Key (FK)
Ship Date Key (FK)
Warehouse Receipt Date Key (FK)
Product Key (FK)
Vendor Key (FK)
Contract Terms Key (FK)
Discount Taken Key (FK)
Contract Number (DD)
Purchase Requisition Number (DD)
Purchase Order Number (DD)
Shipping Notification Number (DD)
Accounts Payable Check Number (DD)
Vendor Payment Quantity
Vendor Gross Payment Dollar Amount
Vendor Payment Discount Dollar Amount
Vendor Net Payment Dollar Amount

Figure 4.2 Multiple fact tables for procurement processes.

Slowly Changing Dimensions

Up to this point we have pretended that each dimension is logically independent from all the other dimensions. In particular, dimensions have been assumed to be independent of time. Unfortunately, this is not the case in the real world. While dimension table attributes are relatively static, they are not fixed forever. Dimension attributes change, albeit rather slowly, over time. Dimensional designers must engage business representatives proactively to help determine the appropriate change-handling strategy. We can't simply jump to the conclusion that the business doesn't care about dimension changes just because its representatives didn't mention it during the requirements process. While we're assuming that accurate change tracking is unnecessary, business users may be assuming that the data warehouse will allow them to see the impact of each and every dimension change. Even though we may not want to hear that change tracking is a must-have because we are not looking for any additional development work, it is obviously better to receive the message sooner rather than later.

When we need to track change, it is unacceptable to put everything into the fact table or make every dimension time-dependent to deal with these changes. We would quickly talk ourselves back into a full-blown normalized structure with the consequential loss of understandability and query performance. Instead, we take advantage of the fact that most dimensions are nearly constant over time. We can preserve the independent dimensional structure with only relatively minor adjustments to contend with the changes. We refer to these nearly constant dimensions as *slowly changing dimensions*. Since Ralph Kimball first introduced the notion of slowly changing dimensions in 1994, some IT professionals—in a never-ending quest to speak in acronymese—have termed them *SCDs*.

For each attribute in our dimension tables, we must specify a strategy to handle change. In other words, when an attribute value changes in the operational world, how will we respond to the change in our dimensional models? In the following section we'll describe three basic techniques for dealing with attribute changes, along with a couple hybrid approaches. You may decide that you need to employ a combination of these techniques within a single dimension table.

Type 1: Overwrite the Value

With the type 1 response, we merely overwrite the old attribute value in the dimension row, replacing it with the current value. In so doing, the attribute always reflects the most recent assignment.

Let's assume that we work for an electronics retailer. The procurement buyers are aligned along the same departmental lines as the store, so the products being acquired roll up into departments. One of the procured products is IntelliKidz software. The existing row in the product dimension table for IntelliKidz looks like the following:

Product Key	Product Description	Department	SKU Number (Natural Key)
12345	IntelliKidz 1.0	Education	ABC922-Z

Of course, there would be numerous additional descriptive attributes in the product dimension, but we've abbreviated the column listing given our page space constraints. As we discussed earlier, a surrogate product key is the primary key of the table rather than just relying on the stock keeping unit (SKU) number. Although we have demoted the SKU number to being an ordinary product attribute, it still has a special significance because it remains the natural key. Unlike all other product attributes, the natural key must remain inviolate. Throughout the discussion of all three SCD types, we assume that the natural key of a dimension remains constant.

Suppose that a new merchandising person decides that IntelliKidz should be moved from the Education software department to the Strategy department on January 15, 2002, in an effort to boost sales. With the type 1 response, we'd simply update the existing row in the dimension table with the new department description. The updated row would look like the following:

Product Key	Product Description	Department	SKU Number (Natural Key)
12345	IntelliKidz 1.0	Strategy	ABC922-Z

In this case, no dimension or fact table keys were modified when IntelliKidz's department changed. The rows in the fact table still reference product key 12345, regardless of IntelliKidz's departmental location. When sales take off following the move to the Strategy department, we have no information to explain the performance improvement because the historical and more recently loaded data both appear as if IntelliKidz has always rolled up into Strategy.

The type 1 response is the simplest approach to dealing with dimension attribute changes. The advantage of type 1 is that it is fast and easy. In the dimension table, we merely overwrite the preexisting value with the current assignment. The fact table is left untouched. The problem with a type 1 response is that we lose all history of attribute changes. Since overwriting obliterates historical attribute values, we're left solely with the attribute values as they exist today. A type 1 response obviously is appropriate if the attribute change is a correction. It also may be appropriate if there is no value in keeping the old description. We need input from the business to determine the value of retaining the old attribute value; we shouldn't make this determination on our own in an IT vacuum. Too often project teams use a type 1 response as the default response for dealing with slowly changing dimensions and end up totally missing the mark if the business needs to track historical changes accurately.

The type 1 response is easy to implement, but it does not maintain any history of prior attribute values.

Before we leave the topic of type 1 changes, there's one more easily overlooked catch that you should be aware of. When we used a type 1 response to deal with the relocation of IntelliKidz, any preexisting aggregations based on the department value will need to be rebuilt. The aggregated data must continue to tie to the detailed atomic data, where it now appears that IntelliKidz has always rolled up into the Strategy department.

Type 2: Add a Dimension Row

We made the claim earlier in this book that one of the primary goals of the data warehouse was to represent prior history correctly. A type 2 response is the predominant technique for supporting this requirement when it comes to slowly changing dimensions.

Using the type 2 approach, when IntelliKidz's department changed, we issue a new product dimension row for IntelliKidz to reflect the new department attribute value. We then would have two product dimension rows for IntelliKidz, such as the following:

Product Key	Product Description	Department	SKU Number (Natural Key)
12345	IntelliKidz 1.0	Education	ABC922-Z
25984	IntelliKidz 1.0	Strategy	ABC922-Z

Now we see why the product dimension key can't be the SKU number natural key. We need two different product surrogate keys for the same SKU or physical barcode. Each of the separate surrogate keys identifies a unique product attribute profile that was true for a span of time. With type 2 changes, the fact table is again untouched. We don't go back to the historical fact table rows to modify the product key. In the fact table, rows for IntelliKidz prior to January 15, 2002, would reference product key 12345 when the product rolled into the Education department. After January 15, the IntelliKidz fact rows would have product key 25984 to reflect the move to the Strategy department until we are forced to make another type 2 change. This is what we mean when we say that type 2 responses perfectly partition or segment history to account for the change.

If we constrain only on the department attribute, then we very precisely differentiate between the two product profiles. If we constrain only on the product description, that is, IntelliKidz 1.0, then the query automatically will fetch both IntelliKidz product dimension rows and automatically join to the fact table for the complete product history. If we need to count the number of products correctly, then we would just use the SKU natural key attribute as the basis of the distinct count rather than the surrogate key. The natural key field becomes a kind of reliable glue that holds the separate type 2 records for a single product together. Alternatively, a most recent row indicator might be another useful dimension attribute to allow users to quickly constrain their query to only the current profiles.

The type 2 response is the primary technique for accurately tracking slowly changing dimension attributes. It is extremely powerful because the new dimension row automatically partitions history in the fact table.

It certainly would feel natural to include an effective date stamp on a dimension row with type 2 changes. The date stamp would refer to the moment when the attribute values in the row become valid or invalid in the case of expiration dates. Effective and expiration date attributes are necessary in the staging area because we'd need to know which surrogate key is valid when we're loading historical fact records. In the dimension table, these date stamps are helpful extras that are not required for the basic partitioning of history. If you use these extra date stamps, just remember that there is no need to constrain on the effective date in the dimension table in order to get the right answer. This is often a point of confusion in the design and use of type 2 slowly changing dimensions.

While including effective and expiration date attributes may feel comfortable to database designers, we should be aware that the effective date on the dimension table may have little to do with the dates in the fact table. Attempting to constrain on the dimension row effective date actually may yield an incorrect result. Perhaps version 2.0 of IntelliKidz software will be released on May 1, 2002. A new operational SKU code (and corresponding data warehouse surrogate key) would be created for the new product. This isn't a type 2 change because the product is a completely new physical entity. However, if we look at a fact table for the retailer, we don't see such an abrupt partitioning of history. The old version 1.0 of the software inevitably will continue to be sold in stores after May 1, 2002, until the existing inventory is depleted. The new version 2.0 will appear on the shelves on May 1 and gradually will supersede the old version. There will be a transition period where both versions of the software will move past the cash registers in any given store. Of course, the product overlap period will vary from store to store. The cash registers will recognize both operational SKU codes and have no difficulty handling the sale of either version. If we had an effective date on the product dimension row, we wouldn't dare constrain on this date to partition sales because the date has no relevance. Even worse, using such a constraint may even give us the wrong answer.

Nevertheless, the effective/expiration date stamps in the dimension may be useful for more advanced analysis. The dates support very precise time slicing of the dimension by itself. The row effective date is the first date the descriptive profile is valid. The row expiration date would be one day less than the row effective date for the next assignment, or the date the product was retired from the catalog. We could determine what the product catalog looked like as of December 31, 2001, by constraining a product table query to retrieve all rows where the row effective date to less than or equal to December 31, 2001, and the row expiration date to greater than or equal to December 31, 2001. We'll further discuss opportunities to leverage effective and expiration dates when we delve into the human resources schema in Chapter 8.

The type 2 response is the workhorse technique to support analysis using historically accurate attributes. This response perfectly segments fact table history because prechange fact rows use the prechange surrogate key. Another type 2 advantage is that we can gracefully track as many dimension changes as required. Unlike the type 1 approach, there is no need to revisit preexisting aggregation tables when using the type 2 approach.

Of course, the type 2 response to slowly changing dimensions requires the use of surrogate keys, but you're already using them anyhow, right? It is not sufficient to use the underlying operational key with two or three version digits because you'll be vulnerable to the entire list of potential operational key issues discussed in Chapter 2. Likewise, it is certainly inadvisable to append an effective date to the otherwise primary key of the dimension table to uniquely identify each version. With the type 2 response, we create a new dimension row with a new single-column primary key to uniquely identify the new product profile. This single-column primary key establishes the linkage between the fact and dimension tables for a given set of product characteristics. There's no need to create a confusing secondary join based on effective or expiration dates, as we have pointed out.

We recognize that some of you may be concerned about the administration of surrogate keys to support type 2 changes. In Chapter 16 we'll discuss a workflow for managing surrogate keys while accommodating type 2 changes in more detail. In the meantime, we want to put your mind somewhat at ease about the administrative burden. When we're staging dimension tables, we're often handed a complete copy of the latest, greatest source data. It would be wonderful if only the changes since the last extract, or deltas, were delivered to the staging area, but more typically, the staging application has to find the changed dimensions. A field-by-field comparison of each dimension row to identify the changes between yesterday's and today's versions would be extremely laborious, especially if we have 100 attributes in a several-million-row dimension table. Rather than checking each field to see if something has changed, we instead compute a checksum for the entire row all at once. A cyclic redundancy checksum (CRC) algorithm helps us quickly recognize that a wide, messy row has changed without looking at each of its constituent fields. In our staging area we calculate the checksum for each row in a dimension table and add it to the row as an administrative column. At the next data load, we compute the CRCs on the incoming records to compare with the prior CRCs. If the CRCs match, all the attributes on both rows are identical; there's no need to check every field. Obviously, any new rows would trigger the creation of a new product dimension row. Finally, when we encounter a changed CRC, then we'll need to deal with the change based on our dimension-change strategy. If we're using a type 2 response for all the attributes, then we'd just create another new row. If we're using a combination of techniques, then we'd have to look at the fields in more detail to determine the appropriate action.

Since the type 2 technique spawns new dimension rows, one downside of this approach is accelerated dimension table growth. Hence it may be an inappropriate technique for dimension tables that already exceed a million rows. We'll discuss an alternative approach for handling change in large, multimillion-row dimension tables when we explore the customer dimension in Chapter 6.

Type 3: Add a Dimension Column

While the type 2 response partitions history, it does not allow us to associate the new attribute value with old fact history or vice versa. With the type 2 response, when we constrain on Department = Strategy, we will not see IntelliKidz facts from before January 15, 2002. In most cases, this is exactly what we want.

However, sometimes we want the ability to see fact data as if the change never occurred. This happens most frequently with sales force reorganizations. District boundaries have been redrawn, but some users still want the ability to see today's sales in terms of yesterday's district lines just to see how they would have done under the old organizational structure. For a few transitional months, there may be a desire to track history in terms of the new district names and conversely to track new data in terms of old district names. A type 2 response won't support this requirement, but the type 3 response comes to the rescue.

In our software example, let's assume that there is a legitimate business need to track both the old and new values of the department attribute both forward and backward for a period of time around the change. With a type 3 response, we do not issue a new dimension row, but rather we add a new column to capture the attribute change. In the case of IntelliKidz, we alter the product dimension table to add a prior department attribute. We populate this new column with the existing department value (Education). We then treat the department attribute as a type 1 response, where we overwrite to reflect the current value (Strategy). All existing reports and queries switch over to the new department description immediately, but we can still report on the old department value by querying on the prior department attribute.

Product Key	Product Description	Department	Prior Department	SKU Number (Natural Key)
12345	IntelliKidz 1.0	Strategy	Education	ABC922-Z

Type 3 is appropriate when there's a strong need to support two views of the world simultaneously. Some designers call this an *alternate reality*. This often occurs when the change or redefinition is soft or when the attribute is a human-applied label rather than a physical characteristic. Although the change has occurred, it is still logically possible to act as if it has not. The type 3 response is distinguished from the type 2 response because both the current and prior descriptions can be regarded as true at the same time. In the case of a sales reorganization, management may want the ability to overlap and analyze results using either map of the sales organization for a period of time. Another common variation occurs when your users want to see the current value in addition to retaining the original attribute value rather than the prior.

The type 3 response is used rather infrequently. Don't be fooled into thinking that the higher type number associated with the type 3 response indicates that it is the preferred approach. The techniques have not been presented in good, better, and best practice sequence. There is a time and place where each of them is the most appropriate response.

 The type 3 slowly changing dimension technique allows us to see new and historical fact data by either the new or prior attribute values.

A type 3 response is inappropriate if you want to track the impact of numerous intermediate attribute values. Obviously, there are serious implementation and usage limitations to creating attributes that reflect the prior minus 1, prior minus 2, and prior minus 3 states of the world, so we give up the ability to analyze these intermediate values. If there is a need to track a myriad of unpredictable changes, then a type 2 response should be used instead in most cases.

Hybrid Slowly Changing Dimension Techniques

In this section we'll discuss two hybrid approaches that combine basic slowly changing dimension techniques. Many IT professionals become enamored of these techniques because they seem to provide the best of all worlds. However, the price we pay for greater flexibility is often greater complexity. While some IT professionals are easily impressed by elegant flexibility, our business users are just as easily turned off by complexity. You should not pursue these options unless the business agrees that they are needed to address their requirements.

Predictable Changes with Multiple Version Overlays

This technique is used most frequently to deal with sales organization realignments, so we'll depart from our IntelliKidz example to present the concept in a more realistic scenario. Consider the situation where a sales organization revises the map of its sales districts on an annual basis. Over a 5-year period, the sales organization is reorganized five times. On the surface, this may seem like a good candidate for a type 2 approach, but we discover through business user interviews that they have a more complex set of requirements, including the following capabilities:

- Report each year's sales using the district map for that year.
- Report each year's sales using a district map from an arbitrary different year.
- Report an arbitrary span of years' sales using a single district map from any chosen year. The most common version of this requirement would be to report the complete span of fact data using the current district map.

We cannot address this set of requirements with a standard type 2 response because it partitions history. A year of fact data can only be reported using the assigned map at that point in time with a type 2 approach. The requirements can't be met with a standard type 3 response because we want to support more than two simultaneous maps.

Sales Rep Dimension
Sales Rep Key
Sales Rep Name
Sales Rep Address...
Current District
District 2001
District 2000
District 1999
District 1998
... and more

Figure 4.3 Sample dimension table with multiple version overlays.

In this case we take advantage of the regular, predictable nature of these changes by geralizing the type 3 approach to have five versions of the district attribute for each sales rep. The sales rep dimension would include the attributes shown in Figure 4.3.

Each sales rep dimension row would include all prior district assignments. The business user could choose to roll up the sales facts with any of the five district maps. If a sales rep were hired in 2000, the dimension attributes for 1998 and 1999 would contain values along the lines of "Not Applicable."

We label the most recent assignment as "Current District." This attribute will be used most frequently; we don't want to modify our existing queries and reports to accommodate next year's change. When the districts are redrawn next, we'd alter the table to add a district 2002 attribute. We'd populate this column with the current district values and then overwrite the current attribute with the 2003 district assignments.

Unpredictable Changes with Single-Version Overlay

This final approach is relevant if you've been asked to preserve historical accuracy surrounding unpredictable attribute changes while supporting the ability to report historical data according to the current values. None of the standard slowly changing dimension techniques enable this requirement independently.

In the case of the electronics retailer's product dimension, we would have two department attributes on each row. The current department column represents the current assignment; the historical department column represents the historically accurate department attribute value.

When IntelliKidz software is procured initially, the product dimension row would look like the following:

Product Key	Product Description	Current Department	Historical Department	SKU Number (Natural Key)
12345	IntelliKidz 1.0	Education	Education	ABC922-Z

When the departments are restructured and IntelliKidz is moved to the Strategy department, we'd use a type 2 response to capture the attribute change by issuing a new row. In this new dimension row for IntelliKidz, the current department will be identical to the historical department. For all previous instances of IntelliKidz dimension rows, the current department attribute will be overwritten to reflect the current structure. Both IntelliKidz rows would identify the Strategy department as the current department.

Product Key	Product Description	Current Department	Historical Department	SKU Number (Natural Key)
12345	IntelliKidz 1.0	Strategy	Education	ABC922-Z
25984	IntelliKidz 1.0	Strategy	Strategy	ABC922-Z

In this manner we're able to use the historical attribute to segment history and see facts according to the departmental roll-up at that point in time. Meanwhile, the current attribute rolls up all the historical fact data for product keys 12345 and 25984 into the current department assignment. If IntelliKidz were then moved into the Critical Thinking software department, our product table would look like the following:

Product Key	Product Description	Current Department	Historical Department	SKU Number (Natural Key)
12345	IntelliKidz 1.0	Critical Thinking	Education	ABC922-Z
25984	IntelliKidz 1.0	Critical Thinking	Strategy	ABC922-Z
31726	IntelliKidz 1.0	Critical Thinking	Critical Thinking	ABC922-Z

With this hybrid approach, we issue a new row to capture the change (type 2) and add a new column to track the current assignment (type 3), where subsequent changes are handled as a type 1 response. Someone once suggested that we refer to this combo approach as type 6 (2 + 3 + 1). This technique allows us to track the historical changes accurately while also supporting the ability to roll up history based on the current assignments. We could further embellish (and complicate) this strategy by supporting additional static department roll-up structures, in addition to the current department, as separate attributes.

Again, while this powerful technique may be naturally appealing to some readers, it is important that we always consider the users' perspective as we strive to arrive at a reasonable balance between flexibility and complexity.

More Rapidly Changing Dimensions

In this chapter we've focused on the typically rather slow, evolutionary changes to our dimension tables. What happens, however, when the rate of change speeds up? If a dimension attribute changes monthly, then we're no longer dealing with a slowly changing dimension that can be handled reasonably with the techniques just discussed. One powerful approach for handling more rapidly changing dimensions is to break off these rapidly changing attributes into one or more separate dimensions. In our fact table we would then have two foreign keys—one for the primary dimension table and another for the rapidly changing attribute(s). These dimension tables would be associated with one another every time we put a row in the fact table. Stay tuned for more on this topic when we cover customer dimensions in Chapter 6.

Summary

In this chapter we discussed several approaches to handling procurement data. Effectively managing procurement performance can have a major impact on an organization's bottom line.

We also introduced several techniques to deal with changes to our dimension table attributes. The slowly changing responses range from merely overwriting the value (type 1), to adding a new row to the dimension table (type 2), to the least frequently used approach in which we add a column to the table (type 3). We also discussed several powerful, albeit more complicated, hybrid approaches that combine the basic techniques.

Order Management

Order management consists of several critical business processes, including order, shipment, and invoice processing. These processes spawn important business metrics, such as sales volume and invoice revenue, that are key performance indicators for any organization that sells products or services to others. In fact, these foundation metrics are so crucial that data warehouse teams most frequently tackle one of the order management processes for their initial data warehouse implementation. Clearly, the topics in this case study transcend industry boundaries.

In this chapter we'll explore several different order management transactions, including the common characteristics and complications you might encounter when dimensionally modeling these transactions. We'll elaborate on the concept of an accumulating snapshot to analyze the order-fulfillment pipeline from initial order through release to manufacturing, into finished goods inventory, and finally to product shipment and invoicing. We'll close the chapter by comparing and contrasting the three types of fact tables: transaction, periodic snapshot, and accumulating snapshot. For each of these fact table types, we'll also discuss the handling of real-time warehousing requirements.

Chapter 5 discusses the following concepts:

- Orders transaction schema
- Fact table normalization considerations
- Date dimension role-playing

- More on product dimensions
- Ship-to / bill-to customer dimension considerations
- Junk dimensions
- Multiple currencies and units of measure
- Handling of header and line item facts with different granularity
- Invoicing transaction schema with profit and loss facts
- Order fulfillment pipeline as accumulating snapshot schema
- Lag calculations
- Comparison of transaction, periodic snapshot, and accumulating snapshot fact tables
- Special partitions to support the demand for near real time data warehousing

Introduction to Order Management

If we take a closer look at the order management function, we see that it's comprised of a series of business processes. In its most simplistic form, we can envision a subset of the data warehouse bus matrix that resembles Figure 5.1.

As we saw in earlier chapters, the data warehouse bus matrix closely corresponds to the organization's value chain. In this chapter we'll focus specifically on the order and invoice rows of the matrix. We'll also describe an accumulating snapshot fact table that combines data from multiple order management processes.

	Date	Product	Customer	Deal	Sales Rep	Ship From	Shipper
Quotes	X	X	X	X	X		
Orders	X	X	X	X	X		
Shipments	X	X	X	X	X	X	X
Invoicing	X	X	X	X	X	X	X

Figure 5.1 Subset of data warehouse bus matrix for order management processes.

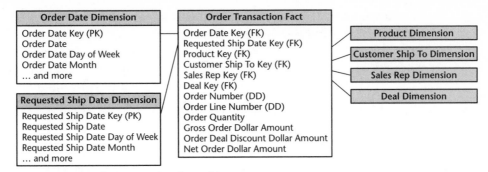

Figure 5.2 Order transaction fact table.

Order Transactions

The first process we'll explore is order transactions. As companies have grown through acquisition, they often find themselves with multiple operational order transaction processing systems in the organization. The existence of multiple source systems often creates a degree of urgency to integrate the disparate results in the data warehouse rather than waiting for the long-term application integration.

The natural granularity for an order transaction fact table is one row for each line item on an order. The facts associated with this process typically include the order quantity, extended gross order dollar amount, order discount dollar amount, and extended net order dollar amount (which is equal to the gross order amount less the discounts). The resulting schema would look similar to Figure 5.2.

Fact Normalization

Rather than storing a list of facts, as in Figure 5.2, some designers want to further normalize the fact table so that there's a single, generic fact amount, along with a dimension that identifies the type of fact. The fact dimension would indicate whether it is the gross order amount, order discount amount, or some other measure. This technique may make sense when the set of facts is sparsely populated for a given fact row and no computations are made between facts. We have used this technique to deal with manufacturing quality test data, where the facts vary widely depending on the test conducted.

However, we generally resist the urge to further normalize the fact table. As we see with orders data, facts usually are not sparsely populated within a row. In this case, if we were to normalize the facts, we'd be multiplying the number of rows in the fact table by the number of fact types. For example, assume that we started with 10 million order line fact table rows, each with six keys and four facts. If we normalized the facts, we'd end up with 40 million fact rows, each with seven keys and one fact. In addition, if we are performing any arithmetic function between the facts (such as discount amount as a percentage of gross order amount), it is far easier if the facts are in the same row because SQL makes it difficult to perform a ratio or difference between facts in different rows. In Chapter 13 we'll explore a situation where a fact dimension makes more sense.

Dimension Role-Playing

By now we all know that a date dimension is found in every fact table because we are always looking at performance over time. In a transaction-grained fact table, the primary date column is the transaction date, such as the order date. Sometimes we also discover other dates associated with each transaction, such as the requested ship date for the order.

Each of the dates should be a foreign key in the fact table. However, we cannot simply join these two foreign keys to the same date dimension table. SQL would interpret such a two-way simultaneous join as requiring both the dates to be identical, which isn't very likely.

Even though we cannot literally join to a single date dimension table, we can build and administer a single date dimension table behind the scenes. We create the illusion of two independent date tables by using views. We are careful to uniquely label the columns in each of the SQL views. For example, order month should be uniquely labeled to distinguish it from requested ship month. If we don't practice good data housekeeping, we could find ourselves in the uncomfortable position of not being able to tell the columns apart when both are dragged into a report.

As we briefly described in Chapter 2, you would define the order date and requested order date views as follows:

```
CREATE VIEW ORDER_DATE (ORDER_DATE_KEY, ORDER_DAY_OF_WEEK,
ORDER_MONTH...)
AS SELECT DATE_KEY, DAY_OF_WEEK, MONTH, . . . FROM DATE
```

and

```
CREATE VIEW REQ_SHIP_DATE (REQ_SHIP_DATE_KEY, REQ_SHIP_DAY_OF_WEEK,
REQ_SHIP_MONTH ...)
AS SELECT DATE_KEY, DAY_OF_WEEK, MONTH, . . . FROM DATE
```

We now have two unique date dimensions that can be used as if they were independent with completely unrelated constraints. We refer to this as *role-playing* because the date dimension simultaneously serves different roles in a single fact table. We'll see additional examples of dimension role-playing sprinkled throughout this book.

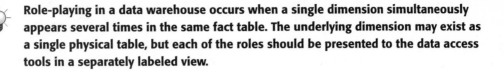 **Role-playing in a data warehouse occurs when a single dimension simultaneously appears several times in the same fact table. The underlying dimension may exist as a single physical table, but each of the roles should be presented to the data access tools in a separately labeled view.**

To handle the multiple dates, some designers are tempted to create a single date table with a key for each unique order date and requested ship date combination. This approach falls apart on several fronts. First, our clean and simple daily date table with approximately 365 rows per year would balloon in size if it needed to handle all the date combinations. Second, such a combination date table would no longer conform to our other frequently used daily, weekly, and monthly date dimensions.

Product Dimension Revisited

A product dimension has participated in each of the case study vignettes presented so far in this book. The product dimension is one of the most common and most important dimension tables you'll encounter in a dimensional model.

The product dimension describes the complete portfolio of products sold by a company. In most cases, the number of products in the portfolio turns out to be surprisingly large, at least from an outsider's perspective. For example, a prominent U.S. manufacturer of dog and cat food tracks nearly 20,000 manufacturing variations of its products, including retail products everyone (or every dog and cat) is familiar with, as well as numerous specialized products sold through commercial and veterinary channels. We've worked with durable goods manufacturers who sell literally millions of unique product configurations.

Most product dimension tables share the following characteristics:

Numerous verbose descriptive columns. For manufacturers, it's not unusual to maintain 100 or more descriptors about the products they sell. Dimension table attributes naturally describe the dimension row, do not vary because of the influence of another dimension, and are virtually constant over time, although as we just discussed in Chapter 4, some attributes do change slowly over time.

One or more attribute hierarchies in addition to many nonhierarchical attributes. It is too limiting to think of products as belonging to a single hierarchy. Products typically roll up according to multiple defined hierarchies. All the hierarchical data should be presented in a single flattened, denormalized product dimension table. We resist creating normalized snowflaked sub-tables for the product dimension. The costs of a more complicated presentation and slower intradimension browsing performance outweigh the minimal storage savings benefits. It is misleading to think about browsing in a small dimension table, where all the relationships can be imagined or visualized. Real product dimension tables have thousands of entries, and the typical user does not know the relationships intimately. If there are 20,000 dog and cat foods in the product dimension, it is not too useful to request a pull-down list of the product descriptions. It would be essential, in this example, to have the ability to constrain on one attribute, such as flavor, and then another attribute, such as package type, before attempting to display the product description listings. Notice that the first two constraints were not drawn strictly from a product hierarchy. Any of the product attributes, regardless of whether they belong to a hierarchy, should be used freely for drilling down and up. In fact, most of the attributes in a large product table are standalone low-cardinality attributes, not part of explicit hierarchies.

The existence of an operational product master aids in maintenance of the product dimension, but a number of transformations and administrative steps must occur to convert the operational master file into the dimension table, including:

Remap the operational product key to a surrogate key. As we discussed in Chapter 2, this smaller, more efficient join key is needed to avoid havoc caused by duplicate use of the operational product key over time. It also might be necessary to integrate product information sourced from different operational systems. Finally, as we just learned in Chapter 4, the surrogate key is needed to track changing product attributes in cases where the operational system has not generated a new product master key.

Add readable text strings to augment or replace numeric codes in the operational product master. We don't accept the excuse that the businesspeople are familiar with the codes. The only reason businesspeople are familiar with codes is that they have been forced to use them! Remember that the columns in a product dimension table are the sole source of query constraints and report labels, so the contents must be legible. Keep in mind that cryptic abbreviations are as bad as outright numeric codes; they also should be augmented or replaced with readable text. Multiple abbreviated codes in a single field should be expanded and separated into distinct fields.

Quality assure all the text strings to ensure that there are no misspellings, impossible values, or cosmetically different versions of the same attribute. In addition to automated procedures, a simple backroom technique for flushing out minor misspellings of attribute values is to just sort the distinct values of the attribute and look down the list. Spellings that differ by a single character usually will sort next to each other and can be found with a visual scan of the list. This supplemental manager's quality assurance check should be performed occasionally to monitor data quality. Data access interfaces and reports rely on the precise contents of the dimension attributes. SQL will happily produce another line in a report if the attribute value varies in any way based on trivial punctuation or spelling differences. We also should ensure that the attribute values are completely populated because missing values easily cause misinterpretations. Incomplete or poorly administered textual dimension attributes lead to incomplete or poorly produced reports.

Document the product attribute definitions, interpretations, and origins in the data warehouse's metadata. Remember that the metadata is analogous to the data warehouse encyclopedia. We must be vigilant about populating and maintaining the metadata.

Customer Ship-To Dimension

The customer ship-to dimension contains one row for each discrete location to which we ship a product. Customer ship-to dimension tables can range from moderately sized (thousands of rows) to extremely large (millions of rows) depending on the nature of the business. A typical customer ship-to dimension is shown in Figure 5.3.

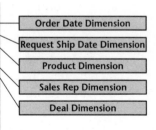

Customer Ship To Dimension	Order Transaction Fact	
Customer Ship To Key (PK)	Order Date Key (FK)	Order Date Dimension
Customer Ship To ID (Natural Key)	Requested Ship Date Key (FK)	Request Ship Date Dimension
Customer Ship To Name	Product Key (FK)	Product Dimension
Customer Ship To Address	Customer Ship To Key (FK)	Sales Rep Dimension
Customer Ship To City	Sales Rep Key (FK)	Deal Dimension
Customer Ship To State	Deal Key (FK)	
Customer Ship To Zip + 4	Order Number (DD)	
Customer Ship To Zip	Order Line Number (DD)	
Customer Ship To Zip Region	Order Quantity	
Customer Ship To Zip Sectional Center	Gross Order Dollar Amount	
Customer Bill To Name	Order Deal Discount Dollar Amount	
Customer Bill To Address Attributes ...	Net Order Dollar Amount	
Customer Organization Name		
Customer Corporate Parent Name		
Customer Credit Rating		
Assigned Sales Rep Name		
Assigned Sales Rep Team Name		
Assigned Sales District		
Assigned Sales Region		

Figure 5.3 Sample customer ship-to dimension.

Several separate and independent hierarchies typically coexist in a customer ship-to dimension. The natural geographic hierarchy is clearly defined by the ship-to location. Since the ship-to location is a point in space, any number of geographic hierarchies may be defined by nesting ever-larger geographic entities around the point. In the United States, the usual geographic hierarchy is city, county, and state. The U.S. ZIP code identifies a secondary geographic breakdown. The first digit of the ZIP code identifies a geographic region of the United States (for example, 0 for the Northeast and 9 for certain western states), whereas the first three digits of the ZIP code identify a mailing sectional center.

Another common hierarchy is the customer's organizational hierarchy, assuming that the customer is a corporate entity. For each customer ship-to, we might have a customer bill-to and customer corporation. For every base-level row in the customer ship-to dimension, both the physical geography and the customer organizational affiliation are well defined, even though the hierarchies roll up differently.

It is natural and common, especially for customer-oriented dimensions, for a dimension to simultaneously support multiple independent hierarchies. The hierarchies may have different numbers of levels. Drilling up and drilling down within each of these hierarchies must be supported in a data warehouse.

The alert reader may have a concern with the implied assumption that multiple ship-tos roll up to a single bill-to in a many-to-one relationship. The real world is rarely quite this clean and simple. There are always a few exceptions involving ship-tos that are associated with more than one bill-to. Obviously, this breaks the simple hierarchical relationship that we have assumed in the earlier denormalized customer ship-to dimension. If this is a rare occurrence, it would be reasonable to generalize the customer ship-to dimension so that the grain of the dimension is each unique ship-to/bill-to combination. If there are two sets of bill-to information associated with a given ship-to location, then there would be two rows in the dimension, one for each combination. On the other hand, if many of the ship-tos are associated with many bill-tos in a robust many-to-many relationship, then ship-to and bill-to probably need to be handled as separate dimensions that are linked together by the fact table. This is the designer's prerogative. With either approach, exactly the same information is preserved at the fact table order line-item level. We'll spend more time on customer organizational hierarchies, including the handling of recursive customer parent-child relationships, in Chapter 6.

Another potential independent hierarchy in the customer ship-to dimension might be the manufacturer's sales organization. Designers sometimes question whether sales organization attributes should be modeled as a separate dimension or the attributes just should be added to the existing customer dimension. Similar to the preceding discussion about bill-tos, the designer should use his or her judgment. If sales reps are highly correlated with customer ship-tos in a one-to-one or many-to-one relationship, combining the sales organization attributes with the customer ship-to dimension is a viable approach. The resulting dimension is only about as big as the larger of the two dimensions. The relationships between sales teams and customers can be browsed efficiently in the single dimension without traversing the fact table.

However, sometimes the relationship between sales organization and customer ship-to is more complicated. The following factors must be taken into consideration:

The one-to-one or many-to-one relationship may turn out to be a many-to-many relationship. As we discussed earlier, if the many-to-many relationship is an exceptional condition, then we may still be tempted to combine the sales rep attributes into the ship-to dimension, knowing that we'd need to treat these rare many-to-many occurrences by issuing another surrogate ship-to key.

If the relationship between sales rep and customer ship-to varies over time or under the influence of a fourth dimension such as product, then the combined dimension is in reality some kind of fact table itself! In this case, we'd likely create separate dimensions for the sales rep and the customer ship-to.

If the sales rep and customer ship-to dimensions participate independently in other business process fact tables, we'd likely keep the dimensions separate. Creating a single customer ship-to dimension with sales rep attributes exclusively around orders data may make some of the other processes and relationships difficult to express.

When entities have a fixed, time-invariant, strongly correlated relationship, they obviously should be modeled as a single dimension. In most other cases, your design likely will be simpler and more manageable when you separate the entities into two dimensions (while remembering the general guidelines concerning too many dimensions). If you've already identified 25 dimensions in your schema, you should give strong consideration to combining dimensions, if possible.

When the dimensions are separate, some designers want to create a little table with just the two dimension keys to show the correlation without using the fact table. This two-dimension table is unnecessary. There is no reason to avoid the fact table to respond to this relationship inquiry. Fact tables are incredibly efficient because they contain only dimension keys and measurements. The fact table was created specifically to represent the correlation between dimensions.

Before we leave the topic of sales rep assignments to customers, users sometimes want the ability to analyze the complex assignment of sales reps to customers over time, even if no order activity has occurred. In this case, we could construct a factless fact table, as we briefly introduced in Chapter 2, to capture the sales rep coverage. The coverage table would provide a complete map of the historical assignments of sales reps to customers, even if some of the assignments never resulted in a sale. As we'll learn in Chapter 13, we'd likely include effective and expiration dates in the sales rep coverage table because coverage assignments change over time.

Deal Dimension

The deal dimension is similar to the promotion dimension from Chapter 2. The deal dimension describes the incentives that have been offered to the customer that theoretically affect the customers' desire to purchase products. This dimension is also sometimes referred to as the *contract*. As shown in Figure 5.4, the deal dimension describes the full combination of terms, allowances, and incentives that pertain to the particular order line item.

The same issues that we faced in the retail promotion dimension also arise with this deal dimension. If the terms, allowances, and incentives are usefully correlated, then it makes sense to package them into a single deal dimension. If the terms, allowances, and incentives are quite uncorrelated and we find ourselves generating the Cartesian product of these factors in the dimension, then it probably makes sense to split such a deal dimension into its separate components. Once again, this is not an issue of gaining or losing information, since the database contains the same information in both cases, but rather the issues of user convenience and administrative complexity determine whether to represent these deal factors as multiple dimensions. In a very large fact table, with tens of millions or hundreds of millions of rows, the desire to reduce the number of keys in the fact table composite key would favor keeping the deal dimension as a single dimension. Certainly any deal dimension smaller than 100,000 rows would be tractable in this design.

Figure 5.4 Sample deal dimension.

Degenerate Dimension for Order Number

Each line item row in the orders fact table includes the order number as a degenerate dimension, as we introduced in Chapter 2. Unlike a transactional parent-child database, the order number in our dimensional models is not tied to an order header table. We have stripped all the interesting details from the order header into separate dimensions such as the order date, customer ship-to, and other interesting fields. The order number is still useful because it allows us to group the separate line items on the order. It enables us to answer such questions as the average number of line items on an order. In addition, the order number is used occasionally to link the data warehouse back to the operational world. Since the order number is left sitting by itself in the fact table without joining to a dimension table, it is referred to as a degenerate dimension.

Degenerate dimensions typically are reserved for operational transaction identifiers. They should not be used as an excuse to stick a cryptic code in the fact table without joining to a descriptive decode in a dimension table.

If the designer decides that certain data elements actually do belong to the order itself and do not usefully fall into another natural business dimension, then order number is no longer a degenerate dimension but rather is a normal dimension with its own surrogate key and attribute columns. However, designers with a strong parent-child background should resist the urge simply to lump the traditional order header information into an order dimension. In almost all cases, the header information belongs in other analytic dimensions rather than merely being dumped into a dimension that closely resembles the transaction order header table.

Junk Dimensions

When we're confronted with a complex operational data source, we typically perform triage to quickly identify fields that are obviously related to dimensions, such as date stamps or attributes. We then identify the numeric measurements in the source data. At this point, we are often left with a number of miscellaneous indicators and flags, each of which takes on a small range of discrete values. The designer is faced with several rather unappealing options, including:

Leave the flags and indicators unchanged in the fact table row. This could cause the fact table row to swell alarmingly. It would be a shame to create a nice tight dimensional design with five dimensions and five facts and then leave a handful of uncompressed textual indicator columns in the row.

Make each flag and indicator into its own separate dimension. Doing so could cause our 5-dimension design to balloon into a 25-dimension design.

Strip out all the flags and indicators from the design. Of course, we ask the obligatory question about removing these miscellaneous flags because they seem rather insignificant, but this notion is often vetoed quickly because someone might need them. It is worthwhile to examine this question carefully. If the indicators are incomprehensible, noisy, inconsistently populated, or only of operational significance, they should be left out.

An appropriate approach for tackling these flags and indicators is to study them carefully and then pack them into one or more *junk dimensions*. You can envision the junk dimension as being akin to the junk drawer in your kitchen. The kitchen junk drawer is a dumping ground for miscellaneous household items, such as rubber bands, paper clips, batteries, and tape. While it may be easier to locate the rubber bands if we dedicated a separate kitchen drawer to them, we don't have adequate storage capacity to do so. Besides, we don't have enough stray rubber bands, nor do we need them very frequently, to warrant the allocation of a single-purpose storage space. The junk drawer provides us with satisfactory access while still retaining enough kitchen storage for the more critical and frequently accessed dishes and silverware.

A junk dimension is a convenient grouping of typically low-cardinality flags and indicators. By creating an abstract dimension, we remove the flags from the fact table while placing them into a useful dimensional framework.

A simple example of a useful junk dimension would be to remove 10 two-value indicators, such as the cash versus credit payment type, from the order fact table and place them into a single dimension. At the worst, you would have 1,024 (2^{10}) rows in this junk dimension. It probably isn't very interesting to browse among these flags within the dimension because every flag occurs with every other flag if the database is large enough. However, the junk dimension is a useful holding place for constraining or reporting on these flags. Obviously, the 10 foreign keys in the fact table would be replaced with a single small surrogate key.

On the other hand, if you have highly uncorrelated attributes that take on more numerous values, then it may not make sense to lump them together into a single junk dimension. Unfortunately, the decision is not entirely formulaic. If you have five indicators that each take on only three values, the single junk dimension is the best route for these attributes because the dimension has only 243 (3^5) possible rows. However, if the five uncorrelated indicators each have 100 possible values, we'd suggest the creation of separate dimensions because you now have 100 million (100^5) possible combinations.

Order Indicator Key	Payment Type Description	Payment Type Group	Inbound/ Outbound Order Indicator	Commission Credit Indicator	Order Type Indicator
1	Cash	Cash	Inbound	Commissionable	Regular
2	Cash	Cash	Inbound	Non-Commissionable	Display
3	Cash	Cash	Inbound	Non-Commissionable	Demonstration
4	Cash	Cash	Outbound	Commissionable	Regular
5	Cash	Cash	Outbound	Non-Commissionable	Display
6	Discover Card	Credit	Inbound	Commissionable	Regular
7	Discover Card	Credit	Inbound	Non-Commissionable	Display
8	Discover Card	Credit	Inbound	Non-Commissionable	Demonstration
9	Discover Card	Credit	Outbound	Commissionable	Regular
10	Discover Card	Credit	Outbound	Non-Commissionable	Display
11	MasterCard	Credit	Inbound	Commissionable	Regular
12	MasterCard	Credit	Inbound	Non-Commissionable	Display
13	MasterCard	Credit	Inbound	Non-Commissionable	Demonstration
14	MasterCard	Credit	Outbound	Commissionable	Regular

Figure 5.5 Sample rows of an order indicator junk dimension.

We've illustrated sample rows from an order indicator dimension in Figure 5.5. A subtle issue regarding junk dimensions is whether you create rows for all the combinations beforehand or create junk dimension rows for the combinations as you actually encounter them in the data. The answer depends on how many possible combinations you expect and what the maximum number could be. Generally, when the number of theoretical combinations is very high and you don't think you will encounter them all, you should build a junk dimension row at extract time whenever you encounter a new combination of flags or indicators.

Another interesting application of the junk dimension technique is to use it to handle the infrequently populated, open-ended comments field sometimes attached to a fact row. Optimally, the comments have been parameterized in a dimension so that they can be used for robust analysis. Even if this is not the case, users still may feel that the comments field is meaningful enough to include in the data warehouse. In this case, a junk dimension simply contains all the distinct comments. The junk dimension is noticeably smaller than the fact table because the comments are relatively rare. Of course, you will need a special surrogate key that points to the "No Comment" row in the dimension because most of your fact table rows will use this key.

Multiple Currencies

Suppose that we are tracking the orders of a large multinational California-based company with sales offices around the world. We may be capturing order transactions in more than 15 different currencies. We certainly wouldn't want to include columns in the fact table for each currency because theoretically there are an open-ended number of currencies.

The most obvious requirement is that order transactions be expressed in both local currency and the standardized corporate currency, such as U.S. dollars in this example. To satisfy this need, we would replace each underlying order fact with a pair of facts, one for the applicable local currency and another for the equivalent standard corporate currency. This would allow all transactions to easily roll up to the corporate currency without complicated application coding. We'd also supplement the fact table with an additional currency dimension to identify the currency type associated with the local-currency facts. A currency dimension is needed even if the location of the transaction is otherwise known because the location does not necessarily guarantee which currency was used.

However, you may find the multicurrency support requirements are more complicated than we just described. We may need to allow a manager in any country to see order volume in any currency. For example, the sales office in Bangkok may monitor sales orders in Thai bhat, the Asia-Pacific region manager in Tokyo may want to look at the region's orders in Japanese yen, and the sales department in California may want to see the orders based on U.S. dollars. Embellishing our initial design with an additional currency conversion fact table, as shown in Figure 5.6, can deliver this flexibility. The dimensions in this fact table represent currencies, not countries, because the relationship between currencies and countries is not one to one. The needs of the sales rep in Thailand and U.S.-based sales management would be met simply by querying the orders fact table. The region manager in Tokyo could roll up all Asia-Pacific orders in Japanese yen by using the special currency conversion table.

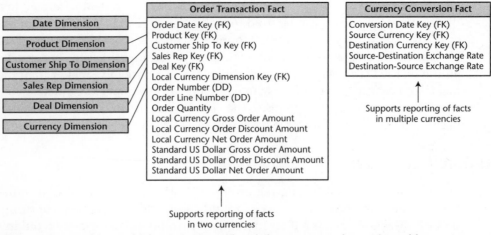

Figure 5.6 Tracking multiple currencies with a daily currency exchange fact table.

Within each fact table row, the amount expressed in local currency is absolutely accurate because the sale occurred in that currency on that day. The equivalent U.S. dollar value would be based on a conversion rate to U.S. dollars for that day. The conversion rate table contains all combinations of effective currency exchange rates going in both directions because the symmetric rates between two currencies are not exactly equal.

Header and Line Item Facts with Different Granularity

It is quite common in parent-child transaction databases to encounter facts of differing granularity. On an order, for example, there may be a shipping charge that applies to the entire order that isn't available at the individual product-level line item in the operational system. The designer's first response should be to try to force all the facts down to the lowest level. We strive to flatten the parent-child relationship so that all the rows are at the child level, including facts that are captured operationally at the higher parent level, as illustrated in Figure 5.7. This procedure is broadly referred to as *allocating*. Allocating the parent order facts to the child line-item level is critical if we want the ability to slice and dice and roll up all order facts by all dimensions, including product, which is a common requirement.

Unfortunately, allocating header-level facts down to the line-item level may entail a political wrestling match. It is wonderful if the entire allocation issue is handled by the finance department, not by the data warehouse team. Getting organizational agreement on allocation rules is often a controversial and complicated process. The data warehouse team shouldn't be distracted and delayed by the inevitable organizational negotiation. Fortunately, in many companies, the need to rationally allocate costs has been recognized already. A task force, independent of the data warehouse team, already may have established activity-based costing measures. This is just another name for allocating.

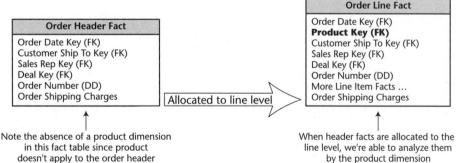

Note the absence of a product dimension in this fact table since product doesn't apply to the order header

When header facts are allocated to the line level, we're able to analyze them by the product dimension

Figure 5.7   Allocating header facts to the line item.

If the shipping charges and other header-level facts cannot be allocated successfully, then they must be presented in an aggregate table for the overall order. We clearly prefer the allocation approach, if possible, because the separate higher-level fact table has some inherent usability issues. Without allocations, we'd be unable to explore header facts by product because the product isn't identified in a header-grain fact table. If we are successful in allocating facts down to the lowest level, the problem goes away.

> **We shouldn't mix fact granularities (for example, order and order line facts) within a single fact table. Instead, we need to either allocate the higher-level facts to a more detailed level or create two separate fact tables to handle the differently grained facts. Allocation is the preferred approach. Optimally, a finance or business team (not the data warehouse team) spearheads the allocation effort.**

Invoice Transactions

If we work for a manufacturing company, invoicing typically occurs when products are shipped from our facility to the customer. We visualize shipments at the loading dock as boxes of product are loaded onto a truck destined for a particular customer address. The invoice associated with the shipment is created at this time. The invoice governs the current shipment of products on that truck on that day to a particular customer address. The invoice has multiple line items, each corresponding to a particular product being shipped. Various prices, discounts, and allowances are associated with each line item. The extended net amount for each line item is also available.

Although we don't show it on the invoice to the customer, a number of other interesting facts are potentially known about each product at the time of shipment. We certainly know list prices; manufacturing and distribution costs may be available as well. Thus we know a lot about the state of our business at the moment of customer shipment.

In the shipment invoice fact table we can see all the company's products, all the customers, all the contracts and deals, all the off-invoice discounts and allowances, all the revenue generated by customers purchasing products, all the variable and fixed costs associated with manufacturing and delivering products (if available), all the money left over after delivery of product (contribution), and customer satisfaction metrics such as on-time shipment.

For any company that ships products to customers or bills customers for services rendered, the optimal place to start a data warehouse typically is with invoices. We often refer to the data resulting from invoicing as the most powerful database because it combines the company's customers, products, and components of profitability.

We choose the grain of the invoice fact table to be the individual invoice line item. A sample invoice fact table associated with manufacturer shipments is illustrated in Figure 5.8.

As you'd expect, the shipment invoice fact table contains a number of dimensions that we've seen previously in this chapter. The conformed date dimension table again would play multiple roles in the fact table. The customer, product, and deal dimensions also would conform so that we can drill across from fact table to fact table and communicate using common attributes. We'd also have a degenerate order number, assuming that a single order number is associated with each invoice line item, as well as the invoice number degenerate dimension.

The shipment invoice fact table also contains some interesting new dimensions we haven't seen yet in our designs. The ship-from dimension contains one row for each manufacturer warehouse or shipping location. This is a relatively simple dimension with name, address, contact person, and storage facility type. The attributes are somewhat reminiscent of the facility dimension describing stores from Chapter 2.

The shipper dimension describes the method and carrier by which the product was shipped from the manufacturer to the customer. Sometimes a shipment database contains only a simple carrier dimension, with attributes about the transportation company. There is only one ship method, namely, truck to customer. However, both manufacturers and customers alike are interested in tracking alternative delivery methods, such as direct store delivery (product delivered directly to the retail outlet), cross-docking (product transferred from one carrier to another without placing it in a warehouse), back hauling (carrier transports the product on a return trip rather than returning empty), and customer pallet creation (product custom assembled and shrink-wrapped on a pallet destined for a retail outlet). Since investments are made in these alternative shipping models, manufacturers (and their customers) are interested in analyzing the businesses along the shipper dimension. The customer satisfaction dimension provides textual descriptions that summarize the numeric satisfaction flags at the bottom of the fact table.

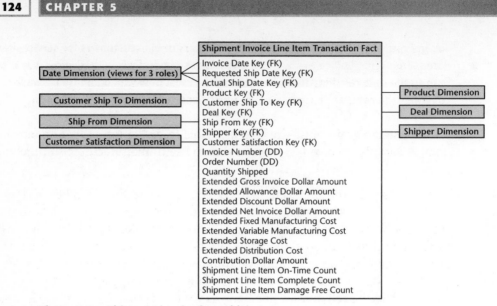

Figure 5.8 Shipment invoice fact table.

Profit and Loss Facts

If your organization has tackled activity-based costing or implemented a robust enterprise resource planning (ERP) system, you are likely in a position to identify many of the incremental revenues and costs associated with shipping finished products to the customer. It is traditional to arrange these revenues and costs in sequence from the top line, which represents the undiscounted value of the products shipped to the customer, down to the bottom line, which represents the money left over after discounts, allowances, and costs. This list of revenues and costs is called a *profit and loss (P&L) statement*. We typically don't make an attempt to carry the P&L statement all the way to a complete view of company profit, including general and administrative costs. For this reason, we will refer to the bottom line in our P&L statement as the *contribution*.

Keeping in mind that each row in the invoice fact table represents a single line item on the shipment invoice, the elements of our P&L statement, as shown in Figure 5.8, have the following interpretations:

Quantity shipped. This is the number of cases of the particular line-item product. We'll discuss the use of multiple equivalent quantities with different units of measure later in the chapter.

Extended gross invoice amount. This is also know as *extended list price* because it is the quantity shipped multiplied by the list unit price. This and all subsequent dollar values are extended amounts or, in other words, unit rates multiplied by the quantity shipped. This insistence on additive values simplifies most access and reporting applications. It is relatively rare for the user to ask for the price from a single row of the fact table. When the user wants an average price drawn from many rows, the extended prices are first added, and then the result is divided by the sum of the shipped quantities.

Extended allowance amount. This is the amount subtracted from the invoice-line gross amount for deal-related allowances. The allowances are described in the adjoined deal dimension. The allowance amount is often called an *off-invoice allowance*. The actual invoice may have several allowances for a given line item. In this example design, we lumped the allowances together. If the allowances need to be tracked separately and there are potentially many simultaneous allowances on a given line item, then an additional dimension structure is needed. An allowance-detail fact table could be used to augment the invoice fact table, serving as a drill-down target for a detailed explanation of the allowance bucket in the invoice fact table.

Extended discount amount. This is the amount subtracted on the invoice for volume or payment-term discounts. The explanation of which discounts are taken is also found in the deal dimension row that points to this fact table row. As discussed in the section on the deal dimension, the decision to code the explanation of the allowances and discount types together is the designer's prerogative. It makes sense to do this if allowances and discounts are correlated and users wish to browse within the deal dimension to study the relationships between allowances and discounts. Note that the discount for payment terms is characteristically a forecast that the customer will pay within the time period called for in the terms agreement. If this does not happen, or if there are other corrections to the invoice, then the Finance Department probably will back out the original invoice in a subsequent month and post a new invoice. In all likelihood, the data warehouse will see this as three transactions. Over time, all the additive values in these rows will add up correctly, but care must be taken in performing rows counts not to impute more activity than actually exists.

All allowances and discounts in this fact table are represented at the line item level. As we discussed earlier, some allowances and discounts may be calculated operationally at the invoice level, not the line-item level. An effort should be made to allocate them down to the line item. An invoice P&L statement that does not include the product dimension poses a serious limitation on our ability to present meaningful P&L slices of the business.

Extended net invoice amount. This is the amount the customer is expected to pay for this line item before tax. It is equal to the gross invoice amount less the allowances and discounts.

The facts described so far likely would be displayed to the customer on the invoice document. The following cost amounts, leading to a bottom-line contribution, are for internal consumption only.

Extended fixed manufacturing cost. This is the amount identified by manufacturing as the pro rata fixed manufacturing cost of the product.

Extended variable manufacturing cost. This is the amount identified by manufacturing as the variable manufacturing cost of the product. This amount may be more or less activity-based, reflecting the actual location and time of the manufacturing run that produced the product being shipped to the customer. Conversely, this number may be a standard value set by a committee of executives. If the manufacturing costs or any of the other storage and distribution costs are too much averages of averages, then the detailed P&Ls in the data warehouse may become meaningless. The existence of the data warehouse tends to illuminate this problem and accelerate the adoption of activity-based costing methods.

Extended storage cost. This is the cost charged to the product for storage prior to being shipped to the customer.

Extended distribution cost. This is the cost charged to the product for transportation from the point of manufacture to the point of shipment. This cost is notorious for not being activity-based. Sometimes a company doesn't want to see that it costs more to do business in Seattle because the manufacturing plant is in Alabama. The distribution cost possibly can include freight to the customer if the company pays the freight, or the freight cost can be presented as a separate line item in the P&L.

Contribution amount. This is the final calculation of the extended net invoice less all the costs just discussed. This is not the true bottom line of the overall company because general and administrative expenses and other financial adjustments have not been made, but it is important nonetheless. This column sometimes has alternative labels, such as *margin*, depending on the company culture.

Profitability—The Most Powerful Data Mart

We should step back and admire the dimensional model we just built. We often describe this design as the *most powerful data mart*. We have constructed a detailed P&L view of our business, showing all the activity-based elements of revenue and costs. We have a full equation of profitability. However, what makes this design so compelling is that the P&L view sits inside a very rich dimensional framework of calendar dates, customers, products, and causal factors. Do you want see customer profitability? Just constrain and group on the customer dimension and bring the components of the P&L into your report. Do you want to see product profitability? Do you want to see deal profitability? All these analyses are equally easy and take the same analytic form in your query and report-writing tools. Somewhat tongue in cheek, we recommend that you not deliver this data mart too early in your career because you will get promoted and won't be able to work directly on any more data warehouses!

Profitability Words of Warning

We must balance the last paragraph with a more sober note. Before leaving this topic, we are compelled to pass along some cautionary words of warning. It goes without saying that most of your users probably are very interested in granular P&L data that can be rolled up to analyze customer and product profitability. The reality is that delivering these P&L statements often is easier said than done. The problems arise with the cost facts. Even with advanced ERP implementations, it is fairly common to be unable to capture the cost facts at this atomic level of granularity. You will face a complex process of mapping, or allocating, the original cost data down to the invoice line level of the shipment invoice. Furthermore, each type of cost may turn out to require a separate extraction from some source system. Ten cost facts may mean 10 different extract and transformation programs. Before you sign up for mission impossible, be certain to perform a detailed assessment of what is available and feasible from your source systems. You certainly don't want the data warehouse team saddled with driving the organization to consensus on activity-based costing as a side project, on top of managing a number of parallel extract implementations. If time permits, profitability is often tackled as a consolidated data mart after the components of revenue and cost have been sourced and delivered separately to business users in the data warehouse.

Customer Satisfaction Facts

In addition to the P&L facts, business users often are interested in customer satisfaction metrics, such as whether the line item was shipped on time, shipped complete, or shipped damage-free. We can add separate columns to the fact table for each of these line item-level satisfaction metrics. These new fact columns are populated with additive ones and zeroes, supporting interesting analyses of line item performance metrics such as the percentage of orders shipped to a particular customer on time. We also would augment the design with a customer satisfaction dimension that combines these flags into a single dimension (ala the junk dimension we discussed earlier) to associate text equivalents with the flags for reporting purposes.

Accumulating Snapshot for the Order Fulfillment Pipeline

We can think of the order management process as a pipeline, especially in a build-to-order manufacturing business, as illustrated in Figure 5.9. Customers place an order that goes into backlog until it is released to manufacturing to be built. The manufactured products are placed in finished goods inventory and then shipped to the customers and invoiced. Unique transactions are generated at each spigot of the pipeline. Thus far we've considered each of these pipeline activities as a separate fact table. Doing so allows us to decorate the detailed facts generated by each process with the greatest number of detailed dimensions. It also allows us to isolate our analysis to the performance of a single business process, which is often precisely what the business users want.

However, there are times when users are more interested in analyzing the entire order fulfillment pipeline. They want to better understand product velocity, or how quickly products move through the pipeline. The accumulating snapshot fact table provides us with this perspective of the business, as illustrated in Figure 5.10. It allows us to see an updated status and ultimately the final disposition of each order.

The accumulating snapshot complements our alternative perspectives of the pipeline. If we're interested in understanding the amount of product flowing through the pipeline, such as the quantity ordered, produced, or shipped, we rely on transaction schemas that monitor each of the pipeline's major spigots. Periodic snapshots give us insight into the amount of product sitting in the pipeline, such as the backorder or finished goods inventories, or the amount of product flowing through a spigot during a predefined time period. The accumulating snapshot helps us better understand the current state of an order, as well as product movement velocities to identify pipeline bottlenecks and inefficiencies.

We notice immediately that the accumulating snapshot looks different from the other fact tables we've designed thus far. The reuse of conformed dimensions is to be expected, but the number of date and fact columns is larger than we've seen in the past. We capture a large number of dates and facts as the

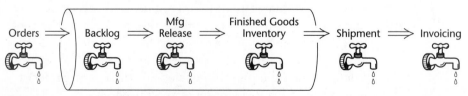

Figure 5.9   Order fulfillment pipeline diagram.

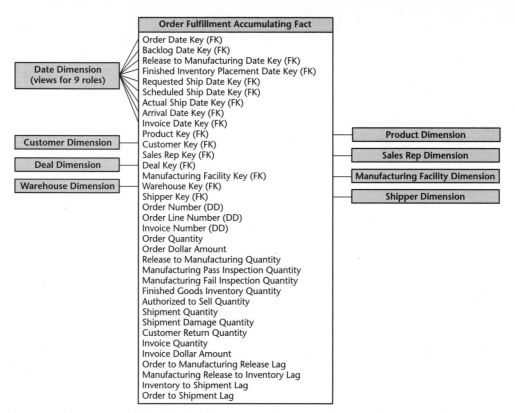

Order Fulfillment Accumulating Fact
Order Date Key (FK)
Backlog Date Key (FK)
Release to Manufacturing Date Key (FK)
Finished Inventory Placement Date Key (FK)
Requested Ship Date Key (FK)
Scheduled Ship Date Key (FK)
Actual Ship Date Key (FK)
Arrival Date Key (FK)
Invoice Date Key (FK)
Product Key (FK)
Customer Key (FK)
Sales Rep Key (FK)
Deal Key (FK)
Manufacturing Facility Key (FK)
Warehouse Key (FK)
Shipper Key (FK)
Order Number (DD)
Order Line Number (DD)
Invoice Number (DD)
Order Quantity
Order Dollar Amount
Release to Manufacturing Quantity
Manufacturing Pass Inspection Quantity
Manufacturing Fail Inspection Quantity
Finished Goods Inventory Quantity
Authorized to Sell Quantity
Shipment Quantity
Shipment Damage Quantity
Customer Return Quantity
Invoice Quantity
Invoice Dollar Amount
Order to Manufacturing Release Lag
Manufacturing Release to Inventory Lag
Inventory to Shipment Lag
Order to Shipment Lag

Date Dimension (views for 9 roles)

Customer Dimension

Deal Dimension

Warehouse Dimension

Product Dimension

Sales Rep Dimension

Manufacturing Facility Dimension

Shipper Dimension

Figure 5.10   Order fulfillment accumulating snapshot fact table.

order progresses through the pipeline. Each date represents a major milestone of the fulfillment pipeline. We handle each of these dates as dimension roles by creating either physically distinct tables or logically distinct views. It is critical that a surrogate key is used for these date dimensions rather than a literal SQL date stamp because many of the fact table date fields will be "Unknown" or "To be determined" when we first load the row. Obviously, we don't need to declare all the date fields in the fact table's primary key.

The fundamental difference between accumulating snapshots and other fact tables is the notion that we revisit and update existing fact table rows as more information becomes available. The grain of an accumulating snapshot fact table is one row per the lowest level of detail captured as the pipeline is entered. In our example, the grain would equal one row per order line item. However, unlike the order transaction fact table we designed earlier with the same granularity, the fact table row in the accumulating snapshot is modified while the order moves through the pipeline as more information is collected from every stage of the lifecycle.

Accumulating snapshots typically have multiple dates in the fact table representing the major milestones of the process. However, just because a fact table has several dates doesn't dictate that it is an accumulating snapshot. The primary differentiator of an accumulating snapshot is that we typically revisit the fact rows as activity takes place.

The accumulating snapshot technique is very useful when the product moving through the pipeline is uniquely identified, such as an automobile with a vehicle identification number, electronics equipment with a serial number, lab specimens with a identification number, or process manufacturing batches with a lot number. The accumulating snapshot helps us understand throughput and yield. If the granularity of an accumulating snapshot is at the serial or lot number, we're able to see the disposition of a discrete product as it moves through the manufacturing and test pipeline. The accumulating snapshot fits most naturally with short-lived processes that have a definite beginning and end. Long-lived processes, such as bank accounts, are better modeled with periodic snapshot fact tables.

Lag Calculations

The lengthy list of date columns is used to measure the spans of time over which the product is processed through the pipeline. The numerical difference between any two of these dates is a number, which can be averaged usefully over all the dimensions. These date lag calculations represent basic measures of the efficiency of the order fulfillment process. We could build a view on this fact table that calculated a large number of these date differences and presented them to the user as if they were stored in the underlying table. These view fields could include such measures as orders to manufacturing release lag, manufacturing release to finished goods lag, and order to shipment lag, depending on the date spans that your organization is interested in monitoring.

Multiple Units of Measure

Sometimes different functional organizations within the business want to see the same performance metrics expressed in different units of measure. For instance, manufacturing managers may want to see the product flow in terms of pallets or shipping cases. Sales and marketing managers, on the other hand, may wish to see the quantities in retail cases, scan units (sales packs), or consumer units (such as individual sticks of gum).

Designers sometimes are tempted to bury the unit-of-measure conversion factors, such as ship case factor, in the product dimension. Users are then required to appropriately multiply (or was it divide?) the order quantity by the conversion factor. Obviously, this approach places a burden on business users, in addition to being susceptible to calculation errors. The situation is further complicated because the conversion factors may change over time, so users also would need to determine which factor is applicable at a specific point in time.

Rather than risk miscalculating the equivalent quantities by placing conversion factors in the dimension table, we recommend that they be stored in the fact table instead. In the orders pipeline fact table example, assume that we had 10 basic fundamental quantity facts, in addition to five units of measure. If we physically stored all the facts expressed in the different units of measure, we'd end up with 50 (10 x 5) facts in each fact row. Instead, we compromise by building an underlying physical row with 10 quantity facts and 4 unit-of-measure conversion factors. We only need four unit-of-measure conversion factors rather than five since the base facts are already expressed in one of the units of measure. Our physical design now has 14 quantity-related facts (10 + 4), as shown in Figure 5.11. With this design, we are able to see performance across the value chain based on different units of measure.

Of course, we would deliver this fact table to the business users through one or more views. The extra computation involved in multiplying quantities by conversion factors is negligible compared with other database management system (DBMS) overhead. Intrarow computations are very efficient. The most comprehensive view actually could show all 50 facts expressed in every unit of measure, but obviously, we could simplify the user interface for any specific user group by only making available the units of measure the group wants to see.

Order Fulfillment Fact
Date Keys (FKs)
Product Key (FK)
More Foreign Keys ...
Degenerate Dimensions ...
Order Quantity
Release to Manufacturing Quantity
Manufacturing Pass Inspection Quantity
Manufacturing Fail Inspection Quantity
Finished Goods Inventory Quantity
Authorized to Sell Quantity
Shipment Quantity
Shipment Damage Quantity
Customer Return Quantity
Invoice Quantity
Retail Case Factor
Shipping Case Factor
Pallet Factor
Car Load Factor

The factors are physically packaged on each fact row. In the user interface, a view multiplies out the combinations.

Figure 5.11   Support for multiple units of measure with fact table conversion factors.

Packaging all the facts and conversion factors together in the same fact table row provides the safest guarantee that these factors will be used correctly. The converted facts are presented in a view(s) to the users.

Finally, another side benefit of storing these factors in the fact table is that it reduces the pressure on the product dimension table to issue new product rows to reflect minor factor modifications. These factors, especially if they evolve routinely over time, behave more like facts than dimension attributes.

Beyond the Rear-View Mirror

Much of what we've discussed in this chapter focuses on effective ways to analyze historical product movement performance. People sometimes refer to these as *rear-view mirror metrics* because they allow us to look backward and see where we've been. As the brokerage industry reminds us, past performance is no guarantee of future results. The current trend is to supplement these historical performance metrics with additional facts that provide a glimpse of what lies ahead of us. Rather than focusing on the pipeline at the time an order is received, some organizations are trying to move further back to analyze the key drivers that have an impact on the creation of an order. For example, in a sales organization, drivers such as prospecting or quoting activity can be extrapolated to provide some visibility to the expected order activity volume. Some organizations are implementing customer relationship management (CRM) solutions in part to gain a better understanding of contact management and other leading indicators. While the concepts are extremely powerful, typically there are feasibility concerns regarding this early predictive information, especially if you're dealing with a legacy data collection source. Because organizations build products and bill customers based on order and invoice data, they often do a much better job at collecting the rear-view mirror information than they do the early indicators. Of course, once the organization moves beyond the rear-view mirror to reliably capture front-window leading indicators, these indicators can be added gracefully to the data warehouse.

Fact Table Comparison

As we mentioned previously, there are three fundamental types of fact tables: transaction, periodic snapshot, and accumulating snapshot. All three types serve a useful purpose; you often need two complementary fact tables to get a complete picture of the business. Table 5.1 compares and contrasts the variations.

Table 5.1 Fact Table Type Comparison

CHARACTERISTIC	TRANSACTION GRAIN	PERIODIC SNAPSHOT GRAIN	ACCUMULATING SNAPSHOT GRAIN
Time period represented	Point in time	Regular, predictable intervals	Indeterminate time span, typically short-lived
Grain	One row per transaction event	One row per period	One row per life
Fact table loads	Insert	Insert	Insert and update
Fact row updates	Not revisited	Not revisited	Revisited whenever activity
Date dimension	Transaction date	End-of-period date	Multiple dates for standard milestones
Facts	Transaction activity	Performance for predefined time interval	Performance over finite lifetime

These three fact table variations are not totally dissimilar because they share conformed dimensions, which are the keys to building separate fact tables that can be used together with common, consistent filters and labels. While the dimensions are shared, the administration and rhythm of the three fact tables are quite different.

Transaction Fact Tables

The most fundamental view of the business's operations is at the individual transaction level. These fact tables represent an event that occurred at an instantaneous point in time. A row exists in the fact table for a given customer or product only if a transaction event occurred. Conversely, a given customer or product likely is linked to multiple rows in the fact table because hopefully the customer or product is involved in more than one transaction.

Transaction data often is structured quite easily into a dimensional framework. The lowest-level data is the most naturally dimensional data, supporting analyses that cannot be done on summarized data. Transaction-level data let us analyze behavior in extreme detail. Once a transaction has been posted, we typically don't revisit it.

Having made a solid case for the charm of transaction-level detail, you may be thinking that all you need is a big, fast DBMS to handle the gory transaction minutiae, and your job is over. Unfortunately, even with transaction-level data, there is still a whole class of urgent business questions that are impractical to answer using only transaction detail. As we indicated earlier, dimensional modelers cannot survive on transactions alone.

Periodic Snapshot Fact Tables

Periodic snapshots are needed to see the cumulative performance of the business at regular, predictable time intervals. Unlike the transaction fact table, where we load a row for each event occurrence, with the periodic snapshot, we take a picture (hence the snapshot terminology) of the activity at the end of a day, week, or month, then another picture at the end of the next period, and so on. The periodic snapshots are stacked consecutively into the fact table. The periodic snapshot fact table often is the only place to easily retrieve a regular, predictable, trendable view of the key business performance metrics.

Periodic snapshots typically are more complex than individual transactions. When transactions equate to little pieces of revenue, we can move easily from individual transactions to a daily snapshot merely by adding up the transactions, such as with the invoice fact tables from this chapter. In this situation, the periodic snapshot represents an aggregation of the transactional activity that occurred during a time period. We probably would build the daily snapshot only if we needed a summary table for performance reasons. The design of the snapshot table is closely related to the design of its companion transaction table in this case. The fact tables share many dimension tables, although the snapshot usually has fewer dimensions overall. Conversely, there often are more facts in a periodic snapshot table than we find in a transaction table.

In many businesses, however, transactions are not components of revenue. When you use your credit card, you are generating transactions, but the credit card issuer's primary source of customer revenue occurs when fees or charges are assessed. In this situation, we can't rely on transactions alone to analyze revenue performance. Not only would crawling through the transactions be time-consuming, but also the logic required to interpret the effect of different kinds of transactions on revenue or profit can be horrendously complicated. The periodic snapshot again comes to the rescue to provide management with a quick, flexible view of revenue. Hopefully, the data for this snapshot schema is sourced directly from an operational system. If it is not, the warehouse staging area must incorporate very complex logic to interpret the financial impact of each transaction type correctly at data load time.

Accumulating Snapshot Fact Tables

Last, but not least, the third type of fact table is the accumulating snapshot. While perhaps not as common as the other two fact table types, accumulating snapshots can be very insightful. As we just observed in this chapter, accumulating snapshots represent an indeterminate time span, covering the complete life of a transaction or discrete product (or customer).

Accumulating snapshots almost always have multiple date stamps, representing the predictable major events or phases that take place during the course of a lifetime. Often there's an additional date column that indicates when the snapshot row was last updated. Since many of these dates are not known when the fact row is first loaded, we must use surrogate date keys to handle undefined dates. It is not necessary to accommodate the most complex scenario that might occur very infrequently. The analysis of these rare outliers can always be done in the transaction fact table.

In sharp contrast to the other fact table types, we purposely revisit accumulating snapshot fact table rows to update them. Unlike the periodic snapshot, where we hang onto the prior snapshot, the accumulating snapshot merely reflects the accumulated status and metrics.

Sometimes accumulating and periodic snapshots work in conjunction with one another. Such is the case when we build the monthly snapshot incrementally by adding the effect of each day's transactions to an accumulating snapshot. If we normally think of the data warehouse as storing 36 months of historical data in the periodic snapshot, then the current rolling month would be month 37. Ideally, when the last day of the month has been reached, the accumulating snapshot simply becomes the new regular month in the time series, and a new accumulating snapshot is started the next day. The new rolling month becomes the leading breaking wave of the warehouse.

Transactions and snapshots are the yin and yang of dimensional data warehouses. Used together, companion transaction and snapshot fact tables provide a complete view of the business. We need them both because there is often no simple way to combine these two contrasting perspectives. Although there is some theoretical data redundancy between transaction and snapshot tables, we don't object to such redundancy because as data warehouse publishers our mission is to publish data so that the organization can analyze it effectively. These separate types of fact tables each provide a different perspective on the same story.

Designing Real-Time Partitions

In the past couple years, a major new requirement has been added the data warehouse designer's list. The data warehouse now must extend its existing historical time series seamlessly right up to the current instant. If the customer has placed an order in the last hour, we need to see this order in the context of the entire customer relationship. Furthermore, we need to track the hourly status of this most current order as it changes during the day.

Even though the gap between the operational transaction-processing systems and the data warehouse has shrunk in most cases to 24 hours, the rapacious needs of our marketing users require the data warehouse to fill this gap with near real-time data.

Most data warehouse designers are skeptical that the existing extract-transform-load (ETL) jobs simply can be sped up from a 24-hour cycle time to a 15-minute cycle time. Even if the data cleansing steps are pipelined to occur in parallel with the final data loading, the physical manipulations surrounding the biggest fact and dimension tables simply can't be done every 15 minutes.

Data warehouse designers are responding to this crunch by building a real-time partition in front of the conventional static data warehouse.

Requirements for the Real-Time Partition

To achieve real-time reporting, we build a special partition that is separated physically and administratively from the conventional static data warehouse tables. Actually, the name *partition* is a little misleading. The real-time partition in many cases should not be a literal table partition in the database sense. Rather, the real-time partition is a separate table subject to special update and query rules.

The real-time partition ideally should meet the following stringent set of requirements. It must:

- Contain all the activity that occurred since the last update of the static data warehouse. We will assume that the static tables are updated each night at midnight.
- Link as seamlessly as possible to the grain and content of the static data warehouse fact tables.
- Be so lightly indexed that incoming data can be continuously dribbled in.

In this chapter we just described the three main types of fact tables: transaction grain, periodic snapshot grain, and accumulating snapshot grain. The real-time partition has a different structure corresponding to each fact table type.

Transaction Grain Real-Time Partition

If the static data warehouse fact table has a transaction grain, then it contains exactly one record for each individual transaction in the source system from the beginning of recorded history. If no activity occurs in a time period, there are no transaction records. Conversely, there can be a blizzard of closely related transaction records if the activity level is high. The real-time partition has exactly the same dimensional structure as its underlying static fact table. It only contains the transactions that have occurred since midnight, when we loaded the regular data warehouse tables. The real-time partition may be completely unindexed both because we need to maintain a continuously open window for loading and because there is no time series (since we only keep today's data in this table). Finally, we avoid building aggregates on this table because we want a minimalist administrative scenario during the day.

We attach the real-time partition to our existing applications by drilling across from the static fact table to the real-time partition. Time-series aggregations (for example, all sales for the current month) will need to send identical queries to the two fact tables and add them together.

In a relatively large retail environment experiencing 10 million transactions per day, the static fact table would be pretty big. Assuming that each transaction grain record is 40 bytes wide (7 dimensions plus 3 facts, all packed into 4-byte fields), we accumulate 400 MB of data each day. Over a year this would amount to about 150 GB of raw data. Such a fact table would be heavily indexed and supported by aggregates. However, the daily tranche of 400 MB for the real-time partition could be pinned in memory. Forget indexes, except for a B-Tree index on the fact table primary key to facilitate the most efficient loading. Forget aggregations too. Our real-time partition can remain biased toward very fast loading performance but at the same time provide speedy query performance.

Since we send identical queries to the static fact table and the real-time partition, we relax and let the aggregate navigator sort out whether either of the tables has supporting aggregates. In the case we have just described, only the large static table needs them.

Periodic Snapshot Real-Time Partition

If the static data warehouse fact table has a periodic grain (say, monthly), then the real-time partition can be viewed as the current hot-rolling month. Suppose that we are working for a big retail bank with 15 million accounts. The static fact table has the grain of account by month. A 36-month time series would result in 540 million fact table records. Again, this table would be indexed extensively and supported by aggregates to provide good query performance. The real-time partition, on the other hand, is just an image of the current developing month, updated continuously as the month progresses. Semiadditive balances and fully additive facts are adjusted as frequently as they are reported. In a retail bank, the core fact table spanning all account types is likely to be quite narrow, with perhaps 4 dimensions and 4 facts, resulting in a real-time partition of 480 MB. The real-time partition again can be pinned in memory.

Query applications drilling across from the static fact table to the real-time partition have a slightly different logic compared with the transaction grain. Although account balances and other measures of intensity can be trended directly across the tables, additive totals accumulated during the current rolling period may need to be scaled upward to the equivalent of a full month to keep the results from looking anomalous.

Finally, on the last day of the month, hopefully the accumulating real-time partition can just be loaded onto the static data warehouse as the most current month, and the process can start again with an empty real-time partition.

Accumulating Snapshot Real-Time Partition

Accumulating snapshots are used for short-lived processes such as orders and shipments. A record is created for each line item on the order or shipment. In the main fact table this record is updated repeatedly as activity occurs. We create the record for a line item when the order is first placed, and then we update it whenever the item is shipped, delivered to the final destination, paid for, or maybe returned. Accumulating snapshot fact tables have a characteristic set of date foreign keys corresponding to each of these steps.

In this case it is misleading to call the main accumulating fact table *static* because this is the one fact table type that is deliberately updated, often repeatedly. However, let's assume that for query performance reasons this update occurs only at midnight when the users are offline. In this case, the real-time partition will consist of only those line items which have been updated today. At the end of the day, the records in the real-time partition will be precisely the new versions of the records that need to be written onto the main fact table either by inserting the records if they are completely new or overwriting existing records with the same primary keys.

In many order and shipment situations, the number of line items in the real-time partition will be significantly smaller than in the first two examples. For example, a manufacturer may process about 60,000 shipment invoices per month. Each invoice may have 20 line items. If an invoice line has a normal lifetime of 2 months and is updated 5 times in this interval, then we would see about 7,500 line items updated on an average working day. Even with the rather wide 80-byte records typical of shipment invoice accumulating fact tables, we only have 600 kB (7,500 updated line items per day x 80 bytes) of data in our real-time partition. This obviously will fit in memory. Forget indexes and aggregations on this real-time partition.

Queries against an accumulating snapshot with a real-time partition need to fetch the appropriate line items from both the main fact table and the partition and can either drill across the two tables by performing a sort merge (outer join) on the identical row headers or perform a union of the rows from the two tables, presenting the static view augmented with occasional supplemental rows in the report representing today's hot activity.

In this section we have made a case for satisfying the new real-time requirement with specially constructed but nevertheless familiar extensions to our existing fact tables. If you drop all the indexes (except for a basic B-Tree index for updating) and aggregations on these special new tables and pin them in memory, you should be able to get the combined update and query performance needed.

Summary

In this chapter we covered a lengthy laundry list of topics in the context of the order management process. We discussed *multiples* on several fronts: multiple references to the same dimension in a fact table (dimension role-playing), multiple equivalent units of measure, and multiple currencies. We explored several of the common challenges encountered when modeling orders data, including facts at different levels of granularity and junk dimensions. We also explored the rich set of facts associated with invoice transactions.

We used the order fulfillment pipeline to illustrate the power of accumulating snapshot fact tables. Accumulating snapshots allow us to see the updated status of a specific product or order as it moves through a finite pipeline. The chapter closed with a summary of the differences between the three fundamental types of fact tables, along with suggestions for handling near real-time reporting with each fact table type.

Customer Relationship Management

L ong before *customer relationship management* (CRM) was a buzzword, organizations were designing and developing customer-centric dimensional models to better understand their customers' behavior. For nearly two decades these models have been used to respond to management's inquiries about which customers were solicited, which responded, and what was the magnitude of their response. The perceived business value of understanding the full spectrum of customers' interactions and transactions has propelled CRM to the top of the charts. CRM has emerged as a mission-critical business strategy that many view as essential to a company's survival.

In this chapter we discuss the implications of CRM on the world of data warehousing. Given the broad interest in CRM, we've allocated more space than usual to an overview of the underlying principles. Since customers play a role in so many business processes within our organizations, rather than developing schemas to reflect all customer interaction and transaction facts captured, we'll devote the majority of this chapter to the all-important customer dimension table.

Chapter 6 discusses the following concepts:

- **CRM overview, including its operational and analytic roles**
- **Customer name and address parsing, along with international considerations**
- **Common customer dimension attributes, such as dates, segmentation attributes, and aggregated facts**
- **Dimension outriggers for large clusters of low-cardinality attributes**

- Minidimensions for attribute browsing and change tracking in large dimensions, as well as variable-width attribute sets
- Implications of using type 2 slowing changing dimension technique on dimension counts
- Behavior study groups to track a set of customers that exhibit common characteristics or behaviors
- Commercial customer hierarchy considerations, including both fixed and variable depth
- Combining customer data from multiple data sources
- Analyzing customer data across multiple business processes

CRM Overview

Regardless of the industry, organizations are flocking to the concept of CRM. They're jumping on the bandwagon in an attempt to migrate from a product-centric orientation to one that is driven by customer needs. While all-encompassing terms like customer relationship management sometimes seem ambiguous or overly ambitious, the premise behind CRM is far from rocket science. It is based on the simple notion that the better you know your customers, the better you can maintain long-lasting, valuable relationships with them. The goal of CRM is to maximize relationships with your customers over their lifetime. It entails focusing all aspects of the business, from marketing, sales, operations, and service, to establishing and sustaining mutually beneficial customer relations. To do so, the organization must develop a single, integrated view of each customer.

CRM promises significant returns for organizations that embrace it in terms of both increased revenue and greater operational efficiencies. Switching to a customer-driven perspective can lead to increased sales effectiveness and closure rates, revenue growth, enhanced sales productivity at reduced cost, improved customer profitability margins, higher customer satisfaction, and increased customer retention. Ultimately, every organization wants more loyal, more profitable customers. Since it often requires a sizable investment to attract new customers, we can't afford to have the profitable ones leave. Likewise, one of CRM's objectives is to convert unprofitable customers into profitable ones.

In many organizations, the view of the customer varies depending on the product line, business unit, business function, or geographic location. Each group may use different customer data in different ways with different results. The evolution from the existing silos to a more integrated perspective obviously requires organizational commitment. CRM is like a stick of dynamite that knocks down the silo walls. It requires the right integration of business processes, people resources, and application technology to be effective.

In many cases, the existing business processes for customer interactions have evolved over time as operational or organization work-arounds. The resulting patchwork set of customer-related processes is often clumsy at best. Merely better automating the current inefficient customer-centric processes actually may be more harmful than doing nothing at all. If you're faced with broken processes, operational adjustments are necessary.

Since it is human nature to resist change, it comes as no surprise that people-related issues often challenge CRM implementations. CRM involves new ways of interacting with your customers. It often entails radical changes to the sales channels. CRM requires new information flows based on the complete acquisition and dissemination of customer touch-point data. Often organization structures and incentive systems are altered dramatically.

Unfortunately, you can't just buy an off-the-shelf CRM product and expect it to be a silver bullet that solves all your problems. While many organizations focus their attention on CRM technology, in the end this may be the simplest component with which to contend compared to other larger issues. Obviously, the best place to start CRM is with a strategy and plan. Tackling the acquisition of technology first actually may impede progress for a successful CRM implementation. Technology should support, not drive, your CRM solution. Without a sound CRM strategy, technology merely may accelerate organizational chaos through the deployment of additional silos.

Earlier in this book we stated that it is imperative for both senior business and IT management to support a data warehousing initiative. We stress this advice again when it comes to a CRM implementation because of the implications of its cross-functional focus. CRM requires clear business vision. Without business strategy, buy-in, and authorization to change, CRM becomes an exercise in futility. Neither the IT community nor the business community is capable of implementing CRM successfully on its own; it demands a joint commitment of support.

Operational and Analytic CRM

It could be said that CRM suffers from a split personality syndrome because it addresses both operational and analytic requirements. Effective CRM relies on the collection of data at every interaction we have with a customer and then the leveraging of that breadth of data through analysis.

On the operational front, CRM calls for the synchronization of customer-facing processes. Often operational systems must be either updated or supplemented to coordinate across sales, marketing, operations, and service. Think about all the customer interactions that occur during the purchase and use of a product or service—from the initial prospect contact, quote generation, purchase transaction, fulfillment, payment transaction, and ongoing customer service. Rather than thinking about these processes as independent silos (or multiple silos that vary by product line), the CRM mind-set is to integrate these customer activities. Each touch point in the customer contact cycle represents an opportunity to collect more customer metrics and characteristics, as well as leverage existing customer data to extract more value from the relationship.

As data is created on the operational side of the CRM equation, we obviously need to store and analyze the historical metrics resulting from our customer interaction and transaction systems. Sounds familiar, doesn't it? The data warehouse sits at the core of CRM. It serves as the repository to collect and integrate the breadth of customer information found in our operational systems, as well as from external sources. The data warehouse is the foundation that supports the panoramic 360-degree view of our customers, including customer data from the following typical sources: transactional data, interaction data (solicitations, call center), demographic and behavioral data (typically augmented by third parties), and self-provided profile data.

Analytic CRM is enabled via accurate, integrated, and accessible customer data in the warehouse. We are able to measure the effectiveness of decisions made in the past in order to optimize future interactions. Customer data can be leveraged to better identify up-sell and cross-sell opportunities, pinpoint inefficiencies, generate demand, and improve retention. In addition, we can leverage the historical, integrated data to generate models or scores that close the loop back to the operational world. Recalling the major components of a warehouse environment from Chapter 1, we can envision the model results pushed back to where the relationship is operationally managed (for example, sales rep, call center, or Web site), as illustrated in Figure 6.1. The model output can translate into specific proactive or reactive tactics recommended for the next point of customer contact, such as the appropriate next product offer or antiattrition response. The model results also are retained in the data warehouse for subsequent analysis.

In other situations, information must feed back to the operational Web site or call center systems on a more real-time basis. This type of operational support is appropriately the responsibility of the operational data store (ODS), as described in Chapter 1. In this case, the closed loop is much tighter than Figure 6.1 because it is a matter of collection and storage and then feedback to the collection system. The ODS generally doesn't require the breadth or depth of customer information available in the data warehouse; it contains a subset of data required by the touch-point applications. Likewise, the integration requirements are typically not as stringent.

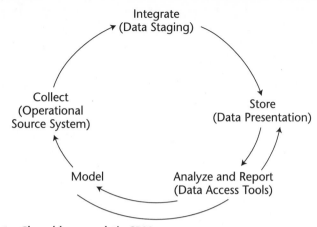

Figure 6.1 Closed-loop analytic CRM.

Obviously, as the organization becomes more centered on the customer, so must the data warehouse. CRM inevitably will drive change in the data warehouse. Data warehouses will grow even more rapidly as we collect more and more information about our customers, especially from front-office sources such as the field force. Our data staging processes will grow more complicated as we match and integrate data from multiple sources. Most important, the need for a conformed customer dimension becomes even more paramount.

Packaged CRM

In response to the urgent need of business for CRM, project teams may be wrestling with a buy versus build decision. In the long run, the build approach may match the organization's requirements better than the packaged application, but the implementation likely will take longer and require more resources, potentially at a higher cost. Buying a packaged application will deliver a practically ready-to-go solution, but it may not focus on the integration and interface issues needed for it to function in the larger IT context. Fortunately, some providers are supporting common data interchange through Extensible Markup Language (XML), publishing their data specifications so that IT can extract dimension and fact data, and supporting customer-specific conformed dimensions.

Buying a packaged solution, regardless of its application breadth, does not give us an excuse to dodge the challenge of creating conformed dimensions, including the customer dimension. If we fail to welcome the packaged application as a full member of the data warehouse, then it is likely to become a stovepipe data mart. The packaged application should not amount to disconnected customer information sitting on another data island. The recent CRM hype is based on the notion that we have an integrated view of the customer. Any purchased component must be linked to a common data warehouse and conformed dimensions. Otherwise, we have just armed our business analysts with access to more inconsistent customer data, resulting in more inconsistent customer analysis. The last thing any organization needs is another data stovepipe, so be certain to integrate any packaged solution properly.

Customer Dimension

The conformed customer dimension is a critical element for effective CRM. A well-maintained, well-deployed conforming customer dimension is the cornerstone of sound customer-centric analysis.

The customer dimension is typically the most challenging dimension for any data warehouse. In a large organization, the customer dimension can be extremely deep (with millions of rows), extremely wide (with dozens or even hundreds of attributes), and sometimes subject to rather rapid change. One leading direct marketer maintains over 3,000 attributes about its customers. Any organization that deals with the general public needs an individual human being dimension. The biggest retailers, credit card companies, and government agencies have monster customer dimensions whose sizes exceed 100 million rows. To further complicate matters, the customer dimension often represents an amalgamation of data from multiple internal and external source systems.

In this next section we focus on numerous customer dimension design considerations. The customer data we maintain will differ depending on whether we operate in a business-to-business (B2B) customer environment, such as distributors, versus a business-to-consumer (B2C) mode. Regardless, many of these considerations apply to both scenarios. We'll begin with name/address parsing and other common customer attributes, including coverage of dimension outriggers. From there we'll discuss minidimension tables to address query performance and change tracking in very large customer dimensions. We'll also describe the use of behavior study group dimensions to track ongoing activity for a group of customers that share a common characteristic. Finally, we'll deal with fixed- and variable-depth commercial customer hierarchies.

Name and Address Parsing

Regardless of whether we're dealing with individual human beings or commercial entities, we typically capture our customers' name and address attributes. The operational handling of name and address information is usually too simplistic to be very useful in the data warehouse. Many designers feel that a liberal design of general-purpose columns for names and addresses, such as Name-1 through Name-3 and Address-1 through Address-6, can handle any situation. Unfortunately, these catchall columns are virtually worthless when it comes to better understanding and segmenting the customer base. Designing the name and location columns in a generic way actually can contribute to data quality problems. Consider the sample design in Table 6.1 with general-purpose columns.

In this design, the name column is far too limited. There is no consistent mechanism for handling salutations, titles, or suffixes. We can't identify what the person's first name is or how she should be addressed in a personalized greeting. If we looked at additional sample data from this operational system, potentially we would find multiple customers listed in a single name field. We also might find additional descriptive information in the name field, such as "Confidential," "Trustee," or "UGMA" (Uniform Gift to Minors Act).

In our sample address fields, inconsistent abbreviations are used in various places. The address columns may contain enough room for any address, but there is no discipline imposed by the columns that will guarantee conformance with postal authority regulations or support address matching or latitude/longitude identification.

Table 6.1 Sample Customer Dimension with Overly General Columns

DIMENSION ATTRIBUTE	EXAMPLE VALUES
Name	Ms. R. Jane Smith, Atty
Address-1	123 Main Rd, North West, Ste 100A
Address-2	P.O. Box 2348
City	Kensington
State	Ark.
ZIP Code	88887-2348
Phone Number	888-555-3333 x776 main, 555-4444 fax

Instead of using a few general-purpose fields, the name and location attributes should be broken down into as many elemental parts as possible. The extract process needs to perform significant parsing on the original dirty names and addresses. Once the attributes have been parsed, then they can be standardized. For example, "Rd" would become "Road" and "Ste" would become "Suite." The attributes also can be verified, such as validating that the ZIP code and associated state combination is correct. Fortunately, name and address data cleansing and scrubbing tools are available on the market to assist with parsing, standardization, and verification.

A sample set of name and location attributes for individuals in the United States is shown in Table 6.2. We've filled in every attribute to make the design clearer, but no single real instance would look like this row.

Table 6.2 Sample Customer Dimension with Parsed Name and Address Elements

DIMENSION ATTRIBUTE	EXAMPLE VALUES
Salutation	Ms.
Informal Greeting Name	Jane
Formal Greeting Name	Ms. Smith
First and Middle Names	R. Jane
Surname	Smith
Suffix	Jr.
Ethnicity	English
Title	Attorney
Street Number	123
Street Name	Main
Street Type	Road
Street Direction	North West
Post Box	2348
Suite	100A
City	Kensington
District	Cornwall
Second District	Berkeleyshire
State	Arkansas
Region	South
Country	United States

(Continues)

Table 6.2 *Continued.*

DIMENSION ATTRIBUTE	EXAMPLE VALUES
Continent	North America
Primary Postal ZIP Code	88887
Secondary Postal ZIP Code	2348
Postal Code Type	United States
Office Telephone Country Code	1
Office Telephone Area Code	888
Office Telephone Number	5553333
Office Extension	776
FAX Telephone Country Code	1
FAX Telephone Area Code	888
FAX Telephone Number	5554444
E-mail address	RJSmith@ABCGenIntl.com
Web Site	www.ABCGenIntl.com
Unique Customer ID	7346531

Commercial customers typically have multiple addresses, such as physical and shipping addresses; each of these addresses would follow much the same logic as the address structure we just developed.

Before leaving this topic, it is worth noting that some organizations maintain the complete set of name and address characteristics in their customer dimension in order to produce mail-ready addresses, as well as support other communication channels such as telephone, fax, and electronic mail, directly from the data warehouse. Here the data warehouse customer dimension becomes a kind of operational system because it is the enterprise-wide authority for valid addresses. This is most likely to happen when no other operational system has taken responsibility for consolidating customer information across the enterprise. In other cases, organizations already have decided to capture solicitation and communication touch points in an operational system. In these environments, the customer dimension in the warehouse may consist of a more reduced subset of attributes meaningful to analysis, as opposed to the complete set of attributes necessary to generate the mailing labels or call list details.

International Name and Address Considerations

Customer geographic attributes become more complicated if we're dealing with customers from multiple countries. Even if you don't have international customers, you may need to contend with international names and addresses somewhere in your data warehouse for international suppliers or human resources personnel records.

When devising a solution for international names and addresses, we need to keep the following in mind, in addition to the name and address parsing requirements we discussed earlier:

Universal representation. The design should be consistent from country to country so that similar data elements appear in predictable, similar places in the customer dimension table.

Cultural correctness. This includes the appropriate salutation and personalization for a letter, electronic mail, or telephone greeting.

Differences in addresses. Different addresses may be required whether they're foreign mailings from the country of origin to the destination country (including idiosyncrasies such as presenting the destination city and country in capital letters), domestic mailings within the destination country, and package delivery services (which don't accept post office boxes).

The attributes we described earlier are still applicable for international names and addresses. In addition, we should include an address block attribute with a complete valid postal address including line breaks rendered in the proper order according to regulations of the destination country. Creating this attribute once in the staging process, based on the correct country-by-country address formation rules, simplifies downstream usage.

Similar to international addresses, telephone numbers must be presented differently depending on where the phone call is originated. We need to provide attributes to represent the complete foreign dialing sequence, complete domestic dialing sequence, and local dialing sequence. Unfortunately, the complete foreign dialing sequence will vary by country of origin.

We have barely scratched the surface concerning the intricacies of international names and addresses. For more detailed coverage, we recommend Toby Atkinson's book on the subject, *Merriam-Webster's Guide to International Business Communications* (Merriam-Webster, 1999).

Other Common Customer Attributes

While geographic attributes are some of the most common attributes found on a customer dimension, here are others you'll likely encounter. Of course, the list of customer attributes typically is quite lengthy. The more descriptive information we capture about our customers, the more robust the customer dimension will be—and the more interesting the analysis.

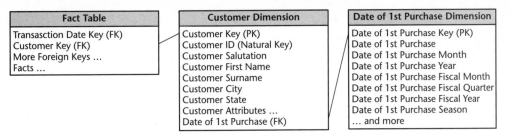

Figure 6.2 Date dimension outrigger.

Dates

We often find dates in the customer dimension, such as date of first purchase, date of last purchase, and date of birth. Although these dates may initially be SQL date format fields, if we want to take full advantage of our date dimension with the ability to summarize these dates by the special calendar attributes of our enterprise, such as seasons, quarters, and fiscal periods, the dates should be changed to foreign key references to the date dimension. We need to be careful that all such dates fall within the span of our corporate date dimension. These date dimension copies are declared as semantically distinct views, such as a "First Purchase Date" dimension table with unique column labels. The system behaves as if there is another physical date table. Constraints on any of these tables have nothing to do with constraints on the primary date dimension table. Shown in Figure 6.2, this design is an example of a dimension outrigger, which we'll discuss further later in this chapter. Dates outside the span of our corporate date dimension should be represented as SQL date fields.

Customer Segmentation Attributes and Scores

Some of the most powerful attributes in a customer dimension are segmentation classifications or scores. These attributes obviously vary greatly by business context. For an individual customer, they may include:

- Gender
- Ethnicity
- Age or other life-stage classifications
- Income or other lifestyle classifications
- Status (for example, new, active, inactive, closed)
- Referring source

- Recency (for example, date of last purchase), frequency (for example, total purchase transaction count), and intensity (for example, total net purchase amount), as well as cluster labels generated by data mining cluster analysis of these recency, frequency, and intensity measures

- Business-specific market segment (such as a preferred customer identifier)

- Scores characterizing the customer, such as purchase behavior, payment behavior, product preferences, propensity to churn, and probability of default. Statistical segmentation models typically generate these scores, which are then tagged onto each customer dimension row as an attribute.

Aggregated Facts as Attributes

Users often are interested in constraining the customer dimension based on aggregated performance metrics, such as wanting to filter on all customers who spent over a certain dollar amount during last year. To make matters worse, perhaps they want to constrain based on how much the customer has purchased during his or her lifetime. Providing aggregated facts as dimension attributes is sure to be a crowd pleaser with the business users. Rather than issuing a separate query to determine all customers who satisfied the spending-habits criteria and then issuing another fact query to further inquire about that group of customers, storing an aggregated fact as an attribute allows users simply to constrain on that spending attribute, just like they might on a geographic attribute. These attributes are to be used for constraining and labeling; they are not to be used in numeric calculations. While there are query usability and performance advantages to storing these attributes, the downside burden falls on the backroom staging processes to ensure that the attributes are accurate, up-to-date, and consistent with the actual fact rows. In other words, they require significant care and feeding. If you opt to include some aggregated facts as dimension attributes, be certain to focus on those which will be used frequently. In addition, you should strive to minimize the frequency with which these attributes need to be updated. For example, an attribute for last year's spending would require much less maintenance than one that identifies year-to-date behavior. Rather than storing attributes down to the specific dollar value, they are sometimes replaced (or supplemented) with more meaningful descriptive values, such as "High Spender," as we just discussed with segmentation attributes. These descriptive values minimize our vulnerability to the fact that the numeric attributes may not tie back exactly to the appropriate fact tables. In addition, they ensure that all users have a consistent definition for high spenders, for example, rather than resorting to their own individual business rules.

Dimension Outriggers for a Low-Cardinality Attribute Set

As we said in Chapter 2, a dimension is said to be *snowflaked* when the low-cardinality columns in the dimension have been removed to separate normalized tables that then link back into the original dimension table. Generally, snowflaking is not recommended in a data warehouse environment because it almost always makes the user presentation more complex, in addition to having a negative impact on browsing performance. Despite this prohibition against snowflaking, there are some situations where you should build a dimension outrigger that has the appearance of a snowflaked table. Outriggers have special characteristics that cause them to be permissible snowflakes.

In Figure 6.3, the dimension outrigger is a set of data from an external data provider consisting of 150 demographic and socioeconomic attributes regarding the customers' county of residence. The data for all customers residing in a given county is identical. Rather than repeating this large block of data for every customer within a county, we opt to model it as an outrigger. There are several factors that cause us to bend our no-snowflake rule. First of all, the demographic data is available at a significantly different grain than the primary dimension data (county versus individual customer). The data is administered and loaded at different times than the rest of the data in the customer dimension. Also, we really do save significant space in this case if the underlying customer dimension is large. If you have a query tool that insists on a classic star schema with no snowflakes, you can hide the outrigger under a view declaration.

💡 **Dimension outriggers are permissible, but they should be the exception rather than the rule. A red warning flag should go up if your design is riddled with outriggers; you may have succumbed to the temptation to overly normalize the design.**

Fact Table	Customer Dimension	County Demographics Outrigger Dimension
Customer Key (FK)	Customer Key (PK)	County Demographics Key (PK)
More Foreign Keys ...	Customer ID (Natural Key)	Total Population
Facts ...	Customer Salutation	Population under 5 Years
	Customer First Name	% Population under 5 Years
	Customer Surname	Population under 18 Years
	Customer City	% Population under 18 Years
	Customer County	Population 65 Years and Older
	County Demographics Key (FK)	% Population 65 Years and Older
	Customer State	Female Population
	... and more	% Female Population
		Male Population
		% Male Population
		Number of High School Graduates
		Number of College Graduates
		Number of Housing Units
		Homeownership Rate
		... and more

Figure 6.3 Permissible snowflaking with a dimension outrigger for cluster of low-cardinality attributes.

Large Changing Customer Dimensions

Multimillion-row customer dimensions present two unique challenges that warrant special treatment. Even if a clean, flat dimension table has been implemented, it generally takes too long to constrain or browse among the relationships in such a big table. In addition, it is difficult to use our tried-and-true techniques from Chapter 4 for tracking changes in these large dimensions. We probably don't want to use the type 2 slowly changing dimension technique and add more rows to a customer dimension that already has millions of rows in it. Unfortunately, huge customer dimensions are even more likely to change than moderately sized dimensions. We sometimes call this situation a *rapidly changing monster dimension*!

Business users often want to track the myriad of customer attribute changes. In some businesses, tracking change is not merely a nice-to-have analytic capability. Insurance companies, for example, must update information about their customers and their specific insured automobiles or homes because it is critical to have an accurate picture of these dimensions when a policy is approved or claim is made.

Fortunately, a single technique comes to the rescue to address both the browsing-performance and change-tracking challenges. The solution is to break off frequently analyzed or frequently changing attributes into a separate dimension, referred to as a *minidimension*. For example, we could create a separate minidimension for a package of demographic attributes, such as age, gender, number of children, and income level, presuming that these columns get used extensively. There would be one row in this minidimension for each unique combination of age, gender, number of children, and income level encountered in the data, not one row per customer. These columns are the ones that are analyzed to select an interesting subset of the customer base. In addition, users want to track changes to these attributes. We leave behind more constant or less frequently queried attributes in the original huge customer table.

Sample rows for a demographic minidimension are illustrated in Table 6.3. When creating the minidimension, continuously variable attributes, such as income and total purchases, should be converted to banded ranges. In other words, we force the attributes in the minidimension to take on a relatively small number of discrete values. Although this restricts use to a set of predefined bands, it drastically reduces the number of combinations in the minidimension. If we stored income at a specific dollar and cents value in the minidimension, when combined with the other demographic attributes, we could end up with as many rows in the minidimension as in the main customer dimension itself. The use of band ranges is probably the most significant compromise associated

Table 6.3 Sample Rows from a Demographic Minidimension

DEMOGRAPHIC KEY	AGE	GENDER	INCOME LEVEL
1	20-24	Male	<$20,000
2	20-24	Male	$20,000-$24,999
3	20-24	Male	$25,000-$29,999
18	25-29	Male	$20,000-$24,999
19	25-29	Male	$25,000-$29,999

with the minidimension technique because once we decide on the value bands, it is quite impractical to change to a different set of bands at a later time. If users insist on access to a specific raw data value, such as a credit bureau score that is updated monthly, it also should be included in the fact table, in addition to being represented as a value band in the demographic minidimension. In Chapter 9 we'll see how to construct on-the-fly value-banding queries against the facts in the fact table, although such queries are much less efficient than directly constraining the value band in our minidimension table.

Every time we build a fact table row, we include two foreign keys related to the customer: the regular customer dimension key and the minidimension demographics key. As shown in Figure 6.4, the demographics key should be part of the fact table's set of foreign keys in order to provide efficient access to the fact table through the demographics attributes. This design delivers browsing and constraining performance benefits by providing a smaller point of entry to the facts. Queries can avoid the huge customer dimension table altogether unless attributes from that table are constrained.

When the demographics key participates as a foreign key in the fact table, another benefit is that the fact table serves to capture the demographic profile changes. Let's presume that we are loading data into a periodic snapshot fact table on a monthly basis. Referring back to our sample demographic minidimension sample rows in Table 6.3, if one of our customers, John Smith, was 24 years old with an income of $24,000, we'd begin by assigning demographics key 2 when loading the fact table. If John has a birthday several weeks later, we'd assign demographics key 18 when the fact table was next loaded. The demographics key on the earlier fact table rows for John would not be changed. In this manner, the fact table tracks the age change. We'd continue to assign demographics key 18 when the fact table is loaded until there's another change in John's demographic profile. If John receives a raise to $26,000 several months later, a new demographics key would be reflected in the next fact table load. Again, the earlier rows would be unchanged. Historical demographic profiles for each customer can be constructed at any time by referring to the fact table and picking up the simultaneous customer key and its contemporary demographics key, which in general will be different from the most recent demographics key.

Customer dimensions are unique in that customer attributes frequently are queried independently of the fact table. For example, users may want to know how many female customers live in Dade County by age bracket. Counts such as these are extremely common with customer segmentation and profiling. Rather than forcing any analysis that combines solely customer and demographic data to link through the fact table, the most recent value of the demographics key also can exist as a foreign key on the customer dimension table. In this case, we refer to the demographics table as a *customer dimension outrigger*, as we discussed earlier in this chapter.

> The *minidimension* terminology refers to when the demographics key is part of the fact table composite key; if the demographics key is a foreign key in the customer dimension, we refer to it as an *outrigger*.

If you embed the most recent demographics key in the customer dimension, you must treat it as a type 1 attribute. If you tracked all the demographics changes over time as a type 2 slowly changing dimension, you would have reintroduced the rapidly changing monster dimension problem that we have been working to avoid! With a type 1 change, as we discussed in Chapter 4, we overwrite the demographics key in the customer row whenever it changes instead of creating a new customer row. We also recommend that these outrigger demographic attributes be labeled as most recent or current values to minimize confusion. Even with unique labeling, be aware that presenting users with two avenues for accessing demographic data, through either the minidimension or the outrigger, can deliver more functionality and complexity than some users can handle.

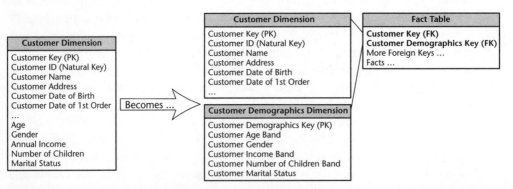

Figure 6.4 Demographic minidimension with a customer dimension.

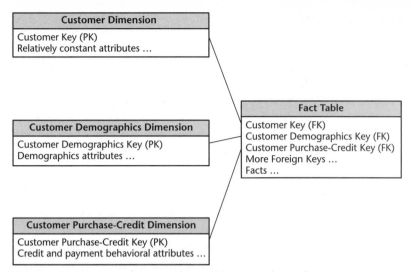

Figure 6.5 Separate demographic and behavioral minidimensions.

The demographic dimension itself cannot be allowed to grow too large. If we have 5 demographic attributes, each with 10 possible values, then the demographics dimension could have 100,000 (10^5) rows. This is a reasonable upper limit for the number of rows in a minidimension. However, there are certainly cases where we need to support more than 5 demographic attributes with 10 values each. In this case, we would build a second demographics dimension, as shown in Figure 6.5. For example, we may have one set of attributes concerning traditional demographic income and lifestyle attributes and another set that focuses on purchase and credit behavioral scores. Multiple minidimensions address the issue of minidimension growth while also clustering like attributes together for a more intuitive user presentation. Another motivation for creating these two minidimensions is that they are potentially sourced from two different data providers with different update frequencies. However, remember to bear in mind our advice from Chapter 2 concerning too many dimensions. We certainly don't want to create a separate minidimension with a foreign key in the fact table for each demographic attribute, such as an age dimension, gender dimension, and income dimension. Likewise, we shouldn't jump immediately on the minidimension technique unless we're dealing with a large or rapidly changing dimension; we can't forget the advantages of maintaining a simple, flat, denormalized dimension table.

The best approach for efficiently browsing and tracking changes of key attributes in really huge dimensions is to break off one or more minidimensions from the dimension table, each consisting of small clumps of attributes that have been administered to have a limited number of values.

Variable-Width Attribute Set

Finally, a minidimension can be created to handle a variable number of customer attributes. Obviously, the longer we have a relationship with a customer, the more descriptive information we know about him or her. If we think about the sales cycle, we have many more prospects than we do customers; however, we know much less about the prospects than we do about our customers. We may have 10 million initial prospects, described by a handful of characteristics, who are worked through the sales pipeline eventually to result in 1 million official customers with a much broader set of known characteristics.

When using external prospect lists, we often are permitted only a one-time use of the list and don't have the legal right to store the prospect information internally. However, if we've generated our own prospect information, it certainly can be stored in the data warehouse. Let's assume that we're capturing metrics, perhaps associated with solicitation or quote-generation events that apply to both prospects and customers. We could store the prospects and customers together in a single contact dimension; however, there is a significant disparity between the numbers of attributes for prospective versus customer contacts. As illustrated in Figure 6.6, we may know only a handful of identification and location attributes about our prospects. On the other hand, we may know 50 additional attributes for a customer, covering purchase, payment, credit and service behaviors, directly elicited profile attributes, and third-party purchased demographic attributes. In the world of electronic retailing, we can equate prospects to be the anonymous Web site visitors as opposed to our registered customers.

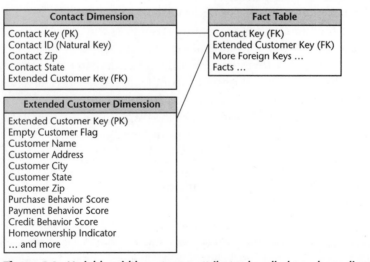

Figure 6.6 Variable-width customer attributes handled as a base dimension and minidimension.

If we assume that many of the final 50 customer attributes are textual, we easily could have a total row width of 1,000 bytes. Suppose that we have 10 million contacts (9 million prospects and 1 million official customers). Obviously, we are concerned that the trailing 50 columns in 90 percent of our contacts have no data. This gets our attention when we're dealing with a 10-GB dimension table. In this case, we may wish to introduce a minidimension.

If we're dealing with a database platform that supports variable-width rows, such as Oracle, we may be able to build a single dimension with the full complement of attributes if the total attributes list is not too long; in some of these cases, we don't need to worry about all the prospects' null columns because they take up virtually zero disk space. However, if we have a fixed-width database, or if the attributes list is very long, we are uncomfortable with all the empty columns for the prospects. In this case, as shown in Figure 6.6, we break the dimension into a 10-million-row base dimension table consisting of attributes that are common to both prospects and customers, along with a 1-million-row customer minidimension that contains the additional attributes we know about our customers. Again, we include two foreign keys in the fact table. Nine of ten fact table rows would join to an empty customer row in the extended customer minidimension.

Implications of Type 2 Customer Dimension Changes

Perhaps your organization sells to tens of thousands of customers rather than tens of millions. In this case, the techniques we discussed in Chapter 4 for tracking dimension changes are still viable. The slowly changing dimension type 2 technique, where another row is added to the dimension table, would remain the predominant technique for tracking change in customer dimensions with less than 100,000 rows. Even if we have a truly large customer dimension, we likely will need to still use the type 2 response to handle very slowly changing attributes left behind in the customer dimension.

As we mentioned earlier, users frequently want to count customers based on their attributes without joining to a fact table. If we used a type 2 response to track customer dimension changes, we would need to be careful to avoid overcounting because we may have multiple rows in the customer dimension for the same individual. Doing a COUNT DISTINCT on a unique customer identifier is a possibility, assuming that the attribute is indeed unique and also hasn't been altered. A most recent row indicator in the customer dimension is also helpful to do counts based on the most up-to-date descriptive values for a customer.

Things get more complicated if we need to do a customer count at a given historical point in time using effective and expiration dates in the customer dimension. For example, if we need to know the number of customers we had at the beginning of 2002, we could constrain the row effective date to less than or equal to "1/1/2002" and the row expiration date to greater than or equal to "1/1/2002" to restrict the result set to only those rows which were valid on January 1, 2002. Note that the comparison operators depend on the business rules used to set our effective/expiration dates. In this example, the row expiration date on the no-longer-valid customer row is one day less than the effective date on the new row. Alternatively, as we discussed earlier, the dates may be surrogate date keys joined to a date dimension outrigger table. In this case, we would use unequal joins between the outrigger date tables and the effective/expiration dates on the customer dimension.

Customer Behavior Study Groups

With customer analysis, simple queries, such as how much have we sold to customers in this geographic area in the past year, rapidly evolve to more complex inquiries, such as how many customers bought more this past month than their average monthly purchase amount from last year. The latter question is much too complicated for business users to express in a single SQL request. Some data access tool vendors allow embedded subqueries, whereas others have implemented multipass SQL capabilities, in which complex requests are broken into multiple select statements and then combined in a subsequent pass.

In other situations, we may want to capture the set of customers from a query or exception report, such as the top 100 customers from last year, customers who spent more than $1,000 last month, or customers who received a specific test solicitation, and then use that group of customers, which we call a *behavior study group*, for subsequent analysis without reprocessing to identify the initial condition. To create a behavior study group, we run a query (or series of queries) to identify the set of customers we want to further analyze and then capture the customer keys of the result set as an actual physical table. We then use this special behavior study group dimension table of customer identifiers whenever we wish to constrain any analysis to that set of specially defined customers, as shown in Figure 6.7.

The secret to building complex behavioral study group queries is to capture the keys of the customers or products whose behavior you are tracking. You then use the captured keys to constrain other fact tables without having to rerun the original behavior analysis.

The behavior study group dimension is attached with an equijoin to the natural key (named "Customer ID" in Figure 6.7) of the customer dimension. This can be even done in a view that hides the explicit join to the behavior dimension. In this way, the resulting dimensional model looks and behaves like an uncomplicated schema. If the study group dimension table is hidden under a view, it should be labeled to uniquely identify it as being associated with the top 100 customers, for example. Virtually any data access tool should be able to analyze this specially restricted schema without paying syntax or user-interface penalties for the complex processing that defined the original subset of customers.

Like many design decisions, this one represents certain compromises. First, this approach requires a user interface for capturing, creating, and administering physical behavior study group tables in the data warehouse. After a complex exception report has been defined, we need the ability to capture the resulting keys into an applet to create the special behavior study group dimension. These study group tables must live in the same space as the primary fact table because they are going to be joined to the customer dimension table directly. This obviously affects the DBA's responsibilities.

Commercial Customer Hierarchies

One of the most challenging aspects of dealing with commercial customers is modeling their internal organizational hierarchy. Commercial customers often have a nested hierarchy of entities ranging from individual locations or organizations up through regional offices, business unit headquarters, and ultimate parent companies. These hierarchical relationships may change frequently as customers reorganize themselves internally or are involved in acquisitions and divestitures.

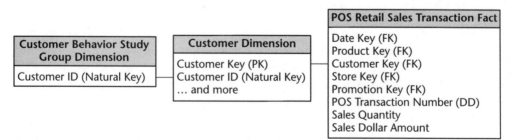

Figure 6.7 Behavior study group dimension consisting of selected keys joined directly to the natural key of the customer dimension.

We'll talk about two approaches to handling customer hierarchies. The first is straightforward but relies heavily on brute force rather than elegance. Still, it may address your requirements adequately with a simplistic approach. The second approach is more advanced and complicated but also much more extensible. If you're not dealing with unpredictable, ragged hierarchies (such as variable customer and cost center hierarchies or manufacturing parts explosion), you may want to skim the coverage on variable-depth hierarchies because it is a bit of a brainteaser.

Fixed-Depth Hierarchies

Although this occurs relatively uncommonly, the lucky ones among us sometimes are confronted with a customer dimension that is highly predictable with a fixed number of levels. Suppose that we track a maximum of three roll-up levels, such as the ultimate corporate parent, business unit headquarters, and regional offices (from top to bottom). In this case, we have three distinct attributes in the customer dimension corresponding to these three levels. For commercial customers with complicated organizational hierarchies, we'd populate all three levels to appropriately represent the three different entities involved at each roll-up level. By contrast, if another customer had a much simpler organization structure, such as a one-location corporation, we'd duplicate the lower-level value to populate the higher-level attributes. In this way, all regional offices will sum to the sum of all business unit headquarters, which will sum to the sum of all ultimate corporate parents. We can report by any level of the hierarchy and see the complete customer base represented.

As we acknowledged up front, this simplistic approach doesn't necessarily address real-world complexity adequately; however, we would be remiss in not mentioning it because it does provide a satisfactory solution for some. The technique described next is more robust, but the robustness comes with baggage. In some situations, the more complex method may be impractical or overkill.

Variable-Depth Hierarchies

Representing an arbitrary, ragged organization hierarchy is an inherently difficult task in a relational environment. For example, we may want to report the revenues for a set of commercial customers who have intricate relationships with each other, such as in Figure 6.8. Each square on the diagram represents an individual customer entity connected in an organizational tree. The illustrated organization has four levels; other customer organizations may have one, ten, or more levels. Let's assume that we sell our products or services to any of these commercial customers. Thus the customer dimension rows can play the role of parent as well as child. We may want to look at the customers and their sales revenue individually. At other times, we may want to summarize revenue to any node in the overall organizational tree.

The computer science approach for handling this unpredictable hierarchy would be to include a recursive parent customer key pointer on each customer dimension row. Although this is a compact and effective way to represent an arbitrary hierarchy, this kind of recursive structure cannot be used effectively with standard SQL. The GROUP BY function in SQL cannot follow the recursive tree structure downward to summarize an additive fact in a companion fact table such as revenue in an organization. Oracle's CONNECT BY SQL extension is able to navigate a recursive pointer in a dimension table, but the CONNECT BY phrase cannot be used in the same SQL statement as a join, which prohibits us from connecting a recursive dimension table to any fact table. While we can fool the parser and perform the join by hiding the CONNECT BY in a VIEW declaration, performance likely would suffer significantly.

Instead of using a recursive pointer, we insert a *bridge table* between the customer dimension and fact tables, as depicted in Figure 6.9. The bridge table has been called a *helper* or *associative table* in the past, but going forward, we'll consistently use the bridge terminology. Use of the bridge table is optional; neither the customer dimension table nor the fact table has to be modified in any way. If the bridge table is left out, the customer dimension table joins to the fact table in the usual way. We can report revenue by customer, but we're unable to navigate the organization hierarchy. When the bridge table is inserted between the customer dimension and fact tables, we're able to analyze revenue results at any hierarchical level using standard SQL, albeit via a more complicated presentation.

The bridge table contains one row for each pathway in Figure 6.8 from a customer entity to each subsidiary beneath it, as well as a row for the zero-length pathway

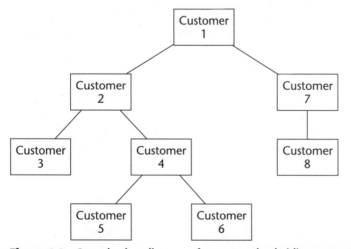

Figure 6.8 Organization diagram of parent and subsidiary companies.

from a customer to itself. Each pathway row contains the customer key of the parent roll-up entity, the customer key of the subsidiary entity, the number of levels between the parent and the subsidiary, a bottom-most flag that identifies a subsidiary with no further nodes beneath it, and finally, a top-most flag to indicate that there are no further nodes above the parent. The sample bridge table rows corresponding to the hierarchy in Figure 6.8 are shown as in Table 6.4.

The number of rows in the bridge table typically is several times larger than the number of rows in the customer dimension. The eight individual parent and subsidiary customers in the Figure 6.8 hierarchy translated into 22 rows in the Table 6.4 bridge table. As an aside, a quick way to calculate the total number of rows for a given customer organization is to multiply the number of values at each level times the depth of the level (counting from the top), and then sum up the resulting products. Let's refer to the Figure 6.8 organization diagram again. At top level 1 of the hierarchy, we have 1 customer (customer 1), which translates into $1 = (1 \times 1)$ row in the bridge table. At the second level, we have 2 customers (customers 2 and 7), which translate into another $4 = (2 \times 2)$ rows in the bridge. At level 3, we have 3 customers (customers 3, 4, and 8), which translate into $9 = (3 \times 3)$ bridge table rows. Finally, at the bottom (fourth) level, we have 2 customers (customers 5 and 6), which translate into an additional $8 = (4 \times 2)$ rows. The sum total number of rows is $22 = (1 + 4 + 9 + 8)$. If you don't believe us, go ahead and count up the number of sample rows in Table 6.4.

When we want to descend the organization hierarchy, we join the tables together as shown in Figure 6.9. We can now constrain the customer table to a particular parent customer and request any aggregate measure of all the subsidiaries at or below that customer. We can use the "# of Levels from Parent" column in the organization bridge table to control the depth of the analysis. Constraining to a value of 1 would give all the direct subsidiaries of the customer. A value greater than zero would give all subsidiary customers but not the original parent. We can use the "Bottom Flag" column to jump directly to all the bottom-most customer entities but omit all higher-level customer entities.

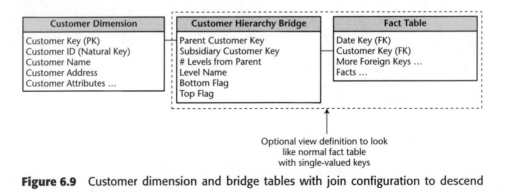

Figure 6.9 Customer dimension and bridge tables with join configuration to descend the tree.

Table 6.4 Sample Bridge Table Rows Corresponding to Hierarchy in Figure 6.8

PARENT CUSTOMER KEY	SUBSIDIARY CUSTOMER KEY	#LEVELS FROM PARENT	BOTTOM FLAG	TOP FLAG
1	1	0	N	Y
1	2	1	N	N
1	3	2	Y	N
1	4	2	N	N
1	5	3	Y	N
1	6	3	Y	N
1	7	1	N	N
1	8	2	Y	N
2	2	0	N	N
2	3	1	Y	N
2	4	1	N	N
2	5	2	Y	N
2	6	2	Y	N
3	3	0	Y	N
4	4	0	N	N
4	5	1	Y	N
4	6	1	Y	N
5	5	0	Y	N
6	6	0	Y	N
7	7	0	N	N
7	8	1	Y	N
8	8	0	Y	N

When we want to ascend the organization hierarchy, we reverse the joins by connecting the customer dimension primary key to the bridge subsidiary key, as shown in Figure 6.10. By constraining the "# of Levels" column in the bridge table to the value of 1, we find the immediate parent of the customer in the customer dimension. When the top-most flag is Y, we have selected the ultimate parent for a given customer.

When issuing SQL statements using the bridge table, we need to be cautious about overcounting the facts. When connecting the tables as shown in Figures 6.9 and 6.10, we must constrain the customer dimension to a single value and then join to the bridge table, which is then joined to the fact table. If we wanted to sum up revenue in the fact table for a given customer and all its subsidiaries, the SQL code would look something like the following:

```
SELECT C.CUSTOMER_NAME, SUM(F.REVENUE)
FROM CUSTOMER C, BRIDGE B, FACT F, DATE D
WHERE C.CUSTOMER_KEY = B.PARENT_KEY
AND B.SUBSIDIARY_KEY = F.CUSTOMER_KEY
AND F.DATE_KEY = D.DATE_KEY //along with joins for other dimensions
AND C.CUSTOMER_NAME = 'ABC General International' //for example
AND D.MONTH = 'January 2002'
GROUP BY C.CUSTOMER_NAME
```

We can request all the revenue from the organizations associated with many parents at once, but we have to get the subsidiary keys distinctly or risk double counting. In the following example we retrieve the January 2002 revenue from all organizations whose parents are located in San Francisco. The SQL code is messier, but it works for both unique and multiple parent customers.

```
SELECT 'San Francisco', SUM(F.REVENUE)
FROM FACT F, DATE D
WHERE F.CUSTOMER_KEY IN
(SELECT DISTINCT B.SUBSIDIARY_KEY
FROM CUSTOMER C, BRIDGE B
      WHERE C.CUSTOMER_KEY = B.PARENT_KEY
        AND C.CUSTOMER_CITY = 'San Francisco') //to sum all SF parents
AND F.DATE_KEY = D.DATE_KEY
AND D.MONTH = 'January 2002'
GROUP BY 'San Francisco'
```

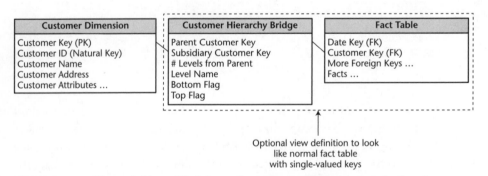

Figure 6.10 Different bridge table join configuration to climb the organizational tree.

There are a number of administrative issues in building and maintaining an organization bridge table. Perhaps the biggest question is, where does the information come from? How do you identify that an organizational change occurred, and then how do you handle the change? If a complete history of changing organizational many-to-many relationships needs to be maintained, then the organization bridge table can be generalized to include effective and expiration dates on each row, as we'll elaborate on in Chapter 13. A most recent indicator to identify the most current organizational roll-up also would be useful. If these dates are administered properly, then every requesting application would have to constrain on a specific date between the effective and expiration dates.

When a group of nodes is moved from one part of an organizational hierarchy to another, only the bridge table rows that refer to paths from outside parents to the moved structure need to be altered. All rows referring to paths within the moved structure are unaffected. Of course, we'd need to add rows if the moved structure had new parentage. This is an advantage over other tree-representation schemas that often require a global renumbering to handle a change such as this.

If two or more parents jointly own a subsidiary, then we can add a weighting factor to the bridge table to reflect the fractional ownership. We'll further elaborate on weighted bridge tables in Chapter 13.

Small and medium-sized parts explosions in a manufacturing application can be modeled using the same kind of bridge table between a part/assembly dimension table and a fact table. The main limitation to using this approach for manufacturing parts explosions is the sheer number of subassemblies and parts. A very large manufacturing parts explosion with hundreds of thousands or millions of parts could result in a bridge table with "more rows than there are molecules in the universe."

Organization hierarchies and parts-explosion hierarchies may be represented with the help of a bridge table. This approach allows the regular SQL grouping and summarizing functions to work through ordinary query tools.

Having made the case for a bridge table to handle recursive variable-depth hierarchies, we'd be the first to admit that it is not a perfect solution. The approach attempts to bridge two inherently distinct structures, fixed rectangular relational tables and free-form hierarchical formations, which is akin to blending oil and water. While the bridge table can be navigated via the standard SQL code generated by many query tools, it is not for the faint of heart. Analytical applications should be preconstructed to shield users from this non-trivial SQL code. Fortunately, a number of nonrelational OLAP tools are providing more robust built-in support for navigating these pesky hierarchies for small to medium-sized dimensions typically with less than 64,000 members.

Combining Multiple Sources of Customer Data

Now that we've designed the customer dimension, it is time to populate it. It is likely that the conformed customer dimension is a distillation of data from several operational systems and possibly outside sources. In the worst case, a unique customer has multiple identifiers in multiple operational touch-point systems. Obviously, one of operational CRM's objectives is create a unique customer identifier and restrict the creation of unnecessary identifiers. In the meantime, the data warehouse team likely will find itself responsible for sorting out and integrating the disparate sources of customer information.

Unfortunately, there's no secret weapon for tackling this data consolidation. The attributes in the customer dimension should represent the best source available for that data in the enterprise. We'll want to integrate a national change of address (NCOA) process to ensure that address changes are captured. Much of the heavy lifting associated with customer data consolidation demands customer-matching or deduplicating logic. Removing duplicates or invalid addresses from large customer lists is critical to eliminating the financial and customer satisfaction costs associated with redundant, misdirected, or undeliverable communications, in addition to avoiding misleading customer counts.

The science of customer matching is more sophisticated than it might first appear. It involves fuzzy logic, address-parsing algorithms, and enormous look-up directories to validate address elements and postal codes, which vary significantly by country. There are specialized commercially available software and service offerings that can perform individual customer or commercial entity matching with remarkable accuracy. Often these products match the address components with standardized census codes, such as state codes, country codes, census tracts, block groups, metropolitan statistical areas (MSAs), and latitude/longitude, which facilitates the merging of external data. As we'll discuss in Chapter 9, there are also householding capabilities that group or link customers who share similar name and address information. Rather than merely performing intrafile matching, some services maintain an enormous external reference file of everyone in the United States to match against. Although these products and services are potentially expensive and complex, it's worthwhile to make the investment if customer matching (as in the foundation of rudimentary CRM) is strategic to your organization. In the end, effective consolidation of customer data depends on a balance of capturing the data as accurately as possible in the source systems coupled with powerful data cleansing/merging tools in the staging process.

Analyzing Customer Data from Multiple Business Processes

As we indicated in earlier chapters, data warehouses should be built process by process, not department by department, on a foundation of conformed dimensions to support cross-process integration. We can imagine querying the sales or support service fact tables to better understand a customer's purchase or service history.

Since the sales and support tables both contain a customer foreign key, we can further imagine joining both fact tables to a common customer dimension to simultaneously summarize sales facts along with support facts for a given customer, as in Figure 6.11. Unfortunately, the many-to-one-to-many join will return the wrong answer in a relational environment because of the differences in fact table cardinality.

Consider the case in which we have a fact table of customer solicitations and another fact table with the customer responses resulting both from the solicitations and other independent sources. There is a one-to-many relationship between customer and solicitation and another one-to-many relationship between customer and response. The solicitation and response fact tables have different cardinalities; in other words, not every solicitation results in a response (unfortunately for the marketing department), and some responses are received for which there is no solicitation. Simultaneously joining the solicitation fact table to the customer dimension, which is in turn joined to the response fact table, does not return the correct answer in a relational DBMS because of the cardinality differences. Fortunately, this problem is easily avoided. We simply issue multipass SQL code to query the solicitation and response tables in separate queries and then outer join the two answer sets. The multipass approach has additional benefits in terms of better controlling performance parameters, in addition to supporting queries that combine data from fact tables in different physical locations.

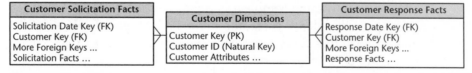

Figure 6.11 Many-to-one-to-many joined tables should *not* be queried with a single SELECT statement.

Be very careful when simultaneously joining a single dimension table to two fact tables of different cardinality. In many cases, relational systems will return the wrong answer. A similar problem arises when joining two fact tables of different granularity together directly.

If users are frequently combining data from multiple business processes, then an additional fact table can be constructed that combines the data once into a second-level, consolidated fact table rather than relying on users to combine the data consistently and accurately on their own. We'll discuss consolidated fact tables further in Chapter 7. Merely using SQL code to drill across fact tables to combine the results makes more sense when the underlying processes are less closely correlated. Of course, when constructing the consolidated fact table, we'd still need to establish business rules to deal with the differing cardinality (for example, does the combined fact table include all the solicitations and responses or only those where both a solicitation and response occurred?).

Summary

In this chapter we focused exclusively on the customer, beginning with an overview of CRM basics. We then delved into design issues surrounding the customer dimension table. We discussed name and address parsing where operational fields are decomposed to their basic elements so that they can be standardized and validated. We explored several other types of common customer dimension attributes, such as dates, segmentation attributes, and aggregated facts. Dimension outriggers that contain a large block of relatively low-cardinality attributes were described as permissible snowflakes in our dimensional designs.

In cases where our customer dimension has millions of rows, we recommended creating a minidimension of frequently analyzed or frequently changing attributes. A minidimension is also appropriate for variable-width attribute sets. The fact table then has two customer-related foreign keys, one for the primary customer dimension and another for the minidimension. We discussed the implications of counting within a customer dimension where additional type 2 rows are created to handle change. We also explored the notion of creating behavioral study group dimensions, which merely consist of customer keys that share a common trait or experience. Finally, we tackled the handling of simple and complex commercial customer hierarchies. The unpredictable, variable-depth customer hierarchies commonly require the use of a bridge table to reflect the recursive hierarchy in a manner that can be queried by standard SQL code.

We briefly discussed the use of external software and service offerings to consolidate customer information effectively while managing duplicate data. Finally, we stepped back into the world of fact tables for a moment to discuss the potential downfalls of querying across two fact tables joined through a common customer dimension table.

Accounting

Financial analysis spans a variety of accounting applications, including the general ledger and detailed subledgers for purchasing and accounts payable, invoicing and accounts receivable, and fixed assets. Since we've already touched on purchase orders and invoices in this book, we'll focus on the general ledger in this chapter. General ledgers were one of the first applications to be computerized decades ago, given the need for accurate handling of a company's financial records. Perhaps some of you are still running your business on a twenty-year-old ledger system. In this chapter we'll discuss the data collected by the general ledger in terms of both journal entry transactions and snapshots at the close of an accounting period. We'll also talk about the budgeting process.

Chapter 7 discusses the following concepts:

- **General ledger periodic snapshots and transactions**
- **Year-to-date facts**
- **Multiple fiscal accounting calendars**
- **Budgeting process and associated data, including net change granularity**
- **Consolidated fact tables that combine metrics from multiple business processes, such as actual and budget data**
- **Role of online analytic processing (OLAP) and packaged analytic financial solutions**

Accounting Case Study

Since finance was an early adopter of technology to better run businesses, it comes as no surprise that early decision support solutions focused on the analysis of financial data. Financial analysts are some of the most data-literate and spreadsheet-savvy individuals around. Often their analysis is disseminated or leveraged by many others in an organization. Managers at all levels need timely access to key financial metrics. In addition to receiving standard reports, managers need the ability to analyze performance trends, variances, and anomalies with relative speed and minimal effort. Unfortunately, the backlog of special requests for financial data is often quite lengthy. As we observe frequently in operational source systems, the data in the general ledger is likely scattered among hundreds of tables. Gaining access to financial data and creating ad hoc reports may require a decoder ring to navigate through the maze of screens. This runs counter to the objective of many organizations to push fiscal responsibility and accountability to line managers.

The data warehouse can provide a single source of usable, understandable financial information, ensuring that everyone is working with the same data based on common definitions and metrics. The audience for financial data is quite diverse in many organizations, ranging from analysts to operational managers to executives. For each group, we need to determine which subset of corporate financial data is needed, in which format, and with what frequency. Analysts and managers will want to view information at a high level and then drill down to journal entries for more detail. For executives, financial data from the data warehouse often feeds their dashboard or scorecard of key performance indicators. Armed with direct access to information, managers can obtain answers to questions more readily than when forced to work through an intermediary. Meanwhile, the finance department can turn its attention to information dissemination and value-added analysis rather than focusing on report creation.

The benefits of improved access to financial data focus on opportunities to better manage risk, streamline operations, and identify potential cost savings. While financial analysis has cross-organization impact, many businesses focus their initial data warehouse implementation on strategic revenue-generating opportunities. Consequently, accounting data is often not the very first subject area tackled by the data warehouse team. Given its proficiency with technology, the finance department often has already performed magic with spreadsheets and personal databases to create work-around analytic solutions, perhaps to its short-term detriment, since these imperfect interim fixes likely are stressed to the limits.

General Ledger Data

The general ledger (G/L) is a core foundation financial system because it ties together the detailed information collected by the purchasing, payables (what you owe to others), and receivables (what others owe you) subledgers or systems. In this case study we'll focus on the general ledger rather than the subledgers, which would be handled as separate business processes and fact tables. As we work through a basic design for G/L data, we discover, once again, that two complementary schemas with periodic snapshot and transaction-grained fact tables working together are required.

General Ledger Periodic Snapshot

We begin by delving into a snapshot of the G/L accounts at the end of each fiscal period (or month if your fiscal accounting periods align with calendar months). Referring once again to our four-step process for designing dimensional models, the business process obviously focuses on the G/L. The grain of this periodic snapshot is one row per accounting period for the most granular level in the G/L's chart of accounts.

Chart of Accounts

The cornerstone of the G/L is the chart of accounts. The G/L's chart of accounts is the epitome of an intelligent key because it usually consists of a series of identifiers. For example, the first set of digits may identify the account, account type (for example, asset, liability, equity, income, or expense), and other account roll-ups. Sometimes intelligence is embedded in the account numbering scheme. For example, account numbers from 1,000 through 1,999 might be asset accounts, whereas account numbers ranging from 2,000 to 2,999 may identify liabilities. Obviously, in the data warehouse, we'd include the account type as a dimension attribute rather than forcing users to filter on the first digit of the account number.

The chart of accounts also likely provides insight regarding the organizational cost center associated with the account. Typically, the organizational elements provide a complete roll-up from cost center to department to division, for example. If the corporate G/L combines data across multiple business units, the chart of accounts also would indicate the business unit or subsidiary company.

Obviously, charts of accounts vary from company to company. They're often extremely complicated. In our case study vignette we assume that the chart of accounts naturally decomposes into two dimensions. One dimension focuses on the attributes of the financial G/L account, whereas the other represents the organizational roll-up. The organization roll-up may be a fixed-depth hierarchy, where we can handle the hierarchy levels as separate attributes in the organization cost center dimension. If the organizational hierarchy is ragged with imbalanced roll-up trees, then we'll need to resort to the bridge table technique from Chapter 6 for dealing with variable-depth hierarchies.

The G/L sometimes tracks financial results for multiple sets of books or subledgers to support different requirements, such as taxation or regulatory agency reporting. We'll treat this as a separate dimension because it is such a fundamental filter.

Period Close

At the end of each accounting period, the finance organization is responsible for finalizing the financial results so that they can be officially reported internally and externally. It typically takes several days at the end of each period to reconcile and balance the books before they can be closed with the finance department's official stamp of approval. From there, finance's focus turns to reporting and interpreting the results. The finance department often produces countless reports and responds to countless variations on the same questions each month.

Financial analysts are constantly looking to streamline the processes for period-end closing, reconciliation, and reporting of G/L results. While operational G/L systems often support these requisite capabilities, they may be cumbersome, especially if you're not dealing with a modern G/L. In this chapter we'll focus on more easily analyzing the closed financial results rather than facilitating the close. However, in many organizations, G/L trial balances are loaded into the data warehouse to leverage the capabilities of the data warehouse's presentation area to find the needles in the G/L haystack and then make the appropriate operational adjustments before the period ends.

The sample schema in Figure 7.1 supports the access and analysis of G/L account balances at the end of each account period. It would be very useful for many kinds of financial analysis, such as account rankings, trending patterns, and period-to-period comparisons.

For the moment, we're just representing actual facts in the Figure 7.1 schema; we'll turn our attention to budget data later in this chapter. Obviously, the balance amount is a semiadditive fact. Although we typically attempt to avoid semiadditive facts, it makes sense to store the balance in this schema because many of the accounts are tracked as a balance. Otherwise, we'd need to go back to the beginning of time to calculate an accurate end-of-period balance.

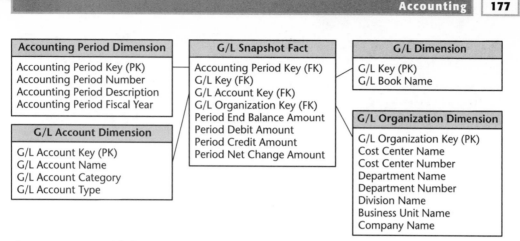

Figure 7.1 General ledger (G/L) periodic snapshot.

Year-to-Date Facts

Designers are often tempted to store *to-date* columns in fact tables. They think that it would be helpful to store quarter-to-date or year-to-date totals on each fact row so that users don't need to calculate them. We need to remember that numeric facts must be consistent with the grain. To-date fields are not true to the grain and are fraught with peril. When fact rows are queried and summarized in arbitrary ways, these untrue-to-the-grain facts produce nonsensical, overstated results. They should be left out of the relational schema design and calculated in the data access application instead.

> **In general, to-date totals should be calculated, not stored in the fact table.**

Multiple Currencies Revisited

If the general ledger consolidates data that has been captured in multiple currencies, we would handle it much as we discussed in Chapter 5. With financial data, we typically want to represent the facts in terms of both the local currency and a standardized corporate currency. In this case, each row in the fact table would represent one set of fact amounts expressed in local currency and a separate set of fact amounts expressed in the equivalent corporate currency. Doing so allows us to summarize the facts in a common corporate currency easily without jumping through hoops in our access applications. Of course, we'd also add a currency dimension as a foreign key in the fact table to identify the local currency type.

General Ledger Journal Transactions

While the end-of-period snapshot addresses a multitude of financial analyses, many users need to dive into the underlying details. If the periodic snapshot

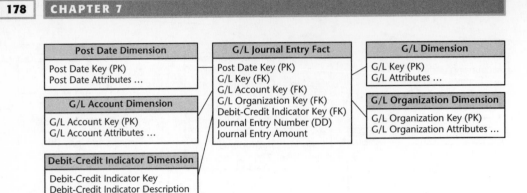

Figure 7.2 General ledger (G/L) journal entry transactions.

data appears unusual or not as expected, analysts will want to look at the detailed transactions to sort through the issue. Others will want access to the details because the summarized monthly balances may obscure large disparities at the granular transaction level. Once again, we complement the periodic snapshot with a detailed journal entry transaction schema. Of course, the accounts payable and receivable subledgers may contain transactions at even lower levels of detail, which would be captured in separate fact tables with additional dimensionality.

In this situation we're still focused on the G/L process; however, the grain of the fact table is now one row for every G/L journal entry transaction. The journal entry transaction identifies the G/L account and the applicable debit or credit amount. As illustrated in Figure 7.2, we'll reuse several dimensions from the last schema, including the account and organization dimensions. If our G/L tracked multiple sets of books, we'd also include the ledger dimension. We're capturing journal entry transactions by transaction posting date, so we'll use a daily-grained date table in this schema. Depending on the business rules associated with the source data, we may need a second role-playing date dimension to distinguish the posting date from the effective accounting date.

The journal entry number likely is a degenerate dimension with no linkage to an associated dimension table. Depending on the source data, we may have a journal entry transaction type and even a description. In this situation we'd create a separate journal entry transaction dimension. Assuming that the descriptions are not just freeform text, this dimension would have significantly fewer rows than the fact table, which would have one row per journal entry line. The specific journal entry number would still be treated as degenerate.

Fact Types

Each row in the journal entry fact table would be identified as either a credit or a debit. Given this inherent sparsity, we'd likely store a single journal entry amount with a debit/credit indicator, unless we're using a database platform, such as Oracle, which supports variable-width columns so that the empty columns take up minimal disk space. The debit/credit indicator would take on two and only two values. We can create a two-row debit/credit decode dimension table, or if your database supports bit-mapped indices, we may just include the industry-standard debit/credit abbreviation (DR/CR) in the fact table with a bit-mapped index for speedy filtering or constraining. We don't want you to perceive that this is an excuse to bypass dimension table decode tables for all low-cardinality dimensions. It makes sense in this case because the abbreviations are understood universally, which isn't usually the case with our internal codes and abbreviations. Ninety-nine percent of the time we'll continue to create dimension tables that contain textual, descriptive decodes.

Multiple Fiscal Accounting Calendars

In this schema we're capturing data by posting date, but users likely also want the ability to summarize the data by fiscal account period. Unfortunately, fiscal accounting periods often do not align with standard Gregorian calendar months. For example, a company may have 13 four-week accounting periods in a fiscal year beginning on September 1 rather than 12 monthly periods beginning on January 1. If we're dealing with a single fiscal calendar, then each day in a year corresponds to a single calendar month, as well as a single accounting period. Given these relationships, the calendar and accounting periods are merely hierarchical attributes on the daily date dimension, as we saw in Chapter 2. The daily date dimension table obviously would conform to a calendar month dimension table, as well as to a fiscal accounting period dimension table.

In other situations we may be dealing with multiple fiscal accounting calendars that vary by subsidiary or line of business. If the number of unique fiscal calendars is a fixed, low number, then we can include each set of uniquely labeled fiscal calendar attributes on a single date dimension. A given row in the daily date dimension could be identified as belonging to accounting period 1 for subsidiary A, but accounting period 7 for subsidiary B.

In a more complex situation with a large number of different fiscal calendars, we could identify the official corporate fiscal calendar in the date dimension. We then have several options to address the subsidiary-specific fiscal calendars. The most common approach is to create a date dimension outrigger with a multipart key consisting of the date and subsidiary keys. There would be one row in this table for each day for each subsidiary. The attributes in this outrigger would consist of fiscal groupings (such as fiscal week end date and fiscal period end date). We'd need a mechanism for filtering on a specific subsidiary in the outrigger. Doing so through a view would then allow the outrigger to be presented as if it were logically part of the date dimension table. A second approach for tackling the subsidiary-specific calendars would be to create separate physical date dimensions, instead of views, for each subsidiary calendar using common set of surrogate date keys. This option likely would be used if your fact data were decentralized by subsidiary. Depending on your data access tool's capabilities, it may be easier to either filter on the subsidiary outrigger as described in the first option or ensure use of the appropriate subsidiary-specific physical date dimension table (the second option). Finally, we could allocate another foreign key in the fact table to a subsidiary fiscal period dimension table. The number of rows in this table would be the number of fiscal periods (approximately 36 for three years) times the number of unique calendars. This approach simplifies user access but puts additional strain on the staging area because it must insert the appropriate fiscal period key during the transformation process.

Financial Statements

One of the primary functions of a G/L system is to produce the organization's official financial reports, such as the balance sheet and income statement. Typically, the operational system handles the production of these reports. We wouldn't want the data warehouse to attempt to replace the reports published by the operational financial system.

However, data warehouse teams sometimes create a complementary database of aggregated data to provide simplified access to report information that can be more widely disseminated throughout the organization. Dimensions in the financial statement database would include the accounting period and cost center. Rather than looking at G/L account-level data, the fact data would be aggregated and tagged with the appropriate financial statement line number and label. In this manner, managers could easily look at performance trends for a given line in the financial statement over time for their organization. Similarly, key performance indicators and financial ratios may be made available at the same level of detail.

Budgeting Process

Modern G/L systems typically include the ability to integrate budget data into the G/L. However, if our G/L either lacks this capability or we've elected not to implement it, we need to provide an alternative mechanism for supporting the budgeting process and variance comparisons.

Within most organizations, the budgeting process is looked at as a series of events. Prior to the start of a fiscal year, each cost center manager typically creates a budget, broken down by budget line items, which is then approved. In reality, budgeting is seldom simply a once-per-year event any more. Budgets are becoming more dynamic because there are budget adjustments as the year progresses, reflecting changes in business conditions or the realities of actual spending versus the original budget. Managers want to see the current budget's status, as well as how the budget has been altered since the first approved version. As the year unfolds, commitments to spend the budgeted monies are made. Finally, payments are processed.

As dimensional modelers, we view the budgeting chain as a series of fact tables. We'll begin with a budget fact table. For an expense budget line item, each row identifies what an organization in the company is allowed to spend for what purpose during a given time frame. Similarly, if the line item reflects an income forecast, which is just another variation of a budget, it would identify what an organization intends to earn from what source during a time frame.

We could further identify the grain to be a status snapshot of each line item in each budget each month. Although this grain has a familiar ring to it (because it feels like a management report), it is a poor choice as the fact table grain. The facts in such a status report are all semiadditive balances rather than fully additive facts. Also, this grain makes it difficult to determine how much has changed since the previous month or quarter because we have to obtain the records from several time periods and then subtract them from each other. Finally, this grain choice would require the fact table to contain many duplicated records when nothing changes in successive months for a given line item.

Instead, the grain we're interested in is the net change of the budget line item in a cost center that occurred during the month. While this suffices for budget reporting purposes, the accountants eventually will need to tie to the budget line item back to a specific G/L account that is affected, so we'll also go down to the G/L account level.

Given the grain, the associated dimensions would include effective month, organization, budget line item, and G/L account, as illustrated in Figure 7.3. The organization dimension is identical to the one used earlier with the G/L data. The G/L dimension is also a reused dimension. The only complication regarding the G/L account dimension is that sometimes a single budget line item has an impact on more than one G/L account. In such a case, we would need to allocate the budget line to the individual G/L accounts. Since the grain of the budget fact table is by G/L account, a single budget line for a cost center may be represented as several rows in the fact table.

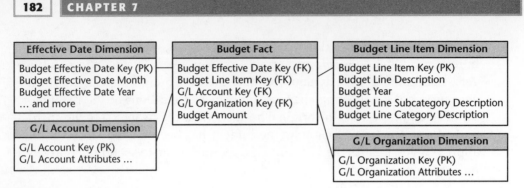

Figure 7.3 Annual budget schema.

The budget line item identifies the purpose of the proposed spending, such as employee wages or office supplies. Typically, several levels of summarization categories are associated with a budget line item. As we discussed in Chapter 5, all the budget line items may not have the same number of levels in their summarization hierarchy, such as when some have only a category roll-up but not a subcategory. In this case we may populate the dimension attributes by replicating the category name in the subcategory column to avoid having line items roll up to a "Not Applicable" subcategory bucket. The budget line-item dimension also would identify the budget year and budget version.

The effective month is the month during which the budget changes are posted. The first entries for a given budget year would show the effective month when the budget is first approved. If the budget is updated or modified as the budget year gets underway, the effective months would occur during the budget year. If we don't adjust the budget at all throughout the year, then the only entries would be the first ones when the budget is approved. This is what we meant when we specified the grain to be the net change. It is critical that you understand this point, or you won't understand what is in this budget fact table or how it is used.

Sometimes budgets are created as annual spending plans; at other times they're broken down by month or by quarter. The schema in Figure 7.3 assumes that the budget is an annual figure, with the budget year identified in the budget line-item dimension. If we need to express the budget data by spending month, we would need to include a second month dimension table that plays the role of spending month.

The budget fact table has a single budget amount fact that is fully additive. If we're budgeting for a multinational organization, the budget amount may be tagged with the expected currency conversion factor for planning purposes. If the budget amount for a given budget line and G/L account is modified during the year, an additional row is added to the budget fact table representing the net change. For example, if the original budget was $200,000, we might have another row in June for a $40,000 increase and then another in October for a negative $25,000 as we tighten our belts going into year-end.

Once the budget year begins, managers make commitments to spend the budget through purchase orders, work orders, or other forms of contracts. Managers are keenly interested in monitoring their commitments and comparing them with the annual budget in order to manage their spending. We can envision a second fact table for the commitments that shares the same dimensions, in addition to dimensions identifying the specific commitment document (purchase order, work order, or contract) and commitment party. In this case the fact would be the committed amount.

Finally, payments are made as monies are transferred to the party named in the commitment. From a practical point of view, the money is no longer available in the budget when the commitment is made. However, the finance department is interested in the relationship between commitments and payments because it manages the company's cash. The dimensions associated with the payments fact table would include the commitment fact table dimensions plus a payment dimension to identify the type of payment and the payee to whom the payment actually was made. In the budgeting chain we expand the list of dimensions as we move from the budget to commitments to payments.

With this design, we can create a number of interesting analyses. To look at the current budgeted amount by department and line item, we constrain on all dates up to the present, adding the amounts by department and line item. Because the grain is the net change in the line items, adding up all the entries over time does exactly the right thing. We end up with the current approved budget amount, and we get exactly those line items in the given departments which have a budget.

To ask for all the changes to the budget for various line items, we simply constrain on a single month. We'll report only those line items which experienced a change during the month.

To compare current commitments with the current budget, we separately sum the commitment amounts and budget amounts from the beginning of time to the current date (or any date of interest). We then combine the two answer sets on the row headers. This is a standard drill-across application using multipass SQL. Similarly, we could drill across commitments and payments.

If you're interested in reading more about building and using the budgeting chain, we recommend *Data Warehouse Design Solutions* (Wiley 1998) by Chris Adamson and Mike Venerable.

Consolidated Fact Tables

In the last section we discussed users comparing metrics generated by separate business processes by drilling across fact tables, such as budget and commitments. If this type of drill-across analysis is extremely common in the user community, it likely makes sense to create a single fact table that combines the metrics once rather than relying on users or their reporting applications to stitch together result sets, especially given the inherent issues of complexity, accuracy, tool capabilities, and performance.

Most typically, business managers are interested in comparing actual to budget variances. At this point we presume that our annual budgets and/or forecasts have been broken down by accounting period. In Figure 7.4 we see the actual and budget amounts, as well as the variance (which is a calculated difference) by the common dimensions. As we discussed earlier, we deliver the to-date fields by leveraging the roll-up attributes on the accounting period dimension.

Again, if we're working for a multinational organization, we likely would see the actual amounts in both local and equivalent standard currency, based on the effective conversion rate. In addition, we may convert the actual results based on the planned currency conversion factor (as described during the budget process). Given the unpredictable nature of currency fluctuations, it is useful to monitor performance based on both the effective and planned conversion rates. In this manner, remote managers aren't penalized for currency rate changes outside their control. Likewise, the finance department can better understand the big-picture impact of unexpected currency conversion fluctuations on the organization's annual plan.

As we introduced in Chapter 3, we refer to fact tables that combine metrics at a common granularity as *consolidated* or *second-level fact tables* (or *consolidated data marts*). While consolidated fact tables can be very useful in terms of both performance and usability, they often represent a dimensionality compromise because they consolidate facts at the least common denominator set of dimensions. One potential risk associated with consolidated fact tables is that project teams sometimes base their designs solely on the granularity of the consolidated fact table while failing to meet user requirements that demand the ability to dive into more granular data. These schemas also run into serious problems if project teams attempt to force a one-to-one correspondence in order to consolidate data with different granularity or dimensionality.

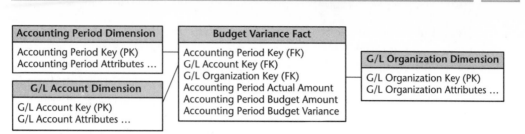

Figure 7.4 Actual versus budget consolidated fact table.

> When facts from multiple business processes are combined in a consolidated fact table, they must live at the same level of granularity and dimensionality. Optimally, the separate facts naturally live at a common grain. Otherwise, we are forced to eliminate or aggregate some dimensions to support the one-to-one correspondence or keep them in separate fact tables. Project teams should not create artificial facts or dimensions in an attempt to force fit the consolidation of differently grained fact data.

Role of OLAP and Packaged Analytic Solutions

While we've been discussing financial data warehouses in the context of relational databases, it is worth noting that multidimensional OLAP vendors have long played a role in this arena. OLAP products have been used extensively for financial reporting, budgeting, and consolidation applications. We often see relational dimensional models feeding financial OLAP data cubes. OLAP cubes are precalculated, which results in fast query performance that is critical for executive use. The data volumes, especially for the G/L balances or financial statement aggregates, typically do not overwhelm the practical size constraints of a multidimensional product. OLAP is well suited to handle complicated organizational roll-ups, as well as complex calculations, including interrow manipulations. Most multidimensional OLAP vendors provide finance-specific capabilities, such as financial functions (for example, net present value or compound growth), the appropriate handling of financial statement data (in the expected sequential order, such as income before expenses), and the proper treatment of debits and credits depending on the account type, as well as more advanced functions such as financial consolidation.

Given the standard nature of G/L processing, purchasing a G/L package rather than attempting to build one from scratch has been a popular route for years. Nearly all the operational package providers also offer a complementary analytic solution, sometimes in partnership with one of the multidimensional OLAP vendors. In many cases these canned analyses based on the cumulative experience of the vendor are a sound way to jump-start a financial data warehouse implementation with potentially reduced cost and risk. The analytic solutions often have tools to assist with the extraction and staging of operational financial data, as well as tools to assist with analysis and interpretation. However, as we discussed in Chapter 6, when leveraging packaged solutions, we need to be cautious about avoiding stovepipe applications. One could easily find oneself in a situation with separate financial, CRM, human resources, and ERP packaged analytic solutions from as many different vendors, none of which integrates with other internal data. We need to conform dimensions across the entire data warehouse environment regardless of whether we're building our own solution or implementing packages. Packaged analytic solutions can turbocharge your data warehouse implementation; however, they do not alleviate the need for conformance. Most organizations inevitably will rely on a combination of building, buying, and integrating for a complete solution.

Summary

In this chapter we focused primarily on financial G/L data in terms of both periodic snapshots and journal entry transactions. We discussed the handling of common G/L data challenges, including multiple currencies, multiple fiscal years, unbalanced organizational trees, and the urge to create to-date totals.

We explored the series of events in a budgeting process chain. We described the use of net-change granularity in this situation rather than creating snapshots of the budget data totals. We also discussed the concept of consolidated fact tables that combine the results of separate business processes when they are analyzed together frequently.

Finally, we discussed the natural fit of multidimensional OLAP products for financial analysis. We also stressed the importance of integrating analytic packages into the overall data warehouse through the use of conformed dimensions.

Human Resources Management

This chapter, which focuses on human resources (HR) data, is the last in the series that deals with cross-industry business applications. Similar to the accounting and finance data described in Chapter 7, HR information is disseminated broadly throughout the organization. Unlike finance, however, we typically don't find a cadre of tech-savvy HR analysts in many organizations.

Most of us operate in a rapidly changing, competitive business environment. We need to better understand our employees' demographics, skills, earnings, and performance in order to maximize their impact. In this chapter we'll explore several dimensional modeling techniques in the context of HR data.

Chapter 8 discusses the following concepts:

- **Dimension tables to track employee transaction facts**
- **Audit dimension**
- **Skill-set keyword dimension outrigger**
- **Handling of survey questionnaire data**

Time-Stamped Transaction Tracking in a Dimension

Thus far the dimensional models we have designed closely resemble each other in that the fact tables have contained key performance metrics that typically can be added across all the dimensions. It is easy for dimensional modelers to get lulled into a kind of *additive complacency*. In most cases, this is exactly how it is supposed to work. However, with HR employee data, many of the facts aren't additive. Most of the facts aren't even numbers, yet they are changing all the time.

To frame the problem with a business vignette, let's assume that we work in the HR department of a large enterprise with more than 100,000 employees. Each employee has a detailed HR profile with at least 100 attributes, including date of hire, job grade, salary, review dates, review outcomes, vacation entitlement, organization, education, address, insurance plan, and many others. In our organization there is a stream of transactions against this employee data. Employees are constantly being hired, transferred, and promoted, as well as adjusting their profiles in a variety of ways.

The highest-priority business requirement is to track and analyze these employee transaction events accurately. This detailed transaction history is the fundamental truth of HR data; it should provide the answer to every possible employee profile inquiry. While these unanticipated questions may be complex, we must be confident the data is available and waiting to be analyzed.

We immediately visualize a schema as depicted in Figure 8.1 where each employee transaction event is captured in a transaction-grained fact table. The granularity of this fact table would be one row per employee transaction. Since no numeric metrics are associated with the transaction, the fact table is factless. The measurements associated with employee transactions are the changes made to the employee profile, such as a new address or job grade promotion.

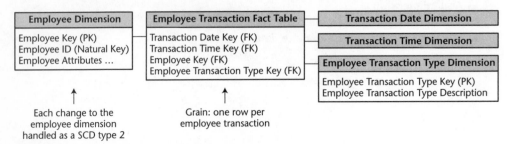

Figure 8.1   Initial draft for tracking employee change transactions.

In this initial draft schema, the dimensions include the transaction date and time, transaction type, and employee. The transaction date and time dimensions refer to the exact date and time of the employee transaction. We assume that these dates and times are fine-grained enough that they guarantee uniqueness of the transaction row for a given employee. The transaction type dimension refers to the variety of transaction that caused the creation of this particular row, such as a promotion or address change. The employee dimension is extremely wide with many attribute columns. The employee identifier used in the HR production system as a constant identifier for the employee is included in this dimension table as an attribute.

We envision using the type 2 slowly changing dimension technique for tracking changed profile attributes in the employee dimension. Consequently, with every employee transaction in the fact table in Figure 8.1, we also create a new type 2 row in the employee dimension that represents the employee's profile as a result of the transaction event. It continues to accurately describe the employee until the next employee transaction occurs at some indeterminate time in the future. The alert reader is quick to point out that we've designed an employee transaction fact table and a type 2 employee dimension table with the exact same number of rows, which are almost always joined to one another. At this point dimensional modeling alarms should be going off. We certainly don't want to have as many rows in a fact table as we do in a related dimension table.

Instead of using the initial schema, we can simplify the design by embellishing the employee dimension table to make it more powerful and thereby doing away with the transaction event fact table. As depicted in Figure 8.2, the employee transaction dimension contains a snapshot of the employee profile following each individual employee transaction. We included the transaction type description in the employee dimension to track the reason for the profile change. There is no numeric metric associated with a profile transaction; the transaction merely results in a new set of employee profile characteristics. In some cases, the affected characteristics are numeric. If the numeric attributes are summarized rather than simply constrained upon, they belong in a fact table instead.

As you'd expect, the surrogate employee transaction key is the primary key of the dimension table, although the natural key is the constant employee ID. We resist the urge to rely on a smart key consisting of the employee ID, transaction code, and transaction date/time. All these attributes are valuable, but they are simply columns in the employee transaction row that participate in queries and constraints like all the other attribute columns.

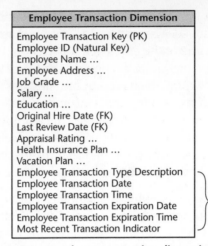

Employee Transaction Dimension

Employee Transaction Key (PK)
Employee ID (Natural Key)
Employee Name ...
Employee Address ...
Job Grade ...
Salary ...
Education ...
Original Hire Date (FK)
Last Review Date (FK)
Appraisal Rating ...
Health Insurance Plan ...
Vacation Plan ...
Employee Transaction Type Description
Employee Transaction Date
Employee Transaction Time   } Indicates the transaction that caused
Employee Transaction Expiration Date   another Employee row to be created
Employee Transaction Expiration Time
Most Recent Transaction Indicator

Figure 8.2 Employee transaction dimension.

A crucial component of this design is the second date and time entry, the transaction expiration date/time. This date/time represents the date/time of the *next* transaction to occur for this employee, whenever that may be. In this way these two date/times in each row define a span during which the employee profile is accurate. The two date/times can be one second apart (if a rapid sequence of transactions is being processed against an employee profile) or many months apart. The transaction expiration date/time in the most current employee profile must be set to an arbitrary time in the future. Although it would seem more elegant to set the expiration date for this row to null, this probably would make the query and reporting applications more complex because they might have to test separately for the null value.

The most recent transaction indicator identifies the latest transaction made against an employee profile. This column allows the most recent or final status of any employee to be retrieved quickly. If a new profile transaction occurs for this employee, the indicator in the former profile row needs to be updated to indicate that it is no longer the latest transaction.

Even in a large organization, this approach doesn't require significant storage. Assume that we have 100,000 employees and perform an average of 10 HR profile transactions on each employee each year. Even if we have a verbose 2,000-byte transaction row, 5 years of profile data only adds up to 10 GB (5 years x 100,000 employees x 2,000 bytes x 10 transactions per year) of raw data in the employee transaction dimension.

On its own, this time-stamped type 2 employee transaction dimension can answer a number of interesting HR inquiries. We obviously can use this table to look in detail at the sequence of transactions against any given employee. We can easily profile the employee population at any precise instant in time. We can choose an exact date at any historical point in time and ask how many employees we have and what their detailed profiles were on that date by constraining the date and time to be equal to or greater than the transaction date/time and less than the transaction expiration date/time. The query can perform counts and constraints against all the rows returned from these date constraints. Given that the dimension rows are snapshots in their own right, we avoid sifting through a complex set of transactions in sequence to construct a snapshot for a particular date in the past.

Adding effective and expiration date/time stamps, along with a transaction description, on each row can embellish the design of a type 2 slowly changing dimension to allow very precise time slicing of the dimension by itself.

Before rushing into this design for an HR application, we need to be thoughtful about the transaction dimension. The underlying HR source system may have a very complex notion of a transaction that isn't really what we want in the data warehouse. For instance, an employee promotion may be implemented in the source system by many microtransactions corresponding to each change in an individual field on the employee record. We don't want to see this detail in the data warehouse. Rather, we want to encapsulate the whole series of microtransactions from the underlying source system and treat them all as a super transaction called *employee promotion*. The new record in our type 2 employee dimension reflects all the relevant changed fields in one step. Identifying these supertransactions may be tricky. Perhaps the best way to identify them is to make sure that there is a field on the HR operational application that captures the high-level action.

Time-Stamped Dimension with Periodic Snapshot Facts

Some of you may be wondering if the employee transaction dimension table isn't really a kind of fact table because it is time-stamped. While technically this may be true, this employee transaction table mainly contains textual values; it is the primary source of query constraints and report labels. Thus it is proper to think of this table as a dimension table that serves as the entry point into the HR fact tables. The employee transaction table can be used with any fact table that requires an employee dimension as long as the employee surrogate key is extended to be the employee transaction surrogate key.

In addition to profiling the employee base in HR, we also need to report summary statuses of the employee base on a regular, monthly basis. We're interested in counts, statistics, and totals, including such things as number of employees, total salary paid during the month, vacation days taken, vacation days accrued, number of new hires, and number of promotions. We want to analyze the data by all possible slices, including time and organization. We need to access totals at the end of each month, even when there is no transaction activity in a given employee's profile during that month.

As shown in Figure 8.3, the HR periodic snapshot consists of a fairly ordinary looking fact table with three dimensions: month, employee transaction, and organization. The month dimension table contains the usual descriptors for the corporate calendar at the month grain. The employee transaction key in a fact table row is the employee transaction key that was effective on the last day of the given reporting month. This guarantees that the month-end report is a correct depiction of all the employee profiles. The organization dimension contains a description of the organization to which the employee belongs at the close of the relevant month.

The facts in this HR snapshot consist of monthly numeric summaries that are difficult to calculate from the underlying transactions. These monthly counts and totals satisfy the bulk of management's inquiries regarding monthly employee statistics. All the facts are additive across all the dimensions or dimension attributes, except for the facts labeled as balances. These balances, like all balances, are semiadditive and must be averaged across the time dimension after adding across the other dimensions.

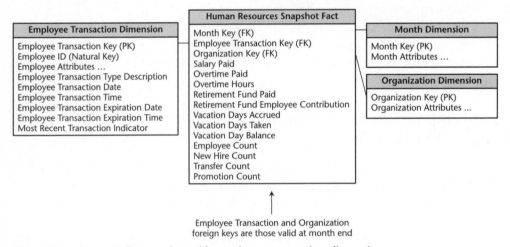

Figure 8.3 HR periodic snapshot with employee transaction dimension.

Audit Dimension

Whenever we build a fact table containing measurements of our business, we surround the fact table with everything we know to be true. We can extend this everything-we-know approach to our fact tables by including key pieces of metadata that are known to be true when an individual fact row is created. For instance, when we create a fact table row, we know the following:

- What source system supplied the fact data
- What version of the extract software created the row
- What version of allocation logic, if any, was used to create the row
- Whether a specific "Not Applicable" fact column is unknown, impossible, corrupted, or not available yet
- Whether a specific fact was altered after the initial load and, if so, why
- Whether the row contains facts more than 2, 3, or 4 standard deviations from the mean or, equivalently, outside various bounds of confidence derived from some other statistical analysis

The first three items describe the lineage of the fact table row; in other words, where did the data come from? The last three items describe our confidence in the quality of data for that fact table row. As illustrated in Figure 8.4, the most efficient way to add this information to a fact table is to create a single audit foreign key in the fact table. The beauty of this design is that the data staging lineage and confidence metadata has now become regular data, which can be queried and analyzed along with the other more familiar dimensions.

The indicators in the audit dimension consist of textual decodes. We are going to constrain and report on these various audit attributes, so we want them to appear as understandable text. Perhaps the extract software attribute might contain the value "Employee extract version 5 using ETL vendorABC release 6.4." The altered status attribute might contain values such as "Not altered" or "Altered due to restatement." In our staging extract-transformation-load (ETL) process, we track these indicators and have them ready when the fact table row is being assembled in its final state. If we are loading a large number of rows each day, almost all the rows will have the same audit foreign key because presumably nearly all the rows will be normal.

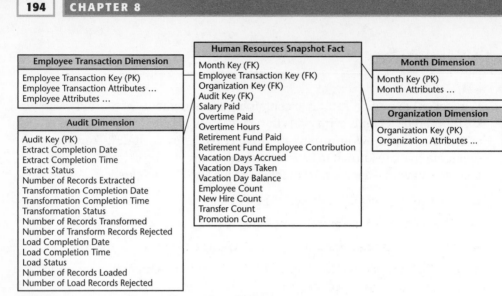

Figure 8.4 HR periodic snapshot with audit dimension.

Keyword Outrigger Dimension

Let's assume that the IT department wants to supplement the employee dimension with descriptive technical skill-set information. The department wants to be able to determine any and all of the key technical skills in which an employee is proficient. It is highly likely that many IT employees have expertise in a wide variety of skills. We can consider these technical skills to be keywords that describe our employees. There will be a number of different keywords, but there will be predictability or structure to them. Some keywords will describe programming languages (for example, Cobol, C++, and Pascal), whereas others will describe operating systems (for example, Unix, Windows, and Linux) or database platforms. We want to search the IT employee population by these descriptive keywords, which we will label as skills in our design.

Since each employee will have a variable, unpredictable number of skills, the skills dimension is a prime candidate to be a multivalued dimension. Keywords, by their nature, usually are open-ended. New keywords are created regularly and added to the database. We'll show two logically equivalent modeling schemes for handling open-ended sets of keywords while at the same time keeping both querying and administration simple. Figure 8.5 shows a multivalued dimension design for handling the skills keywords as an

Figure 8.5 Skills group keyword dimension outrigger.

outrigger to the employee dimension table. As we'll see in Chapter 13 when we further elaborate on multivalued dimension attributes, sometimes the multivalued dimension is joined directly to a fact table.

The skills group identifies a given set of skills keywords. All IT employees who are proficient in Oracle, Unix, and SQL would be assigned the same skills group key. In the skills group outrigger, there would be three rows for this particular group, one for each of the associated keyword skills (Oracle, Unix, and SQL). In this case, just two attributes are associated with each skill, description and category, so we include these attributes in the outrigger directly.

AND/OR Dilemma

Assuming that we have built the schema as shown in Figure 8.5, we are still left with a serious query problem. Query requests against the technical skill-set keywords likely will fall into two categories. The OR queries (for example, Unix OR Linux experience) can be satisfied by a simple OR constraint on the skills description column in the outrigger. However, AND queries (for example, Unix AND Linux experience) are difficult because the AND constraint is a constraint across two rows in the skills outrigger. SQL is notoriously poor at handling constraints across rows. The answer is to create SQL code using unions and intersections, probably in a custom interface that hides the complex logic from the business user. The SQL code would look like this:

```
(SELECT EMPLOYEE_ID, EMPLOYEE_NAME
FROM EMPLOYEE, SKILLS
WHERE EMPLOYEE.SKILLSGROUP = SKILLS.SKILLSGROUP AND SKILL = "UNIX")
UNION / INTERSECTION
(SELECT EMPLOYEE_ID, EMPLOYEE_NAME
FROM EMPLOYEE, SKILLS
WHERE EMPLOYEE.SKILLSGROUP = SKILLS.SKILLSGROUP AND SKILL = "LINUX")
```

Using the UNION lists employees with Unix OR Linux experience, whereas using INTERSECTION identifies employees with Unix AND Linux experience.

Searching for Substrings

We can remove the many-to-many join and the need for UNION/ INTERSECTION SQL by changing the design to a simpler form, as shown in Figure 8.6. Now each row in the skills list outrigger contains one long text string with all the skills keywords for that list key. We use a special delimiter such as a backslash at the beginning of the skills list column and after each skill in the list. Thus the skills list string containing Unix and C++ would look like \Unix\C++\. We presume that a number of employees share a common list of skills. If the lists are not reused frequently, we could collapse the skills list outrigger into the employee dimension merely by including the skills list string as we just described directly in the employee dimension.

String searches can be challenging because of the ambiguity caused by searching on upper or lower case. Is it UNIX or Unix or unix? We can resolve this either by changing all the keywords to one case or by using a special database text string search function that is case-insensitive.

With the design in Figure 8.6, the AND/OR dilemma can be addressed in a single SELECT statement. The OR constraint looks like this:

```
SKILL_LIST LIKE '%\UNIX\% OR SKILL_LIST LIKE '%\LINUX\%'
```

Meanwhile, the AND constraint has exactly the same structure:

```
SKILL_LIST LIKE '%\UNIX\%' AND SKILL_LIST LIKE '%\LINUX\%'
```

The % symbol is a wildcard pattern-matching character defined in SQL that matches zero or more characters. The backslash delimiter is used explicitly in the constraints to exactly match the desired keywords and not get erroneous matches.

The keyword list approach shown in Figure 8.6 will work in any relational database because it is based on standard SQL. However, leading wildcard searches are notorious for being slow when the keyword dimension table gets large. If performance becomes objectionable, you can pursue two approaches if your database allows. First, you can pin the keyword list outrigger in memory so that even though the constraint may invoke an exhaustive search of the dimension, it may be pretty fast. Second, you can build a special pattern index on the keyword list column that provides an index lookup to every conceivable substring, provided that your database can support this type of index.

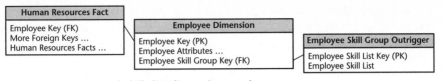

Figure 8.6 Delimited skills list dimension outrigger.

Survey Questionnaire Data

The HR department often collects survey data from the entire employee base, especially when gathering peer and/or management review data. The department wants to analyze these questionnaire responses to determine the average rating for a reviewed employee and the average rating within a department.

In order to analyze questionnaire data, we create a fact table with one row for each question on a respondent's survey, as illustrated in Figure 8.7. There would be two role-playing employee dimensions in the schema corresponding to the responding employee and the reviewed employee. The survey dimension consists of descriptors about the survey instrument. The question dimension would provide the question and its categorization. Presumably, the same question is asked on multiple surveys. The survey and question dimensions can be useful handles for searching for specific topics in a broad database of questionnaires. The response dimension contains the responses and perhaps categories of responses, such as favorable or hostile.

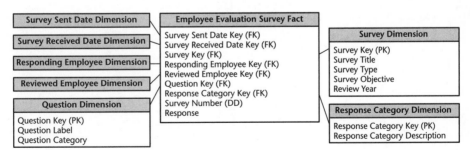

Figure 8.7 HR survey schema.

Creating the simple schema in Figure 8.7 supports robust slicing and dicing of survey data. Variations of this schema design would be useful for analyzing all types of survey data, including customer satisfaction and product usage feedback.

Summary

In this chapter we discussed several concepts in the context of HR data. First, we further elaborated on the advantages of embellishing a dimension table so that it not only captures all the relevant attributes but also tracks transactions that cause profile changes. In the world of HR, this single table will be used to address a number of questions regarding the status and profile of the employee base at any point in time. We described the use of an audit dimension to track data lineage and quality metadata within an HR fact table. This technique obviously is broadly applicable beyond the HR arena. We introduced the use of keyword group or delimited list dimension outriggers to support analysis on multivalued attributes. Finally, we provided a brief overview regarding the analysis of data collected from surveys or questionnaires.

Financial Services

The financial services industry encompasses a wide variety of businesses, including credit card companies, brokerage firms, and mortgage providers. This chapter will focus primarily on retail banks given that most readers have some degree of personal familiarity with this type of financial institution. A full-service bank offers a breadth of products, including checking accounts, savings accounts, mortgage loans, personal loans, credit cards, and safe deposit boxes. This chapter begins with a very simplistic schema. We then explore several schema extensions, including handling of the bank's broad portfolio of heterogeneous products that vary significantly by line of business.

As we embark on a series of industry-focused chapters, we want to remind you that they are not intended to provide full-scale industry solutions. While various dimensional modeling techniques will be discussed in the context of a given industry, the techniques certainly are applicable to other businesses. If you don't work in financial services, you still need to read this chapter. If you do work in financial services, remember that the schemas in this chapter should not be viewed as complete.

Chapter 9 discusses the following concepts:

- **Dimension triage to avoid the "too few dimensions" trap**
- **Household dimensions**
- **Associating individual customers with accounts using a bridge table**
- **Multiple minidimensions in a single fact table**

- Value banding of facts for reporting purposes
- Point-in-time balances using transaction data
- Handling heterogeneous products, each with unique metrics and dimension attributes, across lines of business

Banking Case Study

The bank's initial goal is to build the capability to better analyze the bank's accounts. Users want the ability to slice and dice individual accounts, as well as the residential household groupings to which they belong. One of the bank's major objectives is to market more effectively by offering additional products to households that already have one or more accounts with the bank. After conducting interviews with managers and analysts around the bank, we develop the following set of requirements:

1. Business users want to see 5 years of historical monthly snapshot data on every account.

2. Every account has a primary balance. The business wants to group different types of accounts in the same analyses and compare primary balances.

3. Every type of account (known as *products* within the bank) has a set of custom dimension attributes and numeric facts that tend to be quite different from product to product.

4. Every account is deemed to belong to a single household. There is a surprising amount of volatility in account-household relationships due to changes in marital status and other life-stage factors.

5. In addition to the household identification, users are interested in demographic information as it pertains to both individual customers and households. In addition, the bank captures and stores behavior scores relating to the activity or characteristics of each account and household.

Dimension Triage

Based on the business requirements just listed, the grain and dimensionality of the initial model begin to emerge. We start with a core fact table that records the primary balances of every account at the end of each month. Clearly, the grain of the fact table is one row for each account at the end of each month. Based on this grain declaration, we initially envision a design with only two dimensions—month and account. These two foreign keys form the fact table primary key, as shown in Figure 9.1. A data-centric designer might argue that all the other description information, such as household, branch, and product characteristics, should be embedded as descriptive attributes of the account dimension because each account has only one household, branch, and product associated with it.

While this schema accurately represents the many-to-one and many-to-many relationships in the snapshot data, it does not adequately reflect the natural business dimensions. Rather than collapsing everything into the huge account dimension table, additional analytic dimensions such as product and branch mirror the instinctive way that banking users think about their businesses. These supplemental dimensions provide much smaller points of entry to the fact table. Thus they address both the performance and usability objectives of a dimensional model. Finally, given that the master account dimension in a big bank may approach 10 million members, we worry about type 2 slowly changing dimension (SCD) effects mushrooming this huge dimension into something unworkable. The product and branch attributes are convenient groups of attributes to remove from the account dimension in order to cut down on the type 2 SCD effects. Later in this chapter we'll squeeze the changing demographics and behavioral attributes out of the account dimension for the same reasons.

The product and branch dimensions are two separate dimensions because there is a many-to-many relationship between products and branches. They both change slowly but on different rhythms. Most important, business users think of them as basic, distinct dimensions of the banking business.

In general, most dimensional models end up with between 5 and 15 or so dimensions. If we find ourselves at or below the low end of this range, we should be suspicious that dimensions may have been left out of the design inadvertently. In this case we should consider carefully whether any of the following kinds of dimensions are appropriate supplements to a draft dimensional model:

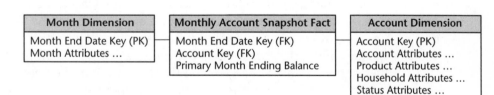

Figure 9.1 Balance snapshot with too few dimensions.

Causal dimensions. These dimensions, such as promotion, contract, deal, store condition, or even weather, provide additional insight into the cause of an event.

Multiple date or time-stamp dimensions. Refer to Chapter 5 for sample fact tables with multiple date stamps, especially when the fact table is an accumulating snapshot.

Degenerate dimensions. These dimensions identify operational transaction control numbers, such as an order, invoice, bill of lading, or ticket, as illustrated initially in Chapter 2.

Role-playing dimensions. Role-playing occurs when a single physical dimension appears several times in a fact table, each represented as a separate logical table with unique column names through views.

Status dimensions. These dimensions identify the current status of a transaction or monthly snapshot within some larger context, such as an account status.

Audit dimension. As discussed in Chapter 8, this dimension is designed to track data lineage and quality.

Junk dimensions. These consist of correlated indicators and flags, as described in Chapter 5.

These supplemental dimensions typically can be added gracefully to a design, even after the data warehouse has gone into production, because they do not change the grain of the fact table. The addition of these dimensions usually does not alter the existing dimension keys or measured facts in the fact table. All existing applications should continue to run without change.

Any descriptive attribute that is single-valued in the presence of the measurements in the fact table is a good candidate to be added to an existing dimension or to be its own dimension.

Based on further study of the bank's requirements, we ultimately choose the following dimensions for our initial schema: month end date, account, household, branch, product, and status. As illustrated in Figure 9.2, at the intersection of these six dimensions, we take a monthly snapshot and record the primary balance and any other metrics that make sense across all products, such as interest paid, interest charged, and transaction count. Remember that account balances are just like inventory balances in that they are not additive across any measure of time. Instead, we must average the account balances by dividing the balance sum by the number of months.

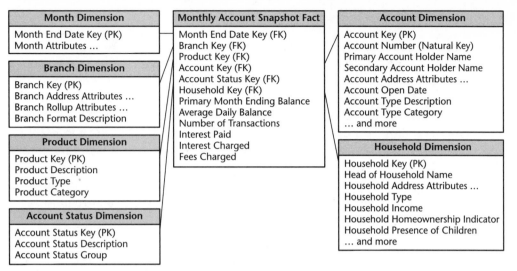

Figure 9.2 Core snapshot fact table for all accounts.

The product dimension consists of a simple product hierarchy that describes all the bank's products, including the name of the product, type, and category. The need to construct a generic product categorization in the bank is the same need that causes grocery stores to construct a generic merchandise hierarchy. The main difference between the bank and grocery store examples is that the bank also develops a large number of custom product attributes for each product type. We'll defer discussion regarding the handling of these custom attributes until the end of this chapter.

The branch dimension is similar to the facility or location dimensions we discussed earlier in this book, such as the retail store or distribution center warehouse.

The account status dimension is a useful dimension to record the condition of the account at the end of each month. The status records whether the account is active or inactive or whether a status change occurred during the month, such as a new account opening or an account closure. Rather than whipsawing the large account dimension or merely embedding a cryptic status code or abbreviation directly in the fact table, we treat status as a full-fledged dimension with descriptive status decodes, groupings, and status reason descriptions as appropriate. In many ways we could consider the account status dimension to be another example of a minidimension, as we introduced in Chapter 6.

Household Dimension

Rather than focusing solely on the bank's accounts, users also want the ability to analyze the bank's relationship with an entire economic unit, or household. They are interested in understanding the overall profile of a household, the magnitude of the existing relationship with the household, and what additional products should be sold to the household. They also want to capture key demographics regarding the household, such as household income, whether the household owns or rents the home, and whether there are children in the household. These demographic attributes change over time; as you might suspect, the users want to track the changes. If the bank focuses on accounts for commercial entities rather than consumers, it likely has similar requirements to identify and link corporate families.

From the bank's perspective, a household may be comprised of several accounts and individual account holders. For example, consider John and Mary Smith as a single household. John has a checking account, and Mary has a savings account. In addition, John and Mary have a joint checking account, credit card, and mortgage with the bank. All five of these accounts are considered to be a part of the same Smith household despite the fact that minor inconsistencies may exist in the operational name and address information.

The process of relating individual accounts to households (or the commercial business equivalent of a residential household) is not to be taken lightly. Householding requires the development of business rules and algorithms to assign accounts to households. As we discussed in Chapter 6, there are specialized products and services to do the matching necessary to determine household assignments. It is very common for a large financial services organization to invest significant resources in specialized capabilities to support its householding needs.

The decision to treat accounts and households as separate dimensions is somewhat a matter of the designer's prerogative. Despite the fact that accounts and households are correlated intuitively, we decide to treat them separately because of the size of the account dimension and the volatility of the account constituents within a household dimension, as referenced earlier. In a large bank, the account dimension is huge, with easily over 10 million rows that group into several million households. The household dimension provides a somewhat smaller point of entry into the fact table without traversing a 10-million-row account dimension table. In addition, given the changing nature of the relationship between accounts and households, we elect to use the fact table to capture the relationship rather than merely including the household attributes on each account dimension row. In this way we avoid using the type 2 SCD approach with the large account dimension.

Multivalued Dimensions

As we just saw in the John and Mary Smith example, an account can have one, two, or more individual account holders, or customers, associated with it. Obviously, we cannot merely include the customer as an account attribute; doing so violates the granularity of the dimension table because more than one individual can be associated with an account. Likewise, we cannot include customer as an additional dimension in the fact table; doing so violates the granularity of the fact table (one row per account per month) again because more than one individual can be associated with any given account. This is a classic example of a multivalued dimension, which we'll develop fully in Chapter 13. For now, suffice it to say that to link an individual customer dimension to an account-grained fact table requires the use of an account-to-customer bridge table, as shown in Figure 9.3. At a minimum, the primary key of the bridge table consists of the surrogate account and customer foreign keys. We'll discuss date/time stamping of bridge table rows in Chapter 13 to capture relationship changes. In addition, we'll elaborate on the use of a weighting factor in the bridge table to enable both correctly weighted reports and impact reports.

> **An open-ended many-valued attribute can be associated with a dimension row by using a bridge table to associate the many-valued attributes with the dimension.**

In some financial services companies, the individual customer is identified and associated with each transaction. For example, credit card companies often issue unique card numbers to each cardholder. John and Mary Smith may have a joint credit card account, but the numbers on their respective pieces of plastic are unique. In this case there is no need for an account-to-customer bridge table because the atomic transaction facts are at the discrete customer grain. Account and customer would both be foreign keys in this fact table.

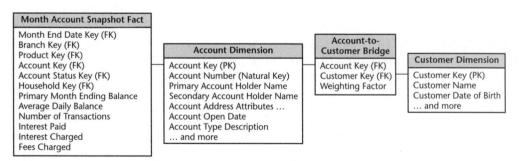

Figure 9.3 Account-to-customer bridge table to associate multiple customers with account-level facts.

Minidimensions Revisited

Similar to our Chapter 6 discussion regarding the customer dimension, there are a wide variety of attributes to describe the bank's accounts, customers, and households, including monthly credit bureau attributes, external demographic data, and calculated scores to identify their behavior, retention, profitability, and delinquency characteristics. Financial services organizations typically are interested in understanding and responding to changes in these attributes over time.

It is unreasonable to rely on the type 2 SCD technique to track changes in the account dimension given the dimension row count and attribute volatility, such as the monthly update of credit bureau attributes. Instead, we break off the browseable and changeable attributes into multiple minidimensions, such as credit bureau and demographics minidimensions, whose keys are included in the fact table. This recommendation was illustrated in Figure 6.4. The minidimensions allow us to slice and dice the fact data based on a lengthy list of attributes while readily tracking attribute changes over time, even though they may be updated at different frequencies. While minidimensions are extremely powerful, we need to be careful that we don't overuse the technique. However, account-oriented financial services are a good environment for using the minidimension technique because the primary fact table is a very long-running periodic snapshot. Thus a fact table row exists for every account every month. This fact row provides a home for all the foreign keys and links them together so that we can always see the account together with all the other minidimensions for any month.

> **Minidimensions should consist of correlated clumps of attributes; each attribute shouldn't be its own minidimension or we'd end up with too many dimensions in the fact table.**

As described in Chapter 6, one of the compromises associated with minidimensions is the need to band attribute values in order to maintain reasonable minidimension row counts. Rather than storing extremely discrete income amounts, such as $31,257.98, we store income ranges, such as $30,000-$34,999 in the minidimension. Similarly, the profitability scores may range from 1 through 1,200, which we band into fixed ranges such as less than or equal to 100, 101-150, 151-200, and so on in the minidimension.

Most organizations find that these banded attribute values support their routine analytic requirements; however, there are two situations where banded values may be inadequate. First, data mining analysis often requires discrete values rather than fixed bands to be most effective. Second, a limited number of power analysts may want to analyze the discrete values to determine if the selected bands are appropriate. In this case we still maintain our banded-value minidimension attributes to support consistent day-to-day analytic reporting, but we also store the key discrete numeric values as facts in the fact table. For example, if each account's profitability score is recalculated each month, we assign the appropriate profitability-range minidimension for that score each month. In addition, we capture the discrete profitability score as a fact in the monthly account snapshot fact table. Finally, if needed, we could include the most recent profitability range or score in the account dimension, where any changes are handled by deliberately overwriting the attribute. Each of these data elements in a schema should be uniquely labeled so that they are distinguishable. Designers always must carefully balance the incremental value of including somewhat redundant facts and attributes versus the cost in terms of additional complexity for both the staging application and user presentation.

Arbitrary Value Banding of Facts

Suppose that business users want the ability to perform value-band reporting on a standard numeric fact, such as the account balance, but are not willing to live with predefined bands. They may want to create a report that looks similar to the following based on the account balance snapshot:

Balance Range	Number of Accounts	Total of Balances
0-1,000	45,678	$10,222,543
1,001-2,000	36,788	$45,777,216
2,001-5,000	11,775	$31,553,884
5,001-10,000	2,566	$22,438,287
10,001 and up	477	$8,336,728

Using the schema in Figure 9.2, it is difficult to create this report directly from the fact table. SQL has no generalization of the GROUP BY clause that clumps additive values into ranges. To further complicate matters, the ranges are of unequal size and have textual names like "10,001 and up". Also, users typically need the flexibility to redefine the bands at query time with different boundaries or levels of precision.

The schema design shown in Figure 9.4 allows us to do flexible value-band reporting. The band definition table can contain as many sets of different reporting bands as desired. The name of a particular group of bands is stored in the band group column. The band definition table is joined to the balance fact using a pair of less-than and greater-than joins. The report uses the band range name as the row header and sorts the report on the band sort column.

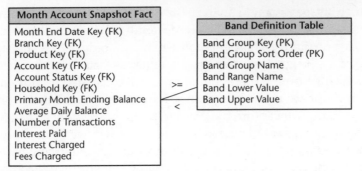

Figure 9.4 Arbitrary value-band reporting using a band definition table.

Controlling the performance of this query can be a challenge. By definition, a value-band query is very lightly constrained. Our example report needed to scan the balances of more than 90,000 accounts. Perhaps only the date dimension was constrained to the current month. Furthermore, the unconventional join to the banding definition table is not the basis of a nice restricting constraint; all it is doing is grouping the 90,000 balances. In this situation you may need to place an index directly on the balance fact. The performance of a query that constrains or groups on the value of a fact, such as balance, will be improved enormously if the database management system (DBMS) can sort and compress the individual fact efficiently. Such an approach was pioneered by the Sybase IQ product in the early 1990s and is now becoming a standard indexing option on several of the competing DBMSs.

Point-in-Time Balances

So far we've restricted our discussions in this financial services chapter to month-end balance snapshots because this level of detail typically is sufficient for analysis. If required, we could supplement the monthly-grained snapshot fact table with a second fact table that provides merely the most current snapshot as of the last nightly update or perhaps is extended to provide daily-balance snapshots for the last week or month. However, what if we face the requirement to report an account's balance at any arbitrarily picked historical point in time?

Creating daily-balance snapshots for a large bank over a lengthy historical time span would be overwhelming given the density of the snapshot data. If the bank has 10 million accounts, daily snapshots translate into approximately 3.65 billion fact rows per year.

Assuming that business requirements already have driven the need to make transaction detail data available for analysis, we could leverage this transaction detail to determine an arbitrary point-in-time balance. To simplify matters, we'll boil the account transaction fact table down to an extremely simple design, as illustrated in Figure 9.5. The transaction type key joins to a small dimension table of permissible transaction types. The transaction sequence number is a continuously increasing numeric number running for the lifetime of the account. The final flag indicates whether this is the last transaction for an account on a given day. The transaction amount is self-explanatory. The balance fact is the ending account balance following the transaction event.

Like all transaction-grained fact tables, we add a row to the fact table in Figure 9.5 only if a transaction occurs. If an account were quiet for two weeks, perhaps January 1 through 14, there would be no rows in the fact table for the account during that time span. However, suppose that we want to know what all the account balances were on January 5? In this case we need to look for the most recent previous transaction fact row for each account on or before our requested date. Here's sample SQL code that does the trick:

```
SELECT A.ACCTNUM, F.BALANCE
FROM FACT F, ACCOUNT A
WHERE F.ACCOUNT_KEY = A.ACCOUNT_KEY
AND F.DATE_KEY
    (SELECT MAX(G.DATE_KEY)
    FROM FACT G
    WHERE G.ACCOUNT_KEY = F.ACCOUNT_KEY
    AND G.DATE_KEY IN
        (SELECT D.DATE_KEY
        FROM DATE D
        WHERE D.FULLDATE <= 'January 5, 2002'))
```

In this example we are taking advantage of a special situation that exists with the surrogate date key. As we discussed in Chapter 2, the date key is a set of integers running from 1 to N with a meaningful, predictable sequence. We assign consecutive integers to the date surrogate key so that we can physically partition a large fact table based on the date. This neatly segments the fact table so that we can perform discrete administrative actions on certain date ranges, such as moving archived data to offline storage or dropping and rebuilding indexes. The date dimension is the only dimension whose surrogate keys have any embedded semi-intelligence. Due to its predictable sequence, it is the only dimension on which we dare place application constraints. We used this ordering in the preceding SQL code to locate the most recent prior end-of-day transaction.

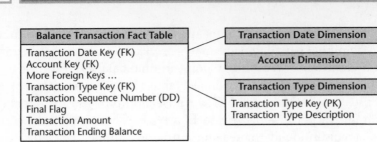

Figure 9.5 Using a transaction fact table for point-in-time balances.

Leveraging the transaction fact table for dual purposes requires that the fact table is absolutely complete and accurate. Every transaction against the account must appear in this fact table, or else the running balance will not be accurate. A late-arriving transaction row would require sweeping forward from the point of insertion in that account and incrementing all the balances and transaction sequence numbers. Note that we haven't explicitly used the transaction sequence number in this discussion, although it is needed in this design to reconstruct the true sequence of transactions reliably and to provide the basis of the fact table's primary key, which is the date, account, and sequence number. We prefer using the sequence number rather than a time-of-day stamp because differences between the sequence numbers are a valid measure of account activity.

This technique is viable in some part because the transaction processing system can readily hand off the current balance metric to the warehouse with each transaction record. Unlike the year-to-date facts we discussed in Chapter 8, in this case of account balances we have no way to determine the balances merely by summarizing recent transactions alone. Rather, we'd need to study the impact of all transactions from the beginning of the account's existence to calculate valid account balances. For some businesses within the financial services arena, even if balances are provided following each transaction, they still may not be valid for point-in-time balance reporting. For example, in the case of a brokerage firm, if a valuation balance is updated following each investment transaction, we cannot rely on that balance for point-in-time reporting because the valuation changes constantly. In this case we'd likely create a snapshot fact table to provide users with regular end-of-period investment valuation balances.

Heterogeneous Product Schemas

In many financial service businesses, a dilemma arises because of the heterogeneous nature of the products or services offered by the institution. As we mentioned in the introduction to this chapter, a typical retail bank offers a myriad of dissimilar products, from checking accounts to mortgages, to the same customers. Although every account at the bank has a primary balance and interest amount associated with it, each product type has a number of special attributes and measured facts that are not shared by other products. For instance, checking accounts have minimum balances, overdraft limits, and service charges; time deposits such as certificates of deposit have few attribute overlaps with checking but instead have maturity dates, compounding frequencies, and current interest rate.

Business users typically require two different perspectives that are difficult to present in a single fact table. The first perspective is the global view, including the ability to slice and dice all accounts simultaneously, regardless of their product type. As we described in Chapter 6, this global view is needed to plan appropriate customer relationship management (CRM) cross-sell and up-sell strategies against the aggregate customer base spanning all possible products. In this situation we need the single core fact table crossing all the lines of business to provide insight into the complete account portfolio, as illustrated earlier in Figure 9.2. Note, however, that the core fact table can present only a limited number of facts that make sense for virtually every line of business. We are unable to accommodate incompatible facts in the core fact table because, in the case of banking, there may be several hundred of these facts when all the possible account types are considered. Similarly, the core product dimension provides an extremely useful analytical point of entry to the facts but is limited to the subset of common product attributes.

The second perspective required by users is the specific line-of-business view that focuses on the in-depth details of one business, such as checking. As we described, there is a long list of special facts and attributes that only make sense for the checking business. These special facts cannot be included in the core fact table; if we did this for each line of business in a retail bank, we would end up with a hundred special facts, most of which would have null values in any specific row. Likewise, if we attempted to include specific line-of-business attributes in the product dimension table, it would have hundreds of special attributes, almost all of which would be empty for any given row. The resulting tables would resemble Swiss cheese, littered with data holes. The solution to this dilemma is to create a custom schema for the checking line of business that is limited to just checking accounts, as shown in Figure 9.6.

Now both the custom checking fact table and the corresponding checking product dimension are widened to describe all the specific facts and attributes that only make sense for checking products. These custom schemas also contain the core facts and attributes so that we can avoid joining tables from the core and custom schemas in order to get the complete set of facts and attributes. Likewise, we would build custom fact and product tables for the other lines of business to support their in-depth analysis requirements. Although creating product-specific schemas sounds complex, only the DBA sees all the tables at once. From the perspective of users, either it's a cross-product analysis that relies on the core fact table and its attendant core product table or the analysis focuses on a particular product type, in which case one of the custom line-of-business subschemas is used. In general, it does not make sense to combine data from one or more custom subschemas because, by definition, the facts and attributes are disjoint (or nearly so).

The keys of the custom product dimensions are the same keys used in the core product dimension, which contains all possible product keys. For example, if the bank offers a $500 minimum balance with no per-check charge checking product, the product would have the same surrogate key in both the core and custom checking product dimensions. As we discussed in Chapter 3, establishing conformed dimensions is essential to an extensible data warehouse architecture. Each custom product dimension is a subset of rows from the core product dimension table. Each custom product dimension contains attributes specific to a particular product type.

This heterogeneous product technique obviously applies to any business that offers widely varied products through multiple lines of business. If we worked for a technology company that sells hardware, software, and services, we can imagine building core sales fact and product dimension tables to deliver the global customer perspective. The core tables would include all facts and dimension attributes that are common across lines of business. The core tables would then be supplemented with schemas that do a deep dive into custom facts and attributes that vary by business. Again, a specific product would be assigned the same surrogate product key in both the core and custom product dimensions.

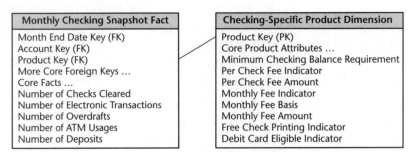

Figure 9.6 Specific line-of-business custom schema for checking products.

A family of core and custom fact tables is needed when a business has heterogeneous products that have naturally different facts and descriptors but a single customer base that demands an integrated view.

We can consider handling the specific line-of-business attributes as a context-dependent outrigger to the product dimension, as illustrated in Figure 9.7. We have isolated the core attributes in the base-product dimension table, and we can include a snowflake key in each base record that points to its proper extended-product outrigger. The snowflake key must connect to the particular outrigger table that a specific product type defines. Usually, you can accomplish this task by constructing a relational view for each product type that hardwires the correct join path.

In the case of account-oriented financial services, when a product is sold to a customer, a new account is opened. In the case of some banking products, such as mortgages, more account-specific descriptive information is collected when the account opening occurs. For example, the bank may offer a 15-year fixed-rate mortgage at a given rate. When the mortgage originates, the bank will know more about the specific property, including the address, appraised value, square footage, home type (for example, single-family, townhouse, condominium, trailer), construction type (for example, wood frame, brick, stucco), date of construction, and acreage. These attribute values differ by account, so they don't belong in the what-the-bank-sells product dimension. As shown in Figure 9.7, we can envision an account dimension outrigger for some account types.

If the lines of business in our retail bank are physically separated so that each has its own data mart, the custom fact and dimension tables likely will not

Account Dimensions
Account Key (PK)
Core Account Attributes ...

Mortgage-Specific Account Outrigger
Mortgage-Specific Account Key (PK)
Property Address ...
Appraised Value
Square Footage
Home Type
Construction Type
Year Constructed Completed
Acreage

Monthly Mortgage Snapshot Fact
Month End Date Key (FK)
Account Key (FK)
Product Key (FK)
More Core Foreign Keys ...
Core Facts ...
Original Loan Amount
Outstanding Loan Amount
Interest Amount
Property Tax Escrow Amount
Insurance Escrow Amount
Property Mortgage Insurance Amount
Property Tax Escrow Paid
Insurance Escrow Paid
Property Mortgage Insurance Paid
Escrow Overage/Shortage Amount
Late Payment Fee
Additional Principal Paid

Product Dimension
Product Key (PK)
Core Product Attributes ...

Mortgage-Specific Product Outrigger
Mortgage-Specific Product Key (PK)
Fixed / Adjustable
Conventional / Jumbo
Rate
Term
FHA Compliant / Eligible
VA Compliant / Eligible

Figure 9.7 Context-dependent dimension outriggers.

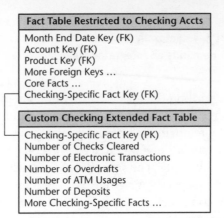

Figure 9.8 Heterogeneous products schema using an extended fact table.

reside in the same space as the core fact and dimension tables. In this case the data in the core fact table would be duplicated exactly once to implement all the custom tables. Remember that the custom tables provide a disjoint partitioning of the products so that there is no overlap between the custom schemas.

If the lines of business share the same physical table space, we can avoid duplicating both the core fact keys and core facts in the custom line-of-business fact tables. We do so by assigning a special join key to each core fact row that uniquely identifies a single account in a single month. Using this join key, we physically link the extended custom facts to the core fact table, as shown in Figure 9.8. When using this technique, we need to ensure that the optimizer resolves the constraints on the core fact table prior to joining to the extended fact table using the special join key.

The query tool or application must know to use this special join key to link to the correct extended fact table for each line of business. While this sounds complicated, it is actually quite natural. By definition with heterogeneous facts, it almost never makes sense to join to more than one extended fact table representing one line of business in a single SQL expression. The names of the facts in the separate extended fact tables, by definition, are different; no single SQL expression can talk to multiple extended fact tables. Thus a requesting application analyzing a specific line of business, such as checking, always would be hard-coded to link to the correct extended fact table.

Heterogeneous Products with Transaction Facts

The heterogeneous product technique just discussed is appropriate for fact tables in which a single logical row contains many product-specific facts. Snapshots usually fit this pattern.

On the other hand, transaction-grained fact tables often have a single fact that is generically the target of a particular transaction. In such cases the fact table has an associated transaction dimension that interprets the amount column. In the case of transaction-grained fact tables, we typically do not need specific line-of-business fact tables. We get by with only one core fact table because there is only one fact. However, we still can have a rich set of heterogeneous products with diverse attributes. In this case we would generate the complete portfolio of custom product dimension tables and use them as appropriate, depending on the nature of the application. In a cross-product analysis, we would use the core product dimension table because it is capable of spanning any group of products. In a single-product analysis, we optionally could use the custom-product dimension table instead of the core dimension if we wanted to take advantage of the custom attributes specific to that product type.

Summary

We began this chapter by discussing the situation in which a fact table has too few dimensions. We provided suggestions for ferreting out additional dimensions using a triage process. Approaches for handling the often complex relationship between accounts, customers, and households were described. We also discussed the use of multiple minidimensions in a single fact table, which is fairly common in financial services schemas.

We illustrated a technique for clustering numeric facts into arbitrary value bands for reporting purposes through the use of a separate band table. We also touched on an approach for leveraging an existing transaction fact table to supply point-in-time balances.

Finally, we provided recommendations for any organization that offers heterogeneous products to the same set of customers. In this case we create a core fact table that contains performance metrics that are common across all lines of business. The companion core dimension table contains rows for the complete product portfolio, but the attributes are limited to those that are applicable across all products. Multiple custom schemas, one for each line of business, complement this core schema with product-specific facts and attributes.

Telecommunications and Utilities

This chapter will flow a bit differently than preceding chapters. We'll still begin with a case study overview, but we won't be designing a dimensional model from scratch this time. Instead, we'll step into a project midstream to conduct a design review, looking for opportunities to improve the initial draft schema. Do you recall reading *Highlights for Children* magazine in your dentist's waiting room long ago? If so, do you remember the *what's wrong with this picture* worksheets where you identified all the out-of-place items, like the chicken driving a car or a snowman on the beach? The bulk of this chapter will focus on a dimensional modeling *what's wrong with this picture* exercise where we'll identify out-of-place design flaws.

We'll use a billing vignette drawn from the telecommunications industry as the basis for the case study; however, it shares similar characteristics with the billing data generated by a utilities company. At the end of this chapter we'll elaborate on managing and leveraging the geographic location information in the warehouse, regardless of the industry.

Chapter 10 discusses the following concepts:

- **Design review exercise**
- **Common design mistakes to look for in a review**
- **Geographic location dimension, including its treatment as a snowflaked outrigger and its interaction with geographic information systems**

Telecommunications Case Study

Given your extensive experience in dimensional modeling (nine chapters so far), you've been recruited to a new position as a dimensional modeler on the data warehouse team for a large wireless telecommunications company. On your first day, after a few hours of human resources paperwork and orientation (including the location of the nearest coffee machine), you're ready to get to work.

The data warehouse team is anxious to pick your brain regarding its initial dimensional design. So far it seems that the project is off to a good start. The company has a strong business and IT sponsorship committee that embraced the concept that a data warehouse must be business-driven; as such, the committee was fully supportive of the business requirements gathering process. Based on the requirements initiative, the team drafted an initial data warehouse bus matrix. It is the first flip chart, as illustrated in Figure 10.1, to hit the wall during the design walk-through with you. The team identified several core business processes and a number of common dimensions. Of course, the complete enterprise-wide matrix would be much larger in terms of both the number of rows and the number of columns, but you're comfortable that the key constituencies' major data requirements have been captured.

The sponsorship committee jointly decided to focus on the first row of the matrix, the customer billing process, for the initial phase of the data warehouse. Business management determined that better access to the metrics resulting from the billing process would have significant impact on the business, especially given the business's recent focus on CRM, as we discussed in Chapter 6. Management wants the ability to see monthly usage and billing metrics (otherwise known as *revenue*) by customer, sales organization, and rate plan to perform sales rep and channel performance analysis and the rate plan analysis. Fortunately, the IT team felt that it was feasible to tackle this business process during the first warehouse iteration.

Some people in the IT organization thought it would be preferable to tackle individual call detail records, such as every call initiated or received by every phone. While this level of highly granular data would provide interesting insights, it was determined by the joint business and IT sponsorship committee that the associated data presents more feasibility challenges while not delivering as much short-term business value.

	Date	Customer	Product	Rate Plan	Sales Channel	Service Line #	Switch	Vendor	GL Account	Organization	Employee	Service Call Type	Service Call Status
Customer Billing	X	X	X	X	X	X							
Call Detail Traffic	X	X	X	X		X	X						
Purchasing	X		X					X	X	X			
Distributor Inventory	X		X		X			X		X			
Channel Sales	X	X	X	X	X	X		X					
Service Calls	X	X	X							X	X	X	X
Repair Items	X	X	X							X	X	X	X

Figure 10.1 Subset of the data warehouse bus matrix.

Based on the direction provided by the sponsorship committee, the team proceeded to look more closely at the customer billing data. Each month, the operational billing system generates a bill for each phone number, also known as *service line*. Since the wireless company has millions of service lines, this represents a significant amount of data. Each service line is associated with a single customer. However, a customer can have multiple wireless service lines, which appear as separate line items on the same bill; each service line has its own set of billing metrics, such as the number of minutes used and monthly service charge. There is a single rate plan associated with each service line on a given bill; this plan can change as customers' usage habits evolve. Finally, a sales rep (and his or her respective sales organization and channel) is associated with each service line in order to evaluate the ongoing billing revenue stream generated by each rep and channel partner.

The team designed a fact table with the grain being one row per bill each month. The data warehouse team proudly unrolls its draft dimensional modeling masterpiece, as shown in Figure 10.2, and looks at you expectantly.

What do you think? Before we move on, please spend several minutes studying the design in Figure 10.2. Try to identify the design flaws and suggest improvements in this "what's wrong with this picture" exercise before reading ahead.

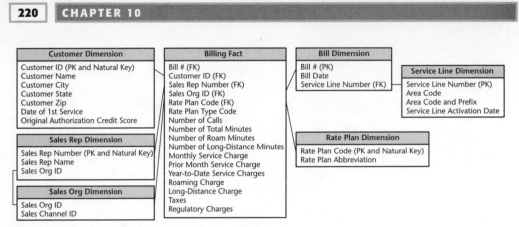

Figure 10.2 Draft schema prior to design review.

General Design Review Considerations

Before we discuss the specific issues and potential recommendations for Figure 10.2, we'll take a moment to outline the design issues we commonly encounter when conducting a design review. Not to insinuate that the data warehouse team in our case study has stepped into all these traps, but it may be guilty of violating several. Again, the design review exercise will be a more effective learning tool if you take a moment to jot down your personal ideas regarding Figure 10.2 before proceeding.

Granularity

One of the first questions we always ask during a design review is, What's the grain of the fact table? Surprisingly, we often get inconsistent answers to this inquiry from the project team. Declaring a clear and concise definition of the grain of the fact table is critical to a productive modeling effort. Likewise, the project team and business liaisons should share a common understanding of this grain declaration.

Of course, if you've read this far, you're aware that we strongly believe that you should build your fact table at the lowest level of granularity possible. However, the definition of the lowest level of granularity possible depends on the business process you are modeling.

In this case study we don't need call-level detail with the granularity of one row for every call to address the business requirements. Instead, a billing fact table is more appropriate. We want to implement the most granular data available for the selected billing process, not just the most granular data available in the enterprise. Of course, if the high-priority business requirements focused on switching network traffic and capacity analysis, then low-level call detail data would be appropriate.

 Going to the lowest level of granularity does not imply finding the greatest amount of detailed data available in the organization.

Fact Granularity

Once the fact table granularity has been established, facts should be identified that are consistent with the grain declaration. In an effort to improve performance or reduce query complexity, aggregated facts such as year-to-date totals sometimes sneak into the fact row. These totals are dangerous because they are not perfectly additive. While a year-to-date total reduces the complexity and run time of a few specific queries, having it in the fact table invites a query to double count the year-to-date column (or worse) when more than one bill date is included in a query. It is very important that once the grain of a fact table is chosen, all the additive facts are presented at a uniform grain.

Dimension Granularity

Each of the dimensions associated with a fact table should take on a single value with each row of fact table measurements. Likewise, each of the dimension attributes should take on one value for a given dimension row. If the attributes have a one-to-many relationship, then this hierarchical relationship can be represented within a single dimension. We generally should look for opportunities to collapse dimension hierarchies whenever possible.

In general, we discourage the snowflaking or normalization of dimension tables. While snowflaking may reduce the disk space consumed by dimension tables, the savings are usually insignificant when compared with the entire data warehouse and seldom offset the disadvantages in ease of use or query performance.

Throughout this book we have occasionally discussed outriggers as permissible snowflakes. Outriggers can play a useful role in your dimensional designs, but keep in mind that the use of outriggers for a cluster of relatively low-cardinality or frequently reused attributes should be the exception rather than the rule. Be careful to avoid abusing the outrigger technique by overusing them in your schemas.

Date Dimension

Design teams sometimes join a generic date dimension to their fact table because they know it's the most common dimension but then can't articulate what the date refers to. Needless to say, this presents real challenges for the data staging team. While we discourage superfluous date dimensions, we encourage the inclusion of robust date roll-up and filter attributes in a meaningful date dimension table.

Fixed Time-Series Buckets Instead of Date Dimension

Other designers sometimes avoid a date dimension table altogether by representing a time series of monthly buckets of facts on a single fact table row. Older operational systems may contain metric sets that are repeated 12 times on a single record to represent month 1, month 2, and so on. There are several problems with this approach. First, the hard-coded identity of the time slots is inflexible. When you fill up all the buckets, you are left with unpleasant choices. You could alter the table to expand the row. Otherwise, you could shift everything over by one column, dropping the oldest data, but this wreaks havoc with your existing query applications. The second problem with this approach is that all the attributes of the date itself are now the responsibility of the application, not the database. There is no date dimension in which to place calendar event descriptions for constraining. Finally, the fixed-slot approach is inefficient if measurements are only taken in a particular time period, resulting in null columns in many rows. Instead, these recurring time buckets should be presented as separate rows in the dimensional fact table.

Degenerate Dimensions

Rather than treating operational transaction numbers, such as the invoice or order number, as degenerate dimensions, teams sometimes want to create a separate dimension for the transaction number. Attributes of the transaction number dimension then include elements from the transaction header record, such as the invoice date, invoice type, and invoice terms.

Remember, transaction numbers are best treated as degenerate dimensions. In your design reviews, be on the lookout for a dimension table that has as many (or nearly as many) rows as the fact table. This should be a warning sign that there may be a degenerate dimension lurking within a dimension table.

Dimension Decodes and Descriptions

All identifiers and codes in the dimension tables should be accompanied by descriptive decodes. We simply need to dismiss the misperception that business users prefer to work with codes. To convince yourself, you should stroll down to their offices to see the decode listings filling their bulletin boards or lining their computer monitors. Most users do not memorize the codes outside of a few favorites. New hires are rendered helpless when assaulted with a lengthy list of meaningless codes.

The good news is that we usually can source decodes from operational systems with minimal additional effort or overhead. Occasionally, the descriptions are not available from an operational system but need to be provided by business partners. In these cases, it is important to determine an ongoing maintenance strategy to maintain data quality.

Finally, we sometimes work with project teams that opt to embed complex filtering or labeling logic in the data access application rather than supporting it via a dimension table. While access tools may provide the ability to decode within the query or reporting application, we recommend that decodes be stored as data elements instead. Applications should be data-driven in order to minimize the impact of decode additions and changes. Of course, decodes that reside in the database also ensure greater report labeling consistency.

Surrogate Keys

Instead of relying on operational keys or identifiers, we recommend the use of surrogate keys throughout your dimensional design. If you are unclear about the reasons for pursuing this strategy, we suggest you backtrack to Chapter 2 to refresh your memory.

Too Many (or Too Few) Dimensions

As we have mentioned, a dimensional model typically has 5 to 15 dimensions. If your design has only two or three dimensions, then you should revisit Chapter 9 for a discussion on dimension triage considerations. If your design has 25 or 30 dimensions, we suggest you review the centipede design in Chapter 2 or the junk dimension in Chapter 5 for ideas to reduce the number of dimensions in your schema.

Draft Design Exercise Discussion

Now that we've reviewed several common dimensional modeling pitfalls that we encounter frequently during design reviews, let's look back to the draft design in Figure 10.2. Several items immediately jump out at us—perhaps so many that it's hard to know where to start.

The first thing we focus on is the grain of the fact table. The design team stated that the grain is one row for each bill each month. However, based on our understanding from the data discovery effort, the lowest level of billing data would be one row per service line on a bill. When we point this out to the project team, the team directs us to the bill number dimension, which includes the service line number. When reminded that each service line has its own set of billing metrics, the team agrees that the more appropriate grain declaration would be one row per service line per bill. We move the service line key into the fact table as a foreign key to the service line dimension.

While discussing the granularity, the bill number dimension is scrutinized, especially since we just moved the service line key into the fact table. As the draft model was originally drawn in Figure 10.2, every time a bill row is loaded into the fact table, a row also would be loaded into the bill number dimension table. It doesn't take much to convince the team that something is wrong with this picture. Even with the modified granularity to include service line, we would still end up with nearly as many rows in both the fact and bill number dimension tables. Instead, we opt to treat the bill number as a degenerate dimension. At the same time, we move the bill date into the fact table and join it to a robust date dimension, which plays the role of a bill date in this schema.

We've been bothered since first looking at the design by the double joins on the sales rep organization dimension table. First of all, the sales rep organizational hierarchy has been snowflaked unnecessarily. We opt to collapse the hierarchy by including the sales rep organization and channel identifiers (along with more meaningful descriptors, hopefully) as additional attributes in the sales rep dimension table. In addition, we can eliminate the unneeded sales rep organization foreign key in the fact table.

The design inappropriately treats the rate-plan type code as a textual fact. Textual facts are seldom a sound design choice. They almost always take up more space in our fact tables than a surrogate key. More important, users generally want to query, constrain, and report against these textual facts. We can provide quicker response and more flexible access by handling these textual values in a dimension table. In addition, additional descriptive attributes usually are associated with the textual fact. In this case study, the rate plan type code and its decode can be treated as roll-up attributes in the rate plan dimension table.

The team spent some time discussing the relationship between the service line and the customer, sales rep, and rate plan dimensions. Since there is a single customer, sales rep, and rate plan associated with a service line number, the dimensions theoretically could be collapsed and modeled as service line attributes. However, collapsing the dimensions would result in a schema with just two dimensions (bill date and service line). Besides, the service line dimension already has millions of rows in it and is growing rapidly. In the end, we opt to treat the customer, sales rep, and rate plan as minidimensions of the service line, as we described in Chapter 6.

We notice that surrogate keys are used inconsistently throughout the design. Many of the draft dimension tables use operational identifiers or system keys as primary keys. We encourage the team to implement surrogate keys for all the dimension primary keys and fact table foreign keys.

The original design was riddled with operational codes and identifiers. In general, adding descriptive names will make the data more legible to the business users. If required by the business, the operational codes can continue to accompany the descriptors as dimension attributes, but they should not be the dimension primary keys.

Finally, we see that there is a year-to-date fact stored in the fact table. While the team felt that this would enable users to report year-to-date figures more easily, in reality, year-to-date facts can be confusing and prone to error. We opt to remove the year-to-date fact. Instead, users can calculate year-to-date amounts on the fly by using a constraint on year in the date dimension or by leveraging the data access tool's capabilities.

After a taxing day, our initial review of the design is complete. Of course, there's more ground to cover, including the handling of changes to the dimension attributes. In the meantime, everyone on the team agrees that the revamped design, illustrated in Figure 10.3, is a vast improvement. We feel that we've earned our first week's pay at our new employer.

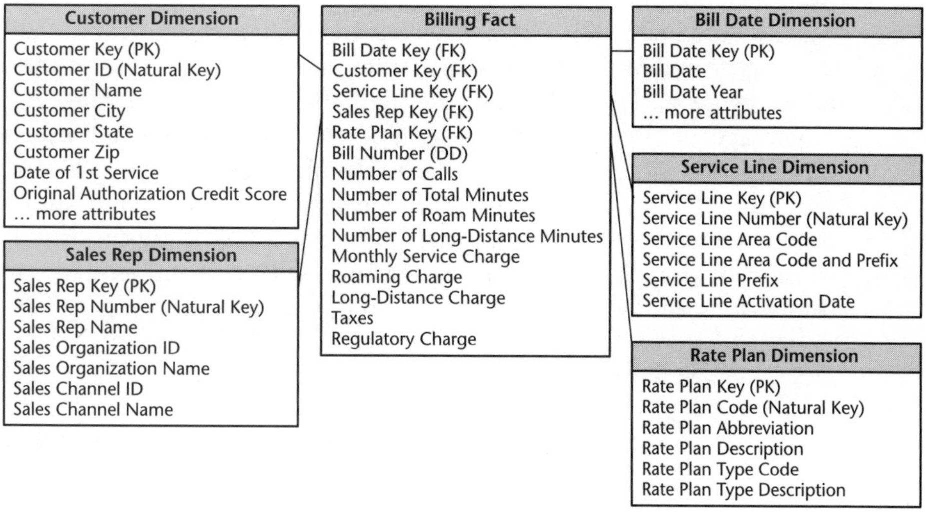

Customer Dimension
Customer Key (PK)
Customer ID (Natural Key)
Customer Name
Customer City
Customer State
Customer Zip
Date of 1st Service
Original Authorization Credit Score
... more attributes

Sales Rep Dimension
Sales Rep Key (PK)
Sales Rep Number (Natural Key)
Sales Rep Name
Sales Organization ID
Sales Organization Name
Sales Channel ID
Sales Channel Name

Billing Fact
Bill Date Key (FK)
Customer Key (FK)
Service Line Key (FK)
Sales Rep Key (FK)
Rate Plan Key (FK)
Bill Number (DD)
Number of Calls
Number of Total Minutes
Number of Roam Minutes
Number of Long-Distance Minutes
Monthly Service Charge
Roaming Charge
Long-Distance Charge
Taxes
Regulatory Charge

Bill Date Dimension
Bill Date Key (PK)
Bill Date
Bill Date Year
... more attributes

Service Line Dimension
Service Line Key (PK)
Service Line Number (Natural Key)
Service Line Area Code
Service Line Area Code and Prefix
Service Line Prefix
Service Line Activation Date

Rate Plan Dimension
Rate Plan Key (PK)
Rate Plan Code (Natural Key)
Rate Plan Abbreviation
Rate Plan Description
Rate Plan Type Code
Rate Plan Type Description

Figure 10.3 Schema following the design review.

Geographic Location Dimension

Let's shift gears and presume that we're now working for a phone company with land lines tied to a specific physical location. In general, the telecommunications industry has a very well-developed notion of location. The same could be said for the utilities industry. Many of its dimensions contain a precise geographic location as part of the attribute set. The location may be resolved to a physical street, city, state, and ZIP code or even to a specific latitude and longitude. Using our dimension role-playing technique, we imagine building a single master location table where data is standardized once and then reused. The location table could be part of the service line telephone number, equipment inventory, network inventory (including poles and switch boxes), real estate inventory, service location, dispatch location, right of way, and even customer entities. Each row in the master location table is a specific point in space that rolls up to every conceivable geographic grouping, such as census tracts and counties. A location could roll up to multiple unique geographic groupings simultaneously.

Location Outrigger

Location more naturally is thought of as a component of a dimension, not as a standalone dimension. The use of an embedded role, such as location, in a variety of unrelated larger dimensions is one of the few places where we support snowflaked outriggers. We recommend creating a join from each of the primary dimension tables that need to describe location to a clone of the location subdimension table. The issues in creating location clones are exactly the same as the ones we described in Chapter 5 for creating date role-playing dimensions. We need separate views for each use of the location table, being careful to create distinguishable column names. A possible advantage of this approach is that if we later embellish the geographic dimensions with census or demographic information, we do so in one place, without touching all the primary dimensions that include a location description. On the other hand, we haven't gained much with this approach if there is little overlap between the geographic locations embedded in various dimensions. In this situation we would pay a performance price for consolidating all the disparate addresses into a single dimension. Likewise, we should check with our database management system to determine its treatment (and associated penalty, if applicable) of the view construct. Ultimately, we need to remain focused on our two driving design principles: ease of use and performance.

Leveraging Geographic Information Systems

While we're on the topic of location dimensions, very few conventional data warehouses currently make the most of their data with a map-driven approach to visualization and presentation. The data warehouse can take advantage of interesting geographic information system (GIS) tools to deliver the information and insights contained in spatially oriented address or route data. This actually may encourage design enhancements and extensions to include attributes that enable richer analysis of our warehouse data via a GIS capability.

Using GIS tools, we can effectively exploit the millions of addresses we already store. We can invoke new graphic presentation tools that allow us to see two-dimensional patterns on a map that simply can't be detected in spreadsheets and conventional reports. In addition, we can attach some new verbs to our existing databases that let us ask spatially enabled questions, such as "Find all the service lines or switches that are within or near a group of counties," without modifying the underlying data.

The process for integrating the warehouse data with a GIS capability will vary depending on which GIS tool is used. Essentially, in order for the GIS to interpret ordinary street addresses, it first standardizes the raw address information from the location dimension into a parsed form. The GIS tool's geocoder then attempts to match the parsed addresses with a standard street network database of geographic points. If all goes well, you get back a set of location objects that can be plotted visually. In other cases you may choose to physically alter and populate the underlying location dimension with geospecific attributes such as points, lines, and polygons. You also may want to consider the spatial capabilities that are implemented within some DBMSs.

If you are a GIS professional sitting on top of mounds of geospatial data, this approach is probably not for you; you likely need to use a mainline GIS solution instead. However, if you are a text-and-numbers data warehouse manager already storing millions of addresses and other attributes of physical locations, then consider this technique to pick the low-hanging fruit that our GIS colleagues have generously provided without modifying your existing data warehouse applications or data architecture.

Summary

This chapter provided the opportunity to conduct a design review using an example case study. We provided a laundry list of common design flaws to scout for when performing a review. We encourage you to use this laundry list to review your own draft schemas in search of potential improvements.

We also discussed the geographic location as a permissible outrigger if it is used repeatedly in dimensional designs. Finally, we suggested opportunities to further leverage this geographic information through the use of a GIS tool.

Transportation

V oyages occur whenever a person or thing travels from one point to another, perhaps with stops in the middle. Obviously, this applies directly to organizations involved in the travel industry. Shippers, as well as internal logistical functions, also will relate to the discussion, as will package delivery services and car rental agencies. Somewhat unexpectedly, many of the characteristics in this chapter's schema are also applicable to telecommunications network route analysis. A phone network can be thought of as a map of possible voyages that a call makes between origin and destination phone numbers.

In this chapter we'll draw on an airline frequent flyer case study to explore voyages and routes because many readers are familiar (perhaps too familiar) with the subject matter. The case study lends itself to a discussion of multiple fact tables at different granularities. We'll also expand on several concepts, such as dimension role-playing and additional date and time dimension considerations. As usual, the intended audience for this chapter should not be limited to the industries just listed.

Chapter 11 discusses the following concepts:

- **Fact tables at different levels of granularity**
- **Combining role-playing dimensions into a superdimension in certain situations**
- **Country-specific date dimensions**
- **Time of day as a fact versus dimension**
- **Dates and times in multiple time zones**

Airline Frequent Flyer Case Study

In this case the airline's marketing department wants to analyze the flight activity of each member of its frequent flyer program. The department is interested in seeing what flights the company's frequent flyers take, which planes they fly, what fare basis they pay, how often they upgrade, how they earn and redeem their frequent flyer miles, whether they respond to special fare promotions, how long their overnight stays are, and what proportion of these frequent flyers have titanium, platinum, gold, or aluminum status.

As usual, we work through the four-step process to tackle the design of this frequent flyer schema. For this case study, the business process would be actual flight activity. We are not focusing on reservation or ticketing activity data that didn't result in a frequent flyer boarding a plane. The data warehouse team will contend with those other sources of data in subsequent phases.

Multiple Fact Table Granularities

When it comes to the grain, we encounter a situation in this case where we are presented with multiple potential levels of fact table granularity. Each of these levels of granularity has different metrics associated with them.

At the most granular level, the airline captures data at the leg level. The leg represents an aircraft taking off at one airport and landing at another without any intermediate stops. Capacity planning and flight scheduling analysts are very interested in this discrete level of information because they're able to look at the number of seats to calculate load factors by leg. We also can include facts regarding the leg's flight duration as well as the number of minutes late at departure and arrival. Perhaps there's even a dimension to easily identify on-time arrivals.

The next level of granularity corresponds to a segment. In this case we're looking at the portion of a trip on a single aircraft. Segments may have one or more legs associated with them. If you take a flight from San Francisco to Minneapolis with a stop in Denver but no aircraft change, you have flown one segment (SFO-MSP) but two legs (SFO-DEN and DEN-MSP). Conversely, if the flight flew nonstop from San Francisco to Minneapolis, you would have flown one segment as well as one leg. The segment represents the line item on an airline ticket coupon; revenue and mileage credit is generated at the segment level.

Next, we can analyze flight activity by trip. The trip provides an accurate picture of customer demand. In our prior example, assume that the flights from San Francisco to Minneapolis required the flyer to change aircraft in Denver. In this case the trip from San Francisco to Minneapolis would entail two segments corresponding to the two aircraft involved. In reality, the passenger just asked to go from San Francisco to Minneapolis; the fact that he or she needed to stop in Denver was merely a necessary evil but certainly wasn't requested. For this reason, sales and marketing analysts are interested in trip-level data.

Finally, the airline collects data for the itinerary, which is equivalent to the entire airline ticket or reservation confirmation number.

The data warehouse team and business representatives decide to begin at the segment-level grain to satisfy the need for improved frequent flyer analysis. This represents the lowest level of data with meaningful metrics for the marketing department. The data warehouse team inevitably will tackle the more granular leg-level data for the capacity planners and flight schedulers at some future point. The conforming dimensions built during this first iteration certainly will be leveraged at that time.

There will be one row in the fact table for each boarding pass collected from frequent flyers. The dimensionality associated with this data is quite extensive, as illustrated in Figure 11.1. If we had instead chosen the grain to be the trip as a multiple-segment event, all the specific details regarding the aircraft, fare basis, class, and other circumstances of each flight would have been suppressed.

We see that the schema uses the role-playing technique extensively. The multiple date, time, and airport dimensions link to views of a single underlying physical date, time, and airport dimension table, respectively, as we discussed originally in Chapter 5.

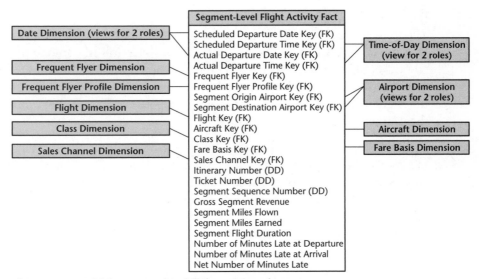

Figure 11.1 Initial segment-level flight activity schema.

The frequent flyer dimension is a garden-variety customer dimension with all the attributes captured about our most valuable flyers. Interestingly, in this case the frequent flyers are motivated to help you maintain this dimension accurately because they want to ensure that they're receiving appropriate mileage credit. For a large airline, this dimension would have tens of millions of rows in it. Marketing wants to analyze activity by frequent flyer tier, which can change during the course of a year. In addition, we learned during the requirements process that the users are interested in slicing and dicing based on the flyers' home airports and whether they belong to the airline's airport club. Therefore, we opt to create a separate frequent flyer profile minidimension, as we discussed in Chapter 6, with one row for each unique combination of frequent flyer elite tier, home airport, and club membership status.

The flight dimension contains information about each flight, such as the aircraft used. Although there is a specific origin and destination associated with each flight, we call these key airport dimensions out separately to simplify the user's view of the data and make access more efficient.

The class of service flown describes whether the passenger sat in coach, business, or first class. The fare basis dimension describes the terms surrounding the fare. It would identify whether it's a full fare, an unrestricted fare, a 21-day advanced-purchase fare with change and cancellation penalties, or a 10 percent off fare due to a special promotion available for tickets purchased at the company's Web site during a given time period. In this case study we decide not to separate the notion of promotion from fare basis. After interviewing business users at the airline, we conclude that fare basis and promotion are inextricably linked and that it does not make sense to separate them in the data.

The sales channel dimension identifies how the ticket was purchased, whether through a travel agency, directly from the airline's toll-free phone number or city ticket office, from the airline's Web site, or via another Internet travel services provider. In addition, several operational numbers are associated with the flight activity data, including the itinerary number, the ticket number, and the segment sequence number.

The facts captured at the segment level of granularity include the gross segment revenue, segment miles flown, and segment miles awarded (in those cases where a minimum number of miles are awarded regardless of the flight distance). To monitor customer service levels, we also might include such facts as the minutes late at departure and arrival, which would be summarized in the case of a multileg segment.

Linking Segments into Trips

Despite the powerful dimensional framework we just designed, we are unable to easily answer one of the most important questions about our frequent fly-ers, namely, where are they going? The segment grain masks the true nature of the trip. If we fetch all the segments of the airline voyage and sequence them by segment number, it is still nearly impossible to discern the trip start and end points. Most complete itineraries start and end at the same airport. If a lengthy stop were used as a criterion for a meaningful trip destination, it would require extensive and tricky processing whenever we tried to summarize a number of voyages by the meaningful stops.

The answer is to introduce two more airport role-playing dimensions: trip ori-gin and trip destination, while keeping the grain at the flight segment level. These are determined during data extraction by looking on the ticket for any stop of more than four hours, which is the airline's official definition of a stopover. The enhanced schema looks like Figure 11.2. We would need to exer-cise some caution when summarizing data by trip in this schema. Some of the dimensions, such as fare basis or class of service flown, don't apply at the trip level. On the other hand, it may be useful to see how many trips from San Francisco to Minneapolis included an unrestricted fare on a segment.

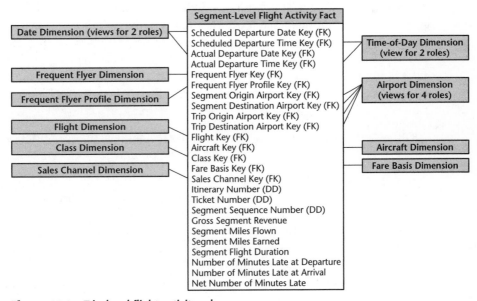

Figure 11.2 Trip-level flight activity schema.

In addition to linking segments into trips as Figure 11.2 illustrates, if the business users are constantly looking at information at the trip level, rather than by segment, we might be tempted to create an aggregate fact table at the trip grain. Some of the earlier dimensions discussed, such as class of service, fare basis, and flight, obviously would not be applicable. The facts would include such metrics as trip gross revenue and additional facts that would appear only in this complementary trip summary table, such as the number of segments in the trip. However, we would only go to the trouble of creating such an aggregate table if there were obvious performance or usability issues when we used the segment-level table as the basis for rolling up the same reports. If a typical trip consisted of three segments, then we might barely see a three times performance improvement with such an aggregate table, meaning that it may not be worth the bother.

Extensions to Other Industries

Using the frequent flyer case study to illustrate a voyage schema makes intuitive sense because most of us have boarded a plane at one time or another. We'll briefly touch on several other variations on this theme.

Cargo Shipper

The schema for a cargo shipper looks quite similar to the frequent flyer schemas just developed. Suppose that a transoceanic shipping company transports bulk goods in containers from foreign to domestic ports. The items in the containers are shipped from an original shipper to a final consignor. The trip can have multiple stops at intermediate ports. It is possible that the containers may be offloaded from one ship to another at a port. Likewise, it is possible that one or more of the legs may be by truck rather than ship.

As illustrated in Figure 11.3, the grain of the fact table is the container on a specific bill-of-lading number on a particular leg of its trip.

The ship mode dimension identifies the type of shipping company and specific vessel. The item dimension contains a description of the items in a container. The container dimension describes the size of the container and whether it requires electrical power or refrigeration. The commodity dimension describes one type of item in the container. Almost anything that can be shipped can be described by harmonized commodity codes, which are a kind of master conformed dimension used by agencies, including U.S. Customs. The consignor,

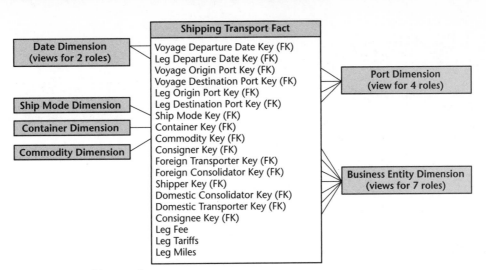

Figure 11.3 Shipper schema.

foreign transporter, foreign consolidator, shipper, domestic consolidator, domestic transporter, and consignee are all roles played by a master business entity dimension that contains all the possible business parties associated with a voyage. The bill-of-lading number is a degenerate dimension. We assume that the fees and tariffs are applicable to the individual leg of the voyage.

Shipping transport schemas like this one characteristically have a large number of dimensions. When all the parties to the voyage have been added, the design can swell to 15 or even 20 dimensions.

Travel Services

If we work for a travel services company, we can envision complementing the customer flight activity schema with fact tables to track associated hotel stays and rental car usage. These schemas would share several common dimensions, such as the date, customer, and itinerary number, along with ticket and segment number, as applicable, to allow hotel stays and car rentals to be interleaved correctly into a airline trip. For hotel stays, the grain of the fact table is the entire stay, as illustrated in Figure 11.4. The grain of a similar car rental fact table would be the entire rental episode. Of course, if we were constructing a fact table for a hotel chain rather than a travel services company, the schema would be much more robust because we'd know far more about the hotel property characteristics, the guest's use of services, and associated detailed charges.

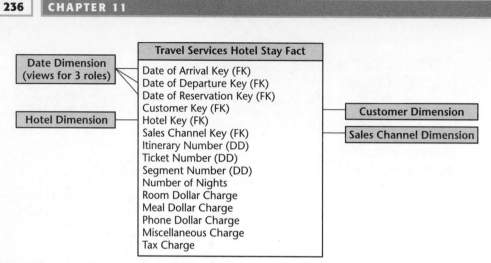

Figure 11.4 Travel services hotel stay schema.

Combining Small Dimensions into a Superdimension

We stated previously that if a many-to-many relationship exists between two groups of dimension attributes, then they should be modeled as separate dimensions with separate foreign keys in the fact table. Sometimes, however, we'll encounter a situation where these dimensions can be combined into a single superdimension rather than treating them as two separate dimensions with two separate foreign keys in the fact table.

Class of Service

The Figure 11.1 draft schema included the class of service flown dimension. Following our first design checkpoint with the business community, we learn that the business users want to analyze the class of service purchased, as well as the class flown. Unfortunately, we're unable to reliably determine the class of service actually used from the original fare basis because the customer may do a last-minute upgrade. In addition, the business users want to easily filter and report on activity based on whether an upgrade or downgrade occurred. Our initial reaction is to include a second role-playing dimension and foreign key in the fact table to support access to both the purchased and flown class of service, along with a third foreign key for the upgrade indicator. In this situation, however, there are only three rows in each class dimension table to indicate first, business, and coach classes. Likewise, the upgrade indicator dimension also would have just three rows in it, corresponding to upgrade, downgrade, or no class change. Since the row counts are so small, we elect instead to combine the dimensions into a single class of service dimension, as illustrated in Figure 11.5.

Class of Service Key	Class Purchased	Class Flown	Purchased-Flown Class Group	Class Change Indicator
1	Coach	Coach	Coach-Coach	No Class Change
2	Coach	Business	Coach-Business	Upgrade
3	Coach	First	Coach-First	Upgrade
4	Business	Coach	Business-Coach	Downgrade
5	Business	Business	Business-Business	No Class Change
6	Business	First	Business-First	Upgrade
7	First	Coach	First-Coach	Downgrade
8	First	Business	First-Business	Downgrade
9	First	First	First-First	No Class Change

Figure 11.5 Sample rows from the combined class dimension.

The Cartesian product of the separate class dimensions only results in a nine-row dimension table (three class purchased rows, three class flown rows). We also have the opportunity in this superdimension to describe the relationship between the purchased and flown classes, such as the class group and class change indicator. In some ways, we can think of this combined class of service superdimension as a type of junk dimension, which we introduced in Chapter 5.

Origin and Destination

Likewise, we can consider the pros and cons of combining the origin and destination airport dimensions. In this situation the data volumes are more significant, so separate role-playing origin and destination dimensions seem more practical. However, the users may need additional attributes that depend on the combination of origin and destination. In addition to accessing the characteristics of each airport, business users also want to analyze flight activity data by the distance between the city-pair airports, as well as the type of city pair (such as domestic or trans-Atlantic). Even the seemingly simple question regarding the total activity between San Francisco (SFO) and Denver (DEN), regardless of whether the flights originated in SFO or DEN, would be challenging with separate origin and destination dimensions. Sure, SQL experts may be able to answer the question programmatically, but what about the less empowered? In addition, even if we're able to derive the correct answer, we lack a standard label for that city-pair route. Some applications may label it SFO-DEN, whereas others might opt for DEN-SFO, San Fran-Denver, Den-SF, and so on. Rather than embedding inconsistent labels in application code, we should put them in a dimension table so that common, standardized labels can be used throughout the organization. It would be a shame to go to the bother of creating a data warehouse and then allow application code to implement inconsistent reporting labels. The business sponsors of the data warehouse won't tolerate that for long.

City-Pair Key	City-Pair Name	Origin Airport	Origin City	Destination Airport	Destination City	Distance (Miles)	Distance Band	City-Pair Type
1	BOS-JFK	BOS	Boston, MA	JFK	New York, NY	191	Less than 200 miles	Domestic
2	BOS-JFK	JFK	New York, NY	BOS	Boston, MA	191	Less than 200 miles	Domestic
3	BOS-LGW	BOS	Boston, MA	LGW	London, UK	3267	3,000 to 3,500 miles	Trans-Atlantic
4	BOS-LGW	LGW	London, UK	BOS	Boston, MA	3267	3,000 to 3,500 miles	Trans-Atlantic
5	BOS-NRT	BOS	Boston, MA	NRT	Tokyo, Japan	6737	More than 6,000 miles	Trans-Pacific

Figure 11.6 Sample rows from the city-pair (route) dimension.

To satisfy the need to access additional city-pair attributes, we have two options. One is merely to add another dimension to the fact table for the city-pair descriptors, including the city-pair name, city-pair type, and distance. The other alternative, as shown in Figure 11.6, is to combine the origin and destination airport attributes in addition to including the supplemental city-pair attributes. In this case, the number of rows in the combined dimension table will grow significantly. Theoretically, the combined dimension could have as many rows as the Cartesian product of the origin and destination airports. Fortunately, in real life the number of rows is much smaller than this theoretical limit. More to the point, we're willing to live with this compromise because the combined city-pair dimension reflects the way the business thinks about the data. We could use this same table as a role-play for a trip city-pair dimension.

As we mentioned, if the actual row counts prohibited a combined dimension, then we could continue to use the separate origin and destination dimensions but include a third dimension in the fact table to support the city-pair attributes rather than relying on the access application for the combination city-pair logic. Besides large data volumes, the other motivation for maintaining separate dimension tables occurs if other business processes require the separate dimensions, although one could argue that the separate dimensions merely must conform to the combined superdimension.

 In most cases, role-playing dimensions should be treated as separate logical dimensions created via views on a single physical table, as we've seen earlier with date dimensions. In isolated situations it may make sense to combine the separate dimensions into a superdimension, notably when the data volumes are extremely small or there is a need for additional attributes that depend on the combined underlying roles for context and meaning.

More Date and Time Considerations

From the earliest chapters in this book we've discussed the importance of having a verbose date dimension, whether it's at the individual day, week, or month granularity, that contains descriptive attributes about the date and private labels for fiscal periods and work holidays. In this final section we'll introduce several additional considerations when dealing with date and time dimensions.

Country-Specific Calendars

If the data warehouse serves multinational needs, we must generalize the standard date dimension to handle multinational calendars in an open-ended number of countries. The primary date dimension contains generic attributes about the date, regardless of the country. If your multinational business spans Gregorian, Hebrew, Islamic, and Chinese calendars, then we would include four sets of days, months, and years in this primary dimension.

Country-specific date dimensions supplement the primary date table. The key to the supplemental dimension is the primary date key, along with the country name. The table would include country-specific date attributes, such as holiday or season names, as illustrated in Figure 11.7. This approach is similar to the handling of multiple fiscal accounting calendars, as described in Chapter 7.

We can join this table to the main calendar dimension or to the fact table directly. If we provide an interface that requires the user to specify a country name, then the attributes of the country-specific supplement can be viewed as logically appended to the primary date table, allowing you to view the calendar through the eyes of a single country at a time. Country-specific calendars can be messy to build in their own right. Things get even messier if we need to deal with local holidays that occur on different days in different parts of a country.

Fact	Date Dimension	Country-Specific Date Outrigger
Date Key (FK)	Date Key (PK)	Date Key (FK)
More Foreign Keys ...	Date	Country Key (PK)
Facts ...	Day of Week	Country Name
	Day Number in Epoch	Civil Holiday Flag
	Week Number in Epoch	Civil Holiday Name
	Month Number in Epoch	Religious Holiday Flag
	Day Number in Calendar Month	Religious Holiday Name
	Day Number in Calendar Year	Workday Indicator
	Day Number in Fiscal Month	Season Name
	Day Number in Fiscal Year	
	Last Day in Week Indicator	
	Last Day in Month Indicator	
	Calendar Week Ending Date	
	Calendar Week Number in Year	
	Calendar Month	
	Calendar Month Number in Year	
	Calendar Year-Month (YYYY-MM)	
	Calendar Quarter	
	Calendar Year-Quarter	
	Calendar Half Year	
	Calendar Year	
	Fiscal Week	
	Fiscal Week Number in Year	
	Fiscal Month	
	Fiscal Month Number in Year	
	Fiscal Year-Month	
	Fiscal Quarter	
	Fiscal Year-Quarter	
	Fiscal Half Year	
	Fiscal Year	
	SQL Date Stamp	
	... and more	

Figure 11.7 Country-specific calendar outrigger.

Time of Day as a Dimension or Fact

We strongly encourage designers to separate time of day from the date dimension to avoid an explosion in the date dimension row count. In earlier examples we've illustrated the time of day as a full-fledged dimension table with one row per discrete time period (for example, each second or minute within a 24-hour period). This is the preferred route if we need to support the roll-up of time periods into more summarized groupings for reporting and analysis, such as 15-minute intervals, hours, or AM/PM. They also could reflect business-specific time groupings, such as the weekday morning rush period for flight activity.

If there's no need to roll up or filter on time-of-day groups, then we have the option to treat time as a simple numeric fact instead. In this situation, the time of day would be expressed as a number of minutes or number of seconds since midnight, as shown in Figure 11.8.

Date and Time in Multiple Time Zones

When operating in multiple countries or even just multiple time zones, we're faced with a quandary concerning transaction dates and times. Do we capture the date and time relative to local midnight in each time zone, or do we express the time period relative to a standard, such as the corporate headquarters date/time or Greenwich Mean Time (GMT)? To fully satisfy users' requirements, the correct answer is probably both. The standard time allows us to see the simultaneous nature of transactions across the business, whereas the local time allows us to understand transaction timing relative to the time of day.

Contrary to popular belief, there are more than 24 time zones (corresponding to the 24 hours of the day) in the world. For example, there is a single time zone in India, offset from GMT by 5.5 or 6.5 hours depending on the time of year. The situation gets even more unpleasant when you consider the complexities of switching to and from daylight saving time. As such, it's unreasonable to think that merely providing an offset in a fact table can support

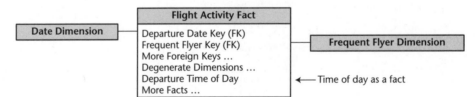

Figure 11.8 Fact table with time of day as a fact.

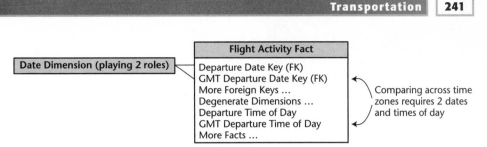

Figure 11.9 Localized and equalized date/time across time zones.

equivalized dates and times. Likewise, the offset can't reside in a time or airport dimension table. The recommended approach for expressing dates and times in multiple time zones is to include separate date and time-of-day dimensions (or time-of-day facts, as we just discussed) corresponding to the local and equivalized dates, as shown in Figure 11.9.

We'll elaborate further on multiple date and time dimension tables to capture both the absolute standard and local clock-on-the-wall dates and times when we discuss a multinational Web retailer in Chapter 14.

Summary

In this chapter we turned our attention to the concept of trips or routes. The expanded case study focused on an airline frequent flyer example, and we briefly touched on similar scenarios drawn from the shipping and travel services industries. We examined the situation in which we have multiple fact tables at multiple granularities with multiple grain-specific facts. We also discussed the possibility of combining dimensions into a single dimension table in cases where the row count volumes are extremely small or when there are additional attributes that depend on the combined dimensions. Again, combining dimensions should be viewed as the exception rather than the rule.

We wrapped up this chapter by discussing several date and time dimension techniques, including country-specific calendar outriggers, treatment of time as a fact versus a separate dimension, and the handling of absolute and relative dates and times.

Education

We step into the world of an educational institution in this chapter. We'll first look at the applicant student pipeline as an accumulating snapshot. When we introduced the accumulating snapshot-grained fact table in Chapter 5, we used an order fulfillment pipeline to illustrate the concept. In this chapter, rather than watching orders move through various states prior to completion, the accumulating snapshot is used to monitor prospective student applicants as they move through standard admissions milestones. The other primary concept discussed in this chapter is the factless fact table. We'll explore several case study illustrations drawn from education to further elaborate on these special fact tables, and we will discuss the analysis of events that didn't occur.

Chapter 12 discusses the following concepts:

- Admission's applicant tracking as an accumulating snapshot
- Factless fact table for student registration and facilities management data
- Handling of nonexistent events, including promotion events from the retail industry

University Case Study

In this chapter we'll pretend that we work for a university, college, or other type of educational institution. Traditionally, there has been less focus on revenue and profit in this arena, but with the ever-escalating costs and competition associated with higher education, universities and colleges are very interested in attracting and retaining high-quality students. In fact, there's a strong interest in understanding and maintaining a relationship well beyond graduation. There's also a dominant need to understand what our student customers are buying in terms of courses each term. Finally, we'll take a look at maximizing the use of the university's capital-intensive facilities.

Accumulating Snapshot for Admissions Tracking

In Chapter 5 we treated the order fulfillment pipeline as an accumulating snapshot. We also described the use of an accumulating snapshot to track a specific item, uniquely identified by a serial or lot number, as it moves through the manufacturing and test pipeline. Let's take a moment to recall the distinguishing characteristics of an accumulating snapshot fact table:

- A single row represents the complete history of something.
- Such a fact table is most appropriate for short-lived processes, such as orders and bills.
- Multiple dates represent the standard scenario milestones of each row.
- Open-ended sets of facts accumulate the interesting measures.
- Each row is revisited and changed whenever something happens.
- Both foreign keys and measured facts may be changed during the revisit.

We can envision these same characteristics applied to the prospective student admissions pipeline. For those who work in other industries, there are obvious similarities to tracking job applicants as they move through the hiring process, and tracking sales prospects as they become customers.

In the case of applicant tracking, prospective students progress through a standard set of admissions hurdles or milestones. Perhaps we're interested in tracking activities around key dates, such as receipt of preliminary admissions test scores, information requested (via Web or otherwise), information sent, interview conducted, on-site campus visit, application received, transcript received, test scores received, recommendations received, first pass review by admissions, review for financial aid, final decision from admissions, accepted, admitted, and enrolled. At any point in time, people in the admissions and enrollment management area are interested in how many applicants are at each stage in the pipeline. The process is much like a funnel, where many applicants enter the pipeline, but far fewer progress through to the final stage. Admission personnel also would like to analyze the applicant pool by a variety of characteristics.

The grain of the accumulating snapshot to track the applicant's lifecycle is one row per prospective student. This granularity represents the lowest level of detail captured when the prospect enters the pipeline. As more information is collected while the prospect progresses toward application, acceptance, and admission, we continue to revisit and update the prospect's status in the fact table row, as illustrated in Figure 12.1.

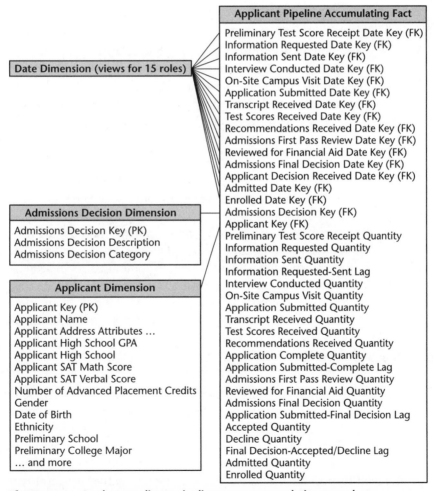

Figure 12.1 Student applicant pipeline as an accumulating snapshot.

Like other accumulating snapshots we've discussed, there are multiple dates in the fact table corresponding to the standard process milestones. We want to analyze the prospect's progress by these dates to determine the pace of movement through the pipeline, and we also want to spot bottlenecks. This is especially important if we see a significant lag involving a candidate whom we're interested in attracting. Each of these dates is treated as a role-playing dimension, using surrogate keys to handle the inevitable unknown dates when we first load the row.

The applicant dimension contains many interesting attributes about our prospective students. Admissions analysts are interested in slicing and dicing these applicant characteristics by geography, incoming credentials (grade point average, college admissions test scores, advanced placement credits, and high school), gender, date of birth, ethnicity, and preliminary major. Analyzing these characteristics at various stages of the pipeline will help admissions personnel adjust their strategies to encourage more (or fewer) students to proceed to the next mile marker.

As we saw previously, accumulating snapshots are appropriate for short-lived processes, such as the applicant pipeline, that have a defined start and end, as well as standard intermediate milestones. This type of fact table allows us to see an updated status and ultimately final disposition of each prospective applicant. We could include a fact for the estimated probability that the prospect will become a student. By adding all these probabilities together, we would see an instantaneous prediction of the following year's enrollment.

Another education-based example of an accumulating snapshot focuses on research proposal activities. Some user constituencies may be interested in viewing the lifecycle of a research grant proposal as it progresses through the grant pipeline from preliminary proposal to grant approval and award receipt. This would support analysis of the number of outstanding proposals in each stage of the pipeline by faculty, department, research topic area, or research funding source. Likewise, we could see success rates by the various dimensions. Having this information in a common repository such as the data warehouse would allow it to be leveraged more readily by a broader university population.

Factless Fact Tables

So far we've designed fact tables that have had a very characteristic structure. Each fact table typically has three to approximately 15 to 20 key columns, followed by one to potentially several dozen numeric, continuously valued, preferably additive facts. The facts can be regarded as measurements taken at the intersection of the dimension key values. From this perspective, the facts are the justification for the fact table, and the key values are simply administrative structure to identify the facts.

There are, however, a number of business processes whose fact tables are similar to those we've been designing with one major distinction: There are no measured facts! We call these *factless fact tables*. In the following examples we'll discuss both event tracking and coverage factless fact tables. We briefly introduced the factless coverage table in Chapter 2 while discussing retail promotion coverage, as well as in Chapter 5 to describe sales rep territory coverage.

Student Registration Events

There are many situations in which events need to be recorded as the simultaneous coming together of a number of dimensional entities. For example, we can track student registrations by term. The grain of the fact table would be one row for each registered course by student and term. As illustrated in Figure 12.2, the fact table has the following dimensionality: term, student, student major and attainment, course, and faculty.

In this scenario we're dealing with fact data at the term level rather than at the more typical calendar day, week, or month granularity. Term is the lowest level available for the registration events. The term dimension still should conform to the calendar date dimension. In other words, each date in our daily calendar dimension should identify the term (for example, Fall AY2002), academic year (for example, AY2002), and term season (for example, Winter). The column labels and values must be identical for the attributes common to both the calendar date and term dimensions.

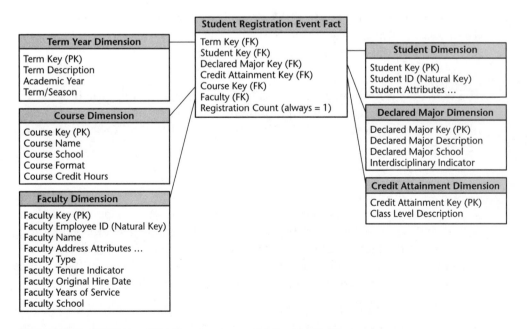

Figure 12.2 Student registration events as a factless fact table.

The student dimension is an expanded version of the applicant dimension that we discussed in the last scenario. We still want to retain all the information we garnered from the application process (for example, geography, credentials, and preliminary major) but supplement it with on-campus information, such as part-time/full-time status, residence, involvement in athletics, declared major, and class level status (for example, sophomore). As we discussed in Chapter 6, we imagine treating some of these attributes as a minidimension(s) because factions throughout the university are interested in tracking changes to them over time, especially when it comes to declared major, class level, and graduation attainment. People in administration and academia are keenly interested in academic progress and retention rates by class, school, department, and major.

A fact table is a reasonable place to represent the robust set of many-to-many relationships among these dimensions. It records the collision of dimensions at a point in time and space. This table could be queried to answer a number of interesting questions regarding registration for the college's academic offerings, such as which students registered for which courses? How many declared engineering majors are taking an out-of-major finance course? How many students have registered for a given faculty member's courses during the last three years? How many students have registered for more than one course from a given faculty member? The only peculiarity in this example is that we don't have a numeric fact tied to this registration data. As such, analyses of this data will be based largely on counts.

 Events often are modeled as a fact table containing a series of keys, each representing a participating dimension in the event. Event tables often have no obvious numeric facts associated with them and hence are called *factless fact tables*.

The SQL for performing counts in this factless fact is asymmetric because of the absence of any facts. When counting the number of registrations for a faculty member, any key can be used as the argument to the COUNT function. For example:

```
SELECT FACULTY, COUNT(TERM_KEY)... GROUP BY FACULTY
```

This gives the simple count of the number of student registrations by faculty, subject to any constraints that may exist in the WHERE clause. An oddity of SQL is that you can count any key and still get the same answer because you are counting the number of keys that fly by the query, not their distinct values. We would need to use a COUNT DISTINCT if we wanted to count the unique instances of a key rather than the number of keys encountered.

The inevitable confusion surrounding the SQL statement, while not a serious semantic problem, causes some designers to create an artificial implied fact, perhaps called *registration count* (as opposed to *dummy*), that is always populated by the value 1. While this fact does not add any information to the fact table, it makes the SQL more readable, such as:

```
SELECT FACULTY, SUM(REGISTRATION_COUNT)... GROUP BY FACULTY
```

At this point the table is no longer strictly factless, but most would agree that the 1 is nothing more than an artifact. The SQL will be a bit cleaner and more expressive with the registration artifact. Perhaps query tools will have an easier time constructing the query with a few simple user gestures. More important, if we build a summarized aggregate table above this fact table, we will need a real column to roll up to meaningful aggregate registration counts.

If a measurable fact does surface during the design, it can be added to the schema, assuming that it is consistent with the grain of student registrations by term. For example, if we have the ability to track tuition revenue, earned credit hours, and grade scores, we could add them to this fact table, but then it's no longer a factless fact table. The addition of these facts would definitely enable more interesting analyses. For example, what is the revenue generated by course or faculty? What is the average grade per class by faculty?

Facilities Utilization Coverage

The second type of factless fact table is the coverage table. We'll draw on a scenario dealing with facility management to serve as an illustration. Universities invest a tremendous amount of capital in their physical plant and facilities. It would be helpful to understand which facilities were being used for what purpose during every hour of the day during each term. For example, which facilities were used most heavily? What was the average occupancy rate of the facilities as a function of time of day? Does use drop off significantly on Fridays when no one wants to teach (or attend) classes?

Once again, the factless fact table comes to the rescue. In this case we'd include one row in the fact table for each facility for standard hourly time blocks during each day of the week during a term regardless of whether the facility is being used or not. We've illustrated the schema in Figure 12.3.

The facility dimension would include all types of descriptive attributes about the facility, such as the building, facility type (for example, classroom, lab, or office), square footage, capacity, and amenities (for example, white board or built-in projector). The utilization status dimension obviously would include a text descriptor with values of "Available" or "Utilized." Meanwhile, multiple organizations may be involved in facilities utilization. Such would be the case if one organization owned the facility during a time block, whereas the same or a different organization was assigned as the facility user.

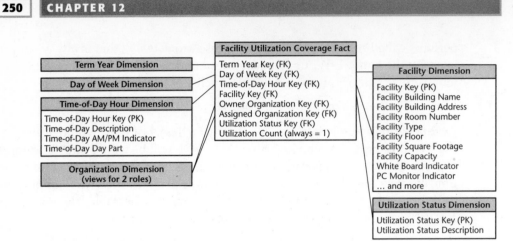

Figure 12.3 Facilities utilization as a coverage factless fact table.

Student Attendance Events

We can visualize a similar schema to track student attendance in a course. In this case the grain would be one row for each student who walks through the course's classroom door each day. This factless fact table would share a number of the same dimensions we discussed with respect to registration events. The primary difference would be that the granularity is by calendar date in this schema rather than merely term. This dimensional model, as illustrated in Figure 12.4, would allow us to answer such questions as which courses were the most heavily attended? Which courses suffered the least attendance attrition over the term? Which students attended which courses? Which faculty member taught the most students?

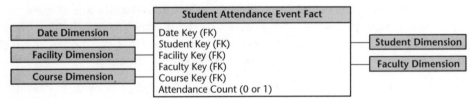

Figure 12.4 Student attendance fact table.

Explicit Rows for What Didn't Happen

Perhaps people are interested in monitoring students who were registered for a course but didn't show up. In this example we can envision adding explicit rows to the fact table for attendance events that didn't occur. Adding rows is viable in this scenario because the nonattendance events have the same exact dimensionality as the attendance events. Likewise, the fact table won't grow at an alarming rate, presuming (or perhaps hoping) that the no shows are a small percentage of the total students registered for a course. In this situation we're no longer dealing with a factless fact table because now the attendance fact would equal either 1 or 0.

While this approach is reasonable in this scenario, creating rows for events that didn't happen is ridiculous in many situations. For example, if we think back to our transportation case study, we certainly don't want to build fact table rows for each flight not taken by a frequent flyer on a given day.

Other Relational Options for What Didn't Happen

In many cases the primary transaction fact table, such as the sales in a grocery store, is very sparsely populated. Only a fraction of the total product portfolio sells in each store each day in most retail environments. There would be overwhelming overhead associated with storing explicit rows for products that didn't sell. The transaction sales fact table is already very large; the last thing we want to do is to spend more money on the resources and disk space to store a bunch of zeroes. As we recall from Chapter 2, we can use a promotion coverage factless fact table to help answer the question of what was being promoted but didn't sell. A row is placed in the coverage table for each product in each store that is on promotion in each time period. This table would be much smaller than adding explicit rows to the existing transaction fact table because it only contains the items on promotion; those not being promoted would be excluded. In addition, perhaps we could substitute a weekly granularity instead of a daily grain if promotions run on a weekly basis. To answer the question regarding what was on promotion but didn't sell, we'd first consult the coverage table for the products on promotion at a given time in that store. We'd then consult the sales fact table to determine what did sell; the set difference between these two lists of products is our answer.

In a relational database environment, we also have the option of using the NOT EXISTS construct in SQL to identify rows that don't exist in a database, such as nonexistent facts or dimension attributes. While this approach alleviates the need for upfront planning and design work to either include explicit rows or construct coverage tables, it's not as pain free as it appears initially. We must ask very specifically what doesn't exist by framing the NOT EXISTS within a larger query. For example, to answer the question about nonexistent sales for promoted products, we must first determine all products sold during a given extended time frame and then issue a subquery within the NOT EXISTS construct to determine all products sold on promotion during a smaller time frame. The danger in using this SQL correlated subquery approach is that we'll miss products that didn't sell at all during the extended time frame. Also, the query is bound to perform slowly because of the complexity. Finally, data access tools may prohibit the use of this construct within their interface. Using the factless promotion coverage table in Figure 12.5, here is the SQL for finding all the products that did not sell on a particular promotion ("Active Promotion") on January 15, 2002 that otherwise sold in the San Antonio Main Outlet sometime during January 2002. If you can understand this SQL, then you are qualified to support this application!

```
SELECT P1.PRODUCT_DESCRIPTION
FROM SALES_FACT F1, PRODUCT P1, STORE S1, DATE D1, PROMOTION R1

WHERE F1.PROD_KEY = P1.PROD_KEY
    AND F1.STORE_KEY = S1.STORE_KEY
    AND F1.DATE_KEY = D1.DATE_KEY
    AND F1.PROMO_KEY = R1.PROMO_KEY
    AND S1.STORE_LOCATION = 'San Antonio Main Outlet'
    AND D1.MONTH = 'January, 2002'

AND NOT EXISTS
        (SELECT R2.PROMO_KEY
          FROM SALES_FACT F2, PROMOTION R2, DATE D2
          WHERE F2.PROMO_KEY = R2.PROMO_KEY
              AND F2.PROD_KEY = F1.PROD_KEY
              AND F2.STORE_KEY = F1.STORE_KEY
              AND F2.DATE_KEY = D2.DATE_KEY
              AND R2.PROMOTION_TYPE = 'Active Promotion'
              AND D2.FULL_DATE = 'January 15, 2002')
```

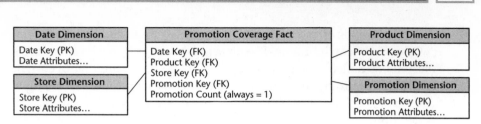

Figure 12.5 Promotion coverage as a factless fact table.

Multidimensional Handling of What Didn't Happen

Multidimensional online analytical processing (OLAP) databases do an excellent job of helping users understand what didn't happen. When the data cube is constructed, the multidimensional database handles the sparsity of the transaction data while minimizing the overhead burden of storing explicit zeroes. As such, at least for fact cubes that are not too sparse, the event and nonevent data is available for user analysis while reducing some of the complexities we just discussed in the relational world.

Other Areas of Analytic Interest

Now that we've taken a tangent to discuss the analysis of what didn't happen, let's return to the world of higher education to bring this chapter to an orderly conclusion. Many of the analytic processes described earlier in this book, such as procurement and human resources, are obviously applicable to the university environment given the desire to better monitor and manage costs. When we focus on the revenue side of the equation, research grants and alumni contributions are key sources, in addition to the tuition revenue.

The majority of research grant analysis is a variation of financial analysis, as we discussed in Chapter 7, but at a lower level of detail, much like a subledger. The grain would include additional dimensions to further describe the research grant, such as the corporate or governmental funding source, research topic, grant duration, and faculty researcher. There is a strong need to better understand and manage the budgeted and actual spending associated with each research project. The objective is to optimize the spending so that a surplus or deficit situation is avoided, while funds are deployed where they will be most productive. Likewise, understanding research spending rolled up by various dimensions is necessary to ensure proper institutional control of such monies.

Better understanding the university's alumni is much like better understanding a customer base, as we described in Chapter 6 regarding CRM. Obviously, there are many interesting characteristics that would be helpful in maintaining a mutually beneficial relationship with our alumni, such as geographic, demographic, employment, interests, and behavioral information, in addition to the data we collected about them as students (for example, incoming credentials, affiliations, school, major, length of time to graduate, and honors). Improved access to a broad range of attributes about the alumni population would allow the university to better target messages and allocate resources. In addition to alumni contributions, we can leverage the information for potential recruiting, job placement, and research opportunities. To this end, we can envision a full-scale CRM operational system to track all the university's touch points with its alumni, working in conjunction with the warehouse's analytic foundation.

Summary

In this chapter we focused on two primary concepts. First, we looked at the accumulating snapshot used to track the application pipeline (or conversely, the research grant activity pipeline). Even though the accumulating snapshot is used much less frequently than the more common transaction and periodic snapshot fact tables, it is very useful in situations where we want to track the current status of a short-lived process with generally accepted standard progress milestones.

Second, we explored several examples of the factless fact table. These fact tables capture the relationship between dimensions in the case of an event or coverage but are unique in that no measurements are collected to serve as actual facts. We also discussed the handling of situations where we want to track events that didn't occur.

Health Care

H ealth care presents several interesting data warehouse design situations. In this chapter we will imagine first that we work for a large health care consortium, then that we work for a billing organization for care providers and hospitals, and finally that we work for a large clinic with millions of complex patient treatment records. Each of these situations will suggest important design techniques applicable to health care and other industries.

Chapter 13 discusses the following concepts:

- Value circle within health care, centered on the patient treatment records
- Accumulating snapshot fact table to handle medical bill line items
- More dimension role-playing as applied to multiple dates and providers
- Multivalued dimensions, such as an open-ended number of diagnoses along with effective dates and weighting factors to support allocations
- Extended fact set to support profitability analysis
- Handling of complex medical events
- Fact dimension to organize extremely sparse, heterogeneous measurements

Health Care Value Circle

A typical large health care consortium is a network of providers, clinics, hospitals, pharmacies, pharmaceutical manufacturers, laboratories, employers, insurance companies, and government agencies. Unlike the value chain we described in Chapter 3, a health care consortium resembles more of a value circle, as illustrated in Figure 13.1. This figure is not a schema diagram! It is a picture of how all these diverse organizations need to share the same critical data: the patient treatment record.

There are two main types of patient treatment records. The treatment billing record corresponds to a line item on a patient bill from a provider's office, a clinic, a hospital, or a laboratory. The treatment medical record, on the other hand, is more comprehensive and includes not only the treatments that result in charges but also all the laboratory tests, findings, and provider's notes during the course of treatment. The issues involved in these two kinds of records are quite different, and we will look at them in separate sections.

Our large health care consortium must be able to share treatment billing records smoothly from organization to organization. Billing records from all the different kinds of providers must have a complete set of common dimensions in order to be processed by the insurance companies and medical bill payers. As individuals move from location to location, employer to employer, and insurance company to government health care program, a coherent picture of that individual's history needs to be creatable at any time. And finally, on the scrimmage line of health care delivery, the medical records of a patient need to be available on short notice for legitimate medical use by any of the primary providers.

Figure 13.1 Typical health care value circle.

The health care value circle differs from the classic linear value chain because there is no obvious ordering in time. However, the issues of conforming the common dimensions remain exactly the same. The health care consortium will be able to function if and only if it can implement a set of conformed dimensions. A representative set of dimensions that must be conformed by the health care consortium include:

- Calendar date
- Patient
- Responsible party (parent, guardian, employee)
- Employer
- Health plan
- Payer (primary, secondary)
- Provider (all forms of health care professionals who administer treatments)
- Treatment (billable procedure, lab test, examination)
- Drug
- Diagnosis
- Outcome
- Location (office, clinic, outpatient facility, hospital)

A billing row probably would need all these dimensions except for the outcome dimension. A medical row would not always identify the employer, health plan, or payer dimensions. And insurance claims processing would need even more dimensions relating to claimants, accidents, lawyers, and the transaction types needed for claims processing. We'll suppress the insurance aspect of health care data warehouses because we will deal with those kinds of subjects in Chapter 15.

In the health care business, some of these dimensions are very hard to conform, whereas others are easier than they look at first glance. The patient and responsible party dimensions are the hardest, at least in the United States, because of the lack of a reliable national identity number and because people are signed up separately in doctors' offices and hospitals and employment situations. The problems with the patient and responsible party dimensions are very similar to the issues we discussed in Chapter 6 regarding the consolidation of multiple sources for customer information. The same customer matching, householding, merge-purge software, and service providers offer similar services to the health care industry. To find out more about these companies, search for name householding or merge-purge on an Internet search engine such as Google (www.google.com).

The diagnosis and treatment dimensions are considerably more structured and predictable than one might expect because the insurance industry and government have mandated their content. Diagnoses usually follow the *International Classification of Diseases, 9th Revision: Clinical Modification*, Volumes 1 and 2 (ICD-9-CM) standard. The U.S. Department of Health and Human Services (HHS) maintains this standard as far as the United States is concerned. The ICD-9-CM standard, Volume 3, defines treatment and management codes.

The *Health Care Financing Administration Common Procedure Coding System* (HCPCS) standard, also updated and distributed by HHS; and *Current Procedural Terminology*, 4th Edition (CPT-4), as updated and distributed by the American Medical Association, cover health-related services and other items, including:

- Physician services
- Physical and occupational therapy services
- Radiological procedures
- Clinical laboratory tests
- Other medical diagnostic procedures
- Hearing and vision services
- Transportation services (including ambulance)
- Medical supplies
- Orthotic and prosthetic devices
- Durable medical equipment

Dentists are able to use the *Code on Dental Procedures and Nomenclature*, as updated and distributed by the American Dental Association, for dental services.

When all the dimensions in our list have been conformed, then any organization with appropriate access privileges can drill across the separate fact tables, linking together the information by matching the row headers of each row. The use of conformed dimensions guarantees that this matching process is well defined. We described this process in Chapter 3 in a product movement context, but the principles are exactly the same when applied to the health care value circle.

Health Care Bill

Let us imagine that we work for a billing organization for health care providers and hospitals. We receive the primary billing transactions from the providers and hospitals, prepare and send the bills to all the responsible payers, and track the progress of the payments made.

Our health care billing data warehouse must meet a number of business objectives. We want to analyze the counts and dollar amounts of all the bills by every dimension available to us, including by patient, provider, diagnosis, treatment, date, and any combinations of all these. We want to see how these bills have been paid and what percentage of the bills have not been collected. We want to see how long it takes to get paid, and we want to see the current status of all unpaid bills, updated every 24 hours. And of course, the queries need to be simple, and the response time must be instantaneous!

As we discussed in Chapter 5, whenever we consider a data source for inclusion in the data warehouse, we have three fundamental choices of grain for the fact table. Remember that the grain of the fact table is the fundamental definition of what constitutes a fact table row. In other words, what is the measurement that we are recording?

The transaction grain is the most fundamental. In the health care bill example, the transaction grain would include every input transaction from the providers and the hospitals, as well as every payment transaction resulting from the bill being sent. Although the world can be reconstructed from individual transactions, this grain may not be the best grain to begin with to meet our business reporting objectives because many of the queries would require rolling the transactions forward from the beginning of the patient's treatment.

The periodic snapshot grain is the grain of choice for long-running time-series processes such as bank accounts and insurance policies. However, the periodic snapshot doesn't do a good job of capturing the behavior of a quickly moving, short-lived process such as orders or medical bills. Most of the interesting activity surrounding a medical bill takes place quickly in one or two months. Also, if the periodic snapshot is available only at month-end, we cannot see the current status of the unpaid bills.

We will choose the accumulating snapshot grain for our health care bill. A single row in our fact table will represent a single line item on a health care bill. Furthermore, this single row will represent the accumulated history of that line item from the moment of creation of the row to the current day. When anything about the line item changes, we revisit the unique accumulating row and modify the row appropriately. From the point of view of the billing organization, we'll assume that the standard scenario of a bill includes:

- Treatment date
- Primary insurance billing date
- Secondary insurance billing date

- Responsible party billing date
- Last primary insurance payment date
- Last secondary insurance payment date
- Last responsible party payment date

We choose these dates to be an adequate description of a normal bill. An accumulating snapshot does not attempt to describe unusual situations fully. If the business users occasionally need to see all the details of a particularly messy bill payment situation, then a companion transaction grained fact table would be needed. The purpose of the accumulating snapshot grain is to place every health care bill into a uniform framework so that the business objectives we described earlier can be satisfied easily.

Now that we have a clear idea of what an individual fact table row represents (for example, the accumulated history of a line item on a health care bill), we can complete the list of dimensions by carefully listing everything we know to be true in the context of this row. In our hypothetical billing organization, we know the responsible party, employer, patient, provider, provider organization, treatment performed, treatment location, diagnosis, primary insurance organization, secondary insurance organization, and master bill ID number. These become our dimensions, as shown in Figure 13.2.

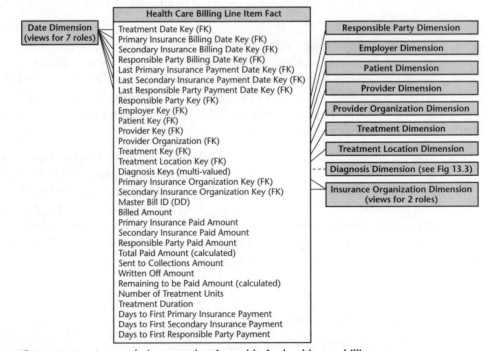

Figure 13.2 Accumulating snapshot fact table for health care billing.

The interesting facts that we choose to accumulate over the history of the line item on the health care bill include the billed amount, primary insurance paid amount, secondary insurance paid amount, responsible party paid amount, total paid amount (calculated), amount sent to collections, amount written off, amount remaining to be paid (calculated), number of treatment units (depending on treatment type), treatment duration, number of days from billing to first primary insurance payment, number of days from billing to first secondary insurance payment, and number of days from billing to first responsible party payment.

We'll assume that a row is created in this fact table when the activity transactions are first received from the providers and hospitals and the initial bills are sent. On a given bill, perhaps the primary insurance company is billed, but the secondary insurance and the responsible party are not billed, pending a response from the primary insurance company. For a period of time after the row is first entered into the database, the last five dates are not applicable. The surrogate date key in the fact table must not be null, but the full date description in the corresponding date dimension table row can indeed be null.

In the next few days and weeks after creation of the row, payments are received, and bills are sent to the secondary insurance company and responsible party. Each time these events take place, the same fact table row is revisited, and the appropriate keys and facts are destructively updated. This destructive updating poses some challenges for the database administrator. The row widths in databases such as Oracle will grow each time an update occurs because numeric facts may be changed from a small number to a larger number. This can cause block splits and fragmentation if enough space is not available at the disk block level to accommodate this growth. If most of these accumulating rows stabilize and stop changing within 90 days (for instance), then a physical reorganization of the database at that time can recover disk storage and improve performance. If the fact table is partitioned on the treatment date key, then the physical clustering (partitioning) probably will be well preserved throughout these changes because we assume that the treatment date is not normally revisited and changed.

Roles Played By the Date Dimension

Accumulating snapshot fact tables always involve multiple date stamps. Our example, which is typical, has seven foreign keys pointing to the date dimension. This is a good place to reiterate several important points:

- The foreign keys in the fact table cannot be actual date stamps because they have to handle the "Not Applicable" case. The foreign keys should be simple integers serving as surrogate keys.

- The surrogate keys assigned in the date dimension should be assigned consecutively in order of date. This is the only dimension where the surrogate keys have any relationship to the underlying semantics of the dimension. We do this so that physical partitioning of a fact table can be accomplished by using one of the date-based foreign keys. In our example we recommend that the treatment date key be used as the basis for physically partitioning the fact table.

- Surrogate keys corresponding to special conditions such as "Not Applicable," "Corrupted," or "Hasn't Happened Yet" should be assigned to the top end of the numeric range so that these rows are physically partitioned together in the hot partition with the most recent data. We do this if these rows are ones that are expected to change.

- We do not join the seven date-based foreign keys to a single instance of the date dimension table. Such a join would demand that all seven dates were the same date. Instead, we create seven views on the single underlying date dimension table, and we join the fact table separately to these seven views, just as if they were seven independent date dimension tables. This allows the seven dates to be independent. We refer to these seven views as *roles* played by the date dimension table.

- The seven view definitions using the date dimension table should cosmetically relabel the column names of each view to be distinguishable so that query tools directly accessing the views will present the column names through the user interface in a way that is understandable to the end user.

Although the role-playing behavior of the date dimension is very characteristic of accumulating snapshot fact tables, other dimensions often play roles in similar ways, such as the payer dimension in Figure 13.2. Later in this chapter we will see how the physician dimension needs to have several roles in complex surgical procedures depending on whether the physician is the primary responsible physician, working in a consulting capacity, or working in an assisting capacity.

Multivalued Diagnosis Dimension

Normally we choose the dimensions surrounding a fact table row by asking, what do we know to be true in the context of the measurement? Almost always we mean, what takes on a single value in the context of the measurement? If something has many values in the context of the measurement, we almost always disqualify that dimension because the many-valuedness means that the offending dimension belongs at a lower grain of measurement.

However, there are a few situations in which the many-valuedness is natural and unavoidable, and we do want to include such a dimension in our design, such as the case when we associated multiple customers with an account in Chapter 9. The diagnosis dimension in our health care billing fact table is another good example. At the moment of treatment, the patient has one or more diagnoses, which are well known. Furthermore, there is good incentive for keeping these diagnoses along with the billing row.

If there were always a maximum of three diagnoses, for instance, we might be tempted to create three diagnosis dimensions, almost as if they were roles. However, diagnoses don't behave like roles. Unfortunately, there are often more than three diagnoses, especially for elderly patients who are hospitalized. Real medical bill-paying organizations sometimes encounter patients with more than 50 diagnoses! Also, the diagnoses don't fit into well-defined roles other than possibly admitting diagnosis and discharging diagnosis. The role-playing dimensions we talked about in the preceding section are categorized much more naturally and disjointly. Finally, the multiple-slots style of design makes for very inefficient applications because the query doesn't know a priori which dimensional slot to constrain for a particular diagnosis.

We handle the open-ended nature of multiple diagnoses with the design shown in Figure 13.3. We replace the diagnosis foreign key in the fact table with a diagnosis group key. This diagnosis group key is connected by a many-to-many join to a diagnosis group bridge table, which contains a separate row for each diagnosis in a particular group.

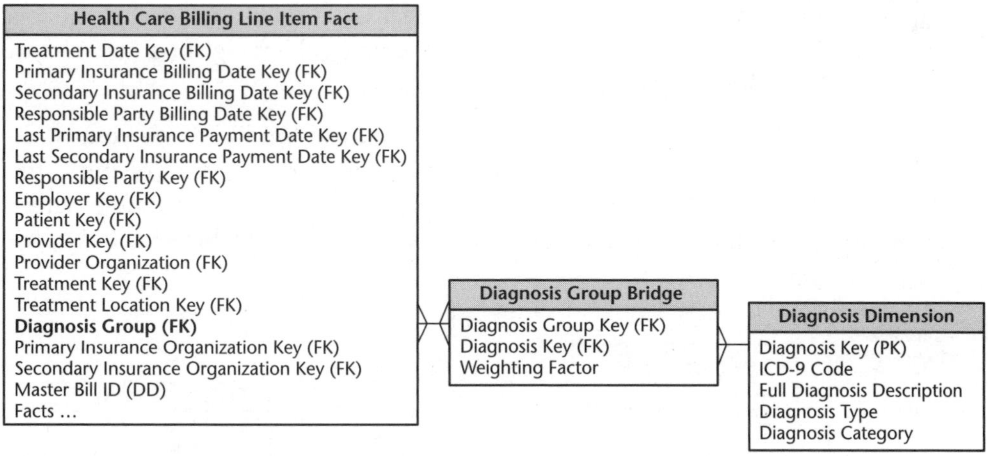

Figure 13.3 Design for a multivalued diagnosis dimension.

If a patient has three diagnoses, then that patient is assigned a diagnosis group with three diagnoses. We assign a numerical weighting factor to each diagnosis in the group such that the sum of all the weighting factors in the group is exactly 1.00. We can then use the weighting factors to allocate any of the numeric additive facts across individual diagnoses. In this way we can add up all billed amounts by diagnosis, and the grand total will be the correct grand total billed amount. This kind of report would be called a *correctly weighted report*.

We see that the weighting factors are simply a way to allocate the numeric additive facts across the diagnoses. Some would suggest that we change the grain of the fact table to be line item by diagnosis rather than just line item. In this case we would take the weighting factors and physically multiply them against the original numeric facts. This is done rarely, for three reasons. First, the size of the fact table would be multiplied by the average number of diagnoses. Second, in some fact tables we have more than one multivalued dimension. The number of rows would get out of hand in this situation, and we would start to question the physical significance of an individual row. Finally, we may want to see the unallocated numbers, and it is hard to reconstruct these if the allocations have been combined physically with the numeric facts.

If we choose not to apply the weighting factors in a given query, we can still summarize billed amounts by diagnosis, but in this case we get what is called an *impact report*. A question such as "What is the total billed amount across all possible treatments in any way involving the diagnosis of XYZ?" would be an example of an impact report.

In Figure 13.3, an SQL view could be defined combining the fact table and the diagnosis group bridge table so that these two tables, when combined, would appear to data access tools as a standard fact table with a normal diagnosis foreign key. Two views could be defined, one using the weighting factors and one not using the weighting factors.

Finally, if the many-to-many join in Figure 13.3 causes problems for your modeling tool that insists on proper foreign-key-to-primary-key relationships, the equivalent design of Figure 13.4 can be used. In this case an extra table whose primary key is diagnosis group is inserted between the fact table and the bridge

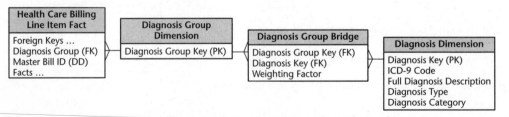

Figure 13.4 Diagnosis group dimension to create a primary key relationship.

table. Now both the fact table and the bridge table have conventional many-to-one joins in all directions. There is no new information in this extra table.

In the real world, a bill-paying organization would decide how to administer the diagnosis groups. If a unique diagnosis group were created for every out-patient treatment, the number of rows could become astronomical and unworkable. Probably the best approach is to have a standard portfolio of diagnosis groups that are used repeatedly. This requires that each set of diagnoses be looked up in the master diagnosis group table. If the existing group is found, it is used. If it is not found, then a new diagnosis group is created.

In a hospital stay situation, however, the diagnosis group probably should be unique to the patient because it is going to evolve over time as a type 2 slowly changing dimension (SCD). In this case we would supplement the bridge table with two date stamps to capture begin and end dates. While the twin date stamps complicate the update administration of the diagnosis group bridge table, they are very useful for querying and change tracking. They also allow us to perform time-span queries, such as identifying all patients who presented a given diagnosis at any time between two dates.

To summarize this discussion of multivalued dimensions, we can list the issues surrounding a multivalued dimension design:

- In the context of the fact table measurement, the multivalued dimension takes on a small but variable number of well-defined values.
- Correctly allocated reports can be created only if weighting factors can be agreed to.
- Weighting factors can be omitted, but then only impact reports can be generated using the multivalued dimension.
- In high-volume situations such as medical bills and bank accounts, a system of recognizing and reusing groups should be used.
- In cases where the relationship represented in the bridge table changes over time, we embellish the bridge table with begin and end dates.

Extending a Billing Fact Table to Show Profitability

Figure 13.5 shows an extended set of facts that might be added to the basic billing schema of Figure 13.2. These include the consumables cost, provider cost, assistant cost, equipment cost, location cost, and net profit before general and administrative (G&A) expenses, which is a calculated fact. If these additional facts can be added to the billing schema, the power of the fact table grows enormously. It now becomes a full-fledged profit-and-loss (P&L) view of the health care business.

Health Care Billing Line Item Fact
Existing 17 Foreign Keys ...
Master Bill ID (DD)
Existing 13 Facts ...
Consumables Cost
Provider Cost
Assistant Cost
Equipment Cost
Location Cost
Net Profit before G&A (calculated)

Figure 13.5 Billing line-item fact table extended at the same grain with activity-based costs for profit and loss.

These costs are not part of the billing process and normally would not be collected at the same time as the billing data. Each of these costs potentially arises from a separate source system. In order to bring this data into the billing fact table, the separately sourced data would have to be allocated down to the billing line item. For activity-based costs such as the ones we have included in the list, it may be worth the effort to do this allocation. All allocations are controversial and to an extent arbitrary, but if agreement can be reached on the set of allocations, the P&L database that results is incredibly powerful. Now the health care organization can analyze profitability by all the dimensions!

Dimensions for Billed Hospital Stays

The first part of this chapter described a comprehensive and flexible design for billed health care treatments that would cover both inpatient and outpatient bills. If an organization wished to focus exclusively on hospital stays, it would be reasonable to tweak the dimensional structure of Figure 13.2 to provide more hospital-specific information. Figure 13.6 shows a revised set of dimensions specialized for hospital stays, with the new dimensions set in bold type.

In Figure 13.6 we show two roles for provider: admitting provider and attending provider. We show provider organizations for both roles because providers may represent different organizations in a hospital setting.

We also have three multivalued diagnosis dimensions on each billed treatment row. The admitting diagnosis is determined at the beginning of the hospital stay and should be the same for every treatment row that is part of the same hospital stay. The current diagnosis describes the state of knowledge of the patient at the time of the treatment. The discharge diagnosis is not known until the patient is discharged and is applied retroactively to all the rows that have been entered as part of the hospital stay.

Figure 13.6   Accumulating snapshot for hospital stays billing.

Complex Health Care Events

In a hospital setting, we may want to model certain very complex events, such as major surgical procedures. In a heart-transplant operation, whole teams of specialists and assistants are assembled for this one event. A different heart transplant may involve a team with a different makeup.

We can model these complex events with the design shown in Figure 13.7. We combine the techniques of role-playing dimensions and multivalued dimensions. We assume that a surgical procedure involves a single responsible physician and variable numbers of attending physicians, assisting professionals, procedures, and equipment types. We also assume that the patient has a multivalued diagnosis before the surgery and a separate multivalued diagnosis after the surgery.

Thus we have six multivalued dimensions, indicated by the bold type in Figure 13.7. The responsible physician, attending physician, and assisting professional dimensions are all roles played by an overall provider dimension. The presurgery and postsurgery multivalued diagnosis dimensions are roles played by a single diagnosis dimension.

Surgical Events Transaction Fact
Treatment Date Key (FK)
Treatment Time of Day Key (FK)
Patient Key (FK)
Responsible Physician Key (FK)
Attending Physician Keys (multivalued)
Assisting Professionals Keys (multivalued)
Location Key (FK)
Procedure Keys (multivalued)
Equipment Keys (multivalued)
Pre-Surgery Diagnosis Keys (multivalued)
Post-Surgery Diagnosis Keys (multivalued)
Outcome
Total Billed Amount
Total Paid Amount (accumulating overwrite)
Consummables Cost
Provider Cost
Assistant Cost
Equipment Cost
Location Cost
Net Profit before G&A (calculated)

Figure 13.7   Surgical events transaction fact table extended to show profit and loss.

Since the grain of the fact table is the surgical procedure itself, it is natural to supply a comprehensive set of facts. We show the extended set of facts that would allow a complete P&L analysis to be done on surgical procedures, assuming that the various costs can be allocated to each surgical event.

We leave out the weighting factors on all the multivalued dimensions in this design. If we tried to provide weighting factors for the multivalued dimensions, we would be implicitly supporting all the complex combinations of weighting values, some of which would be nonsensical. It doesn't seem worth the trouble to claim that the correctly allocated portion of the total billed amount of the surgery conjointly assigned to each possible assistant and each possible piece of equipment has much meaning. Our technique of placing the weighting factors independently in each dimension is only part of the problem. A more practical concern is that most organizations would not be willing to assign dozens or hundreds of weighting factors.

Without the weighting factors, we nevertheless can create many useful impact reports. For instance, what is the total value of all surgeries performed that used a heart-lung machine? We also can ask which physicians, which assisting professionals, and which pieces of equipment were involved in various kinds of surgery. And finally, if we have allocated the costs to each surgery in a rational way, we can ask which types of surgery are profitable or nonprofitable and why.

Medical Records

General medical records are challenging for the data warehouse because of their extreme variability. The records in a patient file take many different forms, ranging from standard-format numeric data captured online, to one-of-a-kind laboratory test results, to free-text comments entered by a health care professional, to graphs and photographs. Given this extreme variability, we don't attempt to do queries and reports simultaneously analyzing every data type. However, we still would like to provide a standard, simple framework for all the records for a given patient. We are driven by the suspicion that if the grain could be defined as an individual record entry for a patient, we should be able to capture most of a medical record in a single fact table.

In such a fact table we might be tempted to provide a fact field for each type of measurement. Some fields would be numeric, and some fields would be flags (or foreign keys to junk dimensions consisting of groups of flags, as described in Chapter 5). However, the sheer variety of possible medical record entries defeats us. We would soon end up with a ridiculously wide fact table row with too many fact fields, almost all of which would be null or zero for any specific medical entry. In addition, this fixed-slot style of design is very inflexible because new measurement types could be added only by physically altering the fact table with the addition of a new field.

Fact Dimension for Sparse Facts

We handle the extreme variability of the medical record entry with a special dimension we call a *fact dimension*. In Figure 13.8 the entry type is a fact dimension that describes what the row means or, in other words, what the fact represents. The entry type dimension also determines which of the four kinds of fact fields (amount, flag, comment, and JPEG file name) are valid for the specific entry and how to interpret each field. For example, the generic amount column is used for every numeric entry. The unit of measure for a given numeric entry is found in the attached entry type dimension row, along with any additivity restrictions. If the entry is a flag (for example, Yes/No or High/Medium/Low), the types of flag values are found in the entry type dimension. If the entry is a free-text comment or a multimedia object such as JPEG graphic image or photograph, the entry type dimension alerts the requesting application to look in these fact table fields.

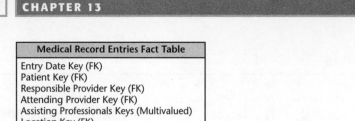

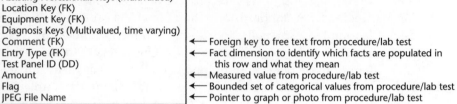

Figure 13.8   Transaction table with sparse, heterogeneous medical record facts and a fact dimension.

This approach is elegant because it is superbly flexible. We can add new measurement types just by adding new rows in the fact dimension, not by altering the structure of the fact table. We also eliminate the nulls in the classic positional fact table design because a row exists only if the measurement exists. However, there are some significant tradeoffs. Using a fact dimension may generate lots of new fact table rows. If an event resulted in 10 numeric measurements, we now have 10 rows in the fact table rather than a single row in the classic design. For extremely sparse situations, such as clinical/laboratory or manufacturing test environments, this is a reasonable compromise. However, as the density of the facts grows, we end up spewing out too many fact rows. At this point we no longer have sparse facts and should return to the classic fact table approach.

Moreover, we must be aware that this approach typically complicates data access applications. Combining two numbers that have been taken as part of a single event is more difficult because now we must fetch two rows from the fact table. SQL likes to perform arithmetic functions within a row, not across rows. In addition, we must be careful not to mix incompatible amounts in a calculation because all the numeric measures reside in a single amount column.

The other dimensions in Figure 13.8 should be fairly obvious. The patient, responsible provider, attending provider, location, equipment, and diagnosis dimensions were all present in various forms in our earlier designs. The test panel ID is a standard degenerate dimension because it probably is just a simple natural key that ties together multiple medical record entries that were all part of a particular test panel.

Free text comments should not be stored in a fact table directly because they waste space and rarely participate in queries. Presumably, the free text comments occur only on some records. Rather, the fact table should have a foreign key that points to a comment dimension, as shown in Figure 13.8.

The use of a JPEG file name to refer to an image, rather than embedding the image as a blob directly in the database, is somewhat of an arbitrary decision. The advantage of using a JPEG file name is that other image creation, viewing, and editing programs can access the image freely. The disadvantage is that a separate database of graphic files must be maintained in synchrony with the fact table.

Going Back in Time

As data warehouse practitioners, we have developed powerful techniques for accurately capturing the historical flow of data from our enterprises. Our numeric measurements go into fact tables, and we surround these fact tables with contemporary descriptions of what we know is true at the time of the measurements. These contemporary descriptions are packaged as dimension tables in our dimensional schemas. In our health care data warehouse, we allow the descriptions of patient, provider, and payer to evolve whenever these entities change their descriptions. Since these changes occur unpredictably and sporadically, we have called these slowly changing dimensions (SCDs).

In Chapter 4 we developed specific techniques for processing overwrites (type 1 SCDs), true changes in the entities at points in time (type 2 SCDs), and changes in the labels we attach to entities (type 3 SCDs). These procedures are an important part of our extract-transform-load (ETL) procedures with every update.

However, what do we do when we receive late-arriving data that should have been loaded into the data warehouse weeks or months ago? Some of our procedures won't work. There are two interesting cases that need to be discussed separately.

Late-Arriving Fact Rows

Using our patient treatment scenario, suppose that we receive today a treatment row that is several months old. In most operational data warehouses we are willing to insert this late-arriving row into its correct historical position, even though our summaries for the prior month will now change. However, we must choose the old contemporary dimension rows that apply to this treatment carefully. If we have been date stamping the dimension rows in our type 2 SCDs, then our processing involves the following steps:

1. For each dimension, find the corresponding dimension row whose date stamp is the latest date stamp less than or equal to the date of the treatment.

2. Using the surrogate keys found in the each of the dimension rows from step 1, replace the natural keys of the late-arriving fact row with the surrogate keys.

3. Insert the late-arriving fact row into the correct physical partition of the database containing the other fact rows from the time of the late-arriving treatment.

There are a few subtle points here. First, we assume that all of our dimension rows contain twin date stamps that indicate the span of time when that particular detailed description was valid. We need to be careful to have an unbroken chain of nonoverlapping begin and end dates for each patient, provider, and payer because we must find the right dimension rows for the new fact row about to be inserted.

A second subtle point goes back to our assumption that we have an operational data warehouse that is willing to insert these late-arriving rows into old months. If your data warehouse has to tie to the books, then you can't change an old monthly total, even if that old total was incorrect. Now you have a tricky situation in which the date dimension on the treatment record is for a booking date, which may be today, but the other patient, provider, and payer dimensions nevertheless should refer to the old descriptions in the way we described earlier. If you are in this situation, you should have a discussion with your finance department manager to make sure that he or she understands what you are doing. An interesting compromise is to carry two date dimensions on treatment records. One refers to the actual treatment date, and the other refers to the booking date. Now we can roll up the treatment records either operationally or by the books.

The third subtle point is the requirement to insert the late-arriving treatment row into the correct physical partition of the database containing its contemporary brothers and sisters. In this way, when you move a physical partition from one form of storage to another or when you perform a backup or restore operation, you will be affecting all the treatment rows from a particular span of time. In most cases this is what you want to do. You can guarantee that all fact rows in a time span occupy the same physical partition if you declare the physical partitioning of the fact table to be based on the date dimension, where the surrogate date keys are assigned in a predictable sequence order.

Late-Arriving Dimension Rows

A late-arriving dimension row presents an entirely different set of issues that, in some ways, are more complex than a late-arriving fact row. Suppose that John Doe's patient dimension row contains a marital flag attribute that always contained the value "Single." We have a number of patient rows for John Doe because this is a slowly changing dimension and other attributes such as John's address and employment status have changed over the past year or two.

Today we are notified that John Doe was married on July 15, 1999 and has been married ever since. To add this new information to the data warehouse requires the following steps:

- Insert a fresh row, with a new surrogate key, for John Doe into the patient dimension with the marital status attribute set to "Married" and the effective date set to "July 15, 1999."

- Scan forward in the patient dimension table from July 15, 1999, finding any other rows for John Doe, and destructively overwrite the marital status field to "Married."

- Find all fact rows involving John Doe from July 15, 1999 to the first next change for him in the dimension after July 15, 1999 and destructively change the patient foreign key in those fact rows to the new surrogate key created in step 1.

This is a fairly messy change, but you should be able to automate these steps in a good programmable ETL environment. We have some subtle issues in this case, too. First, we need to check to see if some other change took place for John Doe on July 15, 1999. If so, then we only need to perform step 2. We don't need a new dimension row in this special case.

Second, since we are using a pair of date stamps in each product dimension row, we need to find the closest previous to July 15 patient row for John Doe and change its end date to July 15, 1999, and we also need to find the closest subsequent to July 15 patient row for John Doe and set the end date for the July 15, 1999 entry to the begin date of that next row. Got it?

Finally, we see from this example why the surrogate keys for all dimensions except date or time cannot be ordered in any way. You never know when you are going to have to assign a surrogate key for a late-arriving row. And since surrogate keys are just assigned in numeric order without any logic or structure, you can easily have a high-valued surrogate key representing a dimension row that is very old.

Hopefully, these late-arriving fact and dimension rows are unusual in most of our data warehouses. If nothing else, they are bothersome because they change the counts and totals for prior history. However, we have taken a pledge as keepers of the data warehouse to present the history of our enterprise as accurately as possible, so we should welcome the old rows because they are making our databases more complete.

Some industries, such as health care, have huge numbers of late-arriving rows. In such cases, these techniques, rather than being specialized techniques for the unusual case, may be the dominant mode of processing.

Summary

Health care not only is an important application area in its own right, but it also provides the data warehouse designer with a number of clear design examples that can be used in many other situations. In this chapter we have seen:

The value circle, where a large number of organizations need to look at the same data in parallel without any strong sense of time sequencing. However, the issues of building a value-circle data warehouse bus architecture with conformed dimensions and conformed facts are exactly the same as the more conventional value chains.

The accumulating snapshot grain of fact table applied to a medical bill line item. This grain was appropriate because of the relatively brief duration of a medical bill compared with something like a bank account, where the periodic snapshot is more appropriate.

Roles played by the date dimension in the accumulating snapshot grain, as well as roles played by the provider and payer dimensions in other fact tables of this chapter. Roles are implemented as separate, specifically named views on a single underlying master dimension.

Multivalued dimensions, especially the diagnosis dimension. In many cases we are able to associate a weighting factor with each of the values in a multivalued dimension entry so as to allow allocations to be calculated on numeric facts in the fact table. We would call this kind of report a correctly weighted report. However, in some cases where we are unwilling to assign weighting factors, the multivalued dimension still lets us produce impact reports.

An extended set of cost-based facts that allow us to implement a P&L schema. Adding these cost-based facts is very attractive, but it is a lot of work. The best costs to add to a design are activity-based costs because these are not too controversial to associate with individual fact rows such as our medical bill line items.

Complex events modeled as single fact table rows containing several multi-valued dimensions. In these cases we often do not build weighting factors into all the multivalued dimensions because the interaction between the weighting factors becomes nonsensical.

Fact dimensions used to organize extremely sparse, heterogeneous measurements into a single, uniform framework. Our example plausibly covered general medical records consisting of standardized numeric measures, one-of-a-kind lab results, categorical textual measurements, free-text comments, and image data.

CHAPTER 14

Electronic Commerce

Web-intensive businesses have access to a new kind of data source that literally records the gestures of every Web site visitor. We call it the *clickstream*. In its most elemental form, the clickstream is every page event recorded by each of the company's Web servers. The clickstream contains a number of new dimensions—such as page, session, and referrer—that are unknown in our conventional data marts. The clickstream is a torrent of data, easily being the largest text and number data set we have ever considered for a data warehouse. Although the clickstream is the most exciting new development in data warehousing, at the same time it can be the most difficult and most exasperating. Does it connect to the rest of the warehouse? Can its dimensions and facts be conformed in a data warehouse bus architecture?

The full story of the clickstream data source and its implementation by companies, such as those involved in electronic commerce, is told in the complete book on this subject, *The Data Webhouse Toolkit*, by Ralph Kimball and Richard Merz (Wiley, 2000). This chapter is a lightning tour of the central ideas drawn from *The Data Webhouse Toolkit*. We start by describing the raw clickstream data source. We show how to design a data mart around the clickstream data. Finally, we integrate this data mart into a larger matrix of more conventional data marts for a large Web retailer and argue that the profitability of the Web sales channel can be measured if you allocate the right costs back to the individual sales of the retailer.

O—⟅ **Chapter 14 discusses the following concepts:**

- Brief tutorial on Web client-server interactions
- Unique characteristics of clickstream data, including the challenges of identifying the visitors, their origin, and their complete session
- Clickstream-specific dimensions, such as the page, event, session, and referral dimensions
- Clickstream fact tables for the complete session, individual page event, and an aggregated summary
- Integrating the clickstream data mart into the rest of the enterprise data warehouse
- Web profitability data mart

Web Client-Server Interactions Tutorial

Understanding the interactions between a Web client (browser) and a Web server (Web site) is essential for understanding the source and meaning of the data in the clickstream. In Figure 14.1 we show a browser, designated "Visitor Browser." We'll look at what happens in a typical interaction from the perspective of a browser user. The browser and Web site interact with each other across the Internet using the Web's communication protocol—the HyperText Transfer Protocol (HTTP).

First, the visitor clicks a button or hypertext link containing a Uniform Resource Locator (URL) to access a particular Web site, shown as black-circled action 1 in Figure 14.1. When this HTTP request reaches the Web site, the server returns the requested item (action 2). In our illustration, this fetches a document in HyperText Markup Language (HTML) format—websitepage.html. Once the document is entirely retrieved, the visitor's browser scans websitepage.html and notices several references to other Web documents that it must fulfill before its work is completed; the browser must retrieve other components of this document in separate requests. Note that the only human action taken here is to click on the original link. All the rest of the actions that follow in this example are computer-to-computer interactions triggered by the click and managed, for the most part, by instructions carried in the initially downloaded HTML document, websitepage.html. In order to speed up Web page responsiveness, most browsers will execute these consequential actions in parallel, typically with up to 4 or more HTTP requests being serviced concurrently.

The visitor's browser finds a reference to an image—a logo perhaps—that, from its URL, is located at Website.com, the same place it retrieved the initial HTML document. The browser issues a second request to the server (action 3), and the server responds by returning the specified image.

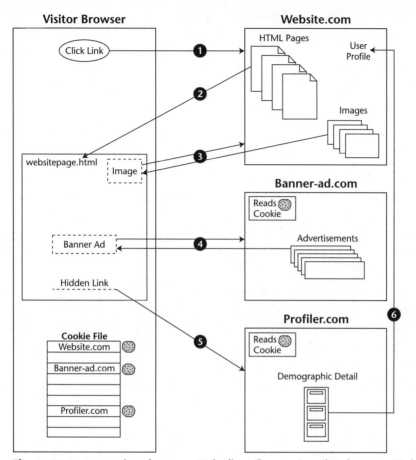

Figure 14.1 Interactions between Web client (browser) and Web server (Web site).

The browser continues to the next reference in websitepage.html and finds an instruction to retrieve another image from Banner-ad.com. The browser makes this request (action 4), and the server at Banner-ad.com interprets a request for the image in a special way. Rather than immediately sending back an image, the banner-ad server first issues a cookie request to the visitor's browser requesting the contents of any cookie that might have been placed previously in the visitor's PC by Banner-ad.com. The banner-ad Web site retrieves this cookie, examines its contents, and uses the contents as a key to determine which banner ad the visitor should receive. This decision is based on the visitor's interests or on previous ads the visitor had been sent by this particular ad server. Once the banner-ad server makes a determination of the optimal ad, it returns the selected image to the visitor. The banner-ad server then logs which ad it has placed along with the date and the clickstream data from the visitor's request. Had the banner-ad server not found its own cookie, it would have sent a new persistent cookie to the visitor's browser for future reference, sent a random banner ad, and started a history in its database of interactions with the visitor's browser.

The HTTP request from the visitor's browser to the banner-ad server carried with it a key piece of information known as the *referrer*. The referrer is the URL of the agent responsible for placing the link on the page. In our example the referrer is Website.com/websitepage.html. The referrer is not the user's browser but rather is the HTML context in which the link to Banner-ad.com was embedded. Because Banner-ad.com now knows who the referrer was, it can credit Website.com for having placed an advertisement on a browser window. This is a single impression. The advertiser can be billed for this impression, with the revenue being shared by the referrer (Website.com) and the advertising server (Banner-ad.com).

If the Web site is sharing Web log information with the referring site, it will be valuable to share page attributes as well. In other words, not only do we want the URL of the referring page, but we also want to know what the purpose of the page was. Was it a navigation page, a partner's page, or a general search page?

While the ad server deals primarily with placing appropriate content, the profiler deals with supplying demographic information about Web site visitors. In our original HTML document, websitepage.html had a hidden field that contained a request to retrieve a specific document from Profiler.com (action 5). When this request reached the profiler server, Profiler.com immediately tried to find its cookie in the visitor's browser. This cookie would contain a user ID placed previously by the profiler that is used to identify the visitor and serves as a key to personal information contained in the profiler's database. The profiler might either return its profile data to the visitor's browser to be sent back to the initial Web site or send a real-time notification to the referrer, Website.com, via an alternative path alerting Website.com that the visitor is currently logged onto Website.com and viewing a specific page (action 6). This information also could be returned to the HTML document to be returned to the referrer as part of a query string the next time an HTTP request is sent to Website.com.

Although Figure 14.1 shows three different sites involved in serving the contents of one document, it is possible, indeed likely, that these functions will be combined into fewer servers. It is likely that advertising and profiling will be done within the same enterprise, so a single request (and cookie) would suffice to retrieve personal information that would more precisely target the ads that are returned. However, it is equally possible that a Web page could contain references to different ad/profile services, providing revenue to the referrer from multiple sources.

Why the Clickstream Is Not
Just Another Data Source

The clickstream is not just another data source that is extracted, cleaned, and dumped into the data warehouse. The clickstream is really an evolving collection of data sources. There are more than a dozen Web server log file formats for capturing clickstream data. These log file formats have optional data components that, if used, can be very helpful in identifying visitors, sessions, and the true meaning of behavior. We are in the infancy of this clickstream game, and it is a sure bet that new logging capabilities and new logging formats will become available on a regular basis. Extensible Markup Language (XML) has the potential for making the structure of our Web pages far more expressive, which is bound to affect the clickstream data source.

Because of the distributed nature of the Web, clickstream data is often collected simultaneously by different physical servers, even when the visitor thinks that he or she is interacting with a single Web site. Even if the log files being collected by these separate servers are compatible, a very interesting problem arises in synchronizing the log files after the fact. Remember that a busy Web server may be processing hundreds of page events per second. It is unlikely that the clocks on separate servers will be in synchrony to a hundredth of a second. *The Data Webhouse Toolkit* explores various technical approaches to solving this synchronization problem.

We also get clickstream data from different parties. Besides our own log files, we may get clickstream data from referring partners or from Internet service providers (ISPs). We also may get clickstream data from Web-watcher services that we have hired to place a special control on certain Web pages that alert them to a visitor opening the page.

Another important form of clickstream data is the search specification given to a search engine that then directs the visitor to the Web site.

Finally, if we are an ISP providing Web access to directly connected customers, we have a unique perspective because we see every click of our familiar captive visitors that may allow much more powerful and invasive analysis of the end visitor's sessions.

The most basic form of clickstream data from a normal Web site is stateless. That is, the log shows an isolated page retrieval event but does not provide a clear tie to other page events elsewhere in the log. Without some other kind of context help, it is difficult or impossible to reliably identify a complete visitor session.

The other big frustration with basic clickstream data is the anonymity of the session. Unless the visitor agrees to reveal his or her identity in some way, we often cannot be sure who he or she is or if we have ever seen the visitor before.

In certain situations we may not even be able to distinguish the clicks of two visitors who are browsing our Web site simultaneously.

Challenges of Tracking with Clickstream Data

Clickstream data contains many ambiguities. Identifying visitor origins, visitor sessions, and visitor identities is something of an interpretive art. Browser caches and proxy servers make these identifications even more challenging.

Identifying the Visitor Origin

If we are very lucky, our site is the default home page for the visitor's browser. Every time the visitor opens his or her browser, our home page is the first thing he or she sees. This is pretty unlikely unless we are the Webmaster for a portal site or an intranet home page, but many sites have buttons that, when clicked, prompt the visitor to set his or her URL as the browser's home page. Unfortunately, there is no easy way to determine from a log whether or not our site is set as a browser's home page.

A visitor may be directed to our site from a search at a portal such as Yahoo! or Alta Vista. Such referrals can come either from the portal's index or table of contents, for which you may have paid a placement fee, or from a word or content search.

For many Web sites, the most common source of visitors is from a browser bookmark. In order for this to happen, the visitor will have to have previously bookmarked the site, and this will occur only after the site's interest and trust levels cross the visitor's bookmark threshold. Unfortunately, when a visitor uses a bookmark, the referrer field is empty, just as if the visitor had typed in the URL by hand.

Finally, the site may be reached as a result of a click-through—a deliberate click on a text or graphic link from another site. This may be a paid-for referral as via a banner ad or a free referral from an individual or cooperating site. In the case of click-throughs, the referring site almost always will be identifiable in the Web site's referrer log data. Capturing this crucial clickstream data is important to verify the efficacy of marketing programs. It also provides crucial data for auditing invoices you may receive from click-through advertising charges.

Identifying the Session

Most web-centric data warehouse applications will require every visitor session (visit) to have its own unique identity tag, similar to a grocery store point-of-sale ticket ID. We call this the *session ID*. The rows of every individual visitor action in a session, whether derived from the clickstream or from an application interaction, must contain this tag. Keep in mind, however, that the operational application generates this session ID, not the Web server.

The basic protocol for the World Wide Web, HTTP, is stateless—that is, it lacks the concept of a session. There are no intrinsic login or logout actions built into the HTTP, so session identity must be established in some other way. There are several ways to do this:

1. In many cases, the individual hits comprising a session can be consolidated by collating time-contiguous log entries from the same host (Internet Protocol, or IP, address). If the log contains a number of entries with the same host ID in a short period of time (for example, one hour), one can reasonably assume that the entries are for the same session. This method breaks down for visitors from large ISPs because different visitors may reuse dynamically assigned IP addresses over a brief time period. In addition, different IP addresses may be used within the same session for the same visitor. This approach also presents problems when dealing with browsers that are behind some firewalls. Notwithstanding these problems, many commercial log analysis products use this method of session tracking, which requires no cookies or special Web server features.

2. Another, much more satisfactory method is to let the Web browser place a session-level cookie into the visitor's Web browser. This cookie will last as long as the browser is open and, in general, won't be available in subsequent browser sessions. The cookie value can serve as a temporary session ID not only to the browser but also to any application that requests the session cookie from the browser. This request must come from the same Web server (actually, the same domain) that placed the cookie in the first place. Using a transient cookie value as a temporary session ID for both the clickstream and application logging allows a straightforward approach to associating the data from both these sources during postsession log processing. However, using a transient cookie has the disadvantage that you can't tell when the visitor returns to the site at a later time in a new session.

3. HTTP's secure sockets layer (SSL) offers an opportunity to track a visitor session because it may include a login action by the visitor and the exchange of encryption keys. The downside to using this method is that to track the session, the entire information exchange needs to be in high-overhead SSL, and the visitor may be put off by security advisories that can pop up when certain browsers are used. In addition, each host server must have its own unique security certificate.

4. If page generation is dynamic, you can try to maintain visitor state by placing a session ID in a hidden field of each page returned to the visitor.

This session ID can be returned to the Web server as a query string appended to a subsequent URL. This method of session tracking requires a great deal of control over the Web site's page-generation methods to ensure that the thread of session ID is not broken. If the visitor clicks on links that don't support this session ID ping-pong, a single session will appear to be multiple sessions. This approach also breaks down if multiple vendors are supplying content in a single session.

5. Finally, the Web site may establish a persistent cookie in the visitor's PC that is not deleted by the browser when the session ends. Of course, it's possible that the visitor will have his or her browser set to refuse cookies or may clean out his or her cookie file manually, so there is no absolute guarantee that even a persistent cookie will survive. Although any given cookie can be read only by the Web site that caused it to be created, certain groups of Web sites can agree to store a common ID tag that would let these sites combine their separate notions of a visitor session into a supersession.

In summary, the most powerful method of session tracking from Web server log records is to set a persistent cookie in the visitor's browser. Other less powerful methods include setting a session-level nonpersistent cookie or nearly associating time-contiguous log entries from the same host. The latter method requires a robust algorithm in the log postprocessor to ensure satisfactory results, in part by deciding when not to take the results seriously.

Identifying the Visitor

Identifying a specific visitor who logs onto our site presents some of the most challenging problems facing a site designer, Webmaster, or manager of data warehousing for the following reasons:

Web visitors wish to be anonymous. They may have no reason to trust us, the Internet, or their PC with personal identification or credit card information.

If we request a visitor's identity, he or she is likely to lie about it. It is believed that when asked their name on an Internet form, men will enter a pseudonym 50 percent of the time and women will use a pseudonym 80 percent of the time.

We can't be sure which family member is visiting our site. If we obtain an identity by association, for instance, from a persistent cookie left during a previous visit, the identification is only for the computer, not for the specific visitor. Any family member or company employee may have been using that particular computer at that moment in time.

We can't assume that an individual is always at the same computer. Server-provided cookies identify a computer, not an individual. If someone accesses the same Web site from an office computer, a home PC, and a laptop computer, a different Web site cookie is probably put into each machine.

Proxy Servers

When a browser makes an HTTP request, that request is not always served from the server specified in a URL. Many ISPs make use of proxy servers to reduce Internet traffic. Proxy servers are used to cache frequently requested content at a location between its intended source and an end visitor. Such proxies are employed commonly by large ISPs such as America Online and Earthlink, and in some cases, an HTTP request may not even leave the visitor's PC. It may be satisfied from the browser's local cache of recently accessed objects.

Proxy servers can introduce three problems, as illustrated in Figure 14.2. First, a proxy may deliver outdated content. Although Web pages can include tags that tell proxy servers whether or not the content may be cached and when content expires, these tags often are omitted by Webmasters or ignored by proxy servers.

Second, proxies may satisfy a content request without properly notifying the originating server that the request has been served by the proxy. When a proxy handles a request, convention dictates that it should forward a message that indicates that a proxy response has been made to the intended server, but this is not reliable. As a consequence, our Webhouse may miss key events that are otherwise required to make sense of the events that comprise a browser/Web site session. Third, if the visitor has come though a proxy, the Web site will not know who made the page request unless a cookie is present.

It is important, therefore, to make liberal use of expiration dates and no-proxy tags in the HTML content of your Web site. This will help ensure that we are getting as much data as possible for our warehouse.

The type of proxy we are referring to in this discussion is called a *forward proxy*. It is outside of our control because it belongs to a networking company or an ISP. Another type of proxy server, called a *reverse proxy*, can be placed in front of our enterprise's Web servers to help them offload requests for frequently accessed content. This kind of proxy is entirely within our control and usually presents no impediment to Webhouse data collection. It should be able to supply the same kind of log information as that produced by a Web server and discussed in the following section.

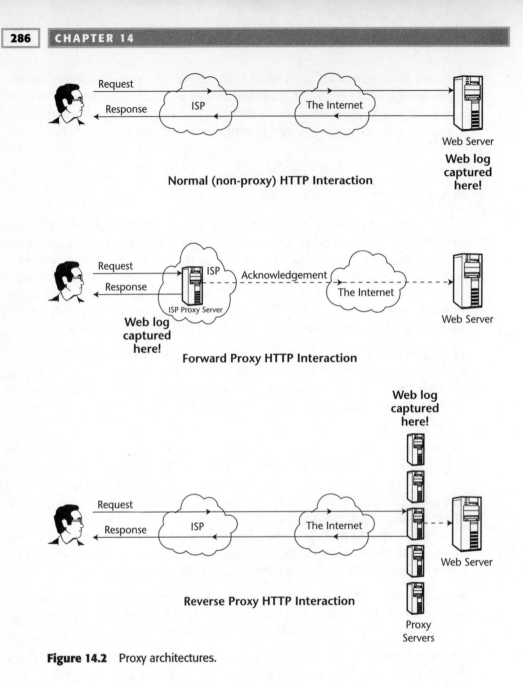

Figure 14.2 Proxy architectures.

Browser Caches

Browser caches also introduce uncertainties in our attempts to track all the events that occur during a visitor session. Most browsers store a copy of recently retrieved objects such as HTML pages and images in a local object cache in the PC's file system. If the visitor returns to a page already in his or her local browser cache (for example, by clicking the Back button), no record of this event will be sent to the server, and the event will not be recorded. This means that we can never be certain that we have a full map of the visitor's actions.

As with proxies, we can attempt to force the browser to always obtain objects from a server rather than from cache by including appropriate "No Cache" HTML tags, but we may not choose to do this because of performance or other content-related reasons.

A similar uncertainty can be introduced when a visitor opens multiple browser windows to the same Web site. The visitor may have multiple views of different pages of the site available on his or her PC screen, but there isn't any way for the Web server to know this.

Specific Dimensions for the Clickstream

Before we design specific clickstream data marts, let's collect together as many dimensions as we can think of that may have relevance in a clickstream environment. Any single dimensional schema will not use all the dimensions at once, but it is nice to have a portfolio of dimensions waiting to be used. The complete list of dimensions for a Web retailer could include:

- Date
- Time of day
- Part
- Vendor
- Transaction
- Status
- Type
- Carrier
- Facilities location
- Product
- Customer
- Media
- Causal

- Service policy
- Internal organization
- Employee
- Page
- Event
- Session
- Referral

All the dimensions in the list, except for the last four, are familiar data warehouse dimensions, most of which we have used already in earlier chapters of this book. The last four, however, are the unique dimensions of the clickstream and warrant some careful attention. We'll also provide preliminary sizing estimates to give a sense of their magnitude.

Page Dimension

The page dimension describes the page context for a Web page event, as shown in Table 14.1. The grain of this dimension is the individual page. Our definition of *page* must be flexible enough to handle the evolution of Web pages from the current, mostly static page delivery to highly dynamic page delivery in which the exact page the customer sees is unique at that instant in time. We will assume even in the case of the dynamic page that there is a well-defined function that characterizes the page, and we will use this to describe the page. We will not create a page row for every instance of a dynamic page because that would yield a dimension with an astronomical number of rows, yet the rows would not differ in interesting ways. What we want is a row in this dimension for each interesting, distinguishable type of page. Static pages probably get their own row, but dynamic pages would be grouped by similar function and type.

When the definition of a static page changes because the Webmaster alters it, the row in the page dimension either can be overwritten or can be treated as a slowly changing dimension. This decision is a matter of policy for the data Webhouse, and it depends on whether the old and new descriptions of the page differ materially and whether the old definition should be kept for historical analysis purposes.

Web site designers and Webhouse developers need to collaborate to assign descriptive codes and attributes to each page served by the Web server, whether the page is dynamic or static. Ideally, Web page developers supply descriptive codes and attributes with each page they create and embed these

Table 14.1 Recommended Design for the Page Dimension

ATTRIBUTE	SAMPLE VALUES
Page Key	Surrogate values, 1-N
Page Source	Static, Dynamic, Unknown, Corrupted, Inapplicable
Page Function	Portal, Search, Product Description, Corporate Information
Page Template	Sparse, Dense
Item Type	Product SKU, Book ISBN Number, Telco Rate Type
Graphics Type	GIF, JPG, Progressive Disclosure, Size Pre-Declared, Combination
Animation Type	Similar to Graphics Type
Sound Type	Similar to Graphics Type
Page File Name	File Name

codes and attributes into the optional fields of the Web log files. This crucial step is at the foundation of the implementation of this page dimension.

The page dimension is small. If the nominal width of a single row is 100 bytes and we have a big Web site with 100,000 pages, then the unindexed data size is 100 x 100,000 = 10 MB. If indexing adds a factor of 3, then the total size of this dimension is about 40 MB.

Event Dimension

The event dimension describes what happened on a particular page at a particular point in time. The main interesting events are open page, refresh page, click link, and enter data. As dynamic pages based on XML become more common, the event dimension will get much more interesting because the semantics of the page will be much more obvious to the Web server. Each field in an XML document can be labeled with a visitor-defined tag. We will want to capture this information in this event dimension, as shown in Table 14.2

Table 14.2 Recommended Design for the Event Dimension

ATTRIBUTE	SAMPLE VALUES
Event Key	Surrogate values, 1-N
Event Type	Open Page, Refresh Page, Click Link, Enter Data, Unknown, Inapplicable
Event Content	Application-dependent fields eventually driven from XML tags

The event dimension is tiny. If the nominal width of a single row is 40 bytes and we have 1,000 distinct events, then the indexed data size is 40 x 1,000 = 0.04 MB. If indexing adds a factor of 3, then the total size of this dimension is only about 0.16 MB.

Session Dimension

The session dimension, illustrated in Table 14.3, provides one or more levels of diagnosis for the visitor's session as a whole. For example, the local context of the session might be requesting product information, but the overall session context might be ordering a product. The success status would diagnose whether the mission was completed. The local context may be decidable from just the identity of the current page, but the overall session context probably can be judged only by processing the visitor's complete session at data extract time. The customer status attribute is a convenient place to label the customer for periods of time, with labels that are not clear immediately either from the page or from the immediate session. Useful statuses include high-value reliable customer, new customer, about to cancel, or in default. All these statuses may be derived from auxiliary data marts in the data Webhouse, but by placing these labels deep within the clickstream, we are able to study the behavior of certain types of customers directly. We do not put these labels in the customer dimension because they may change over very short periods of time. If there were a large number of these statuses, then we would consider creating a separate customer status dimension rather than embedding this information in the session dimension.

This dimension is extremely important because it provides a way to group sessions for insightful analysis. For example, this dimension would be used to ask:

- How many customers consulted our product information before ordering?
- How many customers looked at our product information and never ordered?
- How many customers began the ordering process but did not finish? And where did they stop?

The session dimension is tiny. If the nominal width of a single row is 80 bytes and we have 10,000 identified session combinations, then the indexed data size is 80 x 10,000 = 0.8 MB. If indexing adds a factor of 3, then the total size of this dimension is about 3 MB.

Table 14.3 Recommended Design for the Session Dimension

ATTRIBUTE	SAMPLE VALUES
Session Key	Surrogate values, 1-*N*
Session Type	Classified, Unclassified, Corrupted, Inapplicable
Local Content	Page-derived context, such as requesting product information
Session Context	Trajectory-derived context, such as ordering a product
Action Sequence	Summary label for overall action sequence during session
Success Status	Whether the overall session mission was achieved
Customer Status	High Value, Reliable, In Default

Referral Dimension

Shown in Table 14.4, the referral dimension describes how the customer arrived at the current page. Web server logs usually provide this information. The URL of the previous page is identified, and in some cases, additional information is present. If the referrer was a search engine, then usually the search string is specified. It is not worthwhile to put the raw search specification into our database because the search specifications are so complicated and idiosyncratic that an analyst couldn't usefully query them. We assume that some kind of simplified and cleaned specification is placed in the specification field.

Table 14.4 Recommended Design for the Referral Dimension

ATTRIBUTE	SAMPLE VALUES
Referral Key	Surrogate values, 1-*N*
Referral Type	Intra Site, Remote Site, Search Engine, Corrupted, Inapplicable
Referring URL	www.organization.site.com/linkspage
Referring Site	www.organization.site.com
Referring Domain	Site.com
Search Type	Simple Text Match, Complex Match Logic
Specification	Actual spec used; useful if simple text, questionable otherwise
Target	Where the search found its match, for example, Meta Tags, Body Text, Title

The referral dimension may be fairly large. If the average width of a single row is 100 bytes and if we have 1 million referral rows, then the indexed data size is 100 x 1,000,000 = 100 MB. If indexing adds a factor of 3, then the total size of this dimension is about 400 MB. This is a hard dimension to estimate without actual data because the variability in size comes from the length of the referring URL and the search specification, which may not be present.

Now that we have a portfolio of useful clickstream dimensions, we can first build the primary clickstream data mart directly off the server log files. Then we will integrate this data mart into the family of other data marts in our Web retailer.

Clickstream Fact Table for Complete Sessions

The first fact table in our clickstream data mart will be based solely on the clickstream data derived from our own Web site logs. With an eye toward keeping the first fact table from growing astronomically, we choose the grain to be one row for each completed customer session. This grain is significantly higher than the underlying Web server logs, which record each microscopic page event. However, perhaps we have a big site recording more than 100 million raw page events per day, and we want to start with a more manageable number of rows to be loaded each day. We assume for the sake of argument that the 100 million page events boil down to 5 million complete visitor sessions. This could arise if an average visitor session touched five pages, and there was an average of four basic events recorded per page, including requests for GIF and JPEG graphic images.

The dimensions that are appropriate for this first fact table are calendar date, time of day, customer, page, session, and referrer. Finally, we add a set of measured facts for this session that includes session seconds, pages visited, orders placed, order quantity, and order dollar amount. The completed design is shown in Figure 14.3.

There are a number of interesting aspects to the design shown in Figure 14.3. You may be wondering why the date and time-of-day dimensions play two different roles, identified by semantically independent views, in this schema, as we introduced in Chapter 11. Because we are interested in measuring the precise times of sessions, we must make sure we meet two conflicting requirements. First, we want to make sure that we can synchronize all session dates and times across multiple time zones internationally. Perhaps we have other date and time stamps from other Web servers or from non-Web systems elsewhere in our data warehouse. To achieve true synchronization of events across multiple servers and processes, we must record all session dates and times uniformly in a single time zone such as Greenwich Mean Time (GMT). We interpret the session date and time combinations as the beginning of the session. Since we have the dwell time of the session as a numeric fact, we can tell when the session ended if this is of interest.

The other requirement we will meet with this design is to record the date and time of the session relative to the visitor's wall clock. The best way to represent this information is with a second pair of calendar date and time-of-day foreign keys. Theoretically, we could represent the time zone of the customer in the customer dimension table, but constraints to determine the correct wall clock time would be horrendously complicated. The time difference between two cities (such as London and Sydney) can change by as much as 2 hours at different times of the year depending on when these cities go on and off daylight savings time. This is not the business of the end-user application to work out; it is the business of the database to store this information so that it can be constrained in a simple and direct way.

Inclusion of the page dimension in Figure 14.3 may seem surprising given that the grain of the design is the customer session. However, in a given session, an interesting page is the entry page. We interpret the page dimension in this design as the page with which the session started. In other words, how did the customer hop onto our bus just now? Coupled with the referrer dimension, we now have an interesting ability to analyze how and why the customer accessed our Web site. A more elaborate design also would add an exit page dimension.

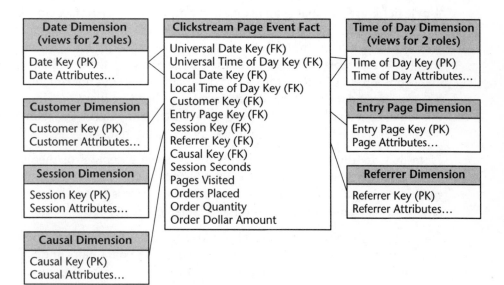

Figure 14.3 Clickstream schema at the session grain.

We may be tempted to add the causal dimension to this design, but if the causal dimension were intended to focus on individual products, it would be inappropriate to add to this design. The symptom that the causal dimension does not mesh with this design is the multivalued nature of the causal factors for a given complete session. If we are running ad campaigns or special deals for several products, how do we represent this multivalued situation if the customer's session involves several products? The right place for a product-oriented causal dimension will be in the more fine-grained table we build in the next fact table example. Conversely, a more broadly focused market causal dimension that described market conditions affecting all products would be appropriate for a session-grained fact table.

The session seconds fact is the total number of seconds the customer spent on the site during this session. There will be many cases where we can't tell when the customer left. Perhaps the customer typed in a new URL. Conventional Web server logs won't detect this (although if the data is being collected by an ISP that can see every click across sessions, then this particular issue goes away). Or perhaps the customer got up out of the chair and didn't return for an hour. Or perhaps the customer just closed the browser without making any more clicks. In all these cases our extract software needs to assign a small and nominal number of seconds to this part of the session so that the analysis is not distorted unrealistically.

The fact table shown in Figure 14.3 has 13 fields. Since all the foreign key fields are surrogate keys, none of them needs to be represented in more than 4 bytes. Similarly, all the measured facts are either integers or scaled integers. Again, 4-byte fields are reasonable for estimation purposes. Thus our fact table is about 52 bytes wide. If we collect 5 million new fact rows each day for our hypothetical large Web site example, then we are adding 260 MB of data (before indexing) to the fact table each day. Over the course of a year, this would amount to 260 MB x 365 = 94.9 GB of unindexed data. This is big, but not ridiculously so. Three years of data, together with indexing overhead, perhaps would consume 600 GB of disk space. Given the pace of Web marketing and Web technology, it seems reasonable to plan on keeping only 3 years of data.

Note that the dimension tables, with the possible exception of the customer dimension, are small by comparison with the main fact table. A fully indexed 50-million-row customer table could occupy 200 GB of storage, about one-third the size of the fact table. All the other dimension tables are negligible by comparison.

We purposely built this first fact table in our clickstream data mart to focus on complete visitor sessions and to keep the size of the data mart under control. The next table we design drops down to the lowest practical granularity we can support in the data Webhouse: the individual page event.

Clickstream Fact Table for Individual Page Events

In this second fact table we will define the granularity to be the individual page event in each customer session. With simple, static HTML pages, we may be able to record only one interesting event per page view, namely, the page view itself. As Web sites employ dynamically created XML-based pages with the ability to establish an ongoing dialogue through the page, the number and types of events will grow.

It is likely that this fact table will become astronomical in size. We will resist the urge to aggregate the table up to a coarser granularity because such a step inevitably involves eliminating dimensions. Actually, the first fact table we built for this data mart represents just such an aggregation. It is a worthwhile fact table, but the analyst cannot ask questions about visitor behavior or individual pages. When the individual page-oriented data set gets too large, then in order to preserve the ability to analyze detailed behavior, either the time span of the data must be restricted or statistical sampling techniques must be used to reduce data size. Although disk storage capacity has been doubling even faster (every 12 months, supposedly) than processing power, our propensity to collect reams of data seems to be doubling at an even faster pace.

Having chosen the grain, we can choose the appropriate dimensions. Our list of dimensions includes calendar date, time of day, customer, page, event, session, session ID, product, causal, and referrer. The completed design is shown in Figure 14.4.

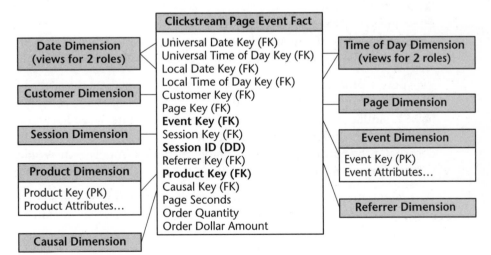

Figure 14.4 Clickstream schema at the page-event grain.

The design in Figure 14.4 looks rather similar to our first design. This similarity between fact tables is typical of dimensional models. One of the charms of dimensional modeling is the boring similarity of the designs. However, this is where they get their power. When the designs have a predictable structure, all the software up and down the data warehouse chain, from extraction, to database querying, to the end-user tools, can exploit this similarity to great advantage. Query and reporting tools, for example, may be able to adapt to a whole family of dimensional designs without any reprogramming.

The two roles played by the calendar date and time-of-day dimensions have the same interpretation as in the first design; one role is the universal synchronized time, probably expressed in GMT, and the other role is the local wall clock time as measured by the customer. In this fact table the date/time combinations refer to the individual page event that is being described by the row we are building.

The page dimension refers to the individual page whose events we are recording. This is the main difference in grain between this fact table and the first one we built. In this fact table we will be able to see all the pages accessed by the customers.

The event dimension describes what happened on the page, as we described earlier in this chapter.

The session dimension describes the outcome of the session. A companion field, the session ID, is a degenerate dimension that does not have a join to a dimension table. The session ID is simply a unique identifier with no semantic content that serves to group together the page events of each customer session in an unambiguous way. We did not need a session ID degenerate dimension in our first fact table because each row in that table already represented a complete session. We recommend that the session dimension be at a higher level of granularity than the session ID because the session dimension is intended to describe classes and categories of sessions, not the characteristics of each individual session.

We show a product dimension in this design under the assumption that this Web site is owned by a Web retailer. A financial services site probably would have a similar dimension. A consulting services site would have a service dimension. An auction site would have a subject or category dimension describing the nature of the items being auctioned. A news site would have a subject dimension, although with different content than an auction site.

We accompany the product dimension with a causal dimension so that we can attach useful marketplace interpretations to the changes in demand we may see for certain products.

For each page event we record the number of seconds that we believe elapse before the next page event. We call this *page seconds* to contrast it with *session seconds* that we used in the first fact table. This is a simple example of paying attention to conformed facts. If we called both these measures simply *seconds*, then we would run the risk of having these seconds added or combined inappropriately. Since these seconds are not precisely equivalent, we name them differently as a warning. In this particular case we would expect the page seconds for a session in this second fact table to add up to the session seconds in the first fact table.

Our final facts are order quantity and order dollar amount. These fields will be zero or null for many of the rows in this fact table simply because the specific page event is not the event that places the order. Nevertheless, it is highly attractive to provide these fields because they tie all-important Web revenue directly to behavior. If the order quantity and dollar amount were only available through the production order-entry system elsewhere in the data Webhouse, it would be inefficient to perform the revenue-to-behavior analysis across multiple large tables. In many database management systems the existence of these kinds of null fields is handled efficiently and may take up literally zero space in the fact table.

We can quickly estimate the size of this fact table. If we use the earlier example of 100 million raw Web log events each day, we probably end up with about 20 million meaningful page events per day after we discard the requests for GIF and JPEG images. Each row in the page-event fact table has 15 fields, which we estimate occupies 15 x 4 bytes = 60 bytes. Thus the total fact table data to be added each day is 20 million x 60 bytes = about 1.2 GB per day. This would amount to 365 x 1.2 GB = 438 GB per year, before indexing. Again, while this is a large number, it is within reach of today's technology.

As we move to more dynamic page delivery with better semantic labels on each of the actions (thanks to XML), undoubtedly we will increase the volume of data available. Perhaps we keep the granularity of the present table at approximately one page view per row rather than making a row for each discrete customer gesture. It is too early at this time to make a definitive prediction of whether we will descend all the way to the individual gesture level with a third and even more granular fact table. Even if our storage and query technologies keep up with the increased volume of data, we need to wait to see if there is sufficient analysis content in the lowest-level behavior data to make it worthwhile. Hopefully, you can see how to extend the techniques of this chapter to handle this case.

Aggregate Clickstream Fact Tables

Both the fact tables we have built thus far in our clickstream data mart are large. There are many business questions we would like to ask that would be forced to summarize millions of rows from these tables. For example, if we want to track the total visits and revenue from major demographic groups of customers accessing our Web site on a month-by-month basis, we certainly can do this with either fact table. In the session-grained fact table we would constrain the calendar date dimension to the appropriate time span (say, January, February, and March of the current year). We would then create row headers from the demographics type field in the customer dimension and the month field in the calendar dimension (to separately label the three months in the output). Finally, we would sum over the total order dollars and count the number of sessions. This all works just fine. However, it is likely to be slow without help from an aggregate table. If this kind of query is frequent, the DBA will be encouraged to build an aggregate table such as shown in Figure 14.5.

We can build this table directly from our first fact table, whose grain is the individual session. To build this aggregate table, we group by month, demographic type, entry page, and session outcome. We count the number of sessions and sum all the other additive facts. This results in a drastically smaller fact table, almost certainly less than 1 percent of the original session-grained fact table. This reduction in size translates directly to a corresponding increase in performance for most queries. In other words, we would expect queries directed to this aggregate table to run at least 100 times faster.

Although it may not have been obvious, we followed a careful discipline in building the aggregate table. This aggregate fact table is connected to a set of shrunken dimensions directly related to the original dimensions in the session-grained fact table. The month table is a conformed subset of the calendar-day table. The demographic table is a conformed subset of the customer table. We assume that the page and session tables are unchanged, although a careful design of the aggregation logic could suggest a conformed shrinking of these tables as well.

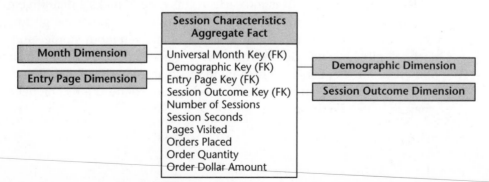

Figure 14.5 Aggregated clickstream schema summarized by session characteristics.

Integrating the Clickstream Data Mart into the Enterprise Data Warehouse

In this section we look at the overall design of a series of data marts implemented for a Web-based computer retailer. The data marts correspond to all the business processes needed by this retailer to run its business. We could illustrate this design by showing each schema as we have done in the preceding examples, but the synergy among the designs would be difficult to see clearly. Instead, we use the data warehouse bus matrix, which we introduced in Chapter 3.

The matrix method lists the data marts down the left side of the matrix and the dimensions used by the data marts across the top of the matrix. The cells of the matrix contain Xs if the particular data mart uses a particular dimension. Note that the matrix describes data marts, not individual fact tables. Typically, a data mart consists of a suite of closely associated fact tables all describing a particular business process. A good way to start the design of a series of data marts is to define first-level data marts that are, as much as possible, related to single sources of data. Once several of these first-level data marts have been implemented, then second-level consolidated data marts, such as profitability, can be built that require data from the first-level marts to be combined. Thus the entries in a given row of the matrix represent the existence of a dimension somewhere in the closely associated suite of tables defining a particular data mart.

Figure 14.6 shows the completed bus matrix for a Web retailer. The matrix has a number of striking characteristics. There are a lot of Xs. An X in a given matrix column is, in effect, an invitation to the meeting for conforming that dimension. The average data mart uses six to eight dimensions. Some of the dimensions, such as date/time, transaction, status/type, organization, and employee, appear in almost every data mart. The product and customer dimensions dominate the whole middle part of the matrix, where they are attached to the data marts that describe customer-oriented activities. At the top of the matrix, suppliers and parts dominate the processes of acquiring the parts that make up products and building them to order for the customer. At the bottom of the matrix we have classic infrastructure and cost-driver data marts that are not tied directly to customer behavior.

We see the Web visitor clickstream data mart sitting squarely among the customer-oriented data marts. It shares the date/time, transaction, product, customer, media, causal, and service policy dimensions with several other data marts nearby. In this sense it should be obvious that the Web visitor clickstream data mart is well integrated into the fabric of the overall data warehouse for this retailer. Applications tying the Web visitor clickstream will be easy to integrate across all these data marts sharing these conformed dimensions because the separate queries to each data mart will be able to be combined across individual rows of the report.

	Date and Time	Part	Vendor	Transaction	Status and Type	Carrier	Facilities Location	Product	Customer	Media	Causal	Service Policy	Internal Organization	Employee	Clickstream (4 dims)
Supplier Purchase Orders	X	X	X	X	X		X						X	X	
Supplier Deliveries	X	X	X	X	X	X	X						X		
Part Inventories	X	X	X	X	X		X						X		
Product Assembly Bill of Materials	X	X	X	X			X	X					X	X	
Product Assembly to Order	X	X	X	X	X		X	X	X				X	X	
Product Promotions	X			X				X	X	X	X		X		
Advertising	X			X				X		X	X		X		
Customer Inquiries	X			X	X		X	X	X		X	X	X	X	
Customer Communications	X			X	X			X	X				X	X	
Web Visitor Clickstream	**X**			**X**				**X**	**X**	**X**	**X**	**X**			**X**
Product Sales Transactions	X			X	X			X	X			X	X	X	
Product Shipments	X			X	X	X	X	X	X			X	X	X	
Customer Billing	X			X	X			X	X			X	X	X	
Customer Payments	X			X	X				X				X	X	
Product Returns	X			X	X		X	X	X			X	X	X	
Product Support	X			X	X		X	X	X			X	X	X	
Service Policy Orders	X			X	X			X	X			X	X	X	
Service Policy Responses	X			X	X		X	X	X			X	X	X	
Employee Labor	X			X	X		X						X	X	
Human Resources	X			X	X		X						X	X	
Facilities Operations	X			X	X		X						X	X	
Web Site Operations	X			X	X		X						X	X	

Figure 14.6 Data warehouse bus matrix for a Web retailer.

The Web visitor clickstream data mart contains the four special clickstream dimensions not found in the other data marts. These dimensions do not pose a problem for applications. Instead, the ability of the Web visitor clickstream data mart to bridge between the Web world and the brick-and-mortar world is exactly the advantage that we are looking for. We can constrain and group on attributes from the four Web dimensions and explore the effect on the other business processes. For example, we can see what kinds of Web experiences produce customers who purchase certain kinds of service policies and then invoke certain levels of service demands.

Electronic Commerce Profitability Data Mart

After the data Webhouse team successfully brings up the initial clickstream data mart and ties this data mart to the sales transaction and customer communication data marts, the team may be ready to tackle the most challenging data mart of all: the Web profitability data mart.

We can build the Web profitability data mart as an extension of the sales transaction data mart. Fundamentally, we are going to allocate all the activity costs and infrastructure costs down to each sales transaction. We could, as an alternative, try to build the Web profitability data mart on top of the clickstream, but this would involve an even more controversial allocation process in which we allocated costs down to each session. It would be hard to assign activity and infrastructure costs to a session that had no obvious product involvement and led to no immediate sale.

A big benefit of extending the sales transaction fact table is that we will get a view of profitability over all our sales channels, not just the Web. In a way, this should be obvious, because we know that we have to sort out the costs and assign them to the various channels anyway. For this reason, we will call the main fact table in our new data mart simply *profitability*.

Thus the grain of the profitability fact table is each individual product sold on a sales ticket to a customer at a point in time. This sounds familiar, doesn't it? This grain is nearly identical to the grain of the first dimensional model we designed. The primary difference is that Chapter 2's schema was limited to the grocer's brick-and-mortar store. In this section the model will include profitability metrics across all channels, including store sales, telesales, and Web sales.

We explored a profitability data mart extensively in Chapter 5. We enumerated a lengthy list of profit and loss (P&L) facts from gross revenue to contribution profit. Figure 14.7 illustrates these same facts in a somewhat broader context. As we saw in Chapter 5, the fact table is organized as a simple P&L statement.

The first fact is our now-familiar quantity sold. The rest of the facts are dollar values, beginning with gross revenue, which is the value of the item as if it were sold at list or catalog price. We account for allowances and promotions to arrive at net revenue, which is the true net price the customer pays times the quantity purchased.

The rest of the P&L table consists of a series of subtractions, where we calculate progressively for more far-reaching versions of profit. We begin by subtracting the product manufacturing cost (if we manufacture it) or, equivalently, the product acquisition cost (if we acquire it from a supplier). We then subtract the product storage cost. At this point many enterprises refer to this partial result as the *gross profit*. One can divide this gross profit by the gross revenue to get the gross margin ratio.

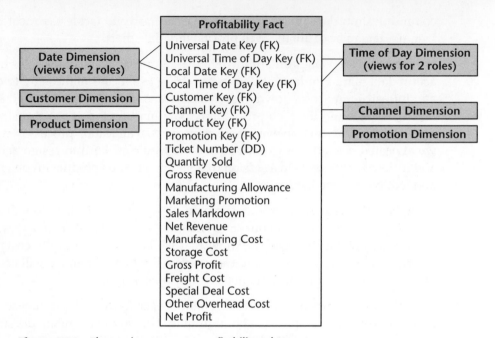

Figure 14.7 Electronic commerce profitability schema.

Obviously, the columns called "Net Revenue" and "Gross Profit" are calculated directly from the fields immediately preceding them in the P&L table. However, should we explicitly store these fields in the database? The answer depends on whether you provide access to this fact table through a view or allow users or applications to access the physical fact table directly. The structure of the P&L table is sufficiently complex that, as the data warehouse provider, you don't want to risk having important measures such as net revenue and gross profit computed incorrectly. If you provide all access through views, you can easily supply the computed columns without physically storing them. However, if your users are allowed to access the underlying physical table, then you should include net revenue, gross profit, and net profit as physical fields.

Below the gross profit we continue subtracting various costs. Typically, the warehouse team must source or estimate each of these costs separately. Remember that the actual entries in any given fact table row are the fractions of these total costs allocated all the way down to the individual fact row grain. Often there is significant pressure on the warehouse team to finish the profitability data mart. To put this another way, there is tremendous pressure to source all these costs. But how good are the costs in the various underlying data sets? Sometimes a cost is only available as a national average, computed for an entire year. Any allocation scheme is going to assign a kind of pro forma value that has no real texture to it. Other costs will be broken down a little better, perhaps to the calendar quarter and by geographic region (if this is relevant). Finally, some costs may be truly activity-based and vary in a highly dynamic, responsive, and realistic way over time.

Web site system costs are an important cost driver in electronic commerce-oriented businesses. Although Web site costs are classic infrastructure costs and therefore are difficult to allocate directly to the product and customer activity, this is a key step in developing a Web-oriented P&L statement. Various allocation schemes are possible, including allocating the Web site costs to various product lines by the number of pages devoted to each product, allocating the costs by pages visited, or allocating the costs by actual Web-based purchases.

Before leaving this design, it is worthwhile to reiterate that Figure 14.7's profitability fact table within a rich dimensional framework is immensely powerful. We can see the breakdown of all the components of revenue, cost, and profit for every conceivable slice and dice supported by the dimensions. We can ask, "How profitable are each of our channels (for example, Web sales, telesales, and store sales) and why?" or "How profitable are all our possible customer segmentations and why?" Of course, the symmetric dimensional approach allows us to combine constraints from as many dimensions as we can. This gives us compound versions of profitability analyses, such as, "Who are the profitable customers in each channel and why?" or "Which promotions work well on the Web but do not work well in other channels and why?"

Summary

The Web retailer example we used in this chapter is illustrative of any business with a significant Web presence. Besides building the clickstream data mart, the central challenge is to integrate the clickstream data effectively into the rest of the business. In this chapter the key concepts included:

The challenge of identifying the Web visitor's origin. In some cases we can look backward through the referral information in the Web log, but in many other cases this information is not supplied.

The challenge of identifying a complete session. HTTP sessions are stateless. The use of cookies is the best mechanism for defining a session, bearing in mind that we cannot explain all the time intervals between page requests.

The challenge of identifying the Web visitor. Even with a cookie, we cannot be sure who the individual is at the other end.

How to deal with proxy servers. A proxy server intercepts the visitor's page requests. We can inhibit the use of proxy servers, or in some cases we can collect the logs.

The design of the page dimension. The key step is to get the Web page designer to assign content codes and attributes to each page and then embed these codes and attributes into the Web server logs.

The design of the session dimension. The key step is to use the record of the complete session, together with some simple criteria, to provide a session diagnosis that can be used to look for sessions of different types.

The design of a clickstream fact table for complete sessions. This fact table is an interesting compromise between a high-level summary of Web site activity and the overwhelming detail provided by a fact table for each page event.

The design of a clickstream fact table for each page event. This ultimate level of detail is the most accurate and complete record of customer behavior. The size problems with this table can be addressed by sampling.

The design of aggregate clickstream fact tables. Much smaller (and faster) fact tables can usefully summarize visitor behavior, such as correlating demographics with productive sessions.

How to integrate the clickstream data mart into the rest of the data warehouse. Using the bus matrix design method, we see which dimensions must be conformed across all the data marts, and we see that the clickstream data mart has a significant overlap with the other data marts.

How to add profitability measures to the product sales data mart so that the contribution of the Web channel can be isolated and analyzed.

Insurance

We will bring together concepts from nearly all the previous chapters to build a data warehouse for a property and casualty insurance company in this final case study. If you are from the insurance industry and jumped directly to this chapter for a quick fix, please accept our apology, but this material depends heavily on ideas from the earlier chapters. You'll need to turn back to the beginning of the book to have this chapter make any sense.

As has been our standard procedure, this chapter is launched with background information for a business case. While the requirements unfold, we'll draft the data warehouse bus matrix, much like we would in a real-life requirements analysis effort. We'll then design a series of dimensional models by overlaying the core techniques learned thus far in a manner similar to the overlay of overhead transparencies.

Chapter 15 reviews the following concepts:

- **Requirements-driven approach to dimensional design**
- **Value-chain implications**
- **Data warehouse bus matrix**
- **Complementary transaction, periodic snapshot, and accumulating snapshot schemas**
- **Four-step design process for dimensional models**
- **Dimension role-playing**
- **Handling of slowly changing dimension attributes**
- **Minidimensions for dealing with large, more rapidly changing dimension attributes**

- Multivalued dimension attributes
- Degenerate dimensions for operational control numbers
- Audit dimensions to track data lineage
- Heterogeneous products with attributes and facts that vary by line of business
- Conformed dimensions and facts
- Consolidated fact tables that combine metrics from separate business processes
- Factless fact tables
- Common mistakes to avoid when designing dimensional models

Insurance Case Study

Let's imagine that we work for a $5 billion property and casualty insurer that offers automobile, homeowners', and personal property insurance. We conduct extensive interviews with representatives and senior management from the claims, field operations, actuarial, finance, and marketing departments. Based on these interviews, we learn that the insurance industry is in a state of flux. New, nontraditional players are entering by leveraging alternative channels, such as the Internet. In the meantime, the industry is consolidating due to globalization, deregulation, and demutualization challenges. Markets are changing, along with customer needs. Numerous interviewees tell us that information is becoming an even more important strategic asset. Regardless of the functional groups, there is a strong desire to use information more effectively to identify opportunities more quickly and respond most appropriately.

The good news is that internal systems and processes already capture the bulk of the data required. Most insurance companies generate tons of nitty-gritty operational data. The bad news is that the data is not integrated. Over the years, political and data-processing boundaries have encouraged the construction of tall barriers around these isolated islands of data. There are multiple disparate sources for information about the company's products, customers, and distribution channels. In the legacy operational systems, the same policyholder may be identified several times in separate automobile, home, and personal property applications. Traditionally, this segmented approach to data was acceptable because the different lines of business functioned largely autonomously. There was little interest in sharing data across units for cross-selling and collaboration in the past. Now we're attempting to better leverage an enormous amount of inconsistent yet somewhat redundant data.

Besides the inherent issues surrounding data integration, business users lack the ability to access data easily when needed. In an attempt to address this shortcoming, several organizations within the insurance company rallied their own resources and hired consultants to solve their individual short-term data needs. In many cases the same data was extracted from the same source systems to be accessed by separate organizations without any strategic overall information-delivery strategy. Unfortunately, no one had the courage to proactively inform senior management of the negative consequences of this approach.

It didn't take long for management to recognize the negative ramifications associated with separate data warehouses because performance results presented at executive meetings differed depending on the analytic source. Management understood that this independent route was not viable as a long-term solution because of the lack of integration, large volumes of redundant data, and difficulty in accessing and interpreting the results. Given the importance of information in this brave new insurance world, management was motivated to deal with the cost implications surrounding the development, support, and analytic inefficiencies of these supposed data warehouses that merely proliferated the operational data islands.

A new chief information officer (CIO) was hired to lead the information charge. Senior management chartered the CIO with the responsibility and authority to break down the historical data silos to "achieve information nirvana." They charged the CIO with the fiduciary responsibility to manage and leverage the organization's information assets more effectively. The CIO developed an overall vision that wed an enterprise strategy for dealing with massive amounts of data, with a response to the immediate need to become an information-rich organization. In the meantime, an enterprise data warehouse team was created to begin designing and implementing the vision.

Senior management has been preaching about a transformation to a more customer-centric focus instead of the traditional product-centric approach in an effort to gain competitive advantage. The CIO jumped on that bandwagon as a catalyst for change and already has had an impact. The message has reached the folks in the trenches. They pledge intent to share data rather than squirreling it away for a single purpose. There is a strong desire for everyone to have a common understanding of the state of the business. They're clamoring to get rid of the isolated pockets of data while ensuring that they have access to detail and summary data at both the enterprise and line-of-business levels.

Insurance Value Chain

The primary value chain of an insurance company is seemingly short and simple. The core processes are to issue policies, collect premium payments, and process claims. The organization is interested in better understanding the metrics spawned by each of these processes. Users want to analyze detailed transactions relating to the formulation of policies, as well as transactions generated by claims processing. They want to measure profit over time by coverage, covered item type (that is, which kinds of houses and automobiles), geographic, demographic, and sales distribution channel characteristics. Of course, the desire to monitor profit implies that both revenues and costs can be identified and tracked. While users are interested in the enterprise perspective, they also want to analyze the heterogeneous nature of the insurance company's lines of business.

Obviously, an insurance company is engaged in many other external processes, such as the investment of premium payments, as well as a host of internally focused activities, such as human resources, finance, and purchasing. For now, we'll focus on the core business related to policies and claims.

The insurance value chain begins with a variety of policy transactions. Based on our current understanding of the requirements and underlying data, we opt to handle all the transactions having an impact on a policy as a single business process (and fact table). If this perspective is too simplistic to accommodate the metrics, dimensionality, or analytics required, we have the option to split the transaction activities into separate fact tables (for example, separate fact tables for quoting, rating, and underwriting). As we discussed in Chapter 3, there are tradeoffs between creating separate fact tables for each natural cluster of transaction types versus lumping the transactions into a single fact table.

While we're on the topic of policies, there is also a need to better understand the premium revenue associated with each policy on a monthly basis. This will be key input into the overall profit picture. In the case of insurance, the business is very transaction-intensive, but the transactions themselves do not represent little pieces of revenue, as was the case with retail or manufacturing sales. We cannot merely add up insurance transactions to determine the revenue amount. The picture is further complicated in insurance because customers pay in advance for services. We encounter this same advance-payment model in organizations that offer magazine subscriptions or extended warranty contracts. Premium payments must be spread out across multiple reporting periods because the organization earns the revenue over time as it provides insurance coverage. The complex relationship between individual transactions and the basic measures of revenue often makes it impossible to answer revenue questions by crawling through the individual transactions. Not only is such crawling time-consuming, but the logic required to interpret the effect of different transaction types on revenue also can be horrendously complicated. The natural conflict between the detailed transaction view and the monthly snapshot perspective almost always requires that we build both kinds of fact tables in the warehouse. In this case, the premium snapshot is not merely a summarization of the policy transactions; it is quite a separate thing that comes from a separate source.

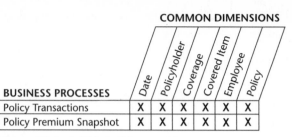

Figure 15.1   Initial draft bus matrix.

Draft Insurance Bus Matrix

Based on the interview findings, along with an understanding of the key source systems, the team begins to draft a data warehouse bus matrix with the core business processes as rows and core dimensions as columns. At this point we're focused on the policy-based processes. We put two rows in the matrix, one corresponding to the policy transactions and another for the monthly policy premium snapshot.

As illustrated in Figure 15.1, the core dimensions include date, policyholder, employee, coverage, covered item, and policy. When drafting the matrix, we don't attempt to include all the dimensions because the matrix could end up with 100 columns or more. Instead, we try to focus on the core common dimensions that are reused in more than one schema.

Policy Transactions

Now let's turn our attention to the first row of the matrix by focusing on the transactions for creating and altering a policy. We assume that the policy is the header for a set of coverages sold to the policyholder. Coverages can be considered the products sold by the insurance company. Homeowner coverages include fire, flood, theft, and personal liability. Automobile coverages include comprehensive, collision damage, uninsured motorist, and personal liability. In a property and casualty insurance company, coverages typically apply to a specific covered item, such as a particular house or car. Both the coverage and covered item are identified carefully in the policy. A particular covered item usually will have several coverages listed in the policy. We assume that a policy can contain multiple covered items.

Just to keep things reasonably simple, an agent sells the policy to the policyholder in this case. Before the policy can be created, a pricing actuary determines the premium rate that will be charged given the specific coverages, covered items, and qualifications of the policyholder. An underwriter, who takes ultimate responsibility for doing business with the policyholder, makes the final approval.

The operational policy transaction system captures the following types of transactions:

- Create policy, alter policy, cancel policy (with reason)
- Create coverage on covered item, alter coverage, cancel coverage (with reason)
- Rate coverage, decline to rate coverage (with reason)
- Underwrite policy, decline to underwrite policy (with reason)

The grain of the policy transaction fact table would be one row for each individual policy transaction. Each atomic transaction should be embellished with as much context as possible to create a complete dimensional description of the transaction. The dimensions associated with the policy transaction business process include the transaction date, effective date, policyholder, employee, coverage, covered item, policy number, and policy transaction type.

Dimension Details and Techniques

Now let's further discuss the dimensions in this schema while taking the opportunity to reinforce concepts from earlier chapters.

Dimension Role-Playing

There are two dates associated with each policy transaction. The policy transaction date is the date when the transaction was entered into the operational system, whereas the policy transaction effective date is when the transaction legally takes effect. These two independent dimensions can be implemented using a single physical date table. Multiple logically distinct tables are then presented to the user through views with unique column names, as described originally in Chapter 5.

The policyholder is the customer in this schema. The policyholder can be multiple people, such as a person and his or her spouse, or the policyholder can be a business entity. The policyholder dimension often qualifies as a large dimension, as is the case with our $5 billion insurer that caters to millions of policyholders.

Slowly Changing Dimensions

Insurance companies typically are very interested in tracking changes to dimensions over time. We'll apply the three basic techniques for handling slowly changing dimension attributes that we introduced in Chapter 4 to the policyholder dimension.

With the type 1 approach, we simply overwrite the preceding dimension attribute value. This is the simplest approach to dealing with attribute changes because the attributes always represent the most current descriptors. For example, perhaps the business agrees to handle changes to the policyholder's date of birth as a type 1 change based on the assumption that any changes to this attribute are intended as corrections. In this manner, all fact table history for this policyholder appears to have always been associated with the updated date-of-birth value.

Since the policyholder's ZIP code is key input to the insurer's pricing and risk algorithms, users are very interested in tracking ZIP code changes, so we opt to use a type 2 approach to this attribute. Type 2 is the most common slowly changing dimension (SCD) approach when there's a requirement for accurate change tracking over time. In this case, when the ZIP code changes, we create a new policyholder dimension row with a new surrogate key and updated geographic attributes. We do not go back and revisit the fact table. Historical fact table rows, prior to the ZIP code change, still reflect the old surrogate key. Going forward, we use the policyholder's new surrogate key so that new fact table rows join to the postchange profile. While this technique is extremely graceful and powerful, it places more burdens on the data staging application. Also, the number of rows in the dimension table grows with each type 2 SCD change. Given that there are already well over 1 million rows in our policyholder dimension table, we may opt to use a minidimension for tracking ZIP code changes, which we'll review shortly.

Finally, let's assume that each policyholder is classified as belonging to a particular segment. Perhaps we historically tagged our nonresidential policyholders as either commercial or government entities. Going forward, the business users want more detailed customer classifications. For instance, the new policyholder segments may differentiate between large multinational, middle market, and small business commercial customers, in addition to nonprofit organizations and governmental agencies. For a period of time, users want the ability to analyze results by either the historical or new segment classifications. In this case we could use a type 3 approach to track the change for a period of time. We add a column to the dimension table, labeled "Historical Policyholder Segment Type," to retain the old classifications. The new classification values would populate the segment attribute that has been a permanent fixture on the policyholder dimension. This approach, while not extremely common, allows us to see performance by either the current or historical segment maps. This is useful when there's been an en masse change, such as the customer classification realignment. Obviously, the type 3 technique becomes overly complex if we need to track more than one version of the historical map or if we need to track before and after changes for multiple dimension attributes.

Minidimensions for Large or Rapidly Changing Dimensions

As we referenced earlier, the policyholder dimension qualifies as a large dimension with more than 1 million rows. The covered item dimension likely also falls into this category because most policyholders insure more than one specific item. In both cases, it is often important to track content values accurately for a subset of attributes. For example, we need an accurate description of some policyholder and covered item attributes at the time the policy was created, as well as at the time of any adjustment or claim. We saw in Chapter 6 that the practical way to track changing attributes in large dimensions was to split the closely monitored, more rapidly changing attributes into one or more minidimensions directly linked to the fact table with a separate surrogate key. The use of minidimensions has an impact on the efficiency of attribute browsing because users typically want to browse and constrain on these changeable attributes, as well as on updating. If all possible combinations of the attribute values in the minidimension have been created already, handling a minidimension change simply means placing a different key in the fact table row from a certain point in time forward. Nothing else needs to be changed or added to the database.

Multivalued Dimension Attributes

We discussed multivalued dimension attributes in Chapter 9 when we associated multiple customers with an account and then again in Chapter 13 when a patient encounter involved multiple diagnoses. We certainly could duplicate the multiple customers per account design for each policy, but in this case study we'll look at yet another multivalued modeling situation: the relationship between commercial customers and their industry classifications.

Each commercial customer may be associated with one or more standard industry classification (SIC) codes. A large, diversified commercial customer could be represented by a dozen or more SIC codes. Much like we did with Chapter 13's diagnosis group, we build an SIC group bridge table to tie together all the SIC codes within an SIC group. This SIC bridge table joins to the customer dimension as an outrigger. It allows us to report fact table metrics by any attribute in the SIC table, either correctly weighted or as an impact report. To handle the case where no valid SIC code is associated with a given customer, we simply create a special SIC dimension row that represents "Unknown."

Let's move on to the coverage dimension. Large insurance companies will have dozens or even hundreds of separate coverage products available to sell for a given type of covered item. If the coverage has specific limits or deductibles, we generally treat these numeric parameters as facts rather than creating a distinct coverage for every different possible value. For example, a basic limit on homeowner's fire protection is the appraised value of the house. Since the appraised value can be thought of as a continuously valued numeric quantity that is measured each time we look at a different policy and can even vary for a given policy over time, we treat limits as legitimate facts.

The covered item is the house, the car, or other specific insured item. The covered item dimension contains one row for each actual covered item. As we mentioned earlier, the covered item dimension is usually somewhat larger than the policyholder dimension, so it's a good place to consider deploying a mini-dimension. In general, it is not desirable to capture the variable descriptions of the physical covered objects as facts because most are textual and are not numeric or continuously valued. In most cases a textual measurement is a description of something drawn from a discrete list of alternatives. The designer should make every effort to put textual measures into dimension tables because they can be correlated more effectively with the other textual attributes in a dimension and require much less space, especially if the proposed fact table text column is a wide, fixed-width field that is often empty. Textual facts can be counted and constrained on, but if they are unpredictable free text, the usual dimensional activities of constraining and grouping on these text values will be of little value. A true text fact is not a very good thing to have in a fact table.

The employee is the individual responsible for creating the transaction. For create policy and create coverage transactions, the responsible employee is the agent. For rating transactions, the employee is the rater. Likewise, the underwriter is the employee involved in underwriting transactions.

Degenerate Dimension

The policy number will be treated as a degenerate dimension if we have extracted all the header information associated with the policy into the other dimensions. We obviously want to avoid creating a policy transaction fact table with just several keys while embedding all the descriptive details (including the policyholder, dates, and coverages) in a policy dimension. In some cases there may be one or two attributes that still belong to the policy and not to another dimension. For example, if the underwriter establishes an overall risk grade for the policy, based on the totality of the coverages and covered items, then this risk grade probably belongs in a policy dimension. Of course, in this scenario we no longer have a degenerate dimension.

The policy transaction type dimension is a small dimension consisting of the transaction types listed earlier together with all the possible reason descriptions for the applicable transactions. Usually, a transaction type dimension contains less than 100 entries, although not always.

Audit Dimension

We always have the option to add keylike information to the transaction fact row, such as an audit key that links to a dimension row created by the extract process. As we described in Chapter 8, each audit dimension row can describe the data lineage of the fact row, including the time of the extract, the source table, and the version of the extract software.

We are now able to present the policy transaction schema, as illustrated in Figure 15.2. The resulting fact table illustrates several characteristics of a classic transaction-grain fact table. First of all, the fact table consists almost entirely of keys. Transaction-level schemas allow us to analyze behavior in extreme detail. As we descend to lower granularity with atomic data, the fact table naturally sprouts more dimensionality. In this case the fact table has a single numeric fact, called *policy transaction amount*. Interpretation of the amount column depends on the type of transaction, as identified in the transaction type dimension. Because there are different kinds of transactions in the same fact table, we usually cannot label the fact with anything more specific. If the transaction-processing system introduces additional types of transactions, they represent a change to the data content but don't necessitate a schema modification.

Heterogeneous Products

While there is strong support for an enterprise-wide perspective at our insurance company, the business users don't want to lose sight of their line-of-business specifics. Insurance companies typically are involved in multiple yet very different lines of business. For example, the detailed parameters of home-owners' coverages differ significantly from automobile coverages. And these both differ substantially from personal property coverage, general liability coverage, and other types of insurance. Although all coverages can be coded into the generic structures we have used so far in this chapter, insurance companies want to track numerous specific attributes (and perhaps facts) that only make sense for a particular coverage and covered item. We can generalize the initial schema developed in Figure 15.2 by using the heterogeneous products technique we discussed in Chapter 9.

Figure 15.2 Policy-creation transaction schema.

In Figure 15.3 we show a schema to handle the specific attributes that describe automobiles and their coverages. For each line of business (or coverage type), we create custom dimension tables for both the covered item and the coverage. When an access application needs the specific attributes of a single coverage type, it uses the appropriate custom dimension tables.

Notice in this transactional schema that we don't need a custom fact table. We only introduce custom dimension tables to handle the special automobile attributes. No new keys need to be generated; logically, all we are doing is extending existing dimension rows.

Alternative (or Complementary) Policy Accumulating Snapshot

Finally, before we leave policy transactions, we want to mention briefly the use of an accumulating snapshot to capture the cumulative effect of the transactions. In this case the grain of the fact table likely would be one row for each coverage/covered item on a policy. We can envision including the following policy-centric dates in the fact table: quoted, rated, underwritten, effective, renewed, and expiration. Many of the other dimensions we discussed also would be applicable to this schema, with the exception of the transaction type dimension. The accumulating snapshot likely would have an expanded fact set. As we discussed in Chapter 5, an accumulating snapshot is effective for collecting information about the key milestones of the policy transaction process. It represents the cumulative lifespan of a policy, covered items, and coverages; however, it does not capture information about each and every transaction that occurred. Unusual transactional events or unexpected outliers from the standard process could be masked with an accumulating perspective. On the other hand, this type of snapshot, sourced from the transactions, provides a clear picture of the durations or lag times between key process events.

Automobile Coverage Dimension	Policy Transaction Fact	Automobile Covered Item Dimension
Coverage Key (PK) Coverage Description Line of Business Description Automobile Deductible Windshield Coverage Included Rental Car Coverage Included	Policy Transaction Date Key (FK) Policy Effective Date Key (FK) Policyholder Key (FK) Employee Key (FK) Coverage Key (FK) Covered Item Key (FK) Policy Transaction Type Key (FK) Policy Transaction Audit Key (FK) Policy Number (DD) Policy Transaction Amount	Covered Item Key (PK) Covered Item Description Vehicle Manufacturer Vehicle Make Vehicle Year Vehicle Classification Engine Size Number of Passenger Capacity Driver's Airbag Indicator

Figure 15.3 Policy transaction schema with custom automobile dimension tables.

Policy Periodic Snapshot

The policy transaction schema is very useful for answering a wide range of questions. However, the blizzard of transactions makes it difficult to quickly determine the status or financial value of a policy at a given point in time. Even if all the necessary detail lies in the transaction data, a snapshot perspective would require rolling the transactions forward from the beginning of history. Not only is this nearly impractical on a single policy, but it is ridiculous to think about generating summary top-line views of key performance metrics in this way.

The answer to this dilemma is to create a second fact table that operates as a companion to the policy transaction table. In this case the business process is the monthly policy premium snapshot. The granularity of the fact table is one row per coverage and covered item on a policy each month.

Conformed Dimensions

Of course, when we approach this second business process within our insurance company, we strive to reuse as many dimensions as makes sense at the periodic snapshot granularity. Hopefully, you have become a conformed dimension enthusiast by now. As we indicated in Chapter 3, conformed dimensions used in separate fact tables either must be identical or must represent a subset of the most granular version of the dimension.

The policyholder, covered item, and coverage dimensions would be identical. We replace the daily date dimension with a conformed month dimension table. We don't need to track all the employees that were somehow involved in policy transactions on a monthly basis, although it may be useful to retain the involved agent, especially since field operations are so focused on ongoing revenue performance analysis. The transaction type dimension would not be used because it does not apply at the periodic snapshot granularity. Instead, we introduce a status dimension so that users can discern quickly the current state of a coverage or policy, such as new policies or cancellations this month and over time.

Conformed Facts

While we're on the topic of conformity, we also need to use conformed facts. If the same facts appear in multiple fact tables, such as some facts that are common to this snapshot fact table as well as the consolidated fact table we'll discuss later in this chapter, then they must have consistent definitions and labels. If the facts are not identical, then they need to be given different names.

Pay-in-Advance Metrics

Business management wants to know how much premium revenue was written (or sold) each month, as well as how much revenue was earned. In this case we can't derive revenue metrics merely by summarizing the detailed policy transactions. While a policyholder may contract and pay for specific coverages on specific covered items for a period of time, the revenue is not earned until the service is provided. In the case of the insurance company, the revenue from a policy is earned month by month as long as the customer doesn't cancel the policy. A correct calculation of a metric such as earned premium would mean fully replicating all the business rules of the operational revenue-recognition system within the data warehouse access application. Typically, the rules for converting a transaction amount into its monthly revenue impact are very complex, especially with coverage upgrades and downgrades. Fortunately, these metrics can be sourced from a separate operational revenue-recognition system.

As we see in the periodic snapshot in Figure 15.4, we include two premium revenue metrics in the fact table to handle the different definitions of written versus earned revenue. Simplistically, if an annual policy for a given coverage and covered item was written on January 1 for a cost of $600, then the written premium for January would be $600, whereas the earned premium is $50 ($600 divided by 12 months). In February, the written premium is zero, whereas the earned premium is still $50. If the policy is canceled on March 31, the earned premium for March is $50, whereas the written premium is a negative $450. Obviously, at this point the earned-revenue stream comes to a crashing halt.

Pay-in-advance business scenarios typically require the combination of a transaction-grained fact table and a monthly snapshot-grained fact table in order to answer questions of transaction frequency and timing, as well as questions of earned income in a given month. We can almost never add enough facts to a snapshot schema to do away with the need for a transaction schema, or vice versa.

Figure 15.4 Periodic policy snapshot schema.

Heterogeneous Products Again

We are again confronted with the need to look at snapshot data by more specific line-of-business attributes. In this case we also need to grapple with snapshot facts that vary by line of business. Because the custom facts for each line are incompatible with each other, for any given snapshot row, most of the fact table would be filled with nulls. In this scenario, the answer is to separate the monthly snapshot fact table physically by line of business. We end up with the single core monthly snapshot schema and a series of custom monthly snapshots, one for each line of business or coverage type. Each of the custom snapshot fact tables is a copy of a segment of the core fact table for just those coverage keys and covered item keys belonging to a particular line of business. We include the core facts as a convenience so that analyses within a coverage type can use both the core and custom facts without having to access two large fact tables. Alternatively, we could handle the extended fact set by adding a special join key to each fact table row, as described in Chapter 9.

Multivalued Dimensions Again

Automobile insurance provides us with another opportunity to discuss multivalued dimensions. Often multiple insured drivers are associated with a policyholder. We can construct a bridge table, as illustrated in Figure 15.5, to capture the relationship between the insured drivers and the policyholder. In this case the insurance company can calculate the weighting factor more realistically based on each driver's share of the total premium cost. We also can assign begin and end dates to the bridge table rows to capture relationship changes over time, as required.

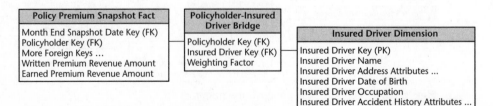

Figure 15.5 Handling multiple drivers associated with a policy.

More Insurance Case Study Background

Unfortunately, the insurance business has a downside. We learn from the interviewees that there's more to life than collecting premium payments. The costs in this industry predominantly result from claims or losses. After a policy with its associated coverages and covered items is in effect, then a claim can be made against a specific coverage and covered item. A claimant, who may be the policyholder or perhaps a new party not previously known to the insurance company, makes the claim. The claimant provides a description of the loss in the claim. The nature of the claim obviously depends on the coverage and covered item.

When the insurance company opens a new claim, a reserve is usually established at this time. The reserve is a preliminary estimate of the insurance company's eventual liability for the claim. As further information becomes known, this reserve can be adjusted.

Before the insurance company pays any claim, there is usually an investigative phase where the insurance company sends out an adjuster to examine the covered item and interview the claimant, policyholder, or other individuals involved. The investigative phase produces a stream of transactions. In complex claims, various outside experts may be required to pass judgment on the claim or the extent of the damage.

In most cases, after the investigative phase, the insurance company issues a number of payments. Many of these payments go to third parties such as doctors, lawyers, or automotive body shop operators. Some payments may go directly to the claimant. A large insurance company may have more than 1,000 individuals who are authorized to issue payments against open claims. For this reason, it is important to clearly identify the employee responsible for every payment made against an open claim.

The insurance company may take possession of the covered item after replacing it for the policyholder or claimant. In many such cases there is a salvage value to the item, which is realized eventually by the insurance company. Salvage payments received are a credit against the claim accounting.

Eventually, the payments are completed, and the claim is closed. If nothing unusual happens, this is the end of the transaction stream generated by the claim. However, in complex cases, further claims are made at later times or claimant lawsuits may force a claim to be reopened. In this case the reserve usually is reset as well. An important measure for an insurance company is how often and under what circumstances claims are reopened and reserves are reset.

Toward the tail end of processing a complex claim, the insurance company may believe that further money will flow back to the insurance company when pending lawsuits or counterclaims are resolved eventually. The insurance company may choose to sell the rights to all such further recoveries to specialists who are prepared to wait out the resolution of the lawsuits or counterclaims. Although such sales take place at a discount, they allow the insurance company to get cash immediately and close its books on the claim. This option is known as *subrogation* and generates its own special transaction.

In addition to analyzing the detailed transactions, the insurance company also wants to understand what happens during the life of a claim. For example, the time lag between the claim open date and the first payment date is an important measure of claims processing efficiency.

Updated Insurance Bus Matrix

With a better understanding of the claims side of the house, we'll revisit the draft matrix from Figure 15.1. Based on the new requirements we've uncovered, we add another row to the matrix to accommodate claims transactions, as shown in Figure 15.6. Many of the dimensions identified earlier in the project will be reused; we added new columns to the matrix for the claim, claimant, and third party.

Project teams sometimes struggle with the level of detail captured in a bus matrix. In the planning phase of an architected data warehouse project, it makes sense to stick with rather high-level business processes (or sources). Multiple fact tables may result from each of these business process rows. As we delve into the implementation phase, we sometimes take a subset of the matrix to a lower level of detail by reflecting all the fact tables resulting from the process as separate matrix rows. At this point the matrix can be enhanced in several ways. We can add columns to reflect the granularity and metrics associated with each fact table. Likewise, we can indicate the use of more summarized conformed dimensions, especially when documenting an aggregated schema. We've illustrated this lower implementation bus matrix in Figure 15.7.

	Date	Policyholder	Coverage	Covered Item	Employee	Policy	Claim	Claimant	3rd Party
Policy Transactions	X	X	X	X	X	X			
Policy Premium Snapshot	X	X	X	X	X	X			
Claims Transactions	X	X	X	X	X	X	X	X	X

Figure 15.6 Updated insurance bus matrix.

Business Process	Fact Table	Granularity	Facts	Date	Policyholder	Coverage	Covered Item	Employee	Policy	Claim	Claimant	3rd Party
Policy Transactions	Corporate Policy Transactions	1 row for every policy transaction	Policy Transaction Amount	X (Trxn Eff)	X	X	X	X	X			
	Auto Policy Transactions	1 row per auto policy transaction	Policy Transaction Amount	X (Trxn Eff)	X	X (Auto)	X (Auto)	X	X			
	Home Policy Transactions	1 row per home policy transaction	Policy Transaction Amount	X (Trxn Eff)	X	X (Home)	X (Home)	X	X			
Policy Premium Snapshot	Corporate Policy Premiums	1 row for every policy, covered item, and coverage each month	Written Premium Revenue Amount, Earned Premium Revenue Amount	X	X	X	X	X (Agent)	X			
	Auto Policy Premiums	1 row per auto policy, auto covered item, and auto coverage each month	Written Premium Revenue Amount, Earned Premium Revenue Amount	X	X	X (Auto)	X (Auto)	X (Agent)	X			
	Home Policy Premiums	1 row per home policy, home covered item, and home coverage each month	Written Premium Revenue Amount, Earned Premium Revenue Amount	X	X	X (Home)	X (Home)	X (Agent)	X			
Claims Transactions	Claim Transactions	1 row for every claim transaction	Claim Transaction Amount	X (Trxn Eff)	X	X	X	X	X	X	X	X
	Claim Accumulating Snapshot	1 row per covered item and coverage on a claim	Original Reserve Amount, Assessed Damage Amount, Reserve Adjustment Amount, Current Reserve Amount, Open Reserve Amount, Claim Amount Paid, Payments Received, Salvage Received, Number of Transactions	X	X	X	X (Agent)	X	X	X	X	
	Accident Event	1 row per loss party and affiliation in an auto claim	Implied Accident Count	X	X	X (Auto)	X (Auto)	X	X (Auto)	X (Auto)	X	X

Figure 15.7 Implementation bus matrix detailing fact tables for each business process.

Claims Transactions

As we learned earlier, the operational claims processing system generates a slew of transactions, including the following transaction types:

- Open claim, reopen claim, close claim
- Set reserve, reset reserve, close reserve
- Set salvage estimate, receive salvage payment
- Adjuster inspection, adjuster interview
- Open lawsuit, close lawsuit
- Make payment, receive payment
- Subrogate claim

We discovered when updating the Figure 15.6 bus matrix that this schema uses a number of dimensions developed for the policy world. We again have two role-playing dates associated with the claims transactions. Unique column labels should distinguish the claims transaction and effective dates from those associated with policy transactions. The employee is the employee involved in the transactional event. As mentioned in the business case, this is particularly interesting for payment authorization transactions. The claims transaction type dimension would include the transaction types and groupings just listed.

As shown in Figure 15.8, there are several new dimensions in the claims transaction fact table. The claim dimension contains a codified description of the claim. Generally, it must map to the coverage and covered item in order to be valid and make sense. The claimant is the party making the claim, typically an individual. The third party is a witness, expert, or payee. The claimant and third-party dimensions usually are dirty dimensions because of the difficulty of reliably identifying and tracking them across different claims, although there certainly would be value in doing so. Unscrupulous potential payees may go out of their way not to identify themselves in a way that would make it easy to tie them to other claims in the insurance company's system.

The heterogeneous product techniques discussed earlier in this chapter are also applicable to claims data. The only difference is that we probably want to extend the claim dimension table, in addition to the covered item and coverage dimension tables, because it seems plausible that there could be special claims attributes that depend on the coverage type.

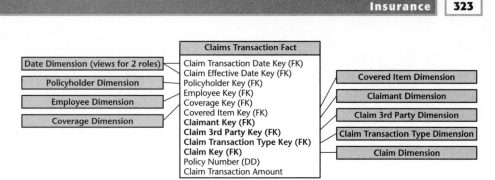

Figure 15.8 Claims transaction schema.

Claims Accumulating Snapshot

As we've seen in the past, even with a robust transaction-level schema, there is a whole class of urgent business questions that can't be answered using only transaction detail. It is difficult to derive claim-to-date performance measures by traversing through every detailed transaction from the beginning of the claim's history and applying the transactions appropriately.

On a periodic basis, perhaps at the close of each day, we can roll forward all the transactions to update an accumulating claims snapshot incrementally. The granularity is one row for each unique combination of policy, coverage, covered item, and claim. The row is created once when the claim is opened and then is updated throughout the life of a claim until it is finally closed.

Many of the dimensions are reusable, conformed dimensions, as illustrated in Figure 15.9. We include more dates in this fact table to track the key milestones in the life of a claim. The dates allow us to observe time lags easily. We've also added a status dimension to quickly identify all open, closed, or reopened claims, for example. Transaction-specific dimensions such as employee, claimant, third party, and claim transaction type are suppressed, whereas the list of additive, numeric measures has been expanded.

In cases where a claim is not so short-lived, such as with long-term disability or care claims that have a multiyear life span, we may represent the snapshot as a periodic monthly snapshot rather than an accumulating variety. The grain of the periodic snapshot would be one row for every working claim each month. The facts would represent numeric, additive facts that occurred during the month, such as amount claimed, amount paid, and change in reserve. In some situations we find ourselves building all three types of fact tables for the same business process.

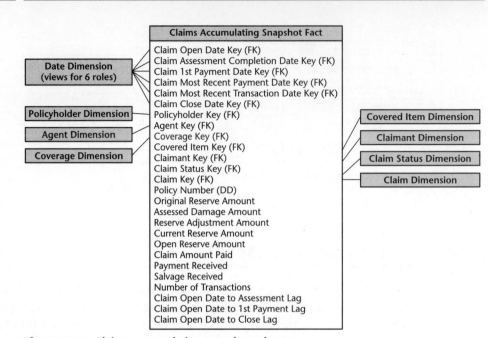

Figure 15.9 Claims accumulating snapshot schema.

Policy/Claims Consolidated Snapshot

With the four fact tables designed thus far (in addition to the heterogeneous extensions), we deliver a robust perspective of the policy and claims transactions, in addition to snapshots from both processes. However, recall that the users expressed a strong interest in profit metrics. While premium and claim financial metrics could be derived by separately querying two fact tables and then combining the result set, we opt to go the next step in the spirit of ease of use and performance. We can construct another fact table to bring the premium revenue and claim loss metrics together, as shown in Figure 15.10. This table has a reduced set of dimensions corresponding to its slightly summarized monthly granularity. As you recall from Chapter 7, we refer to this as a consolidated fact table because it combines data from multiple business processes. It is best to develop consolidated fact tables after the base metrics have been delivered in separate dimensional models.

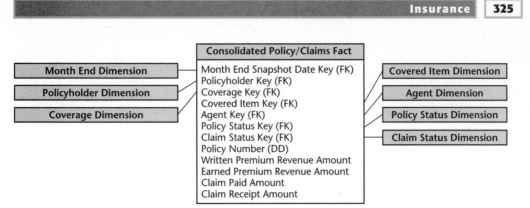

Figure 15.10 Policy/claims consolidated schema.

Factless Accident Events

When we discussed factless fact tables in Chapter 12, we referred to them as the collision of keys at a point in space and time. In the case of an automobile insurer, we can record literal collisions using a factless fact table. In this situation the fact table registers the many-to-many correlations between the loss parties and loss items or, to put it less euphemistically, all the correlations between the people and vehicles involved in an accident.

Several new dimensions appear in the factless fact table shown in Figure 15.11. The loss party describes other individuals who were involved in the accident, possibly as passengers, witnesses, or in another capacity. If the loss party was not associated with a vehicle in the accident, then the loss vehicle key would join to a "No Vehicle" entry in that dimension. The loss affiliation explains the role of the loss party (and loss vehicle, if applicable) to the claim. Again, as we did in Chapter 12, we include a fact that is always valued at 1 to facilitate counting and aggregation. This factless fact table can represent complex accidents involving many individuals and vehicles because the number of involved parties with various roles is open-ended. When there is more than one claimant or loss party associated with an accident, we can optionally treat these dimensions as multivalued dimensions using claimant group and loss party group bridge tables. This has the advantage that the grain of the fact table is preserved as one record per accident claim. Either schema variation could answer questions such as "How many bodily injury claims did we handle where ABC Legal Partners represented the claimant and EZ-Dent-B-Gone body shop performed the repair?"

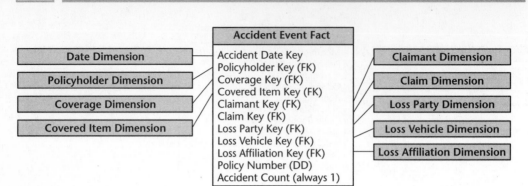

Figure 15.11 Factless fact table for accident events.

Common Dimensional Modeling Mistakes to Avoid

As we close this final chapter on dimensional modeling techniques, we thought it would be helpful to establish boundaries beyond which designers should *not* go. Thus far in this book we've presented concepts by positively stating that you should use technique A in situation X. Now, rather than focusing on to-dos, we turn our attention to not-to-dos by elaborating on dimensional modeling techniques that should be avoided. As we did with Chapter 1's list of pitfalls, we've listed the not-to-dos in reverse order of importance. Be aware, however, that even the less important mistakes can seriously compromise your data warehouse.

Mistake 10: Place text attributes used for constraining and grouping in a fact table. The process of creating a dimensional model is always a kind of triage. The numeric measurements delivered from an operational business process source belong in the fact table. The descriptive textual attributes from the context of the measurements go in dimension tables. Finally, we make a field-by-field decision about the leftover codes and pseudonumeric items, placing them in the fact table if they are more like measurements and in the dimension table if they are more like physical descriptions of something. You shouldn't lose your nerve and leave true text, expecially comment fields, in the fact table. We need to get these text attributes off the main runway of your data warehouse and into dimension tables.

Mistake 9: Limit verbose descriptive attributes in dimensions to save space. You might think that you are being a good, conservative designer by keeping the size of your dimensions under control. However, in virtually every data warehouse, the dimension tables are geometrically smaller than the fact tables. Having a 100-MB product dimension table is insignificant if the fact table is 100 times as large! Your job as designer of an easy-to-use data warehouse is to supply as much verbose descriptive context in each dimension as you can. Make sure every code is augmented with readable descriptive text. Better yet, you probably can remove the codes entirely. Remember that the textual attributes in the dimension tables provide the user interface to data browsing, constraining, or filtering, as well as the content for the row and column headers in your final reports.

Mistake 8: Split hierarchies and hierarchy levels into multiple dimensions. A hierarchy is a cascaded series of many-to-one relationships. For example, many products may roll up to a single brand; and many brands may roll up to a single category. If your dimension is expressed at the lowest level of granularity (for example, product), then all the higher levels of the hierarchy can be expressed as unique values in the product row. Users understand hierarchies. Your job is to present the hierarchies in the most natural and efficient manner. A hierarchy belongs together in a single physical flat dimension table. Resist the urge to snowflake a hierarchy by generating a set of progressively smaller subdimension tables. In this case you would be confusing backroom data staging with front room data presentation! Finally, if more than one roll-up exists simultaneously for a dimension, in most cases it's perfectly reasonable to include multiple hierarchies in the same dimension, as long as the dimension has been defined at the lowest possible grain (and the hierarchies are uniquely labeled).

Mistake 7: Ignore the need to track dimension attribute changes. Contrary to popular belief, business users often want to understand the impact of changes to a subset of the dimension tables' attributes. It is unlikely that your users will settle for dimension tables with attributes that always reflect the current state of the world. We have three techniques for tracking slowly moving attribute changes; don't rely on type 1 exclusively. Likewise, if a group of attributes changes rapidly, don't delay splitting a dimension to allow for a more volatile minidimension. You can't always understand the volatility of your data when you first design the dimensions. Suppose that your product dimension contains a set of attributes called *standard parameters*. At the beginning of the design process you are assured that these standard parameters are fixed for the life of the product. However, after rolling out your data warehouse, you discover that these attributes change several times per year for each product. Sooner, rather than later, you probably should separate your product dimension into two dimensions. The new product standard parameter dimension will keep your original product dimension from burgeoning disastrously if you tried to model it as slowly changing.

Mistake 6: Solve all query performance problems by adding more hardware. Aggregates, or derived summary tables, are the most cost-effective way to improve query performance. Most query tool vendors have explicit support for the use of aggregates, which depend on explicit dimensional modeling constructs. Adding expensive hardware should be done as part of a balanced program that includes building aggregates, creating indices, choosing query-efficient DBMS software, increasing real memory size, increasing CPU speed, and finally, adding parallelism at the hardware level.

Mistake 5: Use operational or smart keys to join dimension tables to a fact table. Novice data warehouse designers are sometimes too literal minded when designing the dimension tables' primary keys that connect to the foreign keys of the fact table. It is counterproductive to declare a whole suite of dimension attributes as the dimension table key and then use them all as the basis of the physical join to the fact table. This includes the unfortunate practice of declaring the dimension key to be the operational key, along with an effective date. All types of ugly problems will arise eventually. You should replace the smart physical key with a simple integer surrogate key that is numbered sequentially from 1 to N, where N is the total number of rows in the dimension table.

Mistake 4: Neglect to declare and then comply with the fact table's grain. All dimensional designs should begin with the business process that generates the numeric performance measurements. Second, specify the exact granularity of that data. Building fact tables at the most atomic, granular level will gracefully resist the ad hoc attack. Third, surround these measurements with dimensions that are true to that grain. Staying true to the grain is a crucial step in the design of a dimensional data model. A subtle but serious error in a dimensional design is to add helpful facts to a fact table, such as rows that describe totals for an extended time span or a large geographic area. Although these extra facts are well known at the time of the individual measurement and would seem to make some applications simpler, they cause havoc because all the automatic summations across dimensions overcount these higher-level facts, producing incorrect results. Each different measurement grain demands its own fact table.

Mistake 3: Design the dimensional model *based on a specific report*. A dimensional model has nothing to do with an intended report! Rather, it is a model of a measurement process. Numeric measurements form the basis of fact tables. The dimensions that are appropriate for a given fact table are the physical context that describes the circumstances of the measurements. We see that a dimensional model is based solidly on the physics of a measurement process and is quite independent of how a user chooses to define a report. A project team once confessed to us that they had built several hundred fact tables to deliver order management data to their users. It turned out that each fact table had been constructed to address a specific report request. The same data was being extracted many, many times to populate all these fact tables. Not surprisingly, the team was struggling to update the databases within the nightly batch window. Rather than designing a quagmire of report-centric schemas, they should have focused on the measurement process(es). The users' requirements could have been handled with a well-designed schema for the atomic data along with a handful (not hundreds) of performance-enhancing aggregations.

Mistake 2: Expect users to query the lowest-level atomic data in a normalized format. The lowest-level data is always the most dimensional and should be the foundation of your dimensional design. Data that has been aggregated in any way has been deprived of some of its dimensions. You can't build a data mart with aggregated data and expect your users and their tools to seamlessly drill down to third normal form data for the atomic details. Normalized models may be helpful for staging the data, but they should never be used for presenting the data to business users.

Mistake 1: Fail to conform facts and dimensions across separate fact tables. This final not-to-do should be presented as two separate mistakes because they are both so dangerous to a successful data warehouse environment, but we've run out of mistake numbers to assign, so we've lumped them into one.

It would be a shame to get this far and then build isolated data stovepipes. We refer to this as snatching defeat from the jaws of victory. If you have a numeric measured fact, such as revenue, in two or more data marts sourced from different underlying systems, then you need to take special care to ensure that the technical definitions of these facts match exactly. If the definitions do not match exactly, then they shouldn't both be referred to as revenue. This is called *conforming the facts*.

Finally, the single most important design technique in the dimensional modeling arsenal is conforming your dimensions. If two or more fact tables have the same dimension, then you must be fanatical about making these dimensions identical or carefully chosen subsets of each other. When you conform your dimensions across fact tables, you will be able to drill across separate data sources because the constraints and row headers mean the same thing and match at the data level. Conformed dimensions are the secret sauce needed for building distributed data warehouses, adding unexpected new data sources to an existing warehouse, and making multiple incompatible technologies function together harmoniously.

Summary

In this final case study we designed a series of insurance dimensional models representing the culmination of many important concepts developed throughout this book. Hopefully, now you feel comfortable and confident using the vocabulary and tools of a dimensional modeler. With dimensional modeling mastered, we turn our attention to all the other activities that occur during the lifecycle of a successful data warehouse project in the next chapter. Before you go forth and be dimensional, it's useful to have this holistic perspective and understanding, even if your job focus is limited to modeling.

Building the Data Warehouse

The gears shift rather dramatically in this chapter. Rather than focusing on dimensional modeling techniques, we turn our attention to everything else that occurs during the course of a data warehouse design and implementation project. We'll walk through the life of a data warehouse project from inception through ongoing maintenance, identifying best practices at each step, as well as potential vulnerabilities. More comprehensive coverage of the data warehouse lifecycle is available in *The Data Warehouse Lifecycle Toolkit*, by Ralph Kimball, Laura Reeves, Margy Ross, and Warren Thornthwaite (Wiley, 1998). This chapter is a crash course drawn from the complete text, which weighs in at a hefty 750+ pages.

Some may perceive that this chapter's content is applicable only to data warehouse project managers. We certainly don't feel that this is the case. Implementing a data warehouse requires tightly integrated activities. We believe that everyone on the project team, including the business analyst, architect, database designer, data stager, and analytic application developer, needs a high-level understanding of the complete lifecycle of a data warehouse. Like the rest of the book, we've written this chapter so that it's accessible to a broad audience.

Chapter 16 covers the following concepts:

- **Business dimensional lifecycle overview**
- **Data warehouse project planning and ongoing communication and management**
- **Tactics for collecting business requirements, including prioritization**

- **Process for developing the technical architecture and then selecting products**
- **Dimensional design workshops**
- **Physical design considerations, including aggregation and indexing**
- **Data staging recommendations**
- **Analytic application design and development**
- **Recommendations for deployment, ongoing maintenance, and future growth**
- **Common mistakes to avoid when building and managing a data warehouse**

Business Dimensional Lifecycle Road Map

When driving to a place we've never been to before, most of us rely on a road map. Similarly, a road map is extremely useful if we're about to embark on the unfamiliar journey of data warehousing. The authors of *The Data Warehouse Lifecycle Toolkit* drew on decades of experience to develop the business dimensional lifecycle approach. We chose the name because it reinforced several of our key tenets for successful data warehousing. First and foremost, data warehouse projects must focus on the needs of the business. Second, the data presented to the business users must be dimensional. Hopefully, this comes as no surprise to any readers at this point! Finally, while data warehousing is an ongoing process, each implementation project should have a finite cycle with a specific beginning and end.

We use the diagram in Figure 16.1 to encapsulate the major activities of the business dimensional lifecycle. The diagram illustrates task sequence, dependency, and concurrency. It serves as a road map to help teams do the right thing at the right time. The diagram does not reflect an absolute timeline. While the boxes are equally wide, there's a vast difference in the time and effort required for each major activity.

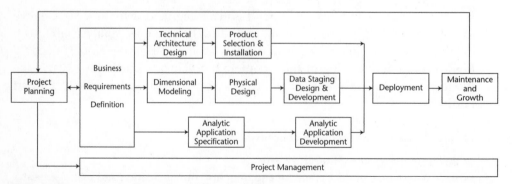

Figure 16.1 Business dimensional lifecycle diagram.

Road Map Major Points of Interest

Before we dive into specifics, let's take a moment to orient ourselves to the road map. The data warehouse lifecycle begins with project planning, as one would expect. During this module we assess the organization's readiness for a data warehouse initiative, establish the preliminary scope and justification, obtain resources, and launch the project. Ongoing project management serves as a foundation to keep the remainder of the lifecycle on track.

The second major task in Figure 16.1 focuses on business requirements definition. Notice the two-way arrow between project planning and business requirements definition because there's much interplay between these two activities. Aligning the data warehouse with business requirements is absolutely crucial. Best-of-breed technologies won't salvage a data warehouse that fails to focus on the business. Data warehouse designers must understand the needs of the business and translate them into design considerations. Business users and their requirements have an impact on almost every design and implementation decision made during the course of a warehouse project. In Figure's 16.1 road map, this is reflected by the three parallel tracks that follow.

The top track of Figure 16.1 deals with technology. Technical architecture design establishes the overall framework to support the integration of multiple technologies. Using the capabilities identified in the architecture design as a shopping list, we then evaluate and select specific products. Notice that product selection is not the first box on the road map. One of the most frequent mistakes made by novice teams is to select products without a clear understanding of what they're trying to accomplish. This is akin to grabbing a hammer whether you need to pound a nail or tighten a screw.

The middle track emanating from business requirements definition focuses on data. We begin by translating the requirements into a dimensional model, as we've been practicing. The dimensional model is then transformed into a physical structure. We focus on performance tuning strategies, such as aggregation, indexing, and partitioning, during the physical design activities. Last but not least, data staging extract-transformation-load (ETL) processes are designed and developed. As we mentioned earlier, the equally sized boxes don't represent equally sized efforts; this is obvious when we think about the workload differential between physical design and data staging activities.

The final set of tasks spawned by the business requirements definition is the design and development of analytic applications. The data warehouse project isn't done when we deliver data. Analytic applications, in the form of parameter-driven templates and analyses, will satisfy a large percentage of the analytic needs of business users.

We bring together the technology, data, and analytic application tracks, along with a good dose of education and support, for a well-orchestrated deployment. From there, ongoing maintenance is needed to ensure that the data warehouse and its user community remain healthy and poised to leverage the investment. Finally, we handle future data warehouse growth by initiating subsequent projects, each returning to the beginning of the lifecycle all over again.

Now that we have a high-level understanding of the road map's overall structure, we'll delve into each of the boxes of Figure 16.1 for more details.

Project Planning and Management

Not surprisingly, we launch the data warehouse with a series of project planning activities. We sometimes refer to these as *marshmallow* tasks because they're soft, sticky, and can gum up the works of a data warehouse project seriously.

Assessing Readiness

Before moving full-steam ahead with significant data warehouse expenditures, it is prudent to take a moment to assess the organization's readiness to proceed. Based on our cumulative experience from hundreds of data warehouses, we've identified five factors that differentiate projects that were predominantly smooth sailing versus those which entailed a constant struggle. These factors are leading indicators of data warehouse success. You don't need high marks on every factor to move forward, but any shortfalls represent risks or vulnerabilities. We'll describe the characteristics in rank order of importance.

The most critical factor for successful data warehousing is to have a strong business sponsor. Business sponsors should have a vision for the potential impact of a data warehouse on the organization. They should be passionate and personally convinced of the project's value while realistic at the same time. Optimally, the business sponsor has a track record of success with other internal initiatives. He or she should be a politically astute leader who can convince his or her peers to support the warehouse.

Sometimes there's strong demand for a data warehouse coming from a single sponsor. Even if this person and his or her opportunity encompass the warehouse characteristics we're looking for, we can still encounter trouble in this scenario because lone sponsors tend to move on, either internally or externally. This is the most common cause for data warehouse stagnation. Some teams are confronted with too much demand coming from all corners of the organization. Assuming that you (or your management) do not attempt to tackle all the demand in one fell swoop, this is a great way to start. Finally, the business sponsor may be missing in action, but this doesn't stop the IT organization from moving forward, nearly guaranteeing a data warehouse false start. This is the riskiest scenario; the project should slow down until the right business sponsor has been identified (or perhaps recruited) and has voiced a commitment to the project.

The second readiness factor is having a strong, compelling business motivation for building a data warehouse. This factor often goes hand in hand with sponsorship. A data warehouse project can't merely deliver a nice-to-have capability; it needs to solve critical business problems in order to garner the resources required for a successful launch and healthy lifespan. Compelling motivation typically creates a sense of urgency, whether the motivation is from external (for example, competitive factors) or internal (for example, inability to analyze cross-organization performance following acquisitions) sources.

The third factor when assessing readiness is feasibility. There are several aspects of feasibility, such as technical or resource feasibility, but data feasibility is the most crucial. Are we collecting real data in real operational source systems to support the business requirements? Data feasibility is a major concern because there is no short-term fix if we're not already collecting reasonably clean source data at the right granularity.

The next factors are not project showstoppers but still influence your probability for success. The fourth factor focuses on the relationship between the business and IT organizations. In your company, does the IT organization understand and respect the business? Conversely, does the business understand and respect the IT organization? The inability to honestly answer yes to these questions doesn't mean that you can't proceed. Rather, it implies that you need to vigilantly keep the business and IT representatives marching to the same drum. In many ways the data warehouse initiative can be an opportunity to mend the fence between these organizations, assuming that you both deliver.

The final aspect of readiness is the current analytic culture within your company. Do business analysts make decisions based on facts and figures, or are their decisions based on intuition, anecdotal evidence, and gut reactions? The businesspeople already immersed in numbers likely will be more receptive to a data warehouse. However, you can be successful with either scenario as long as you prepare for the increased burden of shifting the cultural mindset (with the help of the business sponsor), as well as the need for additional analytic application development, education, and support resources.

If your project is not ready to proceed, typically due to a business sponsor shortfall, we suggest two approaches for shoring up your readiness. The first is to conduct a high-level business requirements analysis and prioritization. We'll talk more about this process in the next major section, so stay tuned. The other alternative is to create a proof of concept. Proofs of concept are quick and dirty demonstrations of the potential capabilities of a data warehouse. They are a sales tool rather than a technical proof of design. Teams use this technique because business users supposedly can't describe what they want without seeing something to react to. While the proof of concept can establish a common understanding, we don't suggest that it be the first tool pulled from your toolbox. Proofs of concept often require more effort than quick and dirty implies. Typically, they're held together with duct tape yet have a tendency to morph into a production system without the requisite rework. It is challenging to manage user expectations appropriately. Those who like to play with tools gravitate to this technique, but you should be aware that there might be more effective and efficient methods to reach the same objective.

Scoping

Once you're comfortable with the organization's readiness, it's time to put boundaries around an initial project. Scoping requires the joint input of both the IT organization and business management. The scope of your data warehouse project should be both meaningful in terms of its value to the organization and manageable. When you are first getting started, you should focus on data from a single business process. Save the more challenging, cross-process projects for a later phase. Sometimes scopes are driven by a target completion date, such as the end of the fiscal year. You can manage the scope to a due date effectively, but doing so may present additional risks. Even with a set time frame, you need to maintain your focus on scoping a project that is both compelling and doable. Sometimes project teams feel that the delivery schedule is cast in concrete before project planning is even initiated. The prioritization process, which we'll describe during business requirements definition, can be used to convince IT and business management that adjustments are required. Finally, remember to avoid the *law of too* when scoping—too firm of a commitment to too brief of a timeline involving too many source systems and too many users in too many locations with too diverse analytic requirements.

Justification

A slew of acronyms surrounds the justification process, but don't let them intimidate you. Justification requires an estimation of the benefits and costs associated with a data warehouse; hopefully, the anticipated benefits grossly outweigh the costs. IT usually is responsible for deriving the expenses. You need to determine approximate costs for the requisite hardware and software. Data warehouses tend to expand rapidly, so be sure the estimates allow some room for short-term growth. Unlike operational system development, where resource requirements tail off after production, ongoing warehouse support needs will not decline appreciably over time.

We rely on the business to determine the financial benefits of a data warehouse. Warehouses typically are justified based on increased revenue or profit opportunities rather than merely focusing on expense reduction. Delivering *a single version of the truth* or *flexible access to information* isn't sufficient financial justification. You need to peel back the layers to determine the quantifiable impact of improved decision making made possible by these sound bites. If you are struggling with warehouse justification, this is likely a symptom that you are focused on the wrong business sponsor or problem.

Staffing

Data warehouse projects require the integration of a cross-functional team with resources from both the business and IT communities. It is common for the same person to fill more than one role, especially as the cost of entry for data warehousing has fallen. The assignment of named resources to roles depends on the project's magnitude and scope, as well as the individual's availability, capacity, and experience.

From the business side of the house, you'll need representatives to fill the following roles:

Business sponsor. The business sponsor is the warehouse's ultimate client, as well as its strongest advocate. Sponsorship sometimes takes the form of an executive steering committee, especially for cross-enterprise initiatives.

Business driver. If you work in a large organization, the sponsor may be too far removed or inaccessible to the project team. In this case the sponsor sometimes delegates his or her less strategic warehouse responsibilities to a middle manager in the organization. This driver should possess the same characteristics as the sponsor.

Business lead. The business project lead is a well-respected person who is highly involved in the project, likely communicating with the project manager on a daily basis. The same person serving as the business driver or subject matter expert sometimes fills this role.

Business users. Optimally, the business users are the enthusiastic fans of the data warehouse. You need to involve them early and often, beginning with the project scope and business requirements. From there, you must find creative ways to maintain their interest and involvement throughout the lifecycle. Remember, user involvement is critical to data warehouse acceptance. Without business users, the data warehouse is a technical exercise in futility.

Several other positions are staffed from either the business or IT organizations. These straddlers can be technical resources that understand the business or business resources that understand technology. Straddler roles include the following:

Business system analyst. This person is responsible for determining the business needs and translating them into architectural, data, and analytic application requirements.

Business subject matter expert. This person is often the current go-to resource for ad hoc analysis. He or she understands what the data means, how it is used, and where data inconsistencies are lurking. Their analytic and data insights are extremely useful, especially during the modeling and analytic application processes.

Analytic application developer. Analytic application developers are responsible for designing and developing the starter set of analytic templates, as well as providing ongoing application support.

Data warehouse educator. The educator(s) must be confident of their data, applications, and access tool knowledge because the business community does not differentiate between these warehouse deliverables.

The following roles typically are staffed from the IT organization (or an external consulting firm). If you are working with consultants due to resource or expertise constraints, you should retain internal ownership of the project. Insist on coaching and extensive skills/knowledge transfer so that you can function more independently on the next project. Finally, you must clearly understand whether you're buying meaningful experience rather than staff augmentation (perhaps with consultants who merely know how to spell OLAP).

Project manager. The project manager is a critical position. He or she should be comfortable with and respected by business executives, as well as technical analysts. The project manager's communication and project management skills must be stellar.

Technical architect. The architect is responsible for the overall technical and security architecture. He or she develops the plan that ties together the required technical functionality and helps evaluate products on the basis of the overall architecture.

Technical support specialists. Technical specialists tend to be nearly encyclopedic about a relatively narrow spectrum of technology.

Data modeler. The data modeler likely comes from a transactional data modeling background with heavy emphasis on normalization. He or she should embrace dimensional modeling concepts and be empathetic to the requirements of the business rather than focused strictly on saving space or reducing the staging workload.

Database administrator. Like the data modeler, the database administrator must be willing to set aside some traditional database administration truisms, such as having only one index on a relational table.

Metadata coordinator. This person ensures that all the metadata is collected, managed, and disseminated. As a watchdog role, the coordinator is responsible for reminding others of their metadata-centric duties.

Data steward. The data steward is responsible for enterprise agreement on the warehouse's conformed dimensions and facts. Clearly, this is a politically challenging role.

Data staging designer. The staging designer is responsible for designing the data staging ETL processes. He or she typically is involved in the make versus buy decision regarding staging software.

Data staging developer. Based on direction from the staging designer, the staging developer delivers and automates the staging processes using either a staging tool or manually programmed routines.

Data warehouse support. Last, but not least, the data warehouse requires ongoing backroom and front room support resources. Most often this role is assigned to individuals who have been involved in the project in an earlier capacity.

Developing and Maintaining the Project Plan

Developing the data warehouse project plan involves identification of all the tasks necessary to implement the data warehouse. Resources are available in the marketplace to help you compile a project task list. For example, the CD-ROM that comes with *The Data Warehouse Lifecycle Toolkit* includes a nearly 200-item task listing.

Any good project manager knows that key team members, such as the data staging designer, should develop the effort estimates for their tasks. The project manager can't dictate the amount of time allowed and expect conformance. The project plan should identify a user acceptance checkpoint after every major milestone and deliverable to ensure that the project is still on track and that the business is still intimately involved.

The data warehouse project demands broad communication. During the project planning phase, we suggest that the project manager establish a communication matrix, such as Table 16.1 illustrates, to help make certain that the communication strategy is executed.

Table 16.1 Example Data Warehouse Communication Plan

CONSTITUENCY	FREQUENCY	FORUM	KEY MESSAGES
Business sponsors	Bimonthly	Face-to-face briefing	Issue resolution, expectation management, funding
Business community	Monthly	Web site	Requisite involvement, expectation management, critical dates
Project team	Weekly	Status meetings	Progress, issue identification and resolution
IT colleagues	Bimonthly	Existing IT staff meeting	Expectation management, resource needs

Data warehouse projects are vulnerable to scope creep largely due to our strong desire to satisfy users' requirements. We need to be most watchful about the accumulation of minor changes that snowball. While no single request is too arduous, taken in total, they may represent a significant change to the project's scope. We have several options when confronted with changes. First, we can increase the scope by adding time, resources, or money to accommodate the change. Otherwise, the total effort can remain unchanged if the users relinquish something that had been in scope to accommodate the change. Finally, we can just say no without really saying no by handling the change as an enhancement request. The most important thing to remember about scope changes is that they shouldn't be made in an IT vacuum. The right answer depends on the situation. Now is the time to leverage your partnership with the business to arrive at an answer with which everyone can live.

The keys to data warehouse project planning and management include:

1. **Having a solid business sponsor**
2. **Balancing high value and doability to define the scope**
3. **Working with the best team possible to develop a detailed project plan**
4. **Being an excellent project manager by motivating, managing, and communicating up, down, and across the organization**

Business Requirements Definition

Embracing the business users to understand their requirements and garner their buy-in is absolutely essential to successful data warehousing. This section focuses on back-to-basics techniques for accomplishing just that.

Requirements Preplanning

Before sitting down with the business community to gather requirements, we suggest that you set yourself up for a productive session by considering the following:

Choose the Forum

We gather requirements by meeting with business user representatives while interweaving data sessions with source system gurus and subject matter experts. This dual-pronged approach gives us insight into the needs of the business in conjunction with the realities of the data. However, we can't ask business managers about the granularity or dimensionality of their critical data. We need to talk to them about what they do, why they do it, how they make decisions, and how they hope to make decisions in the future. Like organizational therapy, we're trying to detect the issues and opportunities.

There are two primary techniques for gathering requirements—interviews or facilitated sessions. Both have their advantages and disadvantages. Interviews encourage lots of individual participation. They are also easier to schedule. Facilitated sessions may reduce the elapsed time to gather requirements, although they require more time commitment from each participant.

Based on our experience, surveys are not a reasonable tool for gathering requirements because they are flat and two-dimensional. The self-selected respondents only answer the questions we've asked in advance. There's no option to probe more deeply, such as when we're face to face. In addition, don't forget that a secondary outcome of gathering requirements is to create a bond between users and the warehousing initiative. This is just not going to happen with surveys.

We generally use a hybrid approach with interviews to gather the gory details and then facilitation to bring the group to consensus. While we'll describe this hybrid approach in more detail, much of the discussion applies to pure facilitation as well. The forum choice depends on the team's skills, the organization's culture, and what you've already subjected your users to. This is a case in which one size definitely does not fit all.

Identify and Prepare
the Requirements Team

Regardless of the approach, you need to identify and prepare the project team members who are involved. If you're doing interviews, you need to identify a lead interviewer whose primary responsibility is to ask the great open-ended questions. Meanwhile, the interview scribe takes copious notes. While a tape recorder may provide more complete coverage of each interview, we don't use one because it changes the meeting dynamics. Our preference is to have a second person in the room with another brain and sets of eyes and ears rather than relying on a whirling machine. We often invite one or two additional project members (depending on the number of interviewees) as observers so that they can hear the users' input directly.

Before you sit down with users, you need to make sure you're approaching the sessions with the right mindset. You shouldn't presume that you already know it all. If done correctly, you will definitely learn during these requirements interviews. On the other hand, you should do some homework by researching available sources, such as the annual report, Web site, and internal organization chart.

Since the key to getting the right answers is asking the right questions, we recommend that questionnaires be formulated before user meetings. The questionnaire should not be viewed as a script. It is a tool to organize your thoughts and serve as a fallback device in case your mind goes blank during the interview session.

Select, Schedule, and Prepare Business Representatives

If this is your first foray into data warehousing (or your first attempt to rescue data stovepipes), you should talk to businesspeople who represent horizontal breadth across the organization. This coverage is critical to formulating the data warehouse bus matrix blueprint. You need to have an early understanding of the common data and vocabulary across the core business functions to build an extensible environment.

Within the target user community, you should cover the organization vertically. Data warehouse project teams naturally gravitate toward the superpower analysts in the business. While their insight is valuable, you can't ignore senior executives and middle management. Otherwise, you are vulnerable to being overly focused on the tactical here-and-now but lose sight of the organization's future strategic direction.

Scheduling the business representatives can be the most onerous requirements task. Be especially nice to your administrator (or your boss's administrator is you're attempting to schedule sessions with executive staff). We prefer to meet with executives on their own, whereas we can meet with a homogeneous group of two to three people for those lower on the organization chart. We allow 1 hour for individual meetings and 1½ hours for the small groups. The scheduler needs to allow ½ hour between meetings for debriefing and other necessities. Interviewing is extremely taxing because you must be completely focused for the duration of the session. Consequently, we only schedule three to four sessions in a day because our brains turn mushy after that.

When it comes to preparing the interviewees, the optimal approach is to conduct a project launch meeting with the users. The business sponsor plays a critical role, stressing his or her commitment and the importance of everyone's participation. The launch meeting disseminates a consistent message about the project. It also generates a sense of the business's ownership of the project. If the launch meeting is a logistical nightmare, the sponsor should distribute a launch memo covering the same topics. Likewise, the interview team must prepare the interviewees by highlighting the topics to be covered in the upcoming session. We do not include a copy of the questionnaire, which is not intended for public dissemination. We do ask the interviewees to bring copies of their key reports and analyses.

Collecting the Business Requirements

It's time to sit down face to face to collect the business requirements. The process usually flows from an introduction through structured questioning to a final wrap-up, as we'll discuss.

Launch

Responsibility for introducing the interview should be established prior to gathering in a conference room. The designated kickoff person should script the primary points to be conveyed in the first couple minutes when you set the tone of the interview meeting. You should focus on the project and interview objectives but not ramble on about the hardware, software, and other technical jargon. The introduction should convey a crisp, business-centric message.

Interview Flow

The objective of an interview is to get business users to talk about what they do and why they do it. A simple, nonthreatening place to begin is to ask about their job responsibilities and organizational fit. This is a lob ball that interviewees can respond to easily. From there, we typically ask about their key performance metrics. Determining how they track progress and success translates directly into the dimensional model. They're telling us about their key business processes and facts without us asking those questions directly.

If we're meeting with a person who has more hands-on data experience, we indirectly probe to better understand the dimensionality of the business, along with hierarchical roll-ups. Again, we go to their world rather than asking them to meet on our turf. Such questions as "How do you distinguish between products (or agents, providers, or facilities)?" or "How do you naturally categorize products?" help identify key dimension attributes and hierarchies.

If the interviewee is more analytic, we ask about the types of analyses he or she currently performs. Understanding the nature of these analyses and whether they are ad hoc or standardized provides input into the data access tool requirements, as well as the application template design process. Hopefully, the interviewee has brought along copies of their key spreadsheets and reports. Rather than stashing them in a folder, it is helpful to understand how the interviewee uses the analysis today, as well as opportunities for improvement. Contrary to the advice of some industry pundits, you cannot design an extensible analytic environment merely by getting users to agree on the top five reports or queries. The users' questions are bound to change. Consequently, we must resist the temptation to narrow our design focus to a supposed top five.

If we're meeting with business executives, we usually don't delve into the details just described. Instead, we ask them about their vision for better leveraging information in the organization. Perhaps the project team is envisioning a totally ad hoc environment, whereas business management is more interested in the delivery of standardized analysis. We need to make sure the data warehouse deliverable matches the business demand and expectations.

We ask each interviewee about the impact of improved access to information. We've likely already received preliminary funding for the project, but it never hurts to capture more potential, quantifiable benefits.

Ground rules for effective interviewing include:

- **Remember your interview role; listen and absorb like a sponge.**
- **Strive for a conversational flow; don't dive too quickly (or pull out a copy of potential data elements).**
- **Verify communication and capture terminology precisely because most organizations use terminology inconsistently.**
- **Establish a peer basis with the interviewee; use his or her vocabulary.**

Wrap-Up

As the interview is coming to a conclusion, we ask each interviewee about his or her success criteria for the project. Of course, each criterion should be measurable. *Easy to use* and *fast* mean something different to everyone, so you should get the interviewees to articulate specifics, such as their expectations regarding the amount of training required to run a predefined report.

At this point in the interview we make a broad disclaimer. The interviewees must understand that just because we discussed a capability in the meeting doesn't guarantee that it'll be included in the first phase of the project. We thank interviewees for their brilliant insights and let them know what's happening next and what their involvement will be. We also take advantage of this opportunity to manage expectations.

Conducting Data-Centric Interviews

While we're focused on understanding the requirements of the business, it is helpful to intersperse sessions with the source system data gurus or subject matter experts to evaluate the feasibility of supporting the business needs. These data-focused interviews are quite different from the ones just described. The goal is to assess that the necessary core data exists before momentum builds behind the requirements. A more complete data audit will occur during the dimensional modeling process. We're trying to learn enough at this point to manage the organization's expectations appropriately.

Postcollection Documentation and Follow-up

Immediately following the interview, the interview team should debrief. You want to ensure that you're on the same page about what was learned, as well as being prepared for any surprises or inconsistencies. It is also helpful to review your notes quickly to fill in any gaps while the interview is still fresh in your memory. Likewise, you should examine the reports gathered to gain further offline insight into the dimensionality that must be supported in the data warehouse.

At this point it is time to document what you heard. While documentation is everyone's least favorite activity, it is critical for both user validation and project team reference materials. There are two levels of documentation that typically result from the requirements process. The first is to write up each individual interview. This activity can be quite time-consuming because the write-up should not be merely a stream-of-consciousness transcript but should make sense to someone who wasn't in the interview. The second level of documentation is a consolidated findings document. We organize the document by first identifying the key business processes. As we mentioned earlier, we tackle the initial phases of a data warehouse on a process-by-process basis. Consequently, it is logical to organize the requirements of the business into the same buckets that will, in turn, become implementation efforts. Notes from all the interviews are reviewed to capture the findings associated with each of the core business processes.

When writing up the findings document, we typically begin with an executive summary, followed by a project overview that discusses the process used and participants involved. The bulk of the report centers on our requirements findings. For each major business process discussed, we describe why business users want to analyze the process results, what capabilities they desire, their current limitations, and potential benefits or impact. We include a list of sample questions that could be answered once the process metrics are available in the data warehouse. Commentary about the feasibility of tackling the data generated by each process is also documented.

We sometimes bring the processes together in a matrix to convey the opportunities across the organization. In this case we're not referring to a data warehouse bus matrix. The rows of the opportunity matrix still identify the business processes. However, in the opportunity matrix, rather than identifying common dimensions as the columns, we instead identify the organizational groups or functions. Surprisingly, the matrix will be quite dense because many groups need access to the same core business process performance metrics.

Prioritization and Consensus

The requirements findings document serves as the basis for presentations back to senior management representatives, as well as for others who participated. Inevitably we've uncovered more than can be tackled in a single iteration, so we need to prioritize our efforts. As we discussed with project scope, you shouldn't make this decision in a vacuum. You need to leverage (or foster) your partnership with the business community to arrive at priorities with which everyone can live.

The requirements wrap-up presentation is positioned as a findings review and prioritization meeting. Participants include relatively high-level business representatives, as well as the data warehouse manager and other involved IT management. The session begins with an overview of each identified business process. You want everyone in the room to have a common understanding of the range of opportunities, as well as what is meant when we say "sales bookings analysis," for example.

Once the findings have been reviewed, it is time to prioritize. The four-cell quadrant technique, illustrated in Figure 16.2, is an effective tool for reaching consensus on a data warehouse development plan that focuses on the right initial opportunities. The quadrant's vertical axis refers to the potential impact or value to the business. The horizontal axis conveys feasibility. Each of the finding's

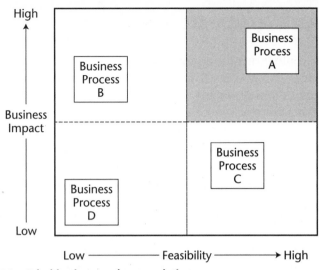

Figure 16.2   Prioritization quadrant analysis.

business process themes is placed in a quadrant based on the representatives' composite agreement on impact and feasibility. The projects that warrant immediate attention are located in the upper right corner because they're high-impact projects, as well as highly feasible. Projects in the lower left cell should be avoided like the plague—they're missions impossible that do little for the business. Likewise, projects in the lower right cell don't justify short-term attention, although project teams sometimes gravitate here because these projects are doable but not very crucial. In other words, no one will notice if the project doesn't go well. Finally, projects in the upper left cell represent meaningful opportunities. These projects have large potential business payback but are currently infeasible. While the data warehouse project team is focused on projects in the shaded upper right cell, other IT teams should address the current feasibility limitations of those in the upper left cell.

Lifecycle Technology Track

The business requirements definition is followed immediately by three concurrent tracks focused on technology, data, and analytic applications, respectively. In the next several sections we'll zero in on the technology track, which includes design of the technical architecture and selection of products that bring the architecture to reality.

Technical Architecture Design

Much like a blueprint for a new home, the technical architecture is the blueprint for the warehouse's technical services and elements. The architecture plan serves as an organizing framework to support the integration of technologies. Like housing blueprints, the technical architecture consists of a series of models that delve into greater detail regarding each of the major components. In both situations, the architecture allows us to catch problems on paper (such as having the dishwasher too far from the sink) and minimize midproject surprises. It supports the coordination of parallel efforts while speeding development through the reuse of modular components. The architecture identifies the immediately required components versus those which will be incorporated at a later date (such as the deck and screened porch). Most important, the architecture serves as a communication tool. Home construction blueprints allow the architect, general contractor, subcontractors, and homeowner to communicate from a common document. The plumber knows that the electrician has power in place for the garbage disposal. Likewise, the data warehouse technical architecture supports communication regarding a consistent set of technical requirements within the team, upward to management, and outward to vendors.

In Chapter 1 we discussed several major components of the technical architecture, including data staging services, data access services, and metadata. In the following section we turn our attention to the process of creating the technical architecture design.

Eight-Step Process for Creating the Technical Architecture

Data warehouse teams approach the technical architecture design process from opposite ends of the spectrum. Some teams simply don't understand the benefits of an architecture and feel that the topic and tasks are too nebulous. They're so focused on data warehouse delivery that the architectures feels like a distraction and impediment to progress, so they opt to bypass architecture design. Instead, they piece together the technical components required for the first iteration with bailing twine and chewing gum, but the integration and interfaces get taxed as we add more data, more users, or more functionality. Eventually, these teams often end up rebuilding because the nonarchitectured structure couldn't withstand the stresses. At the other extreme, some teams want to invest two years designing the architecture while forgetting that the primary purpose of a data warehouse is to solve business problems, not address any plausible (and not so plausible) technical challenge.

Neither end of the architecture spectrum is healthy; the most appropriate response lies somewhere in the middle. We've identified an eight-step process to help you navigate these architectural design waters. Remember, every data warehouse has a technical architecture. The question is whether yours is planned and explicit or merely implicit.

Establish an Architecture Task Force

Based on our experience, it is most useful to have a small task force of two to three people focus on architecture design. Typically, it is the technical architect, working in conjunction with the data staging designer and analytic application developer, to ensure both backroom and front room representation on the task force. This group needs to establish its charter and deliverables time line. It also needs to educate the rest of the team (and perhaps others in the IT organization) about the importance of an architecture.

Collect Architecture-Related Requirements

As you recall from Figure 16.1, defining the technical architecture is not the first box in the lifecycle diagram. The architecture is created to support high-value business needs; it's not meant to be an excuse to purchase the latest, greatest products. Consequently, key input into the design process should come from the business requirements definition findings. However, we listen to the business's requirements with a slightly different filter to drive the architecture design. Our primary focus is to uncover the architectural implications associated with the business's critical needs. We also listen closely for any timing, availability, and performance needs.

In addition to leveraging the business requirements definition process, we also conduct additional interviews within the IT organization. These are purely technology-focused sessions to understand current standards, planned technical directions, and nonnegotiable boundaries. In addition, we can uncover lessons learned from prior information delivery projects, as well as the organization's willingness to accommodate operational change on behalf of the warehouse, such as identifying updated transactions in the source system.

Document Architecture Requirements

Once we leveraged the business requirements definition process and conducted supplemental IT interviews, we need to document our findings. At this point we opt to use a simplistic tabular format. We simply list each business requirement that has an impact on the architecture, along with a laundry list of architectural implications. For example, if there is a need to deliver global sales performance data on a nightly basis following the recent acquisition of several companies, the technical implications might include 24/7 worldwide availability, data mirroring for loads, robust metadata to support global access, adequate network bandwidth, and sufficient staging horsepower to handle the complex integration of operational data.

Develop a High-Level Architectural Model

After the architecture requirements have been documented, we begin formulating models to support the identified needs. At this point the architecture task force often sequesters itself in a conference room for several days of heavy thinking. The team groups the architecture requirements into major components, such as data staging, data access, metadata, and infrastructure. From there the team drafts and refines the high-level architectural model. This drawing is similar to the front elevation page on housing blueprints. It illustrates what the warehouse architecture will look like from the street, but it is dangerously simplistic because significant details are embedded in the pages that follow.

Design and Specify the Subsystems

Now that we understand how the major pieces will coexist, it is time to do a detailed design of the subsystems. For each component, such as data staging services, the task force will document a laundry list of requisite capabilities. The more specific, the better, because what's important to your data warehouse is not necessarily critical to mine. This effort often requires preliminary research to better understand the market. Fortunately, there is no shortage of information and resources available on the Internet, as well as from networking with peers. The subsystem specification results in additional detailed graphic models.

In addition to documenting the capabilities of the primary subsystems, we also must consider our security requirements, as well as the physical infrastructure and configuration needs. Often, we can leverage enterprise-level resources to assist with the security strategy. In some cases the infrastructure choices, such as the server hardware and database software, are predetermined. However, if you're building a large data warehouse, over 1 TB in size, you should revisit these infrastructure platform decisions to ensure that they can scale as required. Size, scalability, performance, and flexibility are also key factors to consider when determining the role of OLAP cubes in your overall technical architecture.

Determine Architecture Implementation Phases

Like the homeowner's dream house, you likely can't implement all aspects of the technical architecture at once. Some are nonnegotiable mandatory capabilities, whereas others are nice-to-haves that can be deferred until a later date. Again, we refer back to the business requirements to establish architecture priorities. We must provide sufficient elements of the architecture to support the end-to-end requirements of the initial project iteration. It would be ineffective to focus solely on data staging services while ignoring the capabilities required for metadata and access services.

Document the Technical Architecture

We need to document the technical architecture, including the planned implementation phases, for those who were not sequestered in the conference room. The technical architecture plan document should include adequate detail so that skilled professionals can proceed with construction of the framework, much like carpenters frame a house based on the blueprint.

Review and Finalize the Technical Architecture

Eventually we come full circle with the architecture design process. With a draft plan in hand, the architecture task force is back to educating the organization and managing expectations. The architecture plan should be communicated, at varying levels of detail, to the project team, IT colleagues, business sponsors, and business leads. Following the review, documentation should be updated and put to use immediately in the product selection process.

Product Selection and Installation

In many ways the architecture plan is similar to a shopping list. We then select products that fit into the plan's framework to deliver the necessary functionality. We'll describe the tasks associated with product selection at a rather rapid pace because many of these evaluation concepts are applicable to any technology selection. The tasks include:

Understand the corporate purchasing process. The first step before selecting new products is to understand the internal hardware and software purchase-approval processes, whether we like them or not. Perhaps expenditures need to be approved by the capital appropriations committee (which just met last week and won't reconvene for 2 months).

Develop a product evaluation matrix. Using the architecture plan as a starting point, we develop a spreadsheet-based evaluation matrix that identifies the evaluation criteria, along with weighting factors to indicate importance. The more specific the criteria, the better. If the criteria are too vague or generic, every vendor will say it can satisfy our needs. Common criteria might include functionality, technical architecture, software design characteristics, infrastructure impact, and vendor viability.

Conduct market research. We must be informed buyers when selecting products, which means more extensive market research to better understand the players and their offerings. Potential research sources include the Internet, industry publications, colleagues, conferences, vendors, and analysts (although be aware that analyst opinions may not be as objective as we're lead to believe). A request for information or request for proposal (RFP) is a classic product-evaluation tool. While some organizations have no choice about their use, we avoid this technique, if possible. Constructing the instrument and evaluating responses are tremendously time-consuming for the team. Likewise, responding to the request is very time-consuming for the vendor. Besides, vendors are motivated to respond to the questions in the most positive light, so the response evaluation is often more of a beauty contest. In the end, the value of the expenditure may not warrant the effort.

Narrow options to a short list and perform detailed evaluations. Despite the plethora of products available in the market, usually only a small number of vendors can meet both our functionality and technical requirements. By comparing preliminary scores from the evaluation matrix, we should focus on a narrow list of vendors about whom we are serious and disqualify the rest. Once we're dealing with a limited number of vendors, we can begin the detailed evaluations. Business representatives should be involved in this process if we're evaluating data access tools. As evaluators, we should drive the process rather than allow the vendors to do the driving (which inevitably will include a drive-by picture of their headquarters building). We share relevant information from the architecture plan so that the sessions focus on our needs rather than on product bells and whistles. Be sure to talk with vendor references, both those provided formally and those elicited from your informal network. If possible, the references should represent similarly sized installations.

Conduct prototype, if necessary. After performing the detailed evaluations, sometimes a clear winner bubbles to the top, often based on the team's prior experience or relationships. In other cases, the leader emerges due to existing corporate commitments. In either case, when a sole candidate emerges as the winner, we can bypass the prototype step (and the associated investment in both time and money). If no vendor is the apparent winner, we conduct a prototype with no more than two products. Again, take charge of the process by developing a limited yet realistic business case study. Ask the vendors to demonstrate their solution using a small sample set of data provided via a flat file format. Watch over their shoulders as they're building the solution so that you understand what it takes. As we advised earlier with proof of concepts, be sure to manage organizational expectations appropriately.

Select product, install on trial, and negotiate. It is time to select a product. Rather than immediately signing on the dotted line, preserve your negotiating power by making a private, not public, commitment to a single vendor. In other words, make your choice but don't let the vendor know that you're completely sold. Instead, embark on a *trial period* where you have the opportunity to put the product to real use in your environment. It takes significant energy to install a product, get trained, and begin using it, so you should walk down this path only with the vendor from whom you fully intend to buy; a trial should not be pursued as another tire-kicking exercise. As the trial draws to a close, you have the opportunity to negotiate a purchase that's beneficial to all parties involved.

Lifecycle Data Track

In the lifecycle diagram found in Figure 16.1, the middle track following the business requirements definition focuses on data. We turn our attention in that direction throughout the next several sections.

Dimensional Modeling

Given the focus of the first 15 chapters of this book, we won't spend much time discussing dimensional modeling techniques here. This is merely a placeholder for all we've discussed earlier. We will, however, take a moment to review the overall dimensional modeling process. We stressed the four-step process previously, but here we'll discuss those steps within a larger project context.

Immediately following the business requirements definition, we should draft (or revisit) the data warehouse bus matrix, as introduced in Chapter 3. We already drafted the matrix rows when documenting and presenting the user's requirements in the context of business processes. Canvassing the core data sources by talking with IT veterans can further flesh out the rows. Likewise, we generate an impressive list of potential dimensions and then mark the intersections.

The final prioritization step of the business requirements activities identified the specific business process that will be tackled first. This, of course, corresponds to a row of the matrix. It also addresses the first question of our four-step dimensional modeling approach: identify the business process.

At this point it's time to do a more thorough analysis of the data generated by this process. While we conducted a high-level audit during the business requirements definition, we need to dig into the nitty-gritty to evaluate granularity, historical consistency, valid values, and attribute availability. Often business subject matter experts or power analysts from the business community can shed light quickly on data inconsistencies or idiosyncrasies based on the challenges they've encountered while attempting to analyze the data.

Once our data-analysis homework is complete, we conduct design workshops to create the dimensional schema. In our experience, it is more effective and efficient to have a small team (consisting minimally of the business system analyst, business subject matter expert, business power analyst, and data modeler) work through the design rather than relying on a solo modeler sitting in his or her ivory tower to design independently. The facilitated group workshop approach seems to arrive at the right design more rapidly. During the earlier case studies, steps 2 through 4 (that is, grain, dimensions, and facts) were tackled in an orderly sequence. In real life, don't be surprised if the design team revisits the granularity declaration once it is immersed in dimensions or facts. While progress is made in each workshop, issues also are identified inevitably. Responsibility for resolving the design issues needs to be assigned. Someone also must be responsible for logging and documenting the complete set of issues and their resolutions. Obviously, the team should leverage the business requirements findings to ensure that the model can support the key needs and questions.

Once the modeling team is reasonably confident about its work product, we communicate and validate the design with a broader audience, first within the IT and data warehouse team and then with others in the business community. To start, the matrix is a prime communication tool with both audiences so that everyone gains an appreciation of the larger, integrated vision and plan. From there, we focus on the specific schema.

We can expect the IT-centric meetings potentially to identify but also hopefully to resolve data issues. The business-user sessions initially will involve a small group of users identified to validate the design. This group should focus on the types of analyses and questions it hopes to ask of the data. When we're ready to present the dimensional design to a larger group of business users, it is often helpful to simplify the schema to hide the join keys and many-to-one crow's feet that have been known to overwhelm users. Simplified illustrations help spoon-feed the design to people who aren't already comfortable with a modeling tool's output.

Documentation on the validated model should identify the table and column names, definitions, and either calculation rules for facts or slowly changing dimension rules for dimension attributes. Typically captured in a modeling tool, this information is some of the first input (or link) to a metadata catalog. As tools and partnerships mature, information will flow more readily between the modeling, staging, access, and metadata tools. The schema documentation is further supplemented by adding the specific source system, fields, and transformation rules to derive the source-to-target mapping in conjunction with the staging team. It is helpful to adopt standard naming conventions for the data elements early in the process.

Physical Design

The dimensional models developed in the preceding section need to be translated into a physical design. In dimensional modeling, the logical and physical designs bear a very close resemblance. We certainly don't want the database administrator to convert our lovely dimensional schema into a normalized structure during the physical design. The physical model will differ from the logical model in terms of the details specified for the physical database, including physical column names (don't be afraid to use lengthy names), data types, key declarations (if appropriate), and the permissibility of nulls. At this point the physical design also contends with such nuts-and-bolts activities as performance tuning, partitioning, and the file layout.

Contrary to public belief, adding more hardware isn't the only weapon in our arsenal for performance tuning. Creating indexes and aggregate tables are far more cost-effective alternatives. We'll briefly review recommendations in both areas, understanding that physical design considerations quickly descend into platform specifics, which are changing rapidly. Also, be aware that aggregation and indexing strategies are bound to evolve as we better understand actual use. However, don't use inevitable change as an excuse to procrastinate on these topics. We must deliver appropriately indexed and aggregated data with the initial rollout to ensure that the warehouse delivers adequate query performance.

Aggregation Strategy

Every data warehouse should contain precalculated and prestored aggregation tables. Given our stringent rules about avoiding mixed fact table granularity, each distinct fact table aggregation should occupy its own physical fact table. When we aggregate facts, we either eliminate dimensionality or associate the facts with a rolled-up dimension. These rolled-up, aggregated dimension tables should be shrunken versions of the dimensions associated with the granular base fact table. In this way, aggregated dimension tables conform to the base dimension tables.

It is impractical to think about building all potential aggregation combinations. If we have a very simple fact table with just four dimensions and each dimension has three attributes that are candidates for aggregation, there are 256 different potential aggregate fact tables. Since we can't possibly build, store, and administer all these aggregates, we need to consider two primary factors when designing our aggregation strategy. First, we need to think about the business users' access patterns. In other words, what data are they frequently summarizing on the fly? The answer to this question can be derived from business requirements analysis insights, as well as from input gained by monitoring actual usage patterns. Second, we need to assess the statistical distribution of the data. For example, how many unique instances do we have at each level of the hierarchy, and what's the compression as we move from one level to the next? If our 50 products roll up into 10 brands, we're only summarizing 5 base rows (on average) to calculate the brand aggregate. In this case it's not worth the effort to physically prestore the aggregate. On the other hand, if we can avoid touching 100 base rows by accessing the aggregate instead, it makes much more sense. The aggregation game boils down to reducing input-output. In general, the disk space required by aggregate tables should be approximately two times the space consumed by the base-level data.

The availability of an aggregate navigator is another consideration in our overall aggregation strategy. Without an aggregate navigator, the number of aggregate schemas for analytic users to manually choose from is very limited—probably no more than two aggregates per base fact table. Aggregate navigator functionality sits between the requesting client and relational database management system. The navigator intercepts the client's SQL request and, wherever possible, modifies it so that it accesses the most appropriate performance-enhancing aggregates. The aggregate navigator makes productive use of the aggregate tables while buffering the client applications. Clients don't need to specifically write their query to access a specific base versus aggregated fact table, requiring that queries be rewritten when aggregates are added or dropped. The navigator handles changes to the aggregate portfolio behind the scenes so that the client can remain oblivious, as it should be.

Finally, we should consider the role of OLAP cubes as part of our aggregation strategy because they are especially well suited for rapid response to summarized data. Some products allow a seamless integration between the aggregated data in the cubes and the detailed schema in a relational structure.

Initial Indexing Strategy

Database administrators may hyperventilate when they learn that dimension tables frequently have more than just one index. Dimension tables will have a unique index on the single-column primary key. In addition, we recommend a B-tree index on high-cardinality attribute columns used for constraints. Bit-mapped indexes should be placed on all medium- and low-cardinality attributes.

Meanwhile, fact tables are the behemoths of the data warehouse, so we need to index them more carefully. The primary key of the fact table is almost always a subset of the foreign keys. We typically place a single, concatenated index on the primary dimensions of the fact table. Since many dimensional queries are constrained on the date dimension, the date foreign key should be the leading index term. In addition, having the date key in the first position speeds the data loading process where incremental data is clumped by date. Since most optimizers now permit more than one index to be used at the same time in resolving a query, we can build separate indexes on the other independent dimension foreign keys in the fact table. Much less frequently, indexes are placed on the facts if they are used for range or banding constraints.

Creating the physical storage plan for the data warehouse is not dissimilar to that for other relational databases. The database administrator will want to consider the database file layout, including striping to minimize input-output contention. Large fact tables typically are partitioned by date, with data segmented by month, quarter, or year into separate storage partitions while appearing to the users as a single table. The advantages of partitioning by date are twofold. Queries will perform better because they only access the partitions required to resolve the query. Likewise, in most cases data loads will run more quickly because we only need to rebuild the index for a partition, not for the entire table. Partitions also can be archived easily. Finally, the database administrator should implement a usage monitoring system as early as possible. Usage monitoring will be important for ongoing performance tuning, as well as for user support, capacity planning, and internal marketing.

Data Staging Design and Development

The final activity in the data track is the design and development of the staging or ETL system. We sometimes refer to staging as the iceberg of the data warehouse project. While the iceberg looks formidable from the ship's helm, we often don't gain a full appreciation of its magnitude until we collide with it and discover the mass that's lurking beneath the water's surface.

As we described in Chapter 1, data staging takes the raw data from operational systems and prepares it for the dimensional model in the data presentation area. It is a backroom service, not a query service, that requires a robust system application. Unfortunately, many teams focus solely on the E and the L of the ETL acronym. Much of the heavy lifting occurs in the transform (T) step, where we combine data, deal with quality issues, identify updated data, manage surrogate keys, build aggregates, and handle errors.

As has been our mantra throughout this chapter, you must first formulate a staging plan. Similar to the technical architecture, we design the staging applications using a series of schematics that start at the high level and then drill into the specifics for each table. You need to decide whether we're buying a data staging tool or building the capabilities on our own. We generally recommend using a commercially available product. While you can't expect to recoup your investment on the first iteration due to the learning curve, a tool will provide greater metadata integration and enhanced flexibility, reusability, and maintainability in the long run.

The other fundamental decision to be made concerns the structure of the data stores that result from or are used to support the staging activities, as we discussed in Chapter 1. Normalizing the source data before it is denormalized for the dimensional model may be appropriate for a particularly thorny relationship or if the source is already normalized, but often is unnecessary. For some, it is unfathomable to think about tackling the staging activities without the use of a normalized structure despite the additional storage space and effort required. In this case the normalized data satisfies a comfort zone need rather than an absolute requirement.

Dimension Table Staging

Since dimensions need to conform and be reused across dimensional models, typically they are the responsibility of a more centralized authority. The dimension authority is responsible for defining, maintaining, and publishing a particular dimension for the appropriate data marts. The act of publishing is actually a kind of synchronous replication because all the downstream marts should have an identical copy of the dimension at the same time.

While the dimension authority has centralized responsibility, there are likely multiple authorities in our organization, each responsible for one or more core dimensions. Dimensions can be processed concurrently. However, all the dimensions involved in a schema must be published prior to staging of the fact data.

Dimension table staging involves the following steps. Staging tools can deliver much of this functionality.

Extract dimensional data from operational source system. The extracted data can be moved to the dimension staging area by either outputting to a file and using File Transfer Protocol (FTP) or doing a stream transfer. Audit statistics from the extract should be collected.

Cleanse attribute values. Appropriate action should be taken to handle the following situations, along with many others: name and address parsing, inconsistent descriptive values, missing decodes, overloaded codes with multiple meanings over time, invalid data, and missing data.

Manage surrogate key assignments. Since we use surrogate keys in the data warehouse, we must maintain a persistent master cross-reference table in the staging area for each dimension. The cross-reference table keeps track of the surrogate key assigned to an operational key at a point in time, along with the attribute profile. If the master cross-reference data were handled as a flat table, the fields would include those identified in Figure 16.3.

As shown in Figure 16.4, we interrogate the extracted dimensional source data to determine whether it is a new dimension row, an update to an existing row, or neither. New records from the operational source are identified easily on the initial pass because the operational source key isn't located in the master cross-reference table. In this case the staging application assigns a new surrogate key and inserts a new row into the master table.

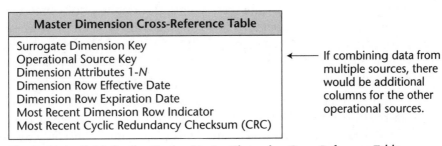

Master Dimension Cross-Reference Table

Surrogate Dimension Key
Operational Source Key
Dimension Attributes 1-*N*
Dimension Row Effective Date
Dimension Row Expiration Date
Most Recent Dimension Row Indicator
Most Recent Cyclic Redundancy Checksum (CRC)

⟵ If combining data from multiple sources, there would be additional columns for the other operational sources.

Figure 16.3 Fields for the Staging Master Dimension Cross-Reference Table

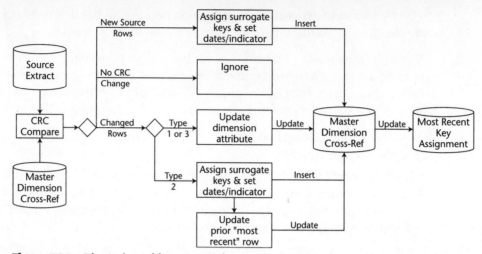

Figure 16.4 Dimension table surrogate key management.

To quickly determine if rows have changed, we rely on a cyclic redundancy checksum (CRC) algorithm. If the CRC is identical for the extracted record and the most recent row in the master table, then we ignore the extracted record. We don't need to check every column to be certain that the two rows match exactly.

If the CRC for the extracted record differs from the most recent CRC in the cross-reference table, then we need to study each column to determine what's changed and then how the change will be handled. If the changed column is a type 1 attribute, then we merely overwrite the attribute value. If the column is to be handled with a type 3 response, changes are made solely in the existing row. However, the processing is a bit trickier with a type 2 change. In this case we add a new row to the master cross-reference table with a new surrogate key reflecting the new attributes values, as well as the appropriate effective date, expiration date, and most recent indicator. The expiration date and most recent indicator on the prior version need to be updated to reflect that the prior row is no longer in effect. If we're using a combination of SCD techniques within a single table, we must establish business rules to determine which change technique takes precedence.

The final step in Figure 16.4 is to update the most recent surrogate key assignment table. This table consists of two columns—the operational source key and its most recent assigned surrogate key. If we've handled changes using the type 2 technique, this table will contain only the most recent row. We create this table to provide fast lookups when assigning fact table surrogate keys.

Build dimension row load images and publish revised dimensions. Once the dimension table reflects the most recent extract (and has been confidently quality assured), it is published to all data marts that use that dimension.

Fact Table Staging

While the dimension tables are replicated to all the appropriate date marts, fact table data is explicitly not duplicated. With the data warehouse bus architecture, the boundaries around a fact table are based on the source business process(es), not on organizational lines. Consequently, fact tables are isolated at unique locations but available to all who need access. Unlike dimension tables that require a centralized authority to guarantee consistency across the organization, fact tables can be managed on a more distributed basis, assuming that each promises to use the dimension authority's conformed dimension and not replicate the same fact table data in multiple locations. We briefly outlined the steps required to stage the fact table data:

1. **Extract fact data from operational source system.**

2. **Receive updated dimensions from the dimension authorities.** We want to ensure that we have the complete set of dimension rows that might be encountered in the fact data.

3. **Separate the fact data by granularity as required.** Operational source systems sometimes include data at different levels of detail within the same file. The granularities should be separated early in the staging process.

4. **Transform the fact data as required.** Common transformations include arithmetic calculations, time conversions, equivalization of currencies or units of measure, normalization of facts (such as the treatment of 12 date-defined buckets on a single operational record), and handling of nulls.

5. **Replace operational source keys with surrogate keys.** To replace the operational keys with surrogate keys, we use the most recent surrogate key assignment table created by the dimension authority. Making one pass over the fact table for each dimension, we quickly substitute the most recent surrogate key for each operational key encountered. We should ensure referential integrity at this point rather than waiting for the data load process. If the fact table's operational key does not locate a match in the surrogate key assignment table, we have several options. The process could be halted. The questionable rows could be written to a reloadable suspense file. Otherwise, we could automatically create a new surrogate key and dimension row for the unmatched operational key. Rather than assigning a single unknown dummy key for all the troublesome operational keys encountered, we assign a different surrogate key for each nonlocated operational key. The

descriptive attribute for this newly assigned surrogate key might read something like "Description Unknown for Operational Key XYZ." In this manner, when the new operational key is described properly, you often can avoid revisiting the surrogate keys in the fact table.

6. **Add additional keys for known context.** We sometimes add surrogate keys that aren't available on the operational record, such as the appropriate promotion key for the point-of-sale transactions or the demographics minidimension key that identifies the customer's current profile. Surrogate keys to indicate "Not Applicable" or "Date to Be Determined" would be assigned as appropriate.

7. **Quality-assure the fact table data.** Of course, we should be generating more row counts and cross-foots to compare with the extract statistics.

8. **Construct or update aggregation fact tables.** The aggregate tables typically are created outside the relational database platform because their construction depends heavily on sort-and-sum sequential processing. Be aware that reversals or prior-period adjustments can wreak havoc on aggregation subsystems.

9. **Bulk load the data.** If fact table key collisions occur during the load, we again have several options. We can halt the process, write the rows to a reloadable suspense file, or additively update the target row.

10. **Alert the users.** Finally, inform the business community that the fact table has been published and is ready for action.

Lifecycle Analytic Applications Track

The final set of parallel activities following the business requirements definition in Figure 16.1 is the analytic application track, where we design and develop the applications that address a portion of the users' analytic requirements. As a well-respected application developer once told us, "Remember, this is the fun part!" We're finally using the investment in technology and data to help users make better decisions. The applications provide a key mechanism for strengthening the relationship between the project team and the business community. They serve to present the data warehouse's face to its business users, and they bring the business needs back into the team of application developers.

While some may feel that the data warehouse should be a completely ad hoc query environment, delivering parameter-driven analytic applications will satisfy a large percentage of the business community's needs. There's no sense making every user start from scratch. Constructing a set of analytic applications establishes a consistent analytic framework for the organization rather than allowing each Excel macro to tell a slightly different story. Analytic applications also serve to encapsulate the analytic expertise of the organization, providing a jump-start for the less analytically inclined.

Analytic Application Specification

Following the business requirements definition, we need to review the findings and collected sample reports to identify a starter set of approximately 10 to 15 analytic applications. We want to narrow our initial focus to the most critical capabilities so that we can manage expectations and ensure on-time delivery. Business community input will be critical to this prioritization process. While 15 applications may not sound like much, the number of specific analyses that can be created from a single template merely by changing variables will surprise you.

Before we start designing the initial applications, it's helpful to establish standards for the applications, such as common pull-down menus and consistent output look and feel. Using the standards, we specify each application template, capturing sufficient information about the layout, input variables, calculations, and breaks so that both the application developer and business representatives share a common understanding.

During the application specification activity, we also must give consideration to the organization of the applications. We need to identify structured navigational paths to access the applications, reflecting the way users think about their business. Leveraging the Web and customizable information portals are the dominant strategies for disseminating application access.

Analytic Application Development

When we move into the development phase for the analytic applications, we again need to focus on standards. Standards for naming conventions, calculations, libraries, and coding should be established to minimize future rework. The application development activity can begin once the database design is complete, the data access tools and metadata are installed, and a subset of historical data has been loaded. The application template specifications should be revisited to account for the inevitable changes to the data model since the specifications were completed.

Each tool on the market has product-specific tricks that can cause it to jump through hoops backwards. Rather than trying to learn the techniques via trial and error, you should invest in appropriate tool-specific education or supplemental resources for the development team.

While the applications are being developed, several ancillary benefits result. Application developers, armed with a robust data access tool, quickly will find needling problems in the data haystack despite the quality assurance performed by the staging application. This is one reason why we prefer to get started on the application development activity prior to the supposed completion of staging. Of course, we need to allow time in the schedule to address any flaws identified by the analytic applications. The developers also will be the first to realistically test query response times. Now is the time to begin reviewing our performance-tuning strategies.

The application development quality-assurance activities cannot be completed until the data is stabilized. We need to make sure that there is adequate time in the schedule beyond the final data staging cutoff to allow for an orderly wrap-up of the application development tasks.

Deployment

The technology, data, and analytic application tracks converge at deployment. Unfortunately, this convergence does not happen naturally but requires substantial preplanning. Perhaps more important, a successful deployment demands the courage and willpower to assess the project's preparedness to deploy honestly. Deployment is similar to serving a large holiday meal to friends and relatives. It can be difficult to predict exactly how long it will take to cook the turkey. Of course, if the turkey's thermometer doesn't indicate doneness, the cook is forced to slow down the side dishes to compensate for the lag. In the case of data warehouse deployment, the data is the main entrée, analogous to the turkey. Cooking (or staging) the data is the most unpredictable task. Unfortunately, in data warehousing, even if the data isn't fully cooked, we often still proceed with deployment because we told the warehouse guests they'd be served on a specific date and time. Because we're unwilling to slow down the pace of deployment, we march into their offices with undercooked data. No wonder users sometimes refrain from coming back for a second helping.

In addition to critically assessing the readiness of the data warehouse deliverable, we also need to package it with education and support for deployment. Since the user community must accept the warehouse for it to be deemed successful, education is critical. The education program needs to focus on the complete warehouse deliverable: data, analytic applications, and the data access tool (as appropriate). If we elect to develop educational materials inhouse, we must allow at least 1 to 2 days of development for each hour of education.

Consider the following for an effective education program:

- **Understand your target audience; don't overwhelm.**
- **Don't train the business community early prior to the availability of data and analytic applications.**
- **Postpone the education (and deployment) if the data warehouse is not ready to be released.**
- **Gain the sponsor's commitment to a "no education, no access" policy.**

The data warehouse support strategy depends on a combination of management's expectations and the realities of the data warehouse deliverables. Support is often organized into a two-tier structure—the first line of expertise resides within the business area, whereas centralized support provides a secondary line of defense. In addition to identifying support resources and procedures, we also need to determine the application maintenance and release plan, as well as ongoing communication strategies.

Much like a software product release goes through a series of phases prior to general availability, so should the data warehouse. The alpha test phase consists of the core project team performing an end-to-end system test. As with any system test, you're bound to encounter problems, so make sure there's adequate time in the schedule for the inevitable rework. With the beta test, we involve a limited set of business users to perform a user acceptance test, especially as it applies to the business relevance and quality of the warehouse deliverables. Finally, the data warehouse is released for general availability, albeit as a controlled rollout.

Maintenance and Growth

We've made it through deployment, so now we're ready to kick back and relax. Not so quickly! Our job is far from complete once we've deployed. We need to continue to invest resources in the following areas:

Support. User support is crucial immediately following the deployment in order to ensure that the business community gets hooked. For the first several weeks following user education, the support team should be working proactively with the users. We can't sit back in our cubicles and assume that no news from the business community is good news. If we're not hearing from them, then chances are that no one is using the data warehouse. Relocate (at least temporarily) to the business community so that the users have easy access to support resources. If problems with the data or applications are uncovered, be honest with the business to build credibility while taking immediate action to correct the problems. Again, if your warehouse deliverable is not of high quality, the unanticipated support demands for data reconciliation and application rework can be overwhelming.

Education. We need to provide a continuing education program for the data warehouse. The curriculum should include formal refresher and advanced courses, as well as repeat introductory courses. More informal education can be offered to the developers and power users to encourage the interchange of ideas.

Technical support. The data warehouse is no longer a nice-to-have but needs to be treated as a production environment, complete with service level agreements. Of course, technical support should proactively monitor performance and system capacity trends. We don't want to rely on the business community to tell us that performance has degraded.

Program support. While the implementation of a specific phase of the data warehouse may be winding down, the data warehouse program lives on. We need to continue monitoring progress against the agreed-on success criteria. We need to market our success. We also need to ensure that the existing implementations remain on track and continue to address the needs of the business. Ongoing checkpoint reviews are a key tool to assess and identify opportunities for improvement with prior deliverables. Data warehouses most often fall off track when they lose their focus on serving the information needs of the business users.

If we've done our job correctly, inevitably there will be demand for growth, either for new users, new data, new applications, or major enhancements to existing deliverables. As we advised earlier when discussing scoping, the data warehouse team should not make decisions about these growth options in a vacuum. The business needs to be involved in the prioritization process. Again, this may be a good time to leverage the prioritization quadrant analysis illustrated in Figure 16.2. If you haven't done so already, it is helpful to have an executive business sponsorship committee in place to share responsibility for the prioritization. Once new priorities have been established, then we go back to the beginning of this chapter and do it all over again! Hopefully, we can leverage much of the earlier work, especially regarding the technical and data architectures.

Common Data Warehousing Mistakes to Avoid

We've told you what to do throughout this chapter; now we'll balance those recommendations with a list of what not to do. We closed Chapter 15 with a list of common dimensional modeling mistakes. Here we've listed mistakes to avoid when building and managing a data warehouse. The mistakes are described as a series of negative caricatures. Please forgive any trace of cynicism you might detect. Our goal is for you to learn from these caricatures based on mistakes made by unnamed data warehouse teams. As George Santayana said, "Those who cannot remember the past are condemned to repeat it." Let's all agree not to repeat any of these mistakes.

As in Chapter 15's list of dimensional modeling mistakes, we've listed these mistakes in reverse order, ending with the most important. However, any of these could be show-stoppers.

Mistake 10: *Accept the premise that those responsible for the enterprise's major source systems are too important and busy to spend time with the data warehouse team. Certainly, they cannot alter their operational procedures significantly for passing data to or from the warehouse.* If your organization really understands and values the data warehouse, then the operational source systems should be effective partners with you in downloading the data needed and in uploading cleaned data as appropriate.

Mistake 9: *After the data warehouse has been rolled out, set up a planning meeting to discuss communications with the business users, if the budget allows.* Newsletters, training sessions, and ongoing personal support of the business community should be gating items for the first rollout of the data warehouse.

Mistake 8: *Make sure the data warehouse support personnel have nice offices in the IT building, which is only a short drive from the business users, and set up a data warehouse support number with lots of touch-tone options.* Data warehouse support people should be physically located in the business departments, and while on assignment, they should spend all their waking hours devoted to the business content of the departments they serve. Such a relationship engenders trust and credibility with the business users.

Mistake 7: *Train every user on every feature of the data access tool in the first training class, defer data content education because the class uses dummy data (the real data won't be ready for another couple of months), and declare success at the completion of the first training class because the data warehouse has been rolled out to business users.* Delay training until your first data mart is ready to go live on real data. Keep the first training session short, and focus only on the simple uses of the access tool. Allocate more time to the data content and analytic applications rather than to the tool. Plan on a permanent series of beginning training classes, as well as follow-up training classes. Take credit for the user acceptance milestone when your users are still using the data warehouse six months after they have been trained.

Mistake 6: *Assume that business users naturally will gravitate toward robust data and develop their own killer analytic applications.* Business users are not application developers. They will embrace the data warehouse only if a set of prebuilt analytic applications is beckoning them.

Mistake 5: *Before implementing the data warehouse, do a comprehensive analysis describing all possible data assets of the enterprise and all intended uses of information, and avoid the seductive illusion of iterative development, which is only an excuse for not getting it right the first time.* Very few organizations and human beings can develop the perfect comprehensive plan for a data warehouse upfront. Not only are the data assets of an organization too vast and complex to describe completely, but also the urgent business drivers will change significantly over the life of the data warehouse. Start with a lightweight data warehouse bus architecture of conformed dimensions and conformed facts, and then build your data warehouse iteratively. You will keep altering and building it forever.

Mistake 4: *Don't bother the senior executives of your organization with the data warehouse until you have implemented it and can point to a significant success.* The senior executives must support the data warehouse effort from the very beginning. If they don't, your organization likely will not be able to use the data warehouse effectively. Get their support prior to launching the project.

Mistake 3: *Encourage the business users to give you continuous feedback throughout the development cycle about new data sources and key performance metrics they would like to access, and make sure to include these requirements in the in-process release.* You need to think like a software developer and manage three very visible stages of developing each data mart: (1) the business requirements gathering stage, where every suggestion is considered seriously, (2) the implementation stage, where changes can be accommodated but must be negotiated and generally will cause the schedule to slip, and (3) the rollout stage, where project features are frozen. In the second and third stages, you must avoid insidious scope creep (and stop being such an accommodating person).

Mistake 2: *Agree to deliver a high-profile customer-centric data mart, ideally customer profitability or customer satisfaction, as your first deliverable.* These kinds of data marts are consolidated, second-level marts with serious dependencies on multiple sources of data. Customer profitability requires all the sources of revenue and all the sources of cost, as well as an allocation scheme to map costs onto the revenue! For the first deliverable, focus instead on a single source of data, and do the more ambitious data marts later.

Mistake 1: *Don't talk to the business users; rather, rely on consultants or internal experts to give you their interpretation of the users' data warehouse requirements.* Your job is to be the publisher of the right data. To achieve your job objectives, you must listen to the business users, who are always right. Nothing substitutes for direct interaction with the users. Develop the ability to listen.

The business users, not you, define the suitability and usability of the data warehouse deliverable. You will be successful only if you serve the business users' needs.

Summary

This chapter provided a high-speed tour of the lifecycle of a data warehouse project. We briefly touched on the key processes and best practices of a data warehouse design and implementation effort. While each project is a bit different from the next, inevitably you'll need to focus attention on each of the major tasks we discussed to ensure a successful initiative.

CHAPTER 17

Present Imperatives and Future Outlook

Despite the dot-com meltdown and the collapse of the Internet hype, it is safe to say that we are still in the middle of a revolution in computing and communications. A majority of the citizens in the United States, Europe, and parts of Asia are using computers directly or are affected directly by them in various ways. The speed and capacities of our computers continue to double every 18 months, and we are aggressively rewiring our infrastructure to support high-bandwidth communications.

The unabated pace of this information revolution has profound implications for data warehousing. Remember, data warehousing (or whatever it may be called in the future) simply means *publishing the right data*. Data warehousing is the central responsibility for doing something useful with all the data we collect. Thus perhaps the good news is that we will all have jobs forever because data warehousing is at the core of IT's responsibility. But the bad news is that data warehousing will be a moving target because our information environment is evolving so rapidly and surely will continue to evolve for many decades.

To try to get a grip on what the next 10 or 20 years may have in store us, let's first lay out as much as we can about what other industry pundits have said recently regarding the next directions of technology. Although this may seem to go counter to the biases in this book (that is, start with the business user's needs, not with technology), in the large sense of the marketplace, the new technology is indeed a reflection of what the users want. Viewed from the perspective of the data warehouse, the entire world is being educated in the new medium of the computer, and a whole set of powerful expectations will define and drive what is a data warehouse.

Second, we must acknowledge and anticipate powerful political forces at work in the world today affecting what we think a computer is and how information should be used. The operative words are *security* and *privacy*. The data warehouse is absolutely in the thick of both security and privacy issues, and if anything, the data warehouse community has been slow to articulate security and privacy solutions. Instead, we have had solutions handed to us by non-data warehouse interests, including infrastructure groups in IT as well as politicians.

Finally, we will try to describe the big cultural trends within data warehousing, including the shake-out of the vendor community, the use of packaged applications and outsourced application service providers, and the trends toward and away from data warehouse centralization.

Ongoing Technology Advances

Let's start with a fun topic: new technology. Did we say gadgets?

Internet appliance. Wafer thin, high performance, always on, real-time audio and video with 24-bit color. Today's personal computers connected to digital subscriber line (DSL) or cable modems already approach these specifications. Increasingly, people will demand portable devices with wireless wideband connections to the Internet. The Internet appliance will become an even more potent combination of information manipulation and communication than it is today. Many data warehouse-driven services will be delivered through this medium, and much data will be collected as a result of the end user's gestures made while using the appliance. The applications of the Internet appliance will include:

All forms of information search and retrieval. These will feature search engines that do a much better job of understanding meaning, both in the search specifications and in document contents.

Electronic mail. Always-on e-mail will encourage a flood of tiny e-mails consisting of single sentence fragments as people converse casually and as parents check on the locations of children, as well as countless other informal types of communication. This behavior is already common with the Japanese DoCoMo device.

Telephony. The Internet appliance will be a full-powered telephone, available anywhere at all times.

Mobile teleconferencing. Two-way and *N*-way face-to-face and voice-to-voice communications will become a significant and valuable mode of using the Internet appliance.

Television. Television will be widely available via the Internet appliance, although it will not replace the standard living room TV.

Movies, literature, and games. The Internet appliance, coupled with wireless access, will be used increasingly for leisure and entertainment, especially on the road. Entertainment, of course, blends into education.

e-Learning. Electronic education will continue to be delivered on demand more and more to remote students.

Radio. Conventional radio broadcasts from all over the world will grow in popularity. The Internet is the successor to shortwave radio.

Shopping. Shopping on the Internet will continue to grow. Consumers increasingly will configure the options they want and arrange delivery of their built-to-order products. Dell provides a case study in a built-to-order, no-intermediary business. eBay will grow to become the worldwide marketplace for person-to-person sales.

Navigation. Since the Internet appliance is portable, always connected, and probably Global Positioning System (GPS)-enabled, it will be an increasingly useful navigation aid, whether for driving or for walking.

Language translation. Slowly but surely, automatic language translation services accessed via the Internet appliance will become accurate and useful.

4000 x 3000 pixel two-page monitors. Large-format, high-resolution display technologies are coming out of the labs today that will increase the usable area and resolution of our desktop PC systems dramatically.

Integration of cameras, video cameras, personal video recorders (PVRs), and PCs. Disk storage and processor bandwidths are very close to being ready at consumer prices for a grand synthesis of high-resolution photography, full video capture, PVRs, and video libraries.

Spoken-language interfaces. Speech recognition is good enough already for voice control of computer commands. A related capability will be voice annotations in documents, a technology that has been waiting in the wings for enough microphones attached to PCs to achieve critical mass.

GPS integration. GPS devices will permeate everything from our automobiles to our portable PCs to our smart credit cards. These devices not only will give end users feedback about where on the surface of the earth they are but also frequently will record and save the locations of important events, such as phone calls and transactions. The increased geocoding of much of our data warehouse data will bring the data warehouse and GPS communities somewhat closer together.

Secure, pervasive e-wallet. Today's uncertainties about revealing your credit card numbers will be forgotten. All of us will have the ability to reliably authenticate ourselves (see the next item) and pay for products and services in any situation. Coincidentally, this will hasten the financial crisis of the conventional post office because paying bills by first class mail will be one of the biggest categories switching over to the electronic form.

Reliable biometric identification. The window of opportunity for smart tokens, such as automatic teller machine (ATM) cards, has passed by already. Especially in these days of concern about making sure the person at the PC is really who he or she says he or she is, there will be widespread use of virtually foolproof biometric devices for personal identification. Today, in 2002, fingerprint recognition seems to be the leader, but retinal recognition seems to be the best long-term technology, assuming that the retinal recognition devices can be built cheaply.

Personal data-collecting transducers everywhere. Over the next several decades, it will be hard to resist the gradually increased use of data-collecting transducers that will record our every move and every gesture. Some of the pressure will come from security cameras or transducers in sensitive public areas. Some of the pressure will come from protective parents needing to track the whereabouts of their children. Criminals perhaps may be released early from jail if they agree to wear a tracking device at all times. Helpful household appliances will turn on the lights and heat up the coffee when we stumble out of bed. Our pantries will keep a running inventory and will generate a pick list for the next grocery store visit. The grocery store itself can interact with this list and optimize our visit. It's a brave new world.

If all 300 million people in the United States generate one record each second 24 hours per day 365 days per year, and assuming that the records thus generated are 40 bytes wide, this would require 378,432 TB of raw data storage each year. And this is a conservative design consisting of only text and numbers, no images or maps.

Micropayments for content. A side effect of the e-wallet may well be the introduction of added-value services in exchange for micropayments of a few cents or fractions of a cent. Our hesitation here is not with the technology but with the culture of the Internet that demands free access to everything. Of course, content providers have to make money somehow, and unless it's advertising, it may have to be micropayments.

Political Forces Demanding Security and Affecting Privacy

At the time of this writing we are in the early stages of responding to the challenges of international terrorism. At the moment, most Americans would be willing give up a little of their civil liberties and privacy in exchange for significantly increased safety. If significant time goes by before another major terrorist assault, the demand for a national ID card or other forms of secure authentication of all persons will fade away. However, if another assault takes place soon, it seems likely that we will want to track everyone, everywhere, at least when they are using public infrastructure. The likely authentication technologies include forgery-proof ID cards with embedded biometric information, as well as camera recognition systems that can identify anyone passing through a security barrier.

In the face of terrorist threats, it is likely that we will tolerate a certain level of tapping of our e-mails as well as our phone calls. It is not likely that we will impose significant new constraints on the use of encryption simply because strong encryption technology is already widely available both in the United States and from foreign countries.

The existence of a national ID number and the encouragement to tie an individual's behavior together with the use of that number is, of course, the familiar use of a conformed dimension on a very grand scale.

Conflict between Beneficial Uses and Insidious Abuses

We often allow our personal information to be gathered only when we consider the beneficial uses. And we usually don't understand or anticipate the insidious abuses of that same gathering of information when we approve it. Consider the following examples:

Personal medical information. The beneficial uses are obvious and compelling. We want our doctors to have complete information about us so that they can provide the most informed care. We recognize that insurance companies need access to our medical records so that they can reimburse the health care providers. Most of us agree that aggregated data about symptoms, diagnoses, treatments, and outcomes is valuable for society as a whole. Furthermore, we see the need to tie these medical records to fairly detailed demographic and behavioral information. Is the patient a smoker? How old is the patient? However, the insidious abuses are nearly as riveting as the benefits. Most of us don't want our personal medical details to be available to anyone other than our doctors. Preferably, insurance claims processing clerks should not be able to view our names, but this is probably unrealistic. We certainly don't want our personal medical information to be sold to marketing-oriented third parties. We don't want to be discriminated against because of our health status, age, or genetic predispositions.

Purchase behavior. The beneficial uses of purchase behavior data allow our favorite retailers to give us personalized service. In fact, when we trust a retailer, we are quite happy to provide a customization profile listing our interests if this focuses the choices down to a manageable number and alerts us to new products in which we would be interested. We want the retailer to know us enough to handle questions, payment issues, delivery problems, and product returns in a low-stress way. However, insidious abuses of our purchase behavior drive us ballistic. We do not wish to be solicited by any third party through junk mail or e-mail or over the telephone.

Safety and security in public facilities. In this day and age, all of us are grateful for a feeling of security in airports, in front of bank teller machines, and in parking garages. We wish the people who deliberately run red traffic lights would stop endangering the rest of us. Most of us accept the presence of cameras and license plate recognition systems in these public places as an effective compromise that increases our safety and security. The legal system, which ultimately reflects our society's values, has solidly supported the use of these kinds of surveillance technologies. However, the insidious abuses of cameras and citizen tracking systems are scary and controversial. We have the technical ability to create a national image database of every citizen and identify most of the faces that cross through airport security gates. How is the accumulated record of our travels going to be used and by whom?

Who Owns Your Personal Data?

There is a natural inclination to believe that each of us owns and has an inalienable right to control all our personal information. However, let's face the harsh reality. This view is naive and impractical in today's society. The forces that collect and share personal information are so pervasive and growing so quickly that we can't even make comprehensive lists of the information-gathering systems, much less define what kinds of collecting and sharing are acceptable.

Think about the three examples discussed earlier. We all routinely sign the waivers that allow providers and insurance companies to share our medical records. Have you read one of these waivers? Usually they allow all forms of records to be used for any purpose for an indefinite period. Just try objecting to the wording on the waiver, especially if you are in the emergency room.

And, honestly, the providers and the insurance companies have a right to own the information because they have committed their resources and exposed themselves to liability on your behalf.

Similarly, the retailer has a right to know who you are and what you bought if you expect any form of credit or delivery relationship with the retailer. If you don't want personalized service, then only engage in anonymous cash transactions at traditional brick-and-mortar stores.

And finally, if you use airports, teller machines, or roads, you implicitly agree to accept the surveillance compromise. Any images collected belong to the government or the bank, at least as far as current law is concerned. An odd corollary of being filmed in a public place is the experience we all have had of walking through a scene being filmed by an amateur photographer. Since a third party has innocently captured our image, do we have any rights of ownership in that image?

What Is Likely to Happen?
Watching the Watchers . . .

In our opinion, there are two major ways in which privacy laws and practices will be developed. Either our lawmakers will lead the way with innovative and insightful legislation such as the Health Insurance Portability and Accountability Act (HIPAA) and the Children's On-Line Privacy Protection Act (COPPA) or the marketplace and media will force organizations to adapt to the perceived privacy concerns of our citizens. It should be said that the government moves slowly, even when it does its job well. HIPAA was enacted in 1996, and COPPA was enacted in 1998. The requirements of these laws still have not been implemented fully in 2002.

Much has been written about the threats to privacy and the impact of new technologies, but a pragmatic and compelling perspective that seems to be gaining a significant following can be found in David Brin's *The Transparent Society: Will Technology Force Us to Choose Between Privacy and Freedom?* (Perseus Books, 1999). Brin argues that an effective compromise between freedom and privacy can be struck by *watching the watchers*. In other words, we accept the inevitability of the beneficial applications of personal information gathering, but we make the whole process much more visible and transparent. In this way we can curb many of the insidious uses of the information. We insist on very visible notifications of information gathering wherever it occurs. We insist on honesty and ethical consistency in following the stated policies. And significantly, we insist on being notified whenever our personal information is used by anyone.

Simson Garfinkel, in *Database Nation* (O'Reilly, 2000), agrees with many of the points raised in Brin's book and further insists that citizens should be able to access, challenge, and correct all instances of their personal information, even if they don't have the absolute right to inhibit its use.

How Watching the Watchers Affects Data Warehouse Architecture

The privacy movement is a potent force that may develop quickly. As data warehouse designers, we may be asked suddenly by management to respond to an array of privacy concerns. How is our data warehouse architecture likely to be affected? Here is a likely list, in our opinion:

- All personal information scattered around our organization will need to be consolidated and centralized into a single database. There should only be one consistent, cleaned set of data about individuals, and any data that is not being used for any identified purpose should be removed from all databases.

- Security roles and policies surrounding this centralized personal information database will need to be defined, enforced, and audited.

- The server containing the centralized personal information database will be need to be physically isolated on its own segment of a local-area network behind a packet filtering gateway that only accepts packets from trusted application servers on the outside.

- Backup and recovery of the centralized personal information server will need a strong form of physical and logical security.

- At least two levels of security sensitivity will need to be defined to implement a new privacy standard in your organization. General demographic information will be assigned a lower level of security. Names, account numbers, and selected financial and health-related information will be assigned a higher level of security.

- An audit database that tracks every use of the personal information must accompany the main database. This audit database must implement the requirement to notify every individual of all uses of his or her personal information, including who the requestor of the information is and what the application is. The audit database may have different access requirements compared with the main database. If the audit database is used in a batch mode, it pumps out usage reports that are e-mailed (or postal mailed) to the affected individual whose information is being used. If the affected individual can query the audit database online, then it is inherently less secure than the main database and probably needs to sit on a different, more public server. It is important that the audit database contains as little compromising content as possible but is focused simply on disclosing the final uses of information.

- An interface must be provided that authenticates the individual requestor and then provides a copy of all his or her personal information stored on the database. A second interface must allow the individual to challenge, comment on, or correct the information.

- A mechanism must exist for the effective expunging of information that is deemed to be incorrect, legally inadmissible, or outdated. Expunged information must be truly expunged so that it cannot surface again at a later time.

Although the data warehouse community traditionally hasn't led the way in advocating social change, we think that it may be a canny look into the future if we each consider whether the preceding list of changes could be implemented in our organizations. Consider it a reasonable future scenario that merits a little advanced planning. If you are more daring, and if you think the privacy debate will end up as the kind of compromise described in Brin's and Garfinkel's books, then have a talk with your CIO and your marketing management about some of these ideas.

Designing to Avoid Catastrophic Failure

We have been used to thinking that our big, important, visible buildings and computers are intrinsically secure just because they are big, important, and visible. This myth has been shattered. If anything, these kinds of buildings and computers are the most vulnerable.

The devastating assault on our infrastructure also has come at a time when the data warehouse has evolved to a near production-like status in many of our companies. The data warehouse now drives customer relationship management and provides near-real-time status tracking of orders, deliveries, and payments. The data warehouse is often the only place where a view of customer and product profitability can be assembled. The data warehouse has become an indispensable tool for running many of our businesses.

Is it possible to do a better job of protecting our data warehouses? Is there a kind of data warehouse that is intrinsically secure and less vulnerable to catastrophic loss?

Catastrophic Failures

Let us list some important threats that can result in a sustained catastrophic failure of a data warehouse, followed by potential practical responses:

Destruction of the facility. A terrorist attack can level a building or damage it seriously through fire or flooding. In these extreme cases, everything on site may be lost, including tape vaults and administrative environments. Painful as it is to discuss, such a loss may include the IT personnel who know passwords and understand the structure of the data warehouse.

Deliberate sabotage by a determined insider. The events of September 11, 2001 showed that the tactics of terrorism include the infiltration of our systems by skilled individuals who gain access to the most sensitive points of control. Once in the position of control, the terrorist can destroy the system, logically and physically.

Cyberwarfare. It is not news that hackers can break into systems and wreak havoc. The events of September 11 should remove any remaining naive assumptions that these incursions are harmless or constructive because they expose security flaws in our systems. There are skilled computer users among our enemies who are actively attempting today to access unauthorized information, alter information, and disable our systems. How many times in recent months have we witnessed denial-of-service attacks from software worms that have taken over servers or personal computers? We do not believe for a minute that these are solely the work of script kiddies. We suspect that some of these efforts are practice runs by cyberterrorists.

Single-point failures (deliberate or not). A final general category of catastrophic loss comes from undue exposure to single-point failures, whether the failures are caused deliberately or not. If the loss of a single piece of hardware, a single communication line, or a single person brings the data warehouse down for an extended period of time, then we have a problem with the architecture.

Countering Catastrophic Failures

Now that we've identified several potential catastrophic failures, let's turn our attention to possible responses:

Profoundly distributed systems. The single most effective and powerful approach to avoiding catastrophic failure of the data warehouse is a profoundly distributed architecture. The enterprise data warehouse must be made up of multiple computers, operating systems, database technologies, analytic applications, communications paths, locations, personnel, and online copies of the data. The physical computers must be located in widely separated locations, ideally in different parts of the United States or across the world. Spreading out the physical hardware with many independent nodes greatly reduces the vulnerability of the warehouse to sabotage and single-point failures. Implementing the data warehouse simultaneously with diverse operating systems (for example, Linux, Unix, and NT) greatly reduces the vulnerability of the warehouse to worms, social engineering attacks, and skilled hackers exploiting specific vulnerabilities. Over the next 20 years, many of the interesting architectural advances in data warehousing will be in building profoundly distributed systems. Although building and administering a profoundly distributed data warehouse sound difficult, we have been arguing for years that we all do this anyway! Very few large enterprise data warehouses are centralized on a single monolithic machine.

Parallel communication paths. Even a distributed data warehouse implementation can be compromised if it depends on too few communication paths. Fortunately, the Internet is a robust communications network that is highly parallelized and adapts itself continuously to its own changing topology. Our impression is that the architects of the Internet are very concerned about system-wide failures due to denial-of-service attacks and other intentional disruptions. Collapse of the overall Internet is probably not the biggest worry. The Internet is locally vulnerable if key switching centers (where high-performance Web servers attach directly to the Internet backbone) are attacked. Each local data warehouse team should have a plan for connecting to the Internet if the local switching center is compromised. Providing redundant multimode access paths such as dedicated lines and satellite links from your building to the Internet further reduces vulnerability.

Extended storage-area networks (SANs). A SAN is typically a cluster of high-performance disk drives and backup devices connected together via very high-speed fiber channel technology. Rather than being a file server, this cluster of disk drives exposes a block-level interface to computers accessing the SAN that makes the drives appear to be connected to the backplane of each computer. SANs offer at least three huge benefits to a hardened data warehouse. A single physical SAN can be 10 kilometers in extent. This means that disk drives, archive systems, and backup devices can be located in separate buildings on a fairly big campus. Second, backup and copying can be performed disk to disk at extraordinary speeds across the SAN. And third, since all the disks on a SAN are a shared resource for attached processors, multiple application systems can be configured to access the data in parallel. This is especially compelling in a true read-only environment.

Daily backups to removable media taken to secure storage. We've known about this one for years, but now it's time to take all this more seriously. No matter what other protections we put in place, nothing provides the bedrock security that offline and securely stored physical media provide. However, before rushing into buying the latest high-density device, give considerable thought as to how hard it will be to read the data from the storage medium one, five, and even ten years into the future.

Strategically placed packet-filtering gateways. We need to isolate the key servers of our data warehouse so that they are not directly accessible from the local-area networks used within our buildings. In a typical configuration, an application server composes queries, which are passed to a separate database server. If the database server is isolated behind a packet-filtering gateway, the database server can only receive packets from the outside world coming from the trusted application server. This means that all other forms of access are either prohibited or must be connected locally to the database server behind the gateway. This means that database administrators with system privileges must have their terminals connected to this inner network so that their administrative actions and passwords typed in the clear cannot be detected by packet sniffers on the regular network in the building.

Role-enabled bottleneck authentication and access. Data warehouses can be compromised if there are too many different ways to access them and if security is not centrally controlled. Note that we didn't say *centrally located*; rather, we said *centrally controlled*. An appropriate solution would be a Lightweight Directory Access Protocol (LDAP) server controlling all outside-the-gateway access to the data warehouse. The LDAP server allows all requesting users to be authenticated in a uniform way regardless of whether they are inside the building or coming in over the Internet from a remote location. Once authenticated, the directory server associates the user with a named role. The application server then makes the decision on a screen-by-screen basis as to whether the authenticated user is entitled to see the information based on his or her role. As our data warehouses grow to thousands of users and hundreds of distinct roles, the advantages of this bottleneck architecture become significant.

There is much we can do to fortify our data warehouses. In the past few years our data warehouses have become too critical to the operations of our organizations to remain as exposed as they have been. We have had the wakeup call.

Intellectual Property and Fair Use

Organizations who create information have tremendous political power and largely have succeeded in asserting permanent ownership rights to the information they create. This kind of information includes recordings of works of art, such as songs, movies, and video productions, as well as news and sports broadcasts, and copyrighted expressions of opinion, such as financial newsletters.

All of this has a pretty significant impact on the data warehouse. One must be extraordinarily careful about collecting information from an outside source. Since most of our organizations have deep pockets, we must be very risk-averse to avoid a lawsuit based on the claim that we appropriated information that did not belong to us or was under license. Because of this, and because media copying technology is being made much more restrictive, the original concept of fair use of information found in a purchased copyrighted work such as a book largely has been eviscerated. Fair use may be still legally valid for an individual, but it may not be possible for a large enterprise.

Although the general public may have felt that Napster was harmless or even beneficial, the courts took an extremely negative view of Napster's file sharing and cut off Napster's air completely. Unless there is some significant change in the law or a successful constitutional challenge, the writing on the wall is clear. Created information belongs to the owner, who has very long-term rights to the absolute control of that information. If you are lucky, you can rent the information, but you won't own it, and there is no practical way to make fair use of that information, at least with the technology we know about today.

Cultural Trends in Data Warehousing

We'll close this chapter by describing the significant cultural trends going on and having an impact on data warehousing.

Managing by the Numbers across the Enterprise

In the past 20 years the business world shifted noticeably to managing by the numbers rather than managing by instinct or by walking the aisles. The whole current generation of business managers has been educated in data-driven analysis and the importance of key performance indicators. The sheer size and complexity of large businesses demand detailed measurements. And finally, micromanaging individual store locations, product subcategories, and even individual customers can result in significant economies.

All this requires a biblical flood of numbers and measurements. Although marketing managers and the other strategic analysts in the business world have been quantitatively oriented for most of the last 20 years, only recently have the rank-and-file operations managers embraced the full potential of the data warehouse. Much of the recent move comes from the new emphasis on integrating all the customer-facing processes of the business into a seamless whole so that both operations people and the customer can see all the processes at once in a single understandable framework. However, achieving full enterprise application integration (EAI) is a very complex process that usually involves replacing the primary online transaction processing (OLTP) operational systems. We are only partway through this process on a global scale. However, competitive and financial pressures to achieve this integration will only increase in the next 20 years. Thus, although this continued evolution of managing by the numbers (you can call it data warehousing, CRM, or EAI) may not be the most high-tech trend in the next 20 years, it is in some ways the most important and pervasive trend we will have to deal with.

Increased Reliance on Sophisticated Key Performance Indicators

Business managers always have had a love-hate relationship with powerful key performance indicators (KPIs), especially those derived from sophisticated mathematical models. If they work, they're fantastic, but as soon as they produce an inexplicable or wrong result, they suffer a disastrous drop in credibility. Data mining and sophisticated forecasting models gradually are gaining a critical mass of respect, especially in certain application areas, such as economic forecasting, promotions analysis, optimal pricing algorithms, fraud detection, and threat analysis. The data mining community seems to have learned the lesson not to oversell their sophisticated techniques but rather to focus on successes that bring money to the bottom line. Generally, we feel that the sophisticated analytic tools are natural clients of the data warehouse. In many cases, the data warehouse serves to hand off observation sets as physical files to these tools, where they are processed and analyzed repeatedly while the main data warehouse is busy serving other clients. The key issues for the data warehouse manager supporting these sophisticated clients are to (1) make sure that these clients actually use the data warehouse as the platform for cleaned data rather than performing primary data extraction themselves,

(2) educate these clients on how to drill across the conformed dimensions of the enterprise to assemble broad and powerful observations, and (3) develop an effective partnership for handing off data in both directions—to the data mining tool and from the data mining tool.

Behavior Is the New Marquee Application

In the 1980s, the dominant data warehouse application was shipments and share. We were delighted just to see how much product went out the door to various markets. In the 1990s, profitability was the dominant data warehouse application. We discovered that with the proper data warehouse design, we could slice and dice the profitability of our businesses by products, customers, promotional events, time, and many other dimensions.

Although shipments, share and profitability certainly remain important, in the 2000s it appears that we have a new marquee application—behavior. Like the earlier applications, behavior means many things and reaches to all corners of our business. Customers have purchase behavior, payment behavior, product return behavior, repurchase behavior, support request behavior, and recommendation behavior. Products have reliability behavior, market appeal behavior, and ordering season behavior. Employees have productivity behavior, selling behavior, vacation taking behavior, and leadership behavior. Web site visitors have click-through behavior, site navigation behavior, privacy behavior, and trust behavior. Behavior is a powerful perspective to add to the shipments and share and profitability applications we already know how to do. Clearly, however, behavior is a more elusive concept. If profitability equals revenue minus expenses, then what is behavior?

Packaged Applications Have Hit Their High Point

During the go-go days of the Internet hype, many IT shops were overwhelmed by the new demands of e-business. Most IT shops knew that they lacked the skills to build their own Web- and CRM-oriented data warehouse systems. This paved the way for application package vendors to address this need with load-and-go packages for Web and CRM analysis. However, with e-business pausing and taking a deep breath, IT shops now have the time to consider more thoughtfully the tradeoffs in relying on an outside vendor's proprietary package for a portion of the data warehouse. We are not taking the position here that packaged applications are bad, but we respectfully suggest that package providers and IT shops need to reach a better middle ground. Here's the main issue: Application package providers cannot be the data warehouse. And this includes the biggest Enterprise Resource Planning (ERP) vendors. The proprietary barriers of most of the application packages defeat the ability of IT to control and publish its enterprise data in an open way. Application packages instead should focus on performing their specific tasks very well and then provide the most flexible and high performance possible way for the IT organization to extract all the data from the package for housing in a separate data warehouse.

Application Integration Has to Be Done by Someone

We mentioned earlier that integrating the enterprise's applications in order to achieve a consistent customer-facing view often requires replacing the production OLTP systems. This is not a cop-out in an effort to get the data warehouse off the hook. Like data quality issues, it is almost impossible to clean up incompatible data issues downstream from the source. Information has been lost. In many cases the matching of data from incompatible systems is not logically possible. In the long run, the data warehouse must follow, not lead, the EAI effort. We do not mean by this to give up on creating conformed dimensions and conformed facts. We are trying to warn you that this task will be far easier if it starts with the production systems. Finally, you should be very concerned if you (the data warehouse manager) are not invited to be on the EAI architecture board of your organization. You are one of the most important clients of this process, and senior management of your organization should understand this.

Data Warehouse Outsourcing Needs a Sober Risk Assessment

At the height of the Internet hype there was a hope that application service providers (ASPs) could take off much of the load of developing and supporting the new kinds of data warehouses required for e-business. Some of these also were affiliated with application package providers (discussed earlier). The potential attraction of a data warehouse ASP remains very real, but again, with the benefit of the pause we are all experiencing, we are assessing the risks of the ASP model as well as the advantages. If we are no longer in a desperate hurry to implement our e-business and our e-warehouse, why are we willing to trust a strategic responsibility to an outsider? Before we throw the baby out with the bath water, let's list the advantages of the ASP model for data warehousing:

- The ASP already has skills that the IT shop does not have and perhaps cannot obtain easily.

- The ASP has configured a complete set of hardware and software components that are known to work well together.

- The ASP has spare hardware capacity to respond to explosive demands from the Web or for disaster recovery.

- The ASP has centralized economies of scale for backup and recovery.

- The costs of the ASP can be isolated and managed in a more visible way than an internal department.

- The ASP takes care of its own personnel management.

Countering these very compelling potential advantages are the risks:

- Defining a data warehouse level-of-service agreement is a sophisticated task, and there isn't a lot of industry experience doing this. No matter what, this agreement should come from your organization, not from the lawyers working for the ASP!

- An ASP can go out of business. A source code escrow agreement is not much consolation in such a case.

- An ASP may upgrade its software on its own schedule. In any case, the ASP probably will not want to make custom modifications to standard software offerings if it is supporting many clients across many applications.

- An ASP may support your competitors. You don't have direct visibility of the security procedures of an ASP.

At this point we are betting against the pure business model of the remote ASP for data warehousing applications. Rather, we think a more viable model giving both parties what they need is for an ASP-like entity to run an inhouse data warehouse implementation where there is significant skills sharing with the local IT staff. In this way, many of the advantages of the ASP model can be realized while lessening the risks.

In Closing

The best way to end this book is to return to the beginning. Sweeping away all the details and techniques, the gold coin for the data warehouse professional is to listen to the business. Consistently listening to the users brings us back to what we are supposed to do. Over the next 20 years, we can navigate through all the technical, organizational, and political changes that will happen if we keep our eyes on the horizon. After all, our job is to publish the right data.

Glossary

24/7 Operational availability 24 hours a day, 7 days a week.

3NF See *Third normal form.*

Accumulating snapshot fact table Type of fact table with multiple dates representing the major milestones of a relatively short-lived process or pipeline. The fact table is revisited and updated as activity occurs. A record is placed in an accumulating snapshot fact table just once, when the item that it represents is first created. Contrast with *Periodic snapshot fact table* and *Transaction-grain fact table.*

Activity-based costs Costs that are reported as a measure of the activity required rather than on an unchanging standard value. See *Allocations.*

Additive (facts) Measurements in a fact table that can be added across all the dimensions. Ratios and unit prices are not generally additive.

Ad hoc queries Queries that are formulated by the user on the spur of the moment. The ad hoc attack refers to the difficulty a database has in anticipating the pattern of queries. The more that queries are ad hoc, the more symmetric the database model must be so that all queries look the same. This is one of the strengths of the dimensional modeling approach.

Aggregate navigator   Layer of software between the client and the relational data that intercepts the client's Structured Query Language (SQL) and transforms that SQL, if it can, to use aggregates that are present somewhere in the data warehouse. The aggregate navigator, by definition, shields the user application from needing to know if an aggregate is present. In this sense, an aggregate behaves like an index. Some relational database suppliers have incorporated aggregate navigation capabilities into their database management systems (DBMSs).

Aggregates   Physical rows in a database, almost always created by summing other records in the database for the purpose of improving query performance. Sometimes referred to as *precalculated summary data*. See *Aggregate navigator*.

Algorithm   Standard method for computing something; essentially a mathematical recipe.

Alias (SQL)   A short alphanumeric identifier in an SQL expression that stands for a physical table name.

Allocated inventory   Inventory that has been assigned for shipment to a particular customer or store before it has actually been shipped.

Allocations   Assignment or proration of measured values (usually costs) to several accounts, customers, products, or transactions. For instance, the overhead costs in a manufacturing plant are often allocated to the various product lines made in the plant.

Allowance   Amount subtracted from the list price of a product, typically as a result of a promotion or a deal. Usually shown on the invoice but called an *off-invoice* allowance.

Analytic application   Prebuilt data access applications intended for less frequent users of the data warehouse. Typically parameter-driven with flexibility to analyze countless permutations. Such an application represents an opportunity to encapsulate the analytic best practices of an organization.

Analytic processing   Using data for analytic purposes to support business decision-making, versus operational processing, where data is used to run the business. Analytic processing often involves trend analysis, period-to-period comparisons, and drilling.

ANSI   American National Standards Institute, the recognized standards-publishing body for a range of businesses, professions, and industries.

Answer set   Rows returned to the end user as a result of an SQL expression presented to a relational DBMS.

Application constraint (SQL)   Portion of the WHERE clause in SQL that defines a constraint on values, usually within a dimension table. To be contrasted with a join constraint.

Architected data marts   See *Data warehouse bus architecture*.

ASCII   American Standard Code for Information Interchange. An 8-bit character set encoding. ASCII can only support 127 characters, which is not enough for international usage. See *Extended ASCII* and *UNICODE*.

Asset   Item that appears on the balance sheet of a company that represents something owned by the company or something owed to the company by someone else. Bank loans are assets from the bank's point of view because they are owed to the bank.

Associative table   See *Bridge table*.

Atomic data   The most detailed granular data captured by a business process. Atomic data must be made available in the data presentation area to respond to unpredictable ad hoc queries.

Attribute   A column (field) in a dimension table.

Audit dimension   A special dimension that tags each fact table row with operational meta data (for example, data lineage and confidence) when the row is created.

Authentication   The step of determining the identity of the requesting client. Single-factor authentication usually is based on a simple password and is the least secure authentication scheme. Two-factor authentication may involve What-You-Know (a password) with What-You-Possess (a plastic card) and is secure enough for banks' automated teller machines. Other two-factor authentication schemes involve What-You-Know with Who-You-Are, using biometric scanning devices, such as fingerprint-, retina-, or voice-based systems.

Average order backlog   Average length of time that orders have been waiting to be fulfilled.

B-tree index   A relational index that is particularly useful for high-cardinality columns. The B-tree index builds a tree of values with a list of row IDs that have the leaf value. B-tree indexes are almost worthless for low-cardinality columns because they take a lot of space and they usually cannot be combined with other indexes at the same time to increase the focus of the constraints. Contrast with *Bitmap index*.

Baseline sales (of a promotion)   Sales volume that would have occurred if there had been no promotion in effect.

Behavior score   Figure of merit that is assigned to a customer based on purchase patterns or credit patterns. Also referred to as a *segmentation score*. Behavior scores can range from simple segmentation labels such as high, medium, or low to complex numerical results of a data-mining application.

Behavior study group   Large group of customers or products that is used in a user analysis or report but which cannot be defined by constraining on dimensional attributes and is too large to be enumerated by an SQL IN clause. The behavioral study group often is defined from an original analysis that isolates interesting purchase behavior or credit behavior.

BI   See *Business intelligence*.

Bitmap index   A relational indexing technique most appropriate for columns with a limited number of potential values (low cardinality). Most optimizers can combine more than one bitmapped index in a single query. Contrast with *B-tree index*.

Brick and mortar   A physically tangible business, such as a store, as opposed to virtual or Web-based businesses. See also *Click and mortar*.

Bridge table   A table with a multipart key capturing a many-to-many relationship that can't be accommodated by the natural granularity of a single-fact table or single-dimension table. Serves to bridge between the fact table and the dimension table in order to allow many-valued dimensions or ragged hierarchies. Sometimes referred to as a *helper* or *associative table*.

Browse query   SELECT DISTINCT query on a single-dimension table to show the user the values of an attribute or combination of attributes.

Browser   Personal computer (PC) client software that communicates with Web servers and displays Web content (text, image, audio, video) on the PC. The main function of the browser is to execute the HyperText Markup Language (HTML) program downloaded from the remote Web server.

Bus   Originally used in the electrical power industry to refer to the common structure providing power; then used in the computer industry to refer to a standard interface specification. In the data warehouse, the bus refers to the standard interface that allows separate data marts to coexist usefully. See *Data warehouse bus architecture*.

Business dimensional lifecycle A methodology for planning, designing, implementing, and maintaining data warehouses, as described in *The Data Warehouse Lifecycle Toolkit* (Wiley, 1998).

Business intelligence (BI) A generic term to describe leveraging the organization's internal and external information assets for making better business decisions.

Business measure Business performance metric captured by an operational system and represented as a fact in a dimensional model.

Business process Major operational activities or processes supported by a source system, such as orders, from which data can be collected for the analytic purposes of the data warehouse. Choosing the business process is the first of four key steps in the design of a dimensional model.

Byte (B) Unit of measure, consisting of 8 bits of data.

Cache In a Web browser, disk space set aside to store temporary copies of Web objects so that if they are requested again, they need not be fetched from the Web but can be obtained locally. More generally, a cache is a temporary storage space for objects or data expected to be used in the near future.

Cannibalization Growth of sales of one product causing the slowing of sales of another product. Usually referring to two products made by the same manufacturer.

Cardinality The number of unique values for a given column in a relational table. Low cardinality refers to a limited number of values, relative to the overall number of rows in the table.

Cartesian product A set comprised of all the possible combinations from multiple constraints.

Causal (factor or dimension) Something that is thought to be the cause of something else. Causal factors in retail sales usually refer to ads, displays, coupons, and price reductions. A causal dimension describes these causal factors.

Centipede fact table A fact table with too many dimensions (often more than 20), leading to a schema that resembles a centipede with numerous foreign keys joined to numerous dimension tables. Centipedes typically result when designers attempt to represent hierarchical relationships with a proliferation of separate dimensions rather than nested within a single dimension.

Chart of accounts   List of accounts used by the general ledger. A uniform chart of accounts is a chart of accounts applied consistently across an organization.

Churn   In a subscription service, the ratio of customers lost to customers gained.

CIO   Chief information officer within an organization.

Click and mortar   A hybrid business with both a Web-based and a physically tangible presence. Contrast with *Brick and mortar*.

Clickstream   The composite body of actions taken by a user at a Web browser. The clickstream can include both the actual clicks (browser requests) and the server responses to those requests. The clickstream takes the form of Web server logs, where each Web server log record corresponds to a single page event.

Click-through   The action of arriving at a Uniform Resource Locator (URL; Web page) by clicking on a button or link, usually located on a different Web site.

Column   Data structure that contains an individual data item within a row (record). Equivalent to a database field.

Composite key   Key in a database table made up of several columns. Same as *Concatenated key*. The overall key in a typical fact table is a subset of the foreign keys in the fact table. In other words, it usually does not require every foreign key to guarantee uniqueness of a fact table row.

Concatenated key   See *Composite key*.

Conformed dimensions   Dimensions are conformed when they are either exactly the same (including the keys) or one is a perfect subset of the other. Most important, the row headers produced in answer sets from two different conformed dimensions must be able to be matched perfectly.

Conformed facts   Facts from multiple fact tables are conformed when the technical definitions of the facts are equivalent. Conformed facts are allowed to have the same name in separate tables and can be combined and compared mathematically. If facts do not conform, then the different interpretations must be given different names.

Consolidated data mart   Data marts that combine business measurements from multiple business processes. Sometimes called a second-level data mart. Contrast with *First-level data mart*.

Constraint   Phrase in the SQL WHERE clause. A constraint is either a join constraint or an application constraint.

Continuously valued (facts)   Numeric measurement that usually is different every time it is measured. Continuously valued measurements should be facts in the fact table as opposed to discrete attributes that belong in a dimension table.

Contribution   Profit in a business measured by subtracting the allowances, discounts, costs of manufacturing, and costs of sales from the gross revenue. See *Profit and loss*.

Cookie   A small text file placed on a user's PC by a Web browser in response to a specific request from a remote Web server. The cookie contents are specified by the Web server and can only be read from Web servers belonging to the domain that is specified in the cookie.

Copybook   Traditional COBOL header file that describes all the columns in an underlying data file.

Core table   The fact table or the dimension table in a heterogeneous product situation that is meant to span all the products at once. Contrast with *Custom line-of-business tables*. See also *Heterogeneous products*.

Cost based optimizer   Software in a relational database that tries to determine how to process the query by assigning estimated costs to various table lookup alternatives.

Coverage table for a promotion   A fact table, typically factless, that records all the products that are on a promotion in a given store, regardless of whether they sold or not.

CRC   See *Cyclic redundancy checksum*.

CRM   See *Customer relationship management*.

Cross-selling   The technique of increasing sales by selling a new product line to existing customers. See also *Up-selling*.

Cube   Name for a dimensional structure on a multidimensional or online analytical processing (OLAP) database platform, originally referring to the simple three-dimension case of product, market, and time.

Custom line-of-business table The fact table or the dimension table in a heterogeneous product situation that contains facts or attributes specific to one set of products, where those facts or attributes are incompatible with the other sets of products. Contrast with *Core tables*. See also *Heterogeneous products*.

Customer master file Company's master list of customers, usually maintained by the order-processing operational system of record.

Customer matching The effort to identify an individual human customer across multiple systems by Social Security Number, address, or other indicators.

Customer relationship management (CRM) Operational and analytic processes that focus on better understanding and servicing customers in order to maximize mutually beneficial relationships with each customer.

Cyclic redundancy checksum (CRC) An algorithm that is useful for checking two complex items, such as customer records, to see if anything has changed. The CRC can be stored with an existing record, and then the CRC can be computed on an incoming record. If there are any differences, the CRCs will be different. This eliminates the requirement to check each constituent field in the record.

Data access tool A client tool that queries, fetches, or manipulates data stored on a relational database, preferably a dimensional model located in the data presentation area. Contrast with a *Data staging tool*.

Data cube See *Cube*.

Data extract Process of copying data from an operational system in order to load it into a data warehouse.

Data mart A logical and physical subset of the data warehouse's presentation area. Originally, data marts were defined as highly aggregated subsets of data, often chosen to answer a specific business question. This definition was unworkable because it led to stovepipe data marts that were inflexible and could not be combined with each other. This first definition has been replaced, and the data mart is now defined as a flexible set of data, ideally based on the most atomic (granular) data possible to extract from an operational source, and presented in a symmetric (dimensional) model that is most resilient when faced with unexpected user queries. Data marts can be tied together using drill-across techniques when their dimensions are conformed. We say these data marts are connected to the data warehouse bus. In its most simplistic form, a data mart represents data from a single business process.

Data mining   A class of undirected queries, often against the most atomic data, that seek to find unexpected patterns in the data. The most valuable results from data mining are clustering, classifying, estimating, predicting, and finding things that occur together. There are many kinds of tools that play a role in data mining. The principal tools include decision trees, neural networks, memory- and cased-based reasoning tools, visualization tools, genetic algorithms, fuzzy logic, and classical statistics. Generally, data mining is a client of the data warehouse.

Data presentation area   The place where warehouse data is organized, stored, and available for direct querying by users, data access tools, and other analytical applications. All querying takes place on the data presentation area. The data in the presentation area must be dimensional and atomic (and possibly summarized, as appropriate) and adhere to the data warehouse bus architecture. Typically referred to as a series of integrated data marts. Contrast with the *Data staging area*.

Data quality assurance   The step during the production data staging process where the data is tested for consistency, completeness, and fitness to publish to the user community.

Data staging area   A storage area and set of processes that clean, transform, combine, deduplicate, household, archive, and prepare source data for use in the data warehouse. The data staging area is everything in between the source system and the data presentation server. No querying should be done in the data staging area because the data staging area normally is not set up to handle fine-grained security, indexing or aggregations for performance, or broad data integration across multiple data sources. Contrast with the *Data presentation area*.

Data staging tool   A software application typically resident on both the client and the server that assists in the production data extract-transform-load processes. Contrast with *Data access tools*.

Data stovepipe   Occurs when data is available in isolated application-specific databases, where little investment has been made to sharing common data, such as customer or product, with other operational systems. Unarchitected, stovepipe data marts are disastrous as they merely perpetuate isolated, incompatible views of the organization.

Data warehouse   The conglomeration of an organization's data warehouse staging and presentation areas, where operational data is specifically structured for query and analysis performance and ease-of-use. See *Enterprise data warehouse*.

Data warehouse bus architecture   The architecture for the data warehouse's presentation area based on conformed dimensions and facts. Without adherence to the bus architecture, a data mart is a standalone stovepipe application.

Data warehouse bus matrix   Tool used to create, document, and communicate the bus architecture, where the rows of the matrix identify the organization's business processes and the columns represent the conformed dimensions. The intersection of relevant dimensions applicable to each business process is then marked.

Database management system (DBMS)   A computer application whose sole purpose is to store, retrieve, and modify data in a highly structured way. Data in a DBMS usually is shared by a variety of applications.

Days' supply (inventory)   The number of days the current inventory level would last at the current rate of sales.

DBA   Database administrator, a senior IT position requiring extensive understanding of database and data warehouse technology, as well as the uses of corporate data.

DD   See *Degenerate dimension*.

Decision support system (DSS)   The original name for data warehousing. In our opinion, it's still the best name because it's the business rationale for the data warehouse—using data to make decisions in an organization. See also *Business intelligence*.

Decode   The textual description associated with an operational code, flag, or indicator.

Degenerate dimension   A dimension key, such as a transaction number, invoice number, ticket number, or bill-of-lading number, that has no attributes and hence does not join to an actual dimension table.

Demand side   Flow of processes in a business starting with finished goods inventory and progressing through to customer sales. Contrast with the *Supply side*.

Demographic minidimension   See *Minidimensions*.

Denormalize   Allowing redundancy in a table so that the table can remain flat, rather than snowflaked or normalized, in order to optimize performance and ease-of-use. Equivalent to *Second normal form (2NF)*.

Depletions   Same as *Shipments*. Usually refers to a warehouse drawing down inventory in response to customer orders.

Dimension An independent entity in a dimensional model that serves as an entry point or as a mechanism for slicing and dicing the additive measures located in the fact table of the dimensional model.

Dimension table A table in a dimensional model with a single-part primary key and descriptive attribute columns.

Dimensional data warehouse Set of tables for decision support designed as star-joined schemas.

Dimensional modeling A methodology for logically modeling data for query performance and ease of use that starts from a set of base measurement events. In the relational DBMS environment, a fact table is constructed generally with one record for each discrete measurement. This fact table is then surrounded by a set of dimension tables describing precisely what is known in the context of each measurement record. Because of the characteristic structure of a dimensional model, it is often called a *star schema*. Dimensional models have proved to be understandable, predictable, extendable, and highly resistant to the ad hoc attack from groups of business users because of their predictable symmetric nature. Dimensional models are the basis of many DBMS performance enhancements, including powerful indexing approaches and aggregations. Dimensional models are the basis for the incremental and distributed development of data warehouses through the use of conformed dimensions and conformed facts. Dimensional models are also the logical foundation for all OLAP systems.

Directory server A server, which can be viewed as a little data warehouse, that keeps track of all the users of a system as well as all the resources available on the system, such as database servers, file servers, printers, and communications resources. The industry standard way to communicate with a directory server is the Lightweight Directory Access Protocol (LDAP).

Dirty customer dimension Customer dimension in which the same person can appear multiple times, probably not with exactly the same name spellings or other attributes.

Discrete (dimension attributes) Data, usually textual, that takes on a fixed set of values, such as the flavor of a product. Discrete textual data always should be handled as attributes in a dimension table as opposed to continuously valued numeric data that belongs in a fact table.

Domain (1) A specific range of Internet addresses assigned to a single Internet user. The domain name is a unique text name, often ending in .com, .org, .gov, or .net. (2) In a dimension, the complete set of legal values from which actual values are derived for an attribute.

Double-barreled joins   Multiple parallel joins between a single dimension table and a fact table.

Drill across   The act of requesting similarly labeled data from two or more fact tables in a single report, almost always involving separate queries that are merged together in a second pass by matching row headers.

Drill down   The act of adding a row header or replacing a row header in a report to break down the rows of the answer set more finely.

Drill up   The act of removing a row header or replacing a row header in a report to summarize the rows of the answer set. Sometimes called *dynamic aggregation*.

DSS   See *Decision support system*.

Dwell time   The length of time that a specific Web page is available for viewing on a user's browser.

Earned income   The income that a company is allowed to report in a given time period based on providing a service during that time period. Money paid in advance cannot be reported as income until it is earned.

End-aisle displays   A form of promotion in grocery and drug stores.

Enterprise application integration (EAI)   In a general sense, the reengineering of operational source systems to deliver enterprise consistency. In a product sense, a set of products that attempt to facilitate transaction-level communication among potentially incompatible operational source systems.

Enterprise data warehouse (EDW)   The conglomeration of an organization's data warehouse staging and presentation areas. Others in the industry refer to the EDW as an centralized, atomic, and normalized layer of the data warehouse, without making it clear if such a system is available for end-user querying and drill-down. We discourage this interpretation of the EDW, preferring to think of the EDW as the largest possible union of staging and presentation services, taken as a whole.

Enterprise resource planning (ERP) application   A class of applications aimed at spanning some or all of the business functions of a complete enterprise. ERP applications often are deployed on relational databases, and the data dictionaries for these applications may contain thousands of tables. An organization acquiring a major ERP application usually must shut down existing legacy applications and restructure fundamental business processes around the ERP system. ERP systems often contain the equivalent of an operational data store (ODS) because they usually are capable of real-time or near-real-time operational reporting, but ERP systems until 2002 have not made good data warehouses because they have not provided acceptable end-user query performance or a flexible environment for importing third-party data.

Entity-relationship (ER) diagram (ERD)   Drawings of boxes and lines to communicate the relationship between tables. Both third normal form (3NF) and dimensional models can be represented as ER diagrams because both consist of joined relational tables. The key difference between the models is the degree of dimension normalization. A dimensional model is a second normal form (2NF) model.

Equal access   The original promise of relational databases: the ability to retrieve data based on any criteria present in the data.

ETL   See *Extract-transform-load*.

Event   See *Page event*.

Event-tracking table   A fact table, frequently factless, where the dimensions of the table are brought together to describe an event, such as an insurance description of an automobile accident.

Extended ASCII   The extension of the American Standard Code for Information Interchange to include European accented characters and other special characters. This encoding uses the high 128 characters in the 8-bit ASCII format. See *ASCII* and *UNICODE*.

Extended cost   The unit cost multiplied by a quantity to give an additive value.

Extensible Markup Language (XML)   A cousin of HTML that provides structured data exchange between parties. XML contains data and meta data but no formatting information. Contrast with *HTML*. XML is a flexible, strongly hierarchical framework for assigning tags to fields within a document. XML does not specify what the tags should be. It is up to various organizations or industry groups to define and use consistent sets of tags, and this effort is the main gating factor slowing the widespread use of XML.

Extract-transform-load (ETL)   Set of processes by which the operational source data is prepared for the data warehouse. The primary processes of the backroom data staging area of the data warehouse, prior to any presentation or querying. Consists of extracting operational data from a source application, transforming it, loading and indexing it, quality-assuring it, and publishing it.

Fact   A business performance measurement, typically numeric and additive, that is stored in a fact table.

Fact dimension   A special dimension used to identify extremely sparse, dissimilar measurements in a single fact table.

Fact table   In a star schema (dimensional model), the central table with numeric performance measurements characterized by a composite key, each of whose elements is a foreign key drawn from a dimension table.

Factless fact table   A fact table that has no facts but captures certain many-to-many relationships between the dimension keys. Most often used to represent events or provide coverage information that does not appear in other fact tables.

File Transfer Protocol (FTP)   TCP/IP protocol that is used for transferring files between computers.

Filter on fact rows   A type of application constraint that constrains on the numeric values of one or more facts. Used for value banding.

First-level data mart   A data mart that is derived from a single primary source system. Contrast with *Consolidated data mart*.

Fixed depth hierarchy   A highly predictable hierarchy with a fixed number of levels. Contrast with *Ragged hierarchy*.

FK   See *Foreign key*.

Flat file   A simple data structure, often implemented on a mainframe, that relies on nonrelational files, such as IBM VSAM files.

Foreign key (FK)   A column in a relational database table whose values are drawn from the values of a primary key in another table. In a star-join schema, the components of a composite fact table key are foreign keys with respect to each of the dimension tables.

Framework   Unifying, guiding architectural approach, as in the data warehouse bus architecture.

FROM clause (SQL)   SQL clause that lists the tables required by the query.

General ledger (G/L)   Ledger that represents the organization's assets, liabilities, equity, income, and expense. The G/L remains balanced through offsetting transactions to debit and credit accounts.

Geographic information system (GIS) A hybrid application combining database and mapping technology. Typically, in a GIS, queries can be constructed from maps, and maps can be delivered as a result of a query.

Gigabyte (GB) One billion bytes.

GIS See *Geographic information system.*

GMROI Gross margin return on inventory, equal to the number of turns of inventory multiplied by the gross margin percent. A measure of the return on each dollar invested in inventory.

Grain The meaning of a single row in a fact table. The declaration of the grain of a fact table is the second of four key steps in the design of a dimensional model.

Granularity The level of detail captured in the data warehouse. See *Grain.*

Greenwich Mean Time (GMT) The local standard time at zero degrees longitude, which runs through the Royal Navy Observatory near London.

Gross margin percent The gross profit expressed as a percentage of gross revenue.

Gross profit The gross revenue less the cost of the goods.

Gross revenue The total revenue paid to a company by its customers. If the gross revenue is calculated before applicable discounts, then the actual amount paid by the customers is called the *net revenue.*

GROUP BY clause (SQL) SQL clause that uniquely lists the unaggregated items in the SELECT list, that is, everything that is not a SUM, COUNT, MIN, MAX, or AVG.

GUI Graphic user interface. A style of computer interface characterized by windows, icons, the use of graphics, and the use of a mouse pointing device.

Helper table See *Bridge table.*

Heterogeneous products A set of products typically characterized by many incompatible product attributes and measurable facts. A characteristic design challenge in financial service environments. See *Core table* and *Custom line-of-business table.*

Hierarchical relationship A relationship where data rolls up into higher levels of summarization in a series of strict many-to-one relationships.

Hierarchies are reflected by additional columns on the atomic dimension table.

Householding   The effort to assign an account or an individual to a household of accounts or individuals for marketing purposes.

HyperText Markup Language (HTML)   A standard markup language for defining the presentation characteristics of Web documents. HTML contains data and formatting but does not contain meta data. Contrast with *XML*. HTML is not a general programming language.

HyperText Transfer Protocol (HTTP)   The communications protocol of the Web. HTTP specifies the way in which a browser and Web site exchange information.

Impact report   When reporting with a bridge table, the weighting factor assigned to the multivalued dimension is ignored. The resulting totals provide a summarization for any case in which the multivalued dimension was involved, regardless of the extent of the involvement. Contrast with *Weighted report*.

Implementation bus matrix   A more detailed version of the data warehouse bus matrix where fact tables are identified for each business process, as well as the fact table granularity and measurements.

Index   A data structure associated with a table that is logically ordered by the values of a key and used to improve database performance and query access speed. B-tree indexes are used for high-cardinality fields, and bitmap indexes are used for medium- and low-cardinality fields.

Internet   The worldwide collection of communication links and services that are tied together using the Internet Protocol (IP).

Internet service provider (ISP)   A company or organization that provides Internet connectivity to the public through the use of telephone lines, cable, or satellites. ISPs often offer a range of services, such as electronic mail, Web hosting, and application access, and provide connectivity to the customer's personal computer using TCP/IP protocols.

IP address   The numeric address of a particular host or subnet on the Internet.

Join constraint (SQL)   The portion of the SQL WHERE clause that bookkeeps the join relationships between the fact table and the dimension tables.

JPEG, JPG   An image-compression format standardized by the Joint Photographic Experts Group. It is particularly suited to complex images such as photographs. A JPEG image can be adjusted to offer high compression with resulting loss of image quality or low compression with high image quality.

Julian day number   A representation of a calendar date as the simple count of days from the beginning of an epoch, such as January 1, 1900. True Julian dates are numbered in the millions and are not used often as the literal basis of date values.

Junk dimension   An abstract dimension with the decodes for a group of low-cardinality flags and indicators, thereby removing the flags from the fact table.

LDAP   Lightweight Directory Access Protocol, a standard currently agreed to by most of the major systems vendors for describing the users of a network and the resources available on a network. See *Directory server*.

Liability   An item that appears on the balance sheet of a company that represents money the company owes to someone else. Bank deposits are liabilities from a bank's point of view because they must be paid back.

Lift of a promotion   The increase of sales over the baseline value that can be attributed to the effects of a promotion.

Line item   An individual line of a control document such as an invoice usually identifying a single product within the invoice. Most often used as the grain of the associated fact table.

Logical design   The phase of a database design concerned with identifying the relationships among the data elements. Contrast with *Physical design*.

Loss party (insurance)   Any individual or entity associated with a claim (a loss), including injured parties, witnesses, lawyers, and other service providers.

Low-cardinality attribute set   A set of attributes that have a very low cardinality relative to the number of rows in the base dimension, such as external demographic data for a set of customers. May be handled as a dimension outrigger. See also *Cardinality*.

Many-to-many relationship   A logical data relationship in which the value of one data element can exist in combination with many values of another data element, and vice versa.

Many-to-one relationship   See *One-to-many relationship*.

Many-valued dimensions Normally, a fact table possesses only connections to dimensions representing a single value, such as a single time or a single product. But occasionally, it is valid to connect a fact table record to a dimension representing an open-ended number of values, such as the number of simultaneous diagnoses a patient may have at the moment of a single treatment. In this case we say that the fact table has a *many-valued dimension*. Also referred to as *Multivalued dimensions*. Typically handled using a bridge table.

Market basket analysis A kind of analysis in retail environments that seeks to understand all the products purchased by a customer in a single shopping event. Market basket analysis is an example of affinity grouping that seeks to find things that happen together.

Market growth A desirable outcome of a promotion that causes overall sales of a product category to grow instead of causing cannibalization.

MBA Master of Business Administration, a graduate college or university degree requiring extensive understanding of how commercial businesses are organized and managed.

Merchandise hierarchy A set of attributes in the product dimension that define an ascending many-to-one relationship. Common to all manufacturing and retail environments.

Meta data Any data maintained to support the operations or use of a data warehouse, similar to an encyclopedia for the data warehouse. Nearly all data staging and access tools require some private meta data in the form of specifications or status. There are few coherent standards for meta data viewed in a broader sense. Distinguished from the primary data in the dimension and fact tables.

Migrate Moving data from one computer to another or from one file format to another.

Minidimensions Subsets of a large dimension, such as customer, that are broken off into separate, smaller artificial dimensions to control the explosive growth of a large, rapidly changing dimension. The continuously changing demographic attributes of a customer are often modeled as a separate minidimension.

Mirrored database A physical organization of data where the entire database is duplicated on separate disk drives. Mirrored databases offer a number of performance and administrative advantages.

Modeling applications   A sophisticated data warehouse client with analytic capabilities that transform or digest the output from the data warehouse. Modeling applications include forecasting models, behavior scoring models that cluster and classify customer purchase behavior or customer credit behavior, allocation models that take cost data from the data warehouse and spread the costs across product groupings or customer groupings, and most data mining tools.

Most recent indicator   An attribute, typically used in conjunction with type 2 slowly changing dimensions, that indicates the most current profile.

Multidimensional database   Database in which the data is presented in data cubes, as opposed to tables in a relational database platform.

Multidimensional OLAP (MOLAP)   Dedicated online analytical processing implementations not dependent on relational databases. Although MOLAP systems do not scale to the sizes that relational databases systems can, they typically offer better performance and more tightly integrated tools than their relational counterparts.

Multipass SQL   Query capability supported by some data access tools in which the results of separate star-schema queries are combined column by column via the conformed dimensions. Not the same thing as a union, which is a row-by-row combination of separate queries.

Multitable join query   One of the two characteristic types of queries in a data warehouse environment. Involves the joining of one or more dimension tables to a single fact table. Contrast with *Browse queries*.

Multivalued dimensions   See *Many-valued dimensions*.

Natural key   The identifier used by the operational systems. Natural keys often have embedded meaning. They may appear as dimension attributes in dimensional models but should not serve as the dimension table primary key, which always should be a surrogate key.

Nonadditive (facts)   A fact that cannot logically be added between rows. May be numeric and therefore usually must be combined in a computation with other facts before being added across rows. If nonnumeric, can only be used in constraints, counts, or groupings.

Normalize   A logical modeling technique that removes data redundancy by separating the data into many discrete entities, each of which becomes a table in a relational DBMS.

Null   A data field or record for which no value exists. We avoid null keys in the fact table by assigning a dimension surrogate key to identify "Not Applicable," "To Be Determined," or other "Empty" conditions.

ODS   See *Operational data store*.

Off-invoice allowances   Typically deal- or promotion-related subtractions from the list price shown on the invoice. Part of deriving the net invoice amount, which is what the customer is supposed to pay on this line item.

Off-invoice discounts   Typically financial terms-related subtractions from the list price shown on the invoice. Part of deriving the net invoice amount, which is what the customer is supposed to pay on this line item.

One-to-many relationship   A logical data relationship in which the value of one data element can exist in combination with many values of another data element, but not vice versa.

Online analytic processing (OLAP)   OLAP is a loosely defined set of principles that provide a dimensional framework for decision support. The term *OLAP* also is used to define a confederation of vendors who offer nonrelational, multidimensional database products aimed at decision support. Contrast with *Online transaction processing*.

Online transaction processing (OLTP)   The original description for all the activities and systems associated with entering data reliably into a database. Most frequently used with reference to relational databases, although OLTP can be used generically to describe any transaction-processing environment. Contrast with *Online analytic processing*.

Operational data store (ODS)   A physical set of tables sitting between the operational systems and the data warehouse or a specially administered hot partition of the data warehouse itself. The main reason for an ODS is to provide immediate reporting of operational results if neither the operational system nor the regular data warehouse can provide satisfactory access. Because an ODS is necessarily an extract of the operational data, it also may play the role of source for the data warehouse.

Operational system of record   An operational system for capturing data about a company's operations and business processes. May not necessarily be a transaction system or a relational system.

ORDER BY clause (SQL)   SQL clause that determines the ordering of rows in the answer set.

Outrigger table   A secondary dimension table attached to a dimension table. An outrigger table is a physical design interpretation of a single logical dimension table. Occurs when a dimension table is snowflaked.

P&L   See *Profit-and-loss schema*.

Page   (1) A Web page is a document in HTML format that can be displayed by a browser. The term *page* also is used to describe a compound document consisting of the HTML document itself and ancillary objects such as images or sounds that are downloaded to the browser as directed by the page's HTML. (2) Basic unit of stored data.

Page event   Refers to a Web page or frame downloaded from a Web server to a browser, exclusive of any ancillary content.

Parent-child database   Hierarchical organization of data typically involving a header and set of line items. The dimensional modeling approach strips all the information out of the header (parent) into separate dimensions and leaves the original parent natural key as a degenerate dimension.

Parsing   Decomposing operational fields, such as a name or address, into standard elemental parts.

Partitioned tables   Tables (and their associated indices) that are managed as physically separate tables but appear logically as a single table. Large fact tables are candidates for partitioning, often by date. Partitioning can improve both query and maintenance performance.

Partitioning of history   The natural correspondence between dimension table entries and fact table rows when a type 2 slowly changing dimension has been implemented. A type 2 slowly changing dimension partitions history because each value of its surrogate key is administered correctly to connect to the correct contemporary span of fact records.

Periodic snapshot fact table   A type of fact table that represents business performance at the end of each regular, predictable time period. Daily snapshots and monthly snapshots are common. Snapshots are required in a number of businesses, such as insurance, where the transaction history is too complicated to be used as the basis for computing snapshots on the fly. A separate record is placed in a periodic snapshot fact table each period regardless of whether any activity has taken place in the underlying account. Contrast with *Transaction fact table* and *Accumulating snapshot fact table*.

Physical design   The phase of a database design following the logical design that identifies the actual database tables and index structures used to implement the logical design.

PK   See *Primary key*.

Point-of-sale (POS) system   The cash registers and associated in-store computers in a retail environment.

Portal   A Web site designed to be the first point of entry for visitors to the Web. Portal sites usually feature a wide variety of contents and search capabilities in order to entice visitors to use them. Portals are often selected as browser home pages.

Price-point analysis   The breakdown of product sales by each discrete transaction price. Requires a fact table with fine enough grain to represent each price point separately.

Primary key (PK)   A column in a database table that is uniquely different for each row in the table.

Product master file   A company's master list of products, usually maintained by a manufacturing or purchase order operational application.

Profit-and-loss (P&L) schema   The P&L, also known as an *income statement*, is the classic logical ordering of revenues and costs to represent a progression from gross revenues down to a bottom line that represents net profit. The profitability schema often is called the most powerful dimensional schema because it allows the business to slice and dice revenue, cost, and profit by their primary dimensions, such as customer and product.

Promotion   An event, usually planned by marketing, that features one or more causal items such as ads, displays, or price reductions. Also thought of as a deal or sometimes as a contract.

Proxy   An alternate Web server that responds to a Web page request in order to reduce the load on a primary Web server or network.

Pseudotransaction   A step needed in some production data extract systems where a nontransactional legacy system is analyzed to see what changed from the previous extract. These changes are then made into artificial (pseudo) transactions in order to be loaded into the data warehouse.

Publishing the right data   The most succinct way to describe the overall responsibility of the data warehouse. The data is right if it satisfies the business's requirements. The act of publishing is driven ultimately by the business user's needs.

Pull-down list   A user-interface effect in a data access tool that displays a list of options for the user. The most interesting pull-down lists in a data warehouse come from browse queries on a dimension attribute.

Query   User request for information stored in a data warehouse. With a relational DBMS, the query is an SQL SELECT statement passed from the data access application (typically on the end user's client machine).

Ragged hierarchy   A hierarchy with an unbalanced and arbitrarily deep structure that usually cannot be described in advance of loading the data. Sometimes referred to as a *variable-depth hierarchy*. Organization charts often are ragged hierarchies. See *Bridge table*.

Real time partitions   A physically separate and specially administered set of tables, apart from the conventional data warehouse, to support more real-time access requirements. See also *Operational data store*.

Reason code   A field used in conjunction with a transaction dimension to describe why the transaction took place. Reason codes are valuable for returns and cancellations and for describing why something changed.

Redundancy   Storing more than one occurrence of the data.

Referential integrity (RI)   Mandatory condition in a data warehouse where all the keys in the fact tables are legitimate foreign keys relative to the dimension tables. In other words, all the fact key components are subsets of the primary keys found in the dimension tables at all times.

Referral   The identity of the previous context of a URL. In other words, if you click on a link in page A and wind up on page B, page B's Web server sees page A as the referral. Web servers can log referrals automatically, which is a very useful way to see why a visitor came to your Web site.

Relational database management system (RDBMS)   Database management system based on the relational model that supports the full range of standard SQL. Uses a series of joined tables with rows and columns to organize and store data.

RI   See *Referential integrity*.

ROI   Return on investment, usually expressed as a rate describing the growth of an investment during its lifetime.

Role-playing dimensions The situation where a single physical dimension table appears several times in a single fact table. Each of the dimension roles is represented as a separate logical table with unique column names through views.

Roll up To present higher levels of summarization. See *Drill up*.

Row A record in a relational table.

Row header The nonaggregated components of the SQL select list. Always listed in the SQL group by clause.

Sales invoice The operational control document that describes a sale. Usually contains multiple line items that each represent a separate product sold.

Scalability The ability to accommodate future growth requirements.

SCD See *Slowly changing dimensions*.

Schema The logical or physical design of a set of database tables, indicating the relationship among the tables.

Second-level mart See *Consolidated data mart*.

SELECT DISTINCT (SQL) SQL statement that suppresses duplicate rows in the answer set.

SELECT list (SQL) List of column specifications that follows SELECT and comes before FROM in an SQL query. Each item in the select list generates a column in the answer set.

Semantic layer An interface layer placed between the user and the physical database structure.

Semiadditive (fact) Numeric fact that can be added along some dimensions in a fact table but not others. Inventory levels and balances cannot be *added* along the time dimension but can be *averaged* usefully over the time dimension.

Session The collection of actions taken by a Web site visitor while visiting the Web site without leaving it. Also called a visit.

Shelf displays Tags, racks, or other promotional mechanisms used in a retail environment.

SKU   See *Stock keeping unit*.

Slice and dice   Ability to access a data warehouse through any of its dimensions equally. Slicing and dicing is the process of separating and combining warehouse data in seemingly endless combinations.

Slowly changing dimensions (SCD)   The tendency of dimension rows to change gradually or occasionally over time. A type 1 SCD is a dimension whose attributes are overwritten when the value of an attribute changes. A type 2 SCD is a dimension where a new row is created when the value of an attribute changes. A type 3 SCD is a dimension where an alternate old column is created when an attribute changes.

Snapshot   See either *Accumulating snapshot fact table* or *Periodic snapshot fact table*.

Snowflake   A normalized dimension where a flat, single-table dimension is decomposed into a tree structure with potentially many nesting levels. In dimensional modeling, the fact tables in both a snowflake and star schema would be identical, but the dimensions in a snowflake are presented in third normal form, usually under the guise of space savings and maintainability. Although snowflaking can be regarded as an embellishment to the dimensional model, snowflaking generally compromises user understandability and browsing performance. Space savings typically are insignificant relative to the overall size of the data warehouse. Snowflaked normalized dimension tables may exist in the staging area to facilitate dimension maintenance.

Sort   To sequence data according to designated criteria.

Source system   An operational system of record whose function it is to capture the transactions or other performance metrics from a business's processes. Alternatively, the source system may be external to the organization but is still capturing information that is needed in the data warehouse.

Sparse   A fact table that has relatively few of all the possible combinations of key values. A grocery store product movement database is considered sparse because only 5 to 10 percent of all the key combinations for product, store, and day will be present. An airline's frequent-flyer database is extremely sparse because very few of the customer, flight number, and day combinations actually appear in the database.

Sparsity failure   A situation that occurs when an aggregate table is created that is not appreciably smaller than the table on which it is based. For instance, if only one SKU in each brand is sold on a given day, then a brand aggregate for a day will be the same size as the base table.

SQL Structured Query Language, the standard language for accessing relational databases.

Star-join schema The generic representation of a dimensional model in a relational database in which a fact table with a composite key is joined to a number of dimension tables, each with a single primary key.

Star schema See *Star-join schema*.

Stock keeping unit (SKU) A standard term in manufacturing and retail environments to describe an individual product.

Subrogation The act of an insurance company selling the rights remaining in a claim, such as the right to sue someone for damages.

Supply side The part of the value chain in a manufacturing company that starts with purchase orders for ingredients and parts and ends with finished goods inventory. Physically, the supply side is the manufacturing operation. Contrast with *Demand side*.

Surrogate key Integer keys that are sequentially assigned as needed in the staging area to populate a dimension table and join to the fact table. In the dimension table, the surrogate key is the primary key. In the fact table, the surrogate key is a foreign key to a specific dimension and may be part of the fact table's primary key, although this is not required. A surrogate key usually cannot be interpreted by itself. That is, it is not a smart key in any way. Surrogate keys are required in many data warehouse situations to handle slowly changing dimensions, as well as missing or inapplicable data. Also known as *artificial keys, integer keys, meaningless keys, nonnatural keys*, and *synthetic keys*.

Syndicated data suppliers Companies that collect data, clean it, package it, and resell it. A.C. Nielsen and IRI are the principal syndicated data suppliers for grocery and drug store scanner data, and IMS Health and Source Informatics (Walsh America) are the principal syndicated data suppliers for pharmaceutical data.

Table Collection of rows (records) that have associated columns (fields).

Takeaway Consumer purchases.

TCP/IP Transmission Control Protocol/Internet Protocol, the basic communication protocol of the Internet, consisting of a transport layer (IP) and an application layer (TCP).

Temporal inconsistency   Tendency of an OLTP database to change its primary data relationships from moment to moment as transactions are processed. This inconsistency has an impact on users in two primary ways: (1) the database is changing constantly as they query it, and (2) old history is not necessarily preserved.

Temporary price reduction (TPR)   Promotional technique in retail environments.

Terabyte (TB)   One trillion (10^{12}) bytes.

Textual (dimension attributes)   Dimension attributes that are actually text or behave like text.

Third normal form (3NF)   Database design approach that eliminates redundancy and therefore facilitates insertion of new rows into tables in an OLTP application without introducing excessive data locking problems. Sometimes referred to as *normalized*.

3NF   See *Third normal form*.

Time shifting of a promotion   Tendency of some promotions to cause the customer to defer purchases until the promotion is on and then not make purchases after the promotion for a prolonged period. In the most serious cases, the promotion accomplishes nothing except to allow the customer to buy products cheaply.

Time stamping   Tagging each record with the time the data was processed or stored.

Topology   The organization of physical devices and connections in a system.

TPR   See *Temporary price reduction*.

Transaction   Indivisible unit of work. A transaction processing system either performs an entire transaction or it doesn't perform any part of the transaction.

Transaction fact table   Type of fact table in which the fact table granularity is one row for the lowest level of detail captured by a transaction. A record in a transaction fact table is present only if a transaction event actually occurs. Contrast with *Periodic snapshot fact table* and *Accumulating snapshot fact table*.

Transshipments   Shipments of product that occur between the warehouses belonging to the manufacturer or retailer.

Trending   Analyzing data representing multiple occurrences in a time series.

Turns (inventory)   Number of times in a given period (usually a year) that the inventory must be completely replenished in order to keep up with the observed rate of sales.

24/7   Operational availability 24 hours a day, 7 days a week.

Twinkling database   The tendency of a transaction-processing database to constantly be changing the data the user is attempting to query.

Type 1   A slowly changing dimension (SCD) technique where the changed attribute is overwritten.

Type 2   A slowly changing dimension (SCD) technique where a new dimension record with a new surrogate key is created to reflect the change.

Type 3   A slowly changing dimension (SCD) technique where a new column is added to the dimension table to capture the change.

UNICODE   The UNICODE worldwide character standard is a character coding system designed to support the interchange, processing, and display of the written texts of the diverse languages of the modern world, including Japanese, Chinese, Arabic, Hebrew, Cyrillic, and many others. In addition, it supports classical and historical texts of many written languages. UNICODE is a 16-bit implementation, which means that 65,535 characters can be supported, unlike ASCII, which can support only 127, or extended ASCII, which supports 255. Release 2.1, the current release of UNICODE, defines 38,887 of the possible characters.

Universal Product Code (UPC)   Standard bar-coded value found on most grocery and drug store merchandise.

Universal Resource Locator (URL)   The text address of a specific object on the World Wide Web. It usually consists of three parts: a prefix describing the TCP protocol to use to retrieve it (for example, HTTP), a domain name (for example, webcom.com), and a document name (for example, index.html). Such a URL would be formatted as http://www.webcom.com/index.html.

UPC   See *Universal product code.*

Up-selling   Selling a product or service to an existing customer, where the goal is to get the customer to purchase a more expensive or higher-value version than previously purchased. See *Cross-selling.*

URL   See *Universal resource locator*.

Value banding (facts)   Grouping facts into flexible value bands as specified in a band definition table.

Value chain   Sequence of processes that describe the movement of products or services through a pipeline from original creation to final sales.

Value circle   In some organizations, the sequence of events or processes more closely resembles a circle, rather than a chain, centered on core data, such as the patient treatment record in health care.

Variable-depth hierarchy   See *Ragged hierarchy*.

Variable-width attribute set   The situation where a varied number of dimension attributes are known, depending on the duration of the relationship, such as the case with prospects who evolve into customers.

VIEW (SQL)   SQL statement that creates logical copies of a table or a complete query that can be used separately in a SELECT statement. Views are semantically independent, so the separate roles of a dimension usually are implemented as views.

Virgin territory   Portion of disk storage that is unoccupied prior to a data load. In a static database experiencing no in-place updates or inserts and with a primary sort order with time as the leading term in the sort, all data loading takes place in virgin territory.

Web   Short for the World Wide Web, the collection of servers and browsers that talk to each other using the HTTP protocol.

Webhouse   The data warehouse evolved to a new form because of the existence of the Web.

Web site   A Web server, or collection of Web servers, that appears to users as an integrated entity with a well-defined system of hyperlinks connecting its components.

Weighted report   When using a bridge table, the facts in the fact table are multiplied by the bridge table's weighting factor to appropriately allocate the facts to the multivalued dimension. Contrast with *Impact report*.

XML   See *Extensible Markup Language*.